THE
EVERYTHING
COOKBOOK

Over 500 easy recipes,
from old-fashioned classics
to today's healthy favorites

Faith Jaycox, Sarah Jaycox,
and Karen Lawson

Adams Media Corporation
Avon, Massachusetts

An Everything® Series Book.
Everything® is a registered trademark of Adams Media Corporation.

Published by Adams Media Corporation
57 Littlefield Street, Avon, MA 02322
www.adamsmedia.com

ISBN: 1-58062-400-6

Printed in the United States of America.

J I H G F E D C

Library of Congress Cataloging-in-Publication data
available upon request from the publisher.

This publication is designed to provide accurate and authoritative information with regard to the subject matter covered. It is sold with the understanding that the publisher is not engaged in rendering legal, accounting, or other professional advice. If legal advice or other expert assistance is required, the services of a competent professional person should be sought.
— From a *Declaration of Principles* jointly adopted by a Committee of the American Bar Association and a Committee of Publishers and Associations

Illustrations by Barry Littmann and Eulala Connor

This book is available at quantity discounts for bulk purchases.
For information, call 1-800-872-5627.

Visit the entire Everything® series at everything.com

*T*his cookbook is lovingly dedicated to Karen's grandmother, Emma Ecker, and to Faith's grandmother and Sarah's great grandmother, Pansy Calvin Fresch. As children we spent many hours in their kitchens watching them as they cooked—almost always without benefit of written recipes! The magic they worked on even the simplest of foods turned every family meal into a feast.

Thanks also to the relatives and friends who generously shared their recipes with us for this project: Maymie Ecker, Ruth Ecker, Grace Freed, Maurine Hatting, Kate Jaycox, Melissa Jaycox, Estelle MacNider, Barbara Sanderson, Gaynell Schandel, Patti McBride Schlosser, and Genevieve Vasiloff Weiss. We remain grateful, too, for the recipes we "inherited" from the late Wilma Ayers, Det Fresch, Louise Hoeft, and Luella Fresch Yoho. Lastly, thanks to all the other friends or friends of friends whose special foods found their way into our files over the years, but whose names have not been as carefully preserved as their recipes.

Contents

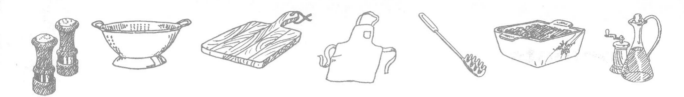

Chapter 1

Cooking Basics: Terms, Techniques, Ingredients, and Nutrition

We all eat. Three full meals a day, and snacks on top on that. Three-plus times a day we make decisions about what to eat. And that translates into decisions about what to cook. And then there's the clock to think about. Most of the time we don't have time to spend hours preparing a meal or to root through countless cookbooks only to end up with four or five separate books cluttering the counter and an impatient group of eaters. As experienced eaters ourselves, we the authors know the time consuming agony of first choosing what to cook, then finding the right recipe, then sorting through complicated directions. That's why we have designed *The Everything® Cookbook* to be an easier answer to good eating. Throughout, we have been guided by two principles: make it basic *and* make it comprehensive.

What makes this cookbook different? First and most importantly, we know real cooks: not chefs in four star restaurants, but the men and women who feed themselves and their families everyday. We know the you's and me's who eat three plus times a day. We know people who are not only body-hungry, but are time-hungry as well, and want good food without much fuss. Of course, although we all love and need at least one quick, standby casserole, there are other ways to kick a quick meal into high gear. And while we know that cooking gourmet meals is challenging and rewarding, we also know it's a special occasion way of cooking that is neither feasible nor desirable everyday. And so we've compiled the recipes that—most days—will bring your basic foods to the table with little hassle and no complaints. For good measure, we've added the occasional zing for when you *do* want to make a resplendent five course feast.

We do not take food lightly, but we also have jobs and kids and dogs and errands. (Actually, one of us is the kid and has been tackling cooking with flavor on a graduate student's budget.) We have learned the fine balance of keeping our meals hot, fresh, and delicious, but also real and filling. We love fresh, whole foods and use them whenever possible. At the same time, frozen vegetables are not the enemy, and we would never scoff at excellent store bought pizza dough. However, we firmly believe that wholesome eating, conve-

nience, and speed can happily coexist in almost any meal.

The Everything® Cookbook is a basic cookbook. That means that you need not be an expert in the kitchen to use it successfully. The first chapter explains basic cooking terms and techniques; you can turn back to it whenever you need to while you are in the process of preparing a recipe. In addition, sidebars are scattered throughout the book to offer specific tips in the spot they are most likely to be needed. We also provide instructions for very basic methods of preparing common foods— how to fry an egg, bake a potato, prepare rice, broil a steak.

Basic, however, is far from boring. Today, basic is not just meat and potatoes—it's Asian cuisine and starter dips, goat cheese salads and stuffed pizzas. That's why The Everything® Cookbook is also a comprehensive cookbook. We've left nothing out—just glance though the chapters: breads, eggs, poultry, pastas. We dress up, dress down, and just plain dress them all. In this book, you will find over 500 recipes from the traditional Thanksgiving Turkey to crowd pleasing Southwestern Quesadillas. You will never

again have to sift through several books to find one recipe for a side of wild rice and one for grilled salmon.

And we've done more than just make The Everything® Cookbook basic and comprehensive; we've included extra "sauce" on the side. Whether you crave the Middle Eastern flavor of Baba Ghanouj or a basic American hamburger, this book will help you add some zest to your meals (or basil, or gruyere, or portobello). We've added tricks of the trade: we've given you more than just recipes—we've given you tips and nuggets of information to infuse the entire cooking process. We've given you variety, for the times when you are cooking for one, or six, or ten. Love sandwiches? There's more to put between bread than peanut butter and jelly!

The Everything® Cookbook will be your cooking ground zero. We eat to survive, but we cook to socialize, to enjoy, and to experiment. This book will get you through dinner with the in-laws, dinner with friends, and dinner with yourself. And you will never have to look elsewhere. It's all here, in one book for the twenty-first century kitchen. We simply ask of you one thing: please, leave a little room for dessert.

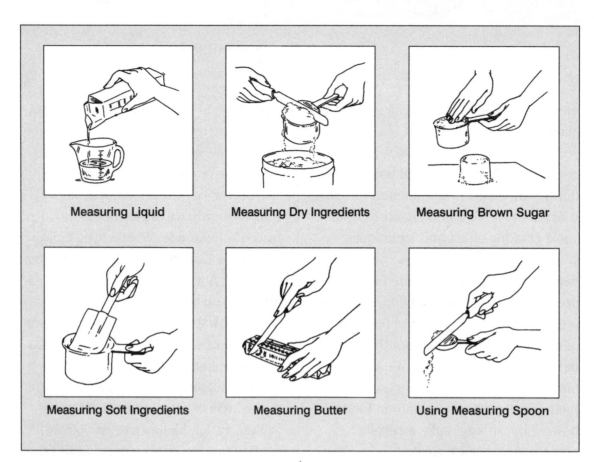

Measuring Liquid

Measuring Dry Ingredients

Measuring Brown Sugar

Measuring Soft Ingredients

Measuring Butter

Using Measuring Spoon

How to Measure It

Don't guess! Accurate measuring is the key to good results.

How to Measure LIQUID Ingredients

1. Use a liquid measuring cup—a glass or plastic cup with graduated markings on the side.
2. Place the cup on a flat, level surface.
3. View the liquid at eye level.

TIP: Liquid measuring cups can be greased with a small amount of oil or shortening before measuring thick liquids like honey.

How to Measure DRY Ingredients

1. Use graduated nesting measuring cups (dry measuring cups).
2. Spoon the ingredient into the appropriate cup, or dip the cup into the container of a dry ingredient.
3. Level it off with a knife or spatula.

EXCEPTION: **Brown sugar** must be packed into the measuring cup, pressing firmly with the fingers. The sugar should retain the shape of the measuring cup when it is dumped.

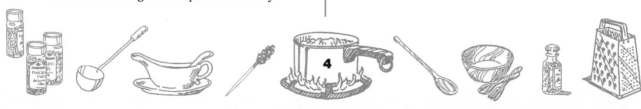

4

Weights and Measures

a dash = less than $\frac{1}{8}$ teaspoon	4 quarts = 1 gallon
3 teaspoons = 1 tablespoon	8 ounces = 1 cup liquid
4 tablespoons = $\frac{1}{4}$ cup	8 ounces = $\frac{1}{2}$ pound
$\frac{1}{3}$ cup = 5 tablespoons + 1 teaspoon	16 ounces = 2 pints or $\frac{1}{2}$ quart liquid
$\frac{1}{2}$ cup = 8 tablespoons	16 ounces = 1 pound
$\frac{2}{3}$ cup = 10 tablespoons + 2 teaspoons	32 ounces = 1 quart
$\frac{1}{2}$ pint = 1 cup	64 ounces = $\frac{1}{2}$ gallon
1 pint = 2 cups	1 liter = 1.06 quarts
1 quart = 4 cups	1 quart = .95 liter

Traditionally, skilled cooks always sifted flour before measuring it, especially when baking. Today, most name-brand flours are presifted. However, flour does settle in packaging. It is a good idea to stir it lightly before spooning it into the measuring cup if you do not sift.

Sifting or resifting flour with other dry ingredients helps distribute the ingredients, like leavening, evenly.

How to Measure SOFT Ingredients

1. Use graduated dry measuring cups
2. Soft bread crumbs, coconut, shredded cheeses, and similar soft ingredients should be lightly pressed down into the selected measuring cup.

EXCEPTION: **Solid shortening** must be firmly packed down into a dry ingredient measuring cup. Scoop it into the selected cup, pack with a spatula or the back of a spoon, then level it off with a spatula or knife.

How to Use Measuring Spoons

1. Use graduated measuring spoons for both liquid and dry ingredients.
2. For dry ingredients, level with a knife or spatula.
3. For liquid ingredients, pour carefully, near but not over the mixing bowl.

How to Heat, Cool, Soften, or Melt It

To juice lemons or oranges more easily, cut the fruit in half, place on a plate, and heat in the microwave on high for 30 seconds before squeezing.

A Preheated Oven has been turned on and allowed to reach the desired temperature before the food is placed inside. Unless a recipe specifies otherwise, ovens should always be preheated. In most ovens 10 to 15 minutes is adequate time to preheat. The heating element will

5

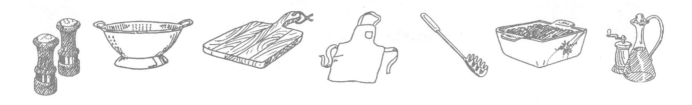

Oven Chart

250°–275° is a VERY SLOW oven

300°–325° is a SLOW oven

350°–375° is a MODERATE oven

400°–425° is a HOT oven

450°–475° is a VERY HOT oven

Zesting

The *zest* of a citrus fruit, used to flavor foods, is from the thin, colored outer peel.

When grating lemon or orange peel to make zest, take only the colorful skin. Do not grate the thicker white membrane under it. Small graters designed especially for citrus can be purchased, but the smallest holes of most conventional kitchen graters can also be used.

temporarily turn off in an electric oven, or will lower in a gas oven, when the set temperature is reached. Setting the thermostat to a higher temperature will not cause the oven to heat more quickly.

Room Temperature Foods have been removed from the refrigerator about 15 minutes before use in a recipe.

Softened Foods like butter or cream cheese have been allowed to stand at room temperature until they are no longer hard to the touch, usually a minimum of 15 minutes.

To soften cold butter or margarine in the microwave: Place 1 stick unwrapped or ½ cup uncovered butter or margarine on a plate. Microwave on low 30 to 45 seconds in a 1,000-watt oven. Adjust time if wattage varies.

To soften cold cream cheese in the microwave: Place unwrapped cheese on an uncovered plate. Heat on high, 15 to 30 seconds for a 3-ounce package or 30 to 45 seconds for an 8-ounce package. Adjust time if oven wattage is not 1,000.

Melted Foods have been thoroughly liquefied.

To melt butter or margarine in the microwave: Place 1 stick unwrapped or ½ cup uncovered butter or margarine in a

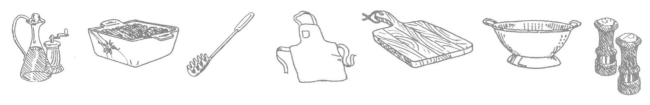

glass liquid measuring cup or bowl. Heat on high for 30 seconds; stir. Heat and stir in additional 10 second intervals if necessary. Adjust time if oven wattage is not 1,000.

To melt chocolate chips in the microwave: Place 1 cup of chips in a glass liquid measuring cup or uncovered bowl. Heat on high for 60 seconds; stir. Heat and stir in additional 45 second intervals until completely melted.

To melt chocolate squares: Place 1 or more squares in a glass liquid measuring cup or uncovered bowl. Heat on high 30 seconds; stir. Heat and stir in additional 30 second intervals until completely melted. Adjust times if oven wattage is not 1,000.

Cooled Foods have been allowed to stand at room temperature for a specified amount of time, or until they can be comfortably touched. Stirring food speeds its cooling time.

Chilled Foods have been allowed to stand in the refrigerator for a specified amount of time, or until both the outside and inside of the food are below room temperature. Stirring food speeds its chilling time.

Thoroughly chilled foods have been allowed to stand in the refrigerator until both the outside and inside of the food have reached the refrigerator's storage temperature. Thorough chilling of heated food usually takes at least an hour or more, depending on the amount of food and shape of the container.

How to Cut It

Bias slice—to cut at a 45 degree angle

Chop—to cut into small irregular pieces with a knife or food processor

Core—to remove the center of a fruit like an apple or pear

Crush—to press or smash seasonings or other foods to release their flavor, using a garlic press, heavy knife, or other implement

Cube—to cut food into squares about $\frac{1}{2}$ inch on the sides

Cut up—to cut into small irregular pieces

Diagonal slice—to cut at a 45 degree angle

Dice—to cut into reasonably uniform pieces of about $\frac{1}{4}$ inch

Grate—to rub a food such as cheese, vegetables, or spices against a sharp-edged

Snipping Herbs

An easy way to snip herbs is to:

- Wash and pat dry the herbs.

- Place the herbs in a coffee mug.

- Point kitchen scissors into the coffee mug.

- Using the scissors, snip the herbs in the mug into small pieces.

kitchen tool called a grater, making small or fine particles

Julienne—to cut into thin strips about two inches long, often compared to matchsticks

Mince—to chop food into very small bits

Score—to cut through the surface of a food (usually about $\frac{1}{4}$ inch deep) to tenderize or make a pattern

Section—to cut the pulp of a peeled citrus fruit away from the membranes that separate its segments

Shred—to cut in narrow, thin strips, usually by using a kitchen shredder. A knife can be used to shred lettuce or cabbage.

Slice—to cut into flat pieces that are usually thin and even

Snip—to cut herbs or other food into small pieces using a kitchen scissors

Tear—to break into pieces using the hands rather than a knife

 A FILET (say "fih-LAY") is a small, boneless piece of meat, such as beef filet mignon.

A FILLET (say "FILL-iht") is a boneless piece of fish or poultry breast. Fillet can also be used as a verb describing the act of removing the bones from the fish or poultry.

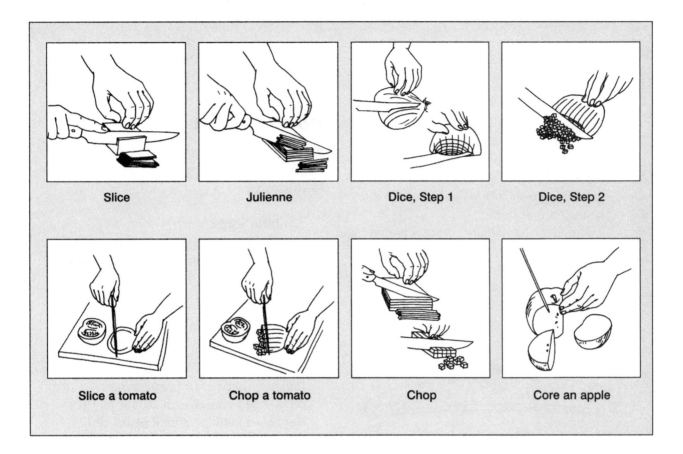

Slice

Julienne

Dice, Step 1

Dice, Step 2

Slice a tomato

Chop a tomato

Chop

Core an apple

Cutting Techniques

Julienne

1. Make thin slices.
2. Stack the slices a few at a time.
3. Cut into matchstick-like pieces.

Cube or Dice

1. Cut into strips the width of the desired cube or dice.
2. Stack a few of the strips or lay them side by side.
3. Cut into cubes or dice.

Chop or Mince

1. Position a chef's knife or other large knife over the food.
2. Lightly hold the knife down near the pointed end and chop by raising and lowering the handle end.

Snip

1. Place herb into a small measuring cup or bowl.
2. Cut quickly with repeated strokes of a kitchen scissors.

Section

1. Peel the citrus fruit and remove any additional white inner skin with a paring knife or parer.
2. Working over a bowl or plate, cut the peeled fruit in half.
3. Holding one half and using a paring knife, slice the top pulp section away from its bottom membrane, then slice the membrane away from the pulp on the top side of the next section.
4. Continue until each pulp section has been removed.

How to Whip Cream

To whip heavy or whipping cream successfully:

- Have the cream very cold.

- Chill the bowl in which it is to be whipped and the mixer beaters.

- Beat on medium speed with an electric mixer until soft peaks form when the beaters are removed.

- Use immediately, or keep in the refrigerator for no more than 1 hour.

How to Mix It

Beat—to stir briskly with a spoon, with a whisk, with a hand egg beater, or with an electric mixer.

To beat eggs:

Lightly (whole eggs)—Use a fork or whisk and beat until whites and yellows are combined but the mixture is not entirely uniform in color or texture.

Well (whole eggs)—Use a fork or whisk and beat until the mixture is uniform in color and texture.

Until soft peaks form (egg whites only)—Use an electric mixer (or hand egg beater) and beat until peaks curl over when the mixer beaters are removed.

Until stiff peaks form (egg whites only)—Use an electric mixer (or hand egg beater) and beat until peaks stand up straight when the mixer beaters are removed.

Until thick and lemon colored (egg yolks only)—Use an electric mixer (or hand egg beater). When beaten sufficiently (about 5 minutes), yolks will become noticeably thicker and lighter in color, and will stream smoothly from the beaters when they are removed.

Blend—to mix two or more ingredients until they make a uniform mixture.

Cream—to beat a fat until it is light and fluffy, often in combination with sugar or other ingredients.

Cut in—to combine a solid fat with dry ingredients, until the fat is in very small pieces about the size of small peas, by using a pastry blender or a fork. Compare with "cream."

Fold—to combine ingredients gently, using a spatula or spoon to lift ingredients from the bottom of the bowl and "fold" them over the top.

Knead—to work dough by continuous folding over and pressing down until it is smooth and elastic. Dough can also be kneaded with electric mixer attachments called dough hooks.

Stir—to mix ingredients at a moderate pace to combine them.

Toss—to mix ingredients by gently lifting them from the bottom of the bowl and allowing them to tumble, usually using two forks or other utensils.

Whip—to beat rapidly with a wire whisk, hand beater, or electric mixer. Whipping increases volume because it adds air to the ingredient(s).

How to Prepare It

Baste—to spoon or pour broth, sauce, or other liquid over food while cooking to prevent dryness or add flavor.

Blacken—to cook Cajun-seasoned foods over a very high heat.

Bread—to coat foods before cooking in bread or cracker crumbs.

Caramelize—to coat the top of a food with sugar and then broil quickly until the sugar is melted. Or, to melt sugar in a saucepan over a low heat until it turns into a golden syrup.

Deglaze—to add liquid to a skillet in which meat has been cooked, stirring to loosen meat bits and make a broth. The broth can be used to make a sauce.

Dot—to place pieces of butter randomly on top of a food.

Drizzle—to pour a liquid topping in thin, irregular lines over a food.

Dust—to sprinkle a dry ingredient lightly and fairly evenly over a food.

Glaze—to spread a thin coating such as jelly on food, making it appear glossy.

Grease—to coat the surface of a pan with shortening or cooking spray to prevent foods from sticking while they bake. To "grease and flour" is to dust the pan lightly with flour after applying the shortening.

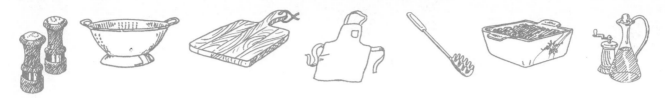

About Pans

Many cooks prefer shiny, uncoated metal pans for most baking. These pans reflect (rather than absorb) heat and give baked goods a tender, golden crust.

Pans with dark coating, such as nonstick pans, cause foods to brown more quickly than shiny pans, because they absorb heat. It is sometimes necessary to reduce the specified oven temperature 25 degrees when using coated pans; check the manufacturer's instructions.

Glass or ceramic pans are technically called *baking dishes*. They can be used interchangeably with metal pans. However, the oven temperature should be reduced 25 degrees *unless the recipe specifies a (glass) baking dish.*

When greasing baking pans, use a solid shortening (like Crisco) or a cooking spray unless the recipe specifies otherwise. Butter or margarine do not work as well because they usually contain salt and can cause sticking. They also burn at lower temperatures.

If you do not wish to apply the shortening with your fingers, use a paper towel or a small plastic bag placed over your hand.

Marinate—to let food stand in a special liquid to flavor it or tenderize it. The liquid is called a *marinade.*

Purée—to make into a thick liquid, usually by using a blender or food processor.

Reduce—to boil a liquid until some of it evaporates, thus concentrating the flavor.

Roux, to make—to combine melted butter, flour, and seasonings over heat to use as a thickening base for sauces.

Sift—to process dry ingredients through a kitchen sifter. Sifting adds air to dry ingredients that have been compressed in storage and also removes any lumps.

Skim—to remove fat or foam that has accumulated on the surface of a liquid, usually using a spoon.

| Bake | Boil | Simmer | Stir-Fry |

How to Cook It

Bake—to cook food with the indirect dry heat of an oven. Covering food while baking it preserves moistness; leaving food uncovered results in a drier or crisp surface.

Barbecue—to cook with barbecue sauce or spices, or to cook slowly on a grill or spit, usually outdoors.

Blanch—to cook fruits, vegetables, or nuts very briefly in boiling water or steam, usually to preserve the color or nutritional value or to remove the skin. Also called *parboiling.*

Boil—to cook a liquid at a temperature at which bubbles rise and break on the surface. *Bring to a boil:* Heat just until bubbling begins. In a full or rolling boil, the bubbles are larger and form quickly and continuously.

Braise—to cook food slowly in a tightly covered pan in a small amount of liquid. Usually, food is first browned in a small amount of fat. Braising tenderizes food and can be done on either the stovetop or in the oven.

Broil—to cook food directly under a direct source of intense heat or flame, producing a browned or crisp exterior and a less well done interior.

Deep-Fry—to cook food in hot, liquefied fat (usually kept at 350 to 375 degrees) deep enough to cover and surround the food completely.

Fry—to cook in hot fat or oil, producing a crisp exterior.

Grill—to cook foods directly above a source of intense heat or flame. Foods can be *pan-grilled* on a stovetop by using a specially designed pan with raised grill ridges.

Oven-Fry—to cook food, usually breaded, in a hot oven with a small amount of fat, usually dotted or drizzled on top of the food.

Pan-Fry—to fry with little or no added fat, using only the fat that accumulates during cooking.

Parboil—see *Blanch.*

Poach—to cook in a simmering (not boiling) liquid.

Roast—to cook meat or poultry in the indirect heat of the oven, uncovered. Roasted foods are not cooked in added liquid (compare *braise*), but are often basted with liquids for flavor and moistness.

Sauté—(say "saw-TAY") to cook in a small amount of fat over high heat.

Scald—to heat a liquid to just below the boiling point, when small bubbles begin to appear around the edges of the pan. When milk is scalded, a film will form on the surface.

Sear—to brown on all sides over high heat to preserve juiciness.

Simmer—to keep a liquid just below the boiling point; a few bubbles will rise and break on the surface.

Steam—to cook food above (not in) boiling or simmering water.

Stew—to cook food, covered, very slowly in liquid.

Stir-Fry—to cook small pieces of food in a hot wok or skillet, using a small amount of fat and a constant stirring motion.

Common Ingredients

Baking Powder is a leavening, or an ingredient that makes a mixture expand or rise by releasing (harmless) carbon dioxide bubbles. It is made from baking soda plus other ingredients, so it cannot be directly substituted for baking soda. Double-acting baking powder acts when ingredients are mixed and again when they are cooked.

Baking Soda is a leavening that works in the presence of acidic ingredients.

Cheeses

Natural cheese is an unblended product that results from solidifying and aging milk curd.

Process cheese is natural cheese that has been reconstituted to stop the aging process, allowing it to have a longer shelf life. It is softer than most natural cheeses. Cheese foods or spreads are process cheeses with additional moisture added.

Fresh cheeses are natural cheeses made from milk curd, but not aged. They include cottage cheese, ricotta, and cream cheese.

Chocolates

Baking cocoa (a powder) is made from the pure "liquor" of the cocoa bean. It contains no cocoa butter, sweetener, or other product.

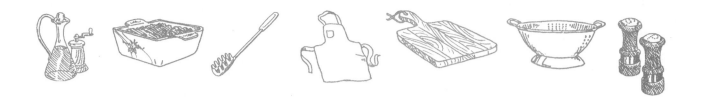

Steaming Tips

- Steaming (or blanching) vegetables or fruits preserves more of their nutritional value.

- If vegetables or fruits are simmered or boiled in water to cover them, much of their vitamin content will go down the drain when the water is drained.

- Raisins, dried cherries or cranberries, and dry (rather than oil-packed) sun-dried tomatoes can be plumped by steaming briefly.

- Folding "steamer inserts" can be used in standard saucepans; specially designed two-part steamer saucepans are also available.

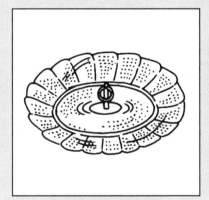

Steamer Insert

Two-Part Steamer Pot

Unsweetened baking chocolate contains butter but no sugar.

Bittersweet, semisweet, sweet, and milk chocolate have butter, sugar, and sometimes milk added to the cocoa bean liquor.

These chocolates should not be substituted for one another without making other adjustments.

Cornstarch is a thickener made from corn, which results in a clear sauce. It takes only about half as much cornstarch as flour to achieve the same amount of thickening.

Cream of Tartar is used primarily to add stability to candies, frostings, and egg whites. It is actually a byproduct of winemaking.

Creams result when milk butterfat is separated from milk liquids.

Half-and-half or light cream is a mixture of milk and cream. It can be substituted for heavy cream, which has more fat and calories, when the cream is used as a liquid in a recipe. It cannot be substituted for heavy cream that must be whipped, however, because the fat content of heavy cream is what allows successful whipping.

Whipping or heavy cream has a very high fat content. When whipped, it doubles in volume.

Sour cream is cream cultured with lactic acid to make it thick and tangy. Low-fat and nonfat varieties are available, but only the low-fat version should be substituted in cooked recipes.

Cream cheese is a cheese, not a cream.

Fats and Oils

Butter, a saturated fat made from cream, is usually considered the best tasting fat. Unless otherwise specified, recipes calling for butter require stick or cube butter.

- Whipped butter cannot be substituted for stick butter in recipes because its volume has been increased with air.
- Salted and unsalted butter can be substituted for each other, although they will, of course, cause a difference in the saltiness in the food's flavor.
- Margarine can usually be substituted for butter, unless a recipe specifically states otherwise, but see the difference between true margarine and vegetable oil margarine below.

Margarine is an unsaturated fat that is a substitute for butter and contains at least 80 percent fat. Only the sticks (not the tubs or squeezable liquids) should be used in preparing recipes.

- Spreads, or vegetable oil margarines, have less than 80 percent fat. Substituting them for butter or true margarine in recipes is not recommended. Cooking results will often differ because spreads contain more water.
- Butter-margarine blends in stick form (not tubs) can be substituted for either butter or margarine in recipes.
- Low-fat or low-calorie butter or margarine should not be used in recipes because

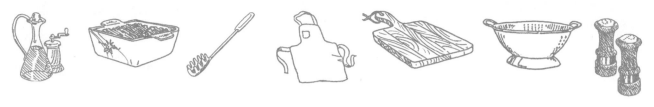

they contain more water and air than regular products.

Shortening is vegetable oil that remains solid at room temperature. Plain and butter-flavored varieties are interchangeable.

Lard is shortening made from animal (pork) fat. It is a saturated fat. Some cooks believe that the flakiest biscuits and pie crusts are made with lard.

Oils are fats from nuts, seeds, or vegetables that remain liquid at room temperature.

- Cooking oil can be made from a single nut, seed, or vegetable, or a blend of several.
- Olive oil is made from black olives and is available in several grades. Extra virgin oil has no added solvents and has a more delicate flavor than lower grades.
- Sesame oil and some nut oils have a distinctive flavor and should not be substituted for regular cooking oil unless the flavor is acceptable in the recipe.
- Spray cooking oils can be used on baking or cooking pans to prevent sticking, or can be sprayed directly on foods.

Flours

All-purpose flour is a blend of hard and soft wheats that can be used for all general cooking and baking. It is usually enriched with vitamins but has no wheat bran or germ. Bleached and unbleached varieties are interchangeable.

Cake flour, bread flour, and pasta flour are made from different kinds of wheat, have different qualities, and perform differently when cooked or baked. Bread flour, for example, absorbs more liquid and contains more gluten-producing proteins that give structure and elasticity. Substituting a specific-purpose flour for another flour in recipes will lead to different and usually unsatisfactory results.

Self-rising flour has salt and leavening added to it. Do not substitute for all-purpose flour without making other adjustments.

Whole-wheat or graham flour is made from the entire wheat kernel and thus includes the bran and germ. It can be substituted for up to half the amount of all-purpose flour called for in most baked goods. However, the resulting product will be denser and flatter, and will have a nuttier flavor.

"Instant" flour has a fine, powdery texture that dissolves easily for sauces and gravies.

Mayonnaise and Salad Dressing are creamy dressings or condiments made primarily from eggs and vinegar. Salad dressing has fewer egg yolks and is lower in fat than mayonnaise. Salad dressing should not be substituted for mayonnaise in cooked dishes because it can separate at high temperatures. They can be used interchangeably in cold dishes.

Milks

Whole, 2 percent or low-fat, and skim milk can all be substituted for each other in recipes.

Buttermilk is low-fat milk that is cultured with lactic acid to give it a tangy flavor and thicken it. Despite its name, it is actually lower in fat than whole milk.

Condensed milk is made from whole or part skim milk with part of the water removed and sugar added. It cannot be substituted for *evaporated milk*, which has had 60 percent of the water removed and is not sweetened. Evaporated milk, when prepared by mixing with an equal amount of water, can be substituted for whole milk.

Sugars and Sweeteners

Granulated sugar is standard white sugar made from sugar cane or beets. When a recipe calls for sugar, use granulated sugar.

Powdered or confectioners' sugar, usually used for icing, is pulverized granulated sugar. It cannot be substituted for granulated sugar in baking without adjusting amounts.

Brown sugar is usually made by adding molasses to granulated sugar. Darker brown sugars contain more molasses and have a more intense flavor. Brown sugar is always measured by packing it into the measuring cup unless a recipe specifies otherwise.

Raw sugar is produced when molasses is removed from sugar cane.

Corn syrup is a liquid sweetener made from corn. Light corn syrup and dark corn syrup can be substituted for each other, but corn syrup should not be substituted for other sweeteners.

Honey is a sweetener that bees make from the nectar of flowers. It is almost twice as sweet as sugar. It cannot be substituted for sugar in a recipe without making other adjustments.

Liquid sweeteners, if well covered, keep indefinitely.

If honey becomes crystalized, set it in a pan of hot water. It can also be microwaved briefly, in 10-second intervals. Do not allow honey to reach a boiling temperature, however, because the flavor will be changed!

Maple syrup is a thick liquid sweetener made from the sap of maple trees. Most commercial syrups are a blend of maple syrup and corn syrup.

Molasses is a sweetener made from sugar cane. It is called sulphured molasses if sulphur fumes are used in the manufacturing process. Dark molasses can be substituted for light molasses, although the dark has a more intense flavor. Blackstrap molasses, however, contains almost no sugar and is not used as a sweetener. It should not be substituted for regular molasses.

Synthetic sugars or artificial sweeteners differ and some cannot be used successfully in cooking. They should be used only

in accordance with the manufacturer's directions.

Tapioca is used as a thickener and is particularly good for foods that will be frozen because it reheats well. For thickening use plain, quick cooking pearl tapioca, not the pudding mix.

Tomatoes

Roma, plum, or Italian tomatoes are the best varieties to use in cooking because they have more pulp and fewer seeds than slicing tomatoes.

Sun-dried tomatoes must be reconstituted if they are not packed in oil. Fresh or canned tomatoes have a very different flavor and cannot be substituted if a recipe calls for sun-dried tomatoes.

Vinegars

Vinegars are acidic condiments and preservatives. When no special vinegar is specified, use cider vinegar, which is made from apple cider.

Balsamic vinegar is made from grapes. It is sweet, dark, and more strongly flavored than cider vinegar.

Rice vinegar is made from rice wine.

White vinegar is made from grain alcohol. It is not often used in recipes and should not be substituted for cider vinegar.

Wine vinegars are made from different varieties of wine.

Fruit and herb vinegars are flavored cider or wine vinegars.

Yeast is a leavening that makes a mixture rise or expand in the presence of warmth, sugar, and liquid. If baking soda or powder is used as leavening in a recipe, yeast is not used.

Nutritional Primer

We are what we eat! Recent research indicates that many serious diseases like heart disease, certain cancers, diabetes, and high blood pressure are diet-related. The typical American diet contains far more fat than is healthy, and surprisingly, about twice as much protein than is necessary.

Proteins are the "building blocks" of the body, which uses them for growth, maintenance, and rebuilding of every cell. The most concentrated sources of protein are animal products. Animal proteins like meat, fish, eggs, and milk contain all of the nine essential amino acids that proteins can provide. They are called complete proteins. Vegetable proteins are present in nuts, seeds, whole grains, and legumes. All vegetable proteins, however—with the one exception of soy—are incomplete. If animal sources of protein are not included in the diet, vegetable proteins must be combined carefully to supply the body with all essential amino acids.

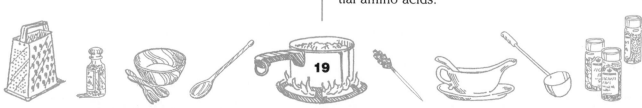

USDA Food Guide to Daily Servings

Recommended Serving Guidelines The USDA has established the following nutritional guidelines for *adults and children over six*: For children ages 2 to 5, calculate ⅔ of the adult serving size as one serving. For children under 2, follow your doctor's advice.

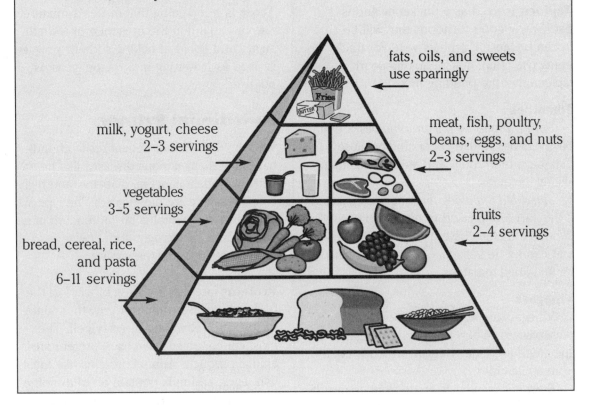

fats, oils, and sweets
use sparingly

milk, yogurt, cheese
2–3 servings

meat, fish, poultry,
beans, eggs, and nuts
2–3 servings

vegetables
3–5 servings

fruits
2–4 servings

bread, cereal, rice,
and pasta
6–11 servings

Carbohydrates provide most of the body's energy. Simple carbohydrates include all kinds of sugars and are sweet. Complex carbohydrates include grain products and some fruits and vegetables like beans and potatoes. Complex carbohydrates must be split apart before they can be absorbed by the body, so they supply energy over a longer period of time than simple carbohydrates. Complex carbohydrates also contain vitamins, minerals, and dietary fiber (or as it used to be called, "roughage.") Fiber is the part of a plant that cannot be digested by humans. Water insoluble fiber, found in fruits, vegetables, and grains, stimulates and regulates the digestive tract. Water soluble fiber, present in fruits, vegetables,

oat bran, and beans, may slow the absorption of sugar into the blood stream and reduce blood cholesterol levels.

Fats although they have a deservedly bad name, are also necessary to good health in appropriate amounts. They provide body insulation, cushioning, and energy reserve, and allow the body to use fat soluble vitamins. In addition, fats make the body feel full or satisfied after eating.

Cholesterol itself is not a fat, but a substance that is present in some fats. It is necessary for proper functioning of nerves and hormones. The human liver can manufacture all the cholesterol the body needs. However, dietary cholesterol is also present in some foods. A high level of cholesterol in the blood is related to cardiovascular disease.

Fats contain both saturated and unsaturated essential fatty acids. *Saturated fats* not only contain dietary cholesterol but also encourage the body to produce more than it needs. All animal fat is saturated fat. Two plant fats—palm and coconut oils—are also heavily saturated. Both are used extensively in processed and packaged bakery products, sweets, snacks, and other junk foods.

Unsaturated fats, which include most vegetable fats, are believed to actually reduce blood cholesterol levels when they replace saturated fat in the diet. *Monounsaturated* fats include fish oils and olive, canola, and peanut oils. *Polyunsaturated* fats include tuna and salmon and sunflower, corn, and sesame oils. However, *partially hydrogenated* vegetable oils (although unsaturated) contain *trans fatty acids*, which research indicates may raise blood cholesterol.

Fat Facts

The average American diet contains far too much fat, but all fats are not alike. Unsaturated fats are better for your body than saturated fats. Animal fats are saturated fats, and most vegetable fats are unsaturated fats. But remember...

Coconut and palm oil are *saturated* vegetable fats and are used in most bakery and processed snack foods.

All oils are 100 percent fat.

Both butter and margarine are 100 percent fat.

Partially hydrogenated oils are used in many shortenings and margarines.

Dietary Guidelines

The American Heart Association recommends a diet in which not more than 30 percent of total caloric intake is from fats. The nutrition labels that now appear on most cans, milk cartons, and other food packages show how much protein, carbohydrate, and fat a serving contains in *gram weight*.

A calorie measures the energy value of food, not its fat content. A calorie is actually the amount of heat needed to raise 1 kilogram of water 1 degree centigrade!

To convert grams to calories, use the following guidelines:
4 calories in 1 gram of protein (eggs, milk, meat, poultry, fish)

4 calories in 1 gram of carbohydrate (starches and sugars)

9 calories in 1 gram of fat

Using a 30 percent guideline, the average 2,000-calorie-per-day diet should contain no more than 600 calories from fat.

Nutrition labels also show the percentage of recommended daily intake contained in a serving of food. These percentages are based on the U.S. Department of Agriculture (USDA) Food and Nutrition Service estimated *average* daily diet of 2,000 calories per day. Actual caloric intake will and should vary with age, gender, weight, and activity level. In general, men and young adults need more calories than women and older adults. Pregnant and breastfeeding women need more calories as well.

Based on 2,000 calories a day, the USDA suggests the following nutrient levels:

Total fat	Less than 65 grams
Saturated fat	Less than 20 grams
Cholesterol	Less than 300 milligrams
Sodium	Less than 2,400 milligrams
Total carbohydrate	300 grams
Dietary fiber	25 grams

Most Americans consume *twice* the maximum recommended sodium intake of 2,400 milligrams per day. (The body actually needs only 500 milligrams per day!) One third of the average intake occurs naturally in foods. Another third is from ordinary table salt added to foods in cooking or eating, and the rest is from processed foods like meats and snack foods. A high sodium intake is sometimes a factor in high blood pressure.

The USDA also recommends:

- maintaining a diet high in grains, vegetables, and fruits
- maintaining a diet low in fat, saturated fat, and cholesterol
- maintaining a diet with a moderate intake of sugar, salt, and sodium
- eating a variety of foods

Yields and Equivalents

Apple
1 medium, chopped = about 1 cup
3 medium = 1 pound
3 medium = $2^3/_4$ cups pared and sliced

Beans, Dried
1 cup = $2^1/_4$ to $2^1/_2$ cups cooked

Butter
1 ounce butter = 2 tablespoons butter or margarine
1 stick butter or margarine = $^1/_4$ pound or 8 ounces
1 cup butter or margarine = 2 sticks or $^1/_2$ pound

Celery
2 medium stalks = $^2/_3$ to $^3/_4$ cup

Chocolate
1 ounce = 1 square
1 cup chips = 6 ounces

Cheese
1 pound American, Cheddar, Colby, Monterey Jack, Swiss, or similar cheeses = 4 cups shredded
1 cup shredded = $^1/_4$ pound

Cranberries
1 cup fresh makes 1 cup sauce
1 pound = 4 cups

Crumbs
1 cup cracker crumbs = 28 saltine crackers or 14 square graham crackers or 24 rich round crackers
1 cup bread crumbs
soft = $1^1/_2$ slices bread
dry = 4 slices bread
$^1/_4$ cup dry bread crumbs = $^3/_4$ cup soft bread crumbs or $^1/_4$ cup cracker crumbs
1 cup vanilla wafer crumbs = 22 wafers

Eggs
1 cup = 4 large eggs
$^1/_4$ cup liquid egg substitute = 1 egg
1 cup egg yolks = 10 to 12 egg yolks
1 cup egg whites = 8 to 10 egg whites

Fruits (see also Apples, Cranberries)
Bananas—3 large or 4 small = 2 cups sliced or $1^1/_3$ mashed
Cherries— $^1/_2$ pound = 1 cup pitted
Grapes—1 pound = 2 cups halved

Recommended Serving Guidelines

Bread, Cereal, Rice, and Pasta: 6 to 11 servings per day

A serving is:
1 slice of bread or 1 dinner roll

$^1/_2$ bagel or English muffin

$^1/_2$ hamburger bun

1 ounce of cereal (about $^3/_4$ to 1 cup of common cereals like corn flakes)

$^1/_2$ cup cooked rice or pasta

Vegetables: 3 to 5 servings per day

A serving is:
1 cup raw salad greens

$^1/_2$ cup chopped or cooked vegetables

$^1/_2$ cup tomato sauce (such as spaghetti sauce)

$^3/_4$ cup vegetable juice

Fruits: 2 to 4 servings per day

A serving is:
1 medium fruit such as apple, banana, pear, peach, orange

$^1/_2$ cup cut up, cooked, canned, or frozen fruit

$^1/_4$ cup dried fruit

$^3/_4$ cup fruit juice

Milk, Yogurt, and Cheese: 2 or 3 servings per day

A serving is:
1 cup milk

1 cup yogurt

1 $^1/_2$ ounces of natural cheese

2 ounces of process cheese

**Meat, Poultry, Seafood, Beans or
Other Legumes, Eggs, and Nuts: 2 or 3 servings per day**

A serving is:
2 to 3 ounces lean meat, fish, or poultry

$^1/_2$ cup cooked dried beans or legumes

2 to 3 eggs (but limit egg intake—they are high in cholesterol)

2 tablespoons of peanut butter

$^1/_3$ cup shelled nuts

Fats and Sweets: Eat sparingly

And remember: **Water** is also an essential body nutrient. Eight glasses or 64 ounces per day is optimal.

Peaches or Pears—1 medium = ½ cup sliced
Rhubarb— ½ pound = 2 to 4 stalks = 1 cup
    cooked
Strawberries—1 quart = 2 cups sliced

Garlic
1 clove fresh = ½ teaspoon chopped = ⅛
    teaspoon garlic powder

Green Pepper
1 large = 1 cup diced

Herbs
1 tablespoon fresh, snipped = 1 teaspoon
    dried or ½ teaspoon ground

Lemon
juice of 1 lemon = about 3 tablespoons
grated peel of 1 lemon = about 1 teaspoon

Macaroni or Tube-Shaped Pastas
1 to 1¼ cups = 4 ounces = 2 to
    2½ cups cooked
16 ounces = about 8 cups cooked

Mushrooms, Fresh
8 ounces = about 2½ cups sliced = about
    1 cup cooked
1 cup sliced and cooked = 4 ounce can,
    drained

Mustard
1 teaspoon dry = 1 tablespoon prepared

Nuts
1 cup chopped = ¼ pound or 4 ounces
1 cup whole or halved = 4 to 5 ounces

Olives
24 small = 2 ounces = about ½ cup sliced

Onion, Green top
1 sliced = about 1 tablespoon
8 sliced, whites only = about ½ cup
4 sliced, whites + 4 inches green top
    = about ½ cup
Regular
1 medium, chopped = ½ cup
1 medium = 1 teaspoon onion powder
    or 1 tablespoon dried minced

Orange
juice of 1 orange = ⅓ to ½ cup
grated peel of 1 orange = about
    2 tablespoons

Potatoes
3 medium = 2 cups sliced or cubed
3 medium = 1¾ cups mashed

Rice
1 cup white rice (long grain) = about
    7 ounces = 3 to 4 cups cooked
1 cup white rice (instant) = 2 cups cooked

1 cup brown rice = 3 cups cooked
1 cup wild rice = 3 to 4 cups cooked
1 pound cooked wild rice = about
   $2^2/_3$ cups dry

Spaghetti and **Noodles**
8 ounces = 4+ cups cooked
1 pound = 8+ cups cooked

Sugar, Powdered
1 pound = 4 cups

Tomatoes
1 cup canned = $1^1/_3$ cups fresh, cut up and
   simmered 5 minutes

Whipping Cream
1 cup = 2 cups whipped

Yeast
1 compressed cake = 1 package or $2^1/_4$
teaspoons regular or quick active dry

Emergency Substitutions

Baking Powder: 1 teaspoon: $^1/_2$ teaspoon
cream of tartar + $^1/_4$ teaspoon baking soda

Balsamic Vinegar: Sherry or cider
vinegar (not white)

Beer: Apple juice or beef broth

Broth: 1 teaspoon granulated or 1 cube
bouillon dissolved in 1 cup water

Brown Sugar, Packed: Equal amount of
granulated sugar

Buttermilk: 1 teaspoon lemon juice or
vinegar plus milk to make 1 cup; let stand
5 minutes

Cajun Seasoning: Equal parts white
pepper, black pepper, ground red pepper,
onion powder, garlic powder, and paprika

Chocolate: For 1 square, unsweetened: 3
tablespoons cocoa plus 1 tablespoon butter
For 1 square, *semisweet*: 1 square unsweetened + 1 tablespoon sugar
For 2 squares, *semisweet*: $^1/_3$ cup semisweet
chips

Corn Syrup: *For light or dark:* 1 cup
sugar + $^1/_4$ cup water
For dark: 1 cup light corn syrup or 1 cup
maple syrup, or $^3/_4$ cup light corn syrup +
$^1/_4$ cup molasses

Cornstarch: For 1 tablespoon: 2 tablespoons all-purpose flour

Cream of Mushroom Soup: For 1 can: 1
cup thick white sauce + 4-ounce can mushrooms, drained and chopped

Dates: *For chopped:* equal amount raisins, prunes, currants, or dried cherries

Eggs: For 1 egg: 2 egg whites or 2 egg yolks or ¼ cup liquid egg substitute

Flour: For cake flour: 1 cup minus 2 tablespoons all-purpose flour

Self-rising flour: 1 cup all-purpose flour + 1 teaspoon baking powder and ½ teaspoon salt

Honey: 1¼ cups sugar + ¼ cup water

Leeks: Equal amount green onions or shallots

Lemon Juice: For 1 teaspoon: 1 teaspoon cider vinegar or white vinegar

Milk: ½ cup evaporated (not condensed) milk plus ½ cup water

Molasses: Equal amount honey

Mushrooms: For 1 cup cooked: 4-ounce can, drained

Poultry Seasoning: For 1 teaspoon: ¾ teaspoon sage + ¼ teaspoon thyme

Prunes: Dates, raisins, or currants

Pumpkin Pie Spice: For 1 teaspoon: ½ teaspoon cinnamon + ¼ teaspoon ground ginger + ⅛ teaspoon ground allspice + ⅛ teaspoon ground nutmeg

Red Pepper Sauce: For 4 drops: ⅛ teaspoon ground cayenne (red) pepper

Sour Cream: Plain yogurt

Tomato Products: For 1 cup juice: ½ cup sauce + ½ cup water
For ½ cup paste: simmer 1 cup sauce till reduced to ½ cup
For 2 cups sauce: ¾ cup paste + 1¼ cup water

Wine: For white: apple juice, apple cider, white grape juice, chicken or vegetable broth, water
For red: apple cider, chicken, beef or vegetable broth, water

Yogurt: Sour cream

Chapter 2
Appetizers, Snacks, and Beverages

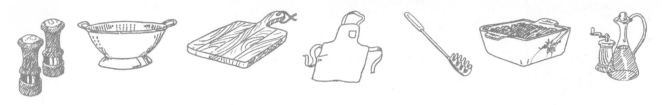

T oday's busy cooks require appetizers that are simple, straightforward, and appealing to most people. Appetizers and first courses should be kept simple as they are intended only to stave off hunger until main courses are served.

Artichoke Dip

Servings: 4

2 15-ounce cans artichoke hearts, drained
    and rinsed
1 red pepper, chopped finely
1 green pepper, chopped finely
3 cloves garlic, minced
2 cups of mayonnaise
white pepper
2 wedges Parmesan cheese (about
    1 pound), grated

Preheat the oven to 325°F. Mix all ingredients except ¼ of the Parmesan cheese. Sprinkle the remaining Parmesan cheese over the top of mixed ingredients and bake in a 9 x 9-inch baking pan or 1½ quart casserole dish for 45 minutes or until golden brown. Serve with crackers or bread.

Spinach Dip

Servings: 6

10-ounce package frozen spinach, thawed
2 cups sour cream
1 cup mayonnaise

1 envelope vegetable soup mix
    (Knorr brand)
1 small white onion, chopped
8-ounce can water chestnuts, drained
    and chopped
2 tablespoons grated Parmesan cheese

Squeeze out water from thawed spinach and do not cook. Add all other ingredients and mix. Serve with raw vegetables, crackers, or a sourdough bread loaf that has been hollowed out and cut into bite-sized pieces. Spinach dip can be served inside the round hollowed out loaf of sourdough bread.

Hummus

Yield: about 2 cups

6–8 large cloves garlic, minced and
    mashed to a paste with ½ teaspoon
    salt added
16–19 ounce can chickpeas,
    rinsed and drained
⅓ cup well-stirred tahini
    (sesame seed paste)*
2 tablespoons fresh lemon juice
2 tablespoons olive oil
2 tablespoons ground cumin

3 tablespoons water
3 tablespoons fresh parsley leaves
salt and pepper to taste

In a food processor or blender, blend together garlic paste, chickpeas, tahini, lemon juice, oil, and cumin, scraping down the sides of the bowl with a rubber scraper until smooth. Add the water, parsley, and salt and pepper and pulse until just combined. Hummus may be made two days ahead and chilled, covered. Serve with pita bread cut into pie-shaped wedges.

*Available at specialty food shops, natural food stores, and some well-stocked supermarkets

Apple Dip

Yield: about 2 cups

8-ounce package cream cheese,
*   regular or light*
$\frac{1}{2}$ cup salad dressing, regular or light
$\frac{1}{2}$ cup finely shredded Cheddar cheese
Yellow Delicious apples

Allow cream cheese to stand at room temperature for 15 minutes. Blend cream cheese thoroughly with the salad dressing. Mix in the cheese, and chill.

Serve with wedges of apples or spread on crackers.

When cut, Yellow Delicious apples do not brown as rapidly as other varieties.

Hot Dungeness Crab Appetizer

Yield: about 2 cups

14-ounce can artichoke hearts
$\frac{1}{2}$ pound Dungeness crabmeat
2 cups mayonnaise
1 small yellow onion, sliced thinly
1 cup shredded Parmesan cheese
minced fresh parsley

Preheat oven to 350°F. Drain artichoke hearts and chop into $\frac{1}{4}$-inch pieces. Drain crab well. Combine all ingredients and mix well. Place in a shallow baking dish and heat in the oven for 6 to 8 minutes or until internal temperature is at least 140°F. Garnish with minced parsley. Serve with assorted breads.

When making dish ahead of time, do not cover with aluminum foil, as crab will discolor.

Babaganouj (Eggplant Dip)

Servings: 6

Serving this with cut vegetables and/or a variety of breads makes a fine meal in itself.

2 small to medium eggplants
juice of 1 large lemon
$\frac{1}{2}$ cup tahini (sesame seed paste)
3 medium cloves garlic, crushed

(continued)

½ cup finely chopped parsley
1 teaspoon salt (or more to taste)
¼ cup finely minced scallion
freshly ground pepper
1 tablespoon olive oil

Preheat oven to 400°F and place aluminum foil on oven bottom. Cut off the stem ends of the eggplants, wash well, and prick them all over with a fork. Place them directly on an oven rack and roast until they are sagging, crumpled, and soft (about 45 minutes).

Remove carefully from the oven and cool until the eggplants can be handled. Scoop out the insides. Combine all other ingredients except the olive oil. Chill thoroughly. Drizzle olive oil over the top before serving.

Variations:

Add 1 cup finely minced onions and 1 cup finely minced mushrooms that have been fried together in olive oil and salt.

Add 1 cup yogurt or sour cream, ½ teaspoon ground cumin, and a few dashes of cayenne pepper.

Roasting eggplant gives it such a wonderful smoky flavor that even people who claim not to like eggplant often eat this dip enthusiastically.

Easy Mustard Dip

Yield: about 1½ cups

1 cup mayonnaise
½ cup Dijon mustard
1 tablespoon prepared horseradish
cut up vegetables
pretzels (optional)

Blend well the mayonnaise, mustard, and horseradish. Chill at least 1 hour. Serve as a dip with vegetables and, if desired, pretzels.

Basic Guacamole

Guacamole is best made with a knife and fork rather than a processor. This standard version allows for a range of "hotness" with the optional addition of jalapeño pepper.

Yield: about 3 cups

¼ small red onion
1 tomato, seeded
2 large avocados (3 if using the smooth green variety with large pits), peeled
1–2 cloves garlic, mashed and chopped
1 tablespoon olive oil
3 tablespoons lime juice
salt and pepper to taste
1 fresh jalapeño, seeded and chopped (optional)

Cut the onion, tomato, and avocado flesh into rough ½-inch chunks. Mash them in a bowl with a sturdy fork, then add the remaining ingredients. Made in this way, the guacamole is particularly good as a substitute for salsa when the main dish is grilled meat or fish.

Do not purée avocados, as an authentic guacamole contains small chunks of avocado. Serve guacamole with tortilla chips.

Sour Cream Dip

Yield: about 2½ cups

2 cups sour cream
¼ cup mayonnaise
2 tablespoons chopped fresh dill or 1 tablespoon dried, crumbled dill
2 tablespoons chopped fresh green onion
2 tablespoon chopped chives
1 tablespoon chopped parsley
salt
freshly ground pepper

Mix the sour cream, mayonnaise, dill, onion, chives, and parsley. Season to taste with salt and pepper, and chill. Serve with fresh raw garden vegetables.

Keep vegetables like carrots, celery, cauliflower, and broccoli (but not tomatoes or mushrooms) in bowls of ice water in the refrigerator to crisp them.

Tomato Bruschetta

Servings: 8

8 slices French bread
2 cloves garlic, halved
1 teaspoon olive oil
2 tablespoons minced onion
1 diced tomato
pinch of oregano, crumbled
pinch of pepper
2 tablespoons grated Parmesan cheese

Toast the bread on both sides. Rub one side of each piece of toast with the cut side of the garlic. Keep hot.

Heat the oil in a nonstick skillet over medium-high heat. Add the onion and cook, stirring until tender, about 10 minutes. Remove from the heat and stir in the tomato, oregano, and pepper. Spoon the tomato mixture over garlic-rubbed side of the toast, dividing evenly. Sprinkle with the cheese and brown slightly under a preheated broiler for 1 minute. Serve immediately.

Cheese Frittata

Servings: 6

Served as an appetizer with cold meats and cheeses, this easy dish makes a tasty and colorful spread.

> 8 eggs
> $^1/_2$ cup shredded fontina cheese
> 1 cup grated Romano or Parmesan cheese
> $^3/_4$ cup cream (half-and-half)
> 2 cups cooked spaghetti or macaroni (5 ounces uncooked)
> 1 teaspoon kosher salt
> $^1/_4$ teaspoon cracked pepper
> 1 tablespoon chopped fresh parsley, tarragon, oregano, or sage
> $^1/_4$ cup olive oil

Preheat oven to 350°F. Whisk the eggs in a large mixing bowl. Add all the remaining ingredients except the olive oil, and stir to combine. Heat the olive oil in a 9-inch cast iron skillet. When the oil is hot, but not smoking, add the egg mixture. Bake the skillet mixture in the oven for 20 to 25 minutes until set.

Cool for 5 to 10 minutes before unmolding. Scrape the edge of the skillet with a rubber spatula to unmold the frittata and loosen it. Slide it onto a serving plate and cut into slices. Serve immediately or allow to cool to room temperature.

Stuffed Mushrooms

Servings: 6

> 1 pound of mushrooms (caps approximately $1^1/_2$ inches across)
> 3 tablespoons butter
> $^1/_2$ cup onion, finely chopped
> $^3/_4$ cup bread crumbs
> $^1/_2$ teaspoon salt
> freshly ground pepper to taste
> 1 teaspoon dried thyme
> $^1/_4$ cup cream (half-and-half)
> $^1/_4$ cup finely grated Parmesan cheese
> 2 tablespoons chopped parsley

Clean the mushrooms and gently pull the stem from each cap, setting the caps aside.

Chop the mushroom stems and set aside. Heat butter in a skillet over medium heat. Add the onion and cook for 1 minute. Add the chopped stems and cook for an additional 2 to 3 minutes. Stir in the bread crumbs, salt, pepper, and thyme, and continue to cook for 1 minute more. Remove from heat and stir in cream and grated cheese.

Using a small spoon, fill each mushroom cap with the mushroom mixture. Place the filled mushrooms on a baking sheet and put under the preheated oven broiler for 5 to 7 minutes or until the tops are browned and caps have softened and are slightly juicy. Sprinkle the tops with chopped parsley and serve hot or warm.

Southwestern Quesadillas

Servings: 6

8-ounce can refried beans
½ cup fresh tomato salsa (page 116)
6 10-inch flour tortillas
2 bunches fresh green onions, chopped
2 tablespoons chopped fresh cilantro
1½ cups grated aged Cheddar cheese
2-ounce can green chili strips
sour cream, guacamole, or salsa for garnish

Place beans and fresh salsa in a bowl, and mash using a potato masher. Spread mixture evenly on the 6 tortillas, leaving a ½ inch border. Sprinkle bean mixture with onions, cilantro, cheese, and green chile strips.

Fold each tortilla (making a half moon) and bake in a 350°F oven or heat on a skillet or griddle on top of the stove until the cheese melts. (Tortillas can also be grilled on a medium-hot greased grill.) Do not heat so long that the outside completely dries out and stiffens.

Cut the finished product into pie-shaped wedges and garnish with sour cream, guacamole, and/or additional salsa.

Taco Scoop

Servings: 3 cups

8-ounce container sour cream
½ teaspoon chili powder
2 medium ripe tomatoes
2 cups shredded lettuce
8 ounces shredded sharp Cheddar cheese
nacho-flavor tortilla chips
1 tablespoon chopped fresh cilantro, parsley, or chives (optional)

Blend together the sour cream and chili powder. Seed and chop the tomatoes, draining on paper towels if necessary. Spread the sour cream in a 13 x 9-inch glass baking dish or on a serving platter. Sprinkle the lettuce, herbs, cheese, and tomatoes on top. Serve with nacho chips for dipping.

Ham Roll-Ups

Yield: about 2 dozen appetizers

3 9-inch flour tortillas
3-ounce package cream cheese
¼ cup sour cream
6 rectangular slices boiled ham (about 6 x 4)
¼ cup chopped fresh chives or sliced green onions
¼ cup shredded Cheddar, Swiss, or Monterey Jack cheese
tomato salsa (optional)

(continued)

Have the tortillas at room temperature. Soften the cream cheese, and combine with the sour cream. Spread on the tortillas. On each tortilla, place two slices of ham. Sprinkle with the chives and cheese. Roll up, wrap in plastic wrap, and chill for at least 3 hours.

To serve, cut into 1-inch slices. If desired, serve with tomato salsa.

Veggie Roll-Ups

Yield: about 24 appetizers

5 9-inch flour tortillas
8-ounce package cream cheese
¹/₄ cup sliced green onion
¹/₄ cup chopped black olives
¹/₂ cup chopped bell pepper—
green, red, yellow, or mixed
tomato salsa, optional

Have the tortillas at room temperature. Soften the cream cheese and spread on the tortillas, dividing evenly. Sprinkle the vegetables evenly over the tortillas. Roll each up tightly and wrap with plastic wrap. Refrigerate at least 3 hours.

To serve, cut in diagonal slices about ³/₄ inch thick. If desired, serve with tomato salsa.

Seafood Roll-Ups

Yield: about 24 appetizers

5 9-inch flour tortillas
8-ounce package cream cheese
¹/₄ cup salad dressing
1 can crabmeat or 1 can shrimp, well
drained and chopped, or 5 ounces
fresh crabmeat, imitation crabmeat, or
cooked shrimp, chopped
2 tablespoons chopped fresh chives
¹/₄ cup chopped red bell pepper
tomato salsa, optional

Have the tortillas at room temperature. Soften the cream cheese and combine with the salad dressing. Blend in the chopped seafood. Spread on the tortillas, dividing evenly. Sprinkle the vegetables evenly over the tortillas. Roll each up tightly and wrap with plastic wrap. Refrigerate at least 3 hours.

To serve, cut in diagonal slices about ³/₄ inch thick. If desired, serve with tomato salsa.

Corned Beef Pâté

Yield: about 2 cups

8 ounces fresh mushrooms
1 tablespoon butter
¹/₂ cup finely chopped onion
¹/₂ cup sour cream
¹/₂ teaspoon dry mustard
¹/₄ teaspoon white pepper

1 tablespoon prepared horseradish
3 tablespoons chopped fresh parsley
12-ounce can corned beef
rye crackers

Chop the mushrooms finely. Melt the butter in a skillet and sauté mushrooms and onions until mushrooms are reduced and cooked. Allow to cool.

Mix the sour cream with the mustard, pepper, horseradish, and parsley, then blend in the corned beef. Blend in the mushroom-onion mixture, mixing thoroughly. Pack into a two-cup mold or adequately sized bowl that has been lined with plastic wrap. Chill at least 3 hours.

Unmold onto a serving plate and serve with rye crackers.

Spinach Balls

A classic "freeze-ahead" recipe

Yield: about 20 balls

> 2 packages frozen spinach, thawed
> 2 cups dry herb-seasoned bread stuffing mix
> 6 eggs
> 1 cup finely chopped onion
> ³/₄ cups butter, melted
> ³/₄ cups grated Parmesan cheese
> 1 cup chopped fresh parsley
> 1¹/₂ teaspoons garlic powder
> ¹/₂ teaspoon thyme
> ¹/₂ teaspoon pepper
> 1 teaspoon salt

Drain the spinach well by squeezing in several thicknesses of paper towels. Chop finely. In a large bowl, combine all ingredients and mix well. Form into small (1¹/₄ inch diameter) balls; place on a cookie sheet and freeze solid.

When frozen, place in plastic freezer bags and store in the freezer until needed.

To bake: Preheat the oven to 375°F. Place frozen balls on a cookie sheet and bake for 20 minutes.

Parmesan Crisps

Yield: about 40 crisps

> 1 loaf French bread baguette
>   (about 12 inches)*
> 1 cup butter
> 1 cup grated Parmesan cheese

Preheat oven to 400°F.

Slice the baguette into ¹/₄-inch slices, discarding the heels. In a small flat-bottomed baking dish, melt the butter. In a similar bowl, place the grated cheese. Quickly dip each side of the bread slices in butter (do not soak!), then in the cheese. Place in a jellyroll pan (do not substitute a cookie sheet because some butter may drain off in cooking).

Bake 5 minutes, then turn slices over. Bake an additional 4 minutes or until browned.

*Note: A baguette is smaller in diameter than a regular loaf of French bread.

Retro Canapés

Perfect to serve with martinis!

Yield: about 20 canapés

> 3 tablespoons salad dressing
> 1 can crabmeat or 1 can shrimp, well
>   drained and chopped, or 5 ounces
>   fresh crabmeat, imitation crabmeat, or
>   cooked shrimp, chopped
> $1/4$ teaspoon white pepper
> salt to taste
> 1 small jar pearl onions
> 1 small jar stuffed green olives
> 1 package melba toast wafers or
>   similar cracker

Blend the salad dressing with the seafood, pepper, and salt. Drain onions and olives well, using paper towels. To assemble, place a heaping teaspoon of the seafood mixture in the center of each wafer and top with either an onion or an olive.

Appetizer Lingo

Canapé (say "cana-PAY" or "CAN-apay"): A small piece of toasted bread, baked pastry, or cracker topped with cheese, meat, fish, or a seasoned spread, and often containing cheese, meat, or fish. A decorative topping, like a pimiento or olive, is often added.

Crudités (say "crew-da-TAY"): Cut up raw vegetables, usually served with a dip.

Hors d'oeuvres (say "or-DURVE"): Small bite-sized foods served before a meal, often with cocktails. Both canapés and crudités are hors d'oeuvres. So are all types of combinations of dips or spreads served with bite-sized fruits, chips, or crackers.

Tamari Cashews

You won't be able to eat just one of these delicious roasted nuts. Serve them with drinks or eat as a protein snack anytime.

Yield: about 3 cups

> 1 tablespoon canola or sunflower oil
> 1 pound broken cashews
> 2 tablespoons soy sauce

Preheat the oven to 350°F. Pour the oil into a baking dish and add the nuts, turning them in the oil. Roast in the oven. for about 15 minutes, turning occasionally, until golden.

Sprinkle the soy sauce over the nuts, turning and coating them. Return to the oven for an additional 5 minutes. Cool and store in a sealable container.

Sweet Summer Cucumbers

Fresh summer cucumbers make this a special seasonal condiment.

Yield: about 6 cups

> 2 cups thinly sliced white onions
> 8 cups thinly sliced cucumbers
> 2 cups sugar
> 1 cup cider vinegar
> 2 tablespoons salt
> 2 teaspoons celery seed

Stir the onions gently into the cucumbers. Mix together the sugar, vinegar, salt, and celery seed. Pour the liquid mixture over the cucumbers and onions and put into a large glass or plastic container in the refrigerator. Let the mixture marinate for a couple of days before eating.

Mustard Pickles

Yield: about 1 quart

> *very small cucumbers*
> *1 tablespoon salt*
> *2 tablespoons sugar*
> *1 tablespoon ground dry mustard*
> *cider vinegar*

Scrub cucumbers well. Mix salt, sugar, and ground mustard together; add to a quart jar half filled with cider vinegar. Add very small cucumbers to vinegar mixture, filling to the point where all cucumbers remain covered with the liquid. Refrigerate and allow cucumbers to marinate for at least two weeks.

Very small cucumbers can be gathered from your garden in summer and refrigerated until you have enough to fill a quart jar.

Wake Up Smoothie

Serves: 1

> *1 cup strong coffee, chilled*
> *1 ripe banana*
> *8-ounce container plain or vanilla yogurt*
> *1 tablespoon powdered instant chocolate milk flavoring, optional*
> *about 4 ice cubes*

Combine all ingredients in a blender and blend on high until smooth.

Tropical Fruit Energizer

Servings: 2

$\frac{1}{2}$ ripe banana, frozen
1 cup fresh fruit (any combination of
    papaya, mango, or passion fruit)
$\frac{1}{2}$ cup nonfat vanilla yogurt
$\frac{1}{4}$ cup papaya, mango, or passion
    fruit nectar*
$\frac{1}{4}$ cup soy protein powder
pinch of powdered ginger

Blend in a blender or food processor and drink immediately.

*Juice "nectars" can be found in the juice section of most well-stocked supermarkets, or in the natural food section of larger grocery stores.

Making Good Coffee

Brewing good coffee is a simple procedure if some basic rules are followed.

- Start with fresh coffee. Vacuum-packed coffee is fine, although if not sealed well and refrigerated, the beans will lose their aroma quickly (aroma is the key to freshness). Buying your own beans and grinding them each time you brew coffee is the best way to insure the freshest cup of coffee.

- Use 2 level tablespoons of coffee to 1 cup of water. If you want stronger coffee, add more coffee grounds, however, do not compensate by brewing the coffee longer, as this only leads to overextraction and bitterness. To make the coffee weaker, use the same proportions, but add additional boiling water *after* the coffee is brewed rather than reducing the amount of coffee grounds.

- The temperature of the water for making coffee with steeped or pressed coffee makers should be approximately 205°F, just under boiling. Taking the boiling kettle off the heat and letting it rest a minute or two will bring the water back to the appropriate temperature range. Use bottled water if your tap water contains salts or minerals.

- Use the right grind for the particular kind of coffee you are making. Use drip for the drip method, regular for the percolator method, coarse for the steeped and pressed methods, and fine for vacuum or espresso methods.

- Coffee that stays too long at a high temperature or is reheated will taste bitter and harsh. Store leftover coffee in an insulated carafe.

- Keep coffee-making equipment very clean, washing after use with a detergent and soaking any filters.

- To make iced coffee, double the amount of coffee and prepare as usual. Let the coffee cool and then add the ice cubes.

- After-dinner coffee made with a liqueur (also called a "cordial") or other alcoholic addition is often served after a special meal.

Irish Coffee

This after-dinner drink goes well with a wide variety of foods.

Servings: 1

1 jigger Irish whiskey
1 teaspoon sugar
1 cup very hot after-dinner coffee
2 tablespoons whipped cream

Pour the whiskey into a glass or mug. Stir in the sugar and add the hot coffee. Top with whipped cream and serve immediately.

Making Good Tea

The best tea is made with leaves steeped in boiling water. Loose tea is best, although tea bags work well if they are put in a warm teapot or mug and boiling water is used. Tea made with a tea bag in a cup of hot water does not do justice to this traditional drink.

- The water used for making tea should always be freshly drawn and brought to a rolling boil in a kettle.
- Use earthenware or china teapots for steeping the tea. Metal is likely to alter the flavor of tea slightly.
- Warm the teapot, mug, or cup by pouring boiling water in and swirling it around before discarding.
- Put a teaspoon of loose tea or one tea bag into the pot for each cup of water

and then gently pour the just-boiled water over the tea. A tea ball for loose tea can also be used. Stir once, cover, and steep 5 minutes. For a single cup, steep 3 to 4 minutes. Do not dunk the bag.

- Pour loose tea into a cup with a tea strainer. If tea is too strong, weaken at this point by adding boiling water. It is easier to weaken strong tea than add tea leaves after it has brewed.
- Serve with cream, milk, sugar, or slices of lemon.
- To make iced tea, double the amount of tea per cup, make as above, and then pour it into a pitcher. Add the ice when cool. If you have little time and want to add ice to the hot tea, triple the amount of tea used when steeping.

Fruit Punch

Yield: about 8 cups

1½ cups sugar
1 quart strong hot tea
1 quart orange juice
1 cup lemon juice
1 quart ginger ale
fresh mint leaves

Dissolve the sugar in the hot tea and mix together with the citrus juices. Pour over a large block of ice. Just before

serving add the ginger ale, and scatter fresh mint leaves on the top.

Raspberry or strawberry fruit syrup* (¹/₂ cup) can be used instead of the sugar. Add additional sugar to taste. If desired, add fresh fruit (strawberries, sliced peaches or mangoes) to the bowl before serving.

*Fruit syrup can be found in the baking supplies section of most well-stocked supermarkets.

Fruit Punch

Yield: 1 gallon

Punch:
6-ounce can frozen lemonade concentrate
8-ounce can crushed pineapple, undrained
10-ounce package frozen strawberries
3 quarts ginger ale, well chilled

Ice Ring:
Ginger ale
6 medium whole strawberries,
 stems removed

Combine the lemonade concentrate, pineapple with juice, and frozen strawberries; blend on high until completely smooth. Refrigerate until ready to serve. When ready to serve, combine in a punch bowl or other container with the ginger ale. If desired, one bottle of champagne can be substituted for one bottle of ginger ale.

To make the ice ring, place the strawberries evenly in a ring mold. Fill to within ¹/₂ inch of the top with ginger ale and freeze overnight, or until solid. (The ice ring is made with ginger ale rather than water so it will not water down the punch as it thaws.)

Variation: Substitute a 16-ounce can of sliced peaches, drained, for the pineapple. If desired, 1 pint of rum, or to taste, can be added.

Homemade Lemonade

Lemonade made this way bears little resemblance to the watered down version purchased in the supermarket. It is worth the effort and tastes wonderful on a hot summer day.

Yield: about 10 cups

5 to 6 large lemons
1³/₄ cup brown sugar or honey
¹/₂ gallon boiling water

Scrub the lemons and halve them. Squeeze the juice and pulp into a large bowl. Add the sugar, and pour half the water over it. Stir until the sugar dissolves. Add the lemon halves and the rest of the water. Stir well, then cover and allow to cool.

Strain, squeezing out the juice from the lemon halves, and serve with ice.

Hot Spiced Cider

Servings: 4

> 1 teaspoon whole cloves
> ¼ teaspoon nutmeg
> dash ginger
> 1 quart cider, fresh pressed if available
> 5 cinnamon sticks
> 4 thin orange slices

Place the cloves, nutmeg, and ginger in a tea ball*. Pour the cider into a large saucepan into which one of the cinnamon sticks has been placed. Hang the tea ball on the side of the pot, being sure that it is submerged in the cider. Float the orange slices on top. Heat to a temperature just below a simmer and allow to cook for at least 15 minutes.

To serve, place one cinnamon stick in each of four mugs and pour cider in, leaving the oranges and cinnamon stick in the pot. (Careful—it will be hot!) If desired, one jigger of bourbon can be added to each mug.

*A tea ball is an inexpensive small roundish metal gadget with many small holes in it, designed to hold loose tea. It is available in grocery, variety, and cooking stores.

For a Hot Summer Day

Minted Litemilk Shake

*A handful of ice cubes
1 cup of skim milk
pinch of salt
a small handful of fresh
    mint leaves*

Combine all the ingredients in a blender. Cover and blend until the ice becomes blended. Pour into a tall mug and garnish with more mint leaves.

Chapter 3

Breads, Muffins, and Coffee Cakes

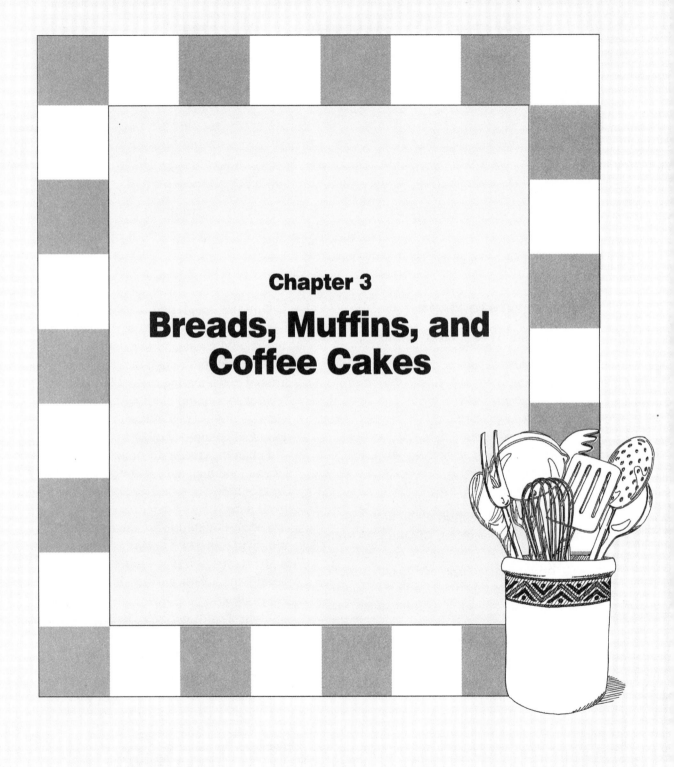

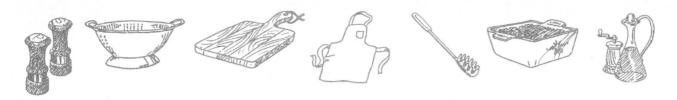

Bread is not just for sandwiches anymore. Delicious muffins are perfect for breakfast or a snack. Flavorful focaccia breads make wonderful pizzas and are great for dipping. Sweet or fruity dessert breads are an ideal finale after a light meal like salad or pasta.

You can add a mix-in or two—like walnuts or raisins—but it's a good idea not to go overboard because too many chunky items can cause the muffin or bread to become too moist or too crumbly after baking. In this chapter you'll find the perfect bread to complement any meal.

Basic White Bread

Yield: 3 small or 2 large loaves

5½–6 cups all-purpose flour
1 package active dry yeast
¼ cup warm water
2 tablespoons sugar
1 tablespoon salt
1¾ cups warm potato water or
    plain water*
2 tablespoons shortening

Place about one third of the flour in a large bowl and set aside. Mix the yeast with ¼ cup warm water in another bowl, stirring well. Add the sugar, salt, and potato water to the yeast. Add the mixture to the flour in the bowl and stir well. Cut in the shortening, using a pastry blender or your hands. Stir in as much of the remaining flour as possible.

Turn the dough onto a lightly floured work surface. Knead 8 to 10 minutes until smooth and elastic, adding flour as necessary. Transfer the dough to a large well-greased bowl, turning to coat both sides. Cover with a damp cloth and place in a warm, draft-free area. Allow to rise until double in volume, about 1 to 1½ hours.

Punch the dough down and let rise a second time until almost doubled in bulk. Grease three 8 x 4-inch or two 9 x 5-inch bread pans.

Punch dough down a second time and divide into two or three loaves. Shape loaves and place into prepared bread pans. Cover and let rise until almost doubled.

Preheat oven to 350°F. Bake 20 to 30 minutes, or until golden brown. Remove from pans and allow to cool on a rack.

(continued)

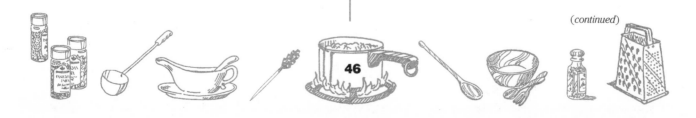

46

Making and Kneading Bread Dough

Begin stirring about half the flour into the dissolved yeast. Beat about 2 minutes, using an electric mixer on medium speed. The dough will still be very batter-like in consistency.

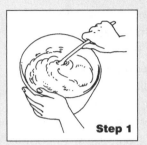
Step 1

1 Mix in as much of the remaining flour as possible, using a wooden spoon. Some cooks prefer to use their hands for this step. The dough will "form" or become stiff enough to leave the sides of the bowl.

Turn onto a lightly floured work surface. *Lightly floured* means you will use approximately 1 tablespoon for each cup of flour in the recipe before you have finished kneading.

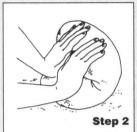
Step 2

2 Knead the dough by folding it over toward you and pushing down with the heels of your hands. Then turn the dough about an eighth turn and repeat. Continue this process until the dough is satiny and elastic and no longer sticks to the board, usually about 8 to 10 minutes. Some air bubbles or blisters will appear under the surface of the dough.

Step 3

3 Grease a large bowl well. Place the dough in it, turning a time or two to grease the dough's surface lightly. Cover with a damp cloth and allow to rise in a warm place, about 75° to 80°F.

4 Allow dough to rise until doubled in size, usually about 2 hours. Do not allow to overrise; it will begin to collapse and the bread's texture will not be satisfactory. To test, press fingertips into the dough about $1/2$ inch. If the imprint remains, the dough has risen the proper amount.

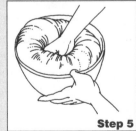
Step 4

5 Make a fist and punch down the dough in the center, then fold the edges over and down into the middle, and turn the dough over in the bowl. Punching down and kneading the bread again removes large air bubbles and creates a fine texture.

Step 5

If **directed by a recipe**, knead the dough a second time, usually no more than 2 minutes. Knead in the bowl, if it is large enough, or turn onto the work surface. (Some breads do not require a second kneading.) Return to the bowl, cover, and let rise a second time until almost but not quite doubled.

To make cinnamon raisin bread: When stirring in the bulk of the flour, add 1 cup of raisins. In a separate bowl, mix together ⅓ cup sugar and 2½ teaspoons cinnamon. Divide dough in half. With a rolling pin roll each half into a rectangular shape about ½ inch thick. After dough is shaped into rectangles, sprinkle each with about 1 tablespoon of water and part of the sugar mixture before rolling. Roll each rectangle up and place in a 9 x 5-inch loaf pan.

 Save the water in which you boil potatoes to use in making white bread. Potato water improves the action of yeast. It also adds a subtle flavor and keeps home-baked bread moist longer.

Whole-Wheat Bread

Adapted from an old-fashioned "sponge" recipe

Yield: 2 loaves

    2 cups warm water
    1 package dry yeast
    3 cups all-purpose or bread flour
    2 tablespoons sugar
    2 teaspoons salt
    ½ cup hot water
    ½ cup brown sugar
    3 tablespoons shortening
    3 cups whole-wheat flour

To the 2 cups warm water, add the yeast, crumbling well. Stir in the all-purpose flour, sugar, and salt. Beat the mixture by hand or with an electric mixer until smooth. Set the mixture in a warm place until it becomes foamy and bubbly, up to an hour.

To the ½ cup hot water, add the brown sugar and shortening; stir. Allow to cool to lukewarm. Add to the bubbly flour mixture, which is called a sponge. Stir in the whole-wheat flour and beat by hand until smooth, but *do not knead.*

Divide the dough into two lightly greased bread pans, cover, and set in a warm place until doubled in size.

Preheat the oven to 350°F and bake 50 minutes.

History Lesson: The sponge process of making bread was more popular in Great Grandma's day, when foodstuffs were less processed and the quality of yeast was less consistently reliable. The yeast works in a batter and the dough rises only once. The sponge process results in a loaf that is lighter but coarser grained.

 Always place bread pans and muffin tins in the center of the oven to allow heat circulation.

Shaping the Bread into a Loaf
Traditional Method

Divide the dough into sections as indicated in the recipe.

1 Flatten the dough into a rectangle shape (about 9 ″ x 18 ″) with your hands or with a rolling pin. If necessary, turn the dough so that one of the shorter ends is facing you.

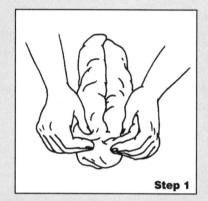

Step 1

2 Roll the dough toward you *tightly*. Seal the seam by pinching. Turn the loaf seam side down. Press each end with the side of your stiffened hand. Tuck the edges under the loaf and place in the pan seam side down. The ends of the bread should touch the short ends of the pan.

Cover and let rise again until almost, but not quite, doubled in size. The dough should fill out the corners of the pan and an imprint should remain if you press the bread lightly.

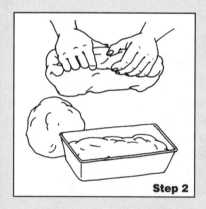

Step 2

49

Oatmeal Bread

Yield: 3 loaves

4 cups milk
1½ cups rolled oats, quick cooking or regular
¾ cup molasses
¼ cup shortening
2 teaspoons salt
1 cup raisins or currants

1 package active dry yeast, dissolved in ¼ cup warm water
1 cup whole-wheat flour
6–7 cups all-purpose flour
melted butter

Scald the milk. Remove from heat and stir in oats, molasses, shortening, salt, and raisins, mixing until well combined. Allow to cool about 10 minutes or until lukewarm, stirring occasionally.

Add the dissolved yeast to the oat mixture. Stir in the whole-wheat flour and enough all-purpose flour to make a workable dough. Turn onto a floured board and knead until smooth and elastic.

Place the dough in a greased bowl and cover. Allow it to double in size in a warm place. Grease 3 loaf pans.

Punch down dough and shape into 3 loaves, placing them in prepared pans. Cover and allow to rise again until almost doubled. Total time required for rising will be up to 3 hours.

Preheat the oven to 400°F. Bake at 400°F for 10 minutes, then reduce oven heat to 375°F and bake for an additional 40 minutes. Remove from pans and brush tops lightly with melted butter. Allow to cool on a rack.

Bread Pan Tips

Metal pans with dark finishes or coatings and glass pans will result in crustier, browner loaves than shiny metal pans.

Remove bread from the pan immediately and cool on a rack to maintain a crisp crust. Breads left to cool slightly in the pan will soften.

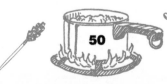

Irish Soda Bread

Yield: 1 large circular loaf

3 cups flour
3 teaspoons baking powder
1 teaspoon baking soda
$\frac{1}{4}$ cup sugar
$\frac{1}{8}$ teaspoon salt
$\frac{1}{4}$ cup shortening
1 egg
$1\frac{1}{2}$ cups buttermilk
1 cup raisins or currants
1 tablespoon caraway seed

Preheat oven to 375°F.

Combine flour, baking powder, baking soda, sugar, and salt. Cut in the shortening and set aside. Beat the egg well and add the buttermilk. Add egg mixture to dry ingredients along with raisins and caraway. Combine thoroughly.

Turn onto a floured work surface and knead briefly, for about 1 minute. Shape into a round loaf and place into a greased 9- or 10-inch skillet or pan. With a sharp knife, cut a cross extending over the top and sides of the bread and brush with milk. Bake for 50 to 60 minutes.

Cornmeal Soda Bread

$1\frac{1}{2}$ cups fine white flour
$1\frac{1}{2}$ cups stone-ground corn flour
1 teaspoon sea salt
$\frac{1}{2}$ teaspoon soda
$1\frac{1}{4}$–$1\frac{1}{2}$ cups buttermilk
milk

Preheat oven to 350°F. Grease and flour 1 9-inch round cake pan.

Combine dry ingredients in a large bowl and whisk to thoroughly combine, breaking up any lumps you may find. Add the buttermulk in a steady stream while stirring with a wooden spoon. Stir until just combined, then spoon into the prepared cake pan. Brush the top with milk and bake for 55 minutes or until a toothpick inserted in the center comes out clean.

Soda breads can be ready quickly and are good accompaniment to a bowl of homemade soup and slices of aged Cheddar cheese.

Herb-Flavored Focaccia

Focaccia bread has become a popular favorite for use in pizzas and as a delicious accompaniment to Italian or any other meals. To make this more crispy, drizzle a little olive oil on the crust before baking; to make it softer, brush the crust with oil immediately after it comes out of the oven. Focaccia, a wonderful sandwich bread alternative, can transform a simple entrée into a special treat.

Yield: 2 loaves

> 1 package active dry yeast
> 1 cup lukewarm water (105°F)
> 2 tablespoons olive oil
> 2½ cups all-purpose flour, plus additional flour for kneading
> 1 teaspoon salt
> 2 tablespoons chopped fresh chives
> 1½ teaspoons finely chopped fresh rosemary
> extra-virgin olive oil for brushing
> coarse salt

In a large mixing bowl, stir the yeast into ¼ cup of the lukewarm water. Let stand until creamy, about 10 minutes. Stir in the remaining ¾ cup lukewarm water and the olive oil. Add the salt and 1 cup of the flour and whisk until smooth. Add the chives and rosemary and mix well. Stir in the remaining flour, ½ cup at a time, until the dough comes together in a rough mass.

On a lightly-floured work surface, knead the dough until smooth, 8 to 10 minutes. Lightly oil a bowl, place the dough in it, and turn the dough to coat with oil. Cover the bowl with plastic wrap and put in a warm place to rise until doubled in bulk, about 1½ hours.

Divide the dough into 2 equal portions and knead slightly. If using for pizza, the dough is now ready to be stretched and topped as directed in recipes for pizza. If it is to be stored, follow storing directions for Neapolitan pizza dough (Chapter 15). If you prefer a thinner, more resilient focaccia, stretch out the dough onto a larger pan.

If plain focaccia is preferred, lightly oil two 8-inch cake pans. Place the dough into the two pans, and gently stretch it out to the edges, pulling it from the center outward to achieve an even thickness. If the dough springs back toward the center and is difficult to work with, cover and set it aside for 10 minutes to relax, then continue coaxing the dough out to an even thickness. Cover the pans with kitchen towels and let rise until almost doubled in bulk and very soft and puffy, about 45 minutes.

Preheat the oven to 475°F. Using your fingertips, dimple the dough in several places, leaving indentations about ½ inch deep. Again cover the pans with towels and let rise

for 20 minutes longer. Bake until golden brown and cooked through, 15 to 18 minutes. Remove from the oven and immediately brush the tops with a generous amount of extra virgin olive oil, then sprinkle with coarse salt. Serve hot or at room temperature.

Cornbread

Yield: 4 servings

¾ cup yellow cornmeal
⅔ cup flour
¼ cup sugar
2 teaspoons baking powder
½ teaspoon salt
⅔ cup milk
½ cup whipping cream
1 egg yolk
6 tablespoons unsalted butter, melted
2 egg whites

Preheat oven to 425°F. Combine cornmeal, flour, sugar, baking powder, and salt in a large bowl.

Mix milk, cream, and egg yolk in another bowl. Whisk in melted butter. Add dry ingredients. Gently mix together and do not overmix.

Whip egg whites until stiff peaks form. Fold into batter using a rubber spatula. Pour batter into a greased 8-inch-square baking pan. Bake 20 minutes or until toothpick inserted in center comes out clean. Cut into squares.

The best way to achieve firm, fine-textured egg whites is to beat room temperature whites in a copper bowl. If you do not have a copper bowl, add a little cream of tartar.

Garlic Cheese Bread

Yield: 1 loaf

4 medium cloves garlic
½ cup butter
1 loaf French bread, unsliced
⅓ cup grated Parmesan cheese
1 teaspoon dried or 1 tablespoon fresh snipped parsley

Preheat oven to 375°F. Peel the garlic cloves and slice in half. Soften the butter.

With a bread knife, make diagonal cuts 1 inch apart in the bread, but do not cut completely through the bottom of the loaf. Rub each slice and the top of the loaf with the cut garlic. After rubbing, mince the garlic and combine with the softened butter, parsley, and cheese. Spread between each slice, reserving a little to spread on top of the loaf.

Wrap foil around the bread, but leave the top open. Bake 15 to 20 minutes.

Hint: Prepare the butter mixture in advance to allow flavors to blend. Cover well and refrigerate; soften before using.

Buttermilk Soda Bread

1½ cups fine white flour
1½ cups stone-ground corn flour
1 teaspoon sea salt
½ teaspoon soda
1¼–1½ cups buttermilk
milk

Preheat oven to 350°F. Grease and flour 1 9-inch round cake pan.

Combine dry ingredients in a large bowl and whisk to thoroughly combine, breaking up any lumps you may find. Add the buttermilk in a steady stream while stirring with a wooden spoon. Stir until just combined, then spoon into the prepared cake pan. Brush the top with milk and bake for 55 minutes or until a toothpick inserted in the center comes out clean.

 Soda breads can be ready quickly and are a good accompaniment to a bowl of homemade soup and slices of aged Cheddar cheese.

Irish Brown Bread

2 cups stone-ground whole-wheat flour
1 cup fine white pastry flour
1 teaspoon baking soda
½ teaspoon sea salt
1¼ to 1½ cups buttermilk
milk

Preheat oven to 350°F. Grease and flour 1 9-inch round cake pan.

Combine dry ingredients in a large bowl and whisk thoroughly to combine, breaking up lumps. Add the buttermilk in a steady stream while stirring with a wooden spoon. Stir until just combined, then spoon into the prepared cake pan. Brush the top with milk and bake for 55 minutes or until a toothpick inserted in the center comes out clean.

Irish cooks say this bread is best if it is allowed to cool and "set" for 4 to 6 hours.

Basic Raised Rolls

Yield: 24 to 32 rolls

3½–4 cups flour, divided
⅓ cup sugar
1 teaspoon salt
1 package regular or quick-acting dry yeast
1 cup milk
⅓ cup butter or shortening
1 egg
extra butter (for crescent rolls)

Mix 2 cups of the flour with the sugar, salt, and yeast. In a saucepan, heat the milk and butter until the butter is almost melted. Beat the egg lightly. Add the egg and the milk mixture to the dry ingredients. Beat with an electric mixer at medium speed for 1 minute, scraping the bowl often, then beat on high speed for 1 additional minute. By hand, stir in as much of the remaining flour as necessary to make a dough that can be easily handled.

Turn dough onto a lightly floured surface and knead until smooth and elastic, at least 5 minutes. As you knead, work in additional flour as necessary to obtain a fairly stiff dough. Place the dough into a greased bowl. Cover and let double in size in a warm place, about 1 hour.

Punch the dough down. Working on a lightly floured surface, cut the dough in half. **Choose one of the following two shapes for the rolls,** then continue.

Cloverleaf Rolls: Makes 24 rolls. Grease 24 muffin cups on both the bottom and sides. Cut each half of dough into 36 pieces. Shape into balls and place 3 in each muffin cup. Skip the next paragraph, then continue as directed.

Crescent or Butterhorn Rolls: Makes 24 to 32 rolls. Grease 2 cookie sheets. Roll each half of dough into a 12-inch circle. Brush with very soft, but not melted, butter. Cut each circle into 12 to 16 wedges as desired. Beginning at the outer (larger) edge, roll up loosely and place with point side down on the cookie sheet. Continue as directed below.

Continuation of general directions: Cover pans of rolls and allow to rise in a warm place until just double in size (about 30 minutes.) Preheat the oven to 375°F. Bake rolls for 12 to 18 minutes, or until golden brown (time will vary with type and size of rolls).

Whole Wheat Raised Rolls: **Substitute** 1 cup of whole-wheat flour for 1 cup of all-purpose flour that is stirred by hand into the dough formed with an electric mixer. Continue as directed above.

Batter Pan Rolls: Use only 1 cup of all-purpose or whole-wheat flour when stirring flour by hand into the dough formed with an electric mixer. **Don't Knead the dough.** Spoon batter into 18 muffin cups that have been well greased on both the bottoms and sides, filling them about half full. Cover and allow to rise in a warm place until almost double (about 45 minutes).

Preheat the oven to 375°F. Brush tops with milk and bake for about 15 minutes, or until golden brown.

Quick Fix Biscuits

Yield: 4 biscuits

16-ounce package refrigerator biscuits
1/4 cup butter
1/2 teaspoon dried onion flakes or minced fresh onion
1/2 teaspoon dill, rosemary, or Italian seasoning

Preheat oven to 425°F. Separate the biscuits and cut each into 4 pieces. In an 8- or 9-inch round pie or cake pan or a ring mold, melt the butter. Into the butter stir the onion and herbs. Roll the biscuit pieces quickly in the mixture and arrange them, touching, in the pan. Bake for about 12 minutes, or until browned.

Cinnamon Rolls

Yield: 16 rolls

8–8 ½ cups all-purpose flour
2 cups warm milk (105–115°F)
⅔ cup sugar
1 teaspoon salt
2 packages active dry yeast
3 large eggs, slightly beaten
2 sticks butter (1 cup), melted and cooled

Filling:

1½ cups brown sugar
1 stick butter (½ cup), melted
¾ teaspoon cinnamon

Frosting:

1 cup confectioners' sugar
1 tablespoon milk
¼ teaspoon vanilla extract

Combine 2 cups of the flour, milk, sugar, salt, and yeast in a large bowl; mix well. Add eggs and butter. Stir in as much of the remaining flour as needed to form a soft dough. Turn dough out onto a lightly floured surface and knead for 5 to 8 minutes, adding a little flour as necessary, until smooth and elastic. Transfer to a large greased bowl and turn to coat both sides. Cover with a towel and place in a draft-free area. Allow the dough to rise until double in volume, about 1 hour.

Punch dough down with fist, and turn dough out onto a lightly floured surface. Knead 10 to 15 times. Cover with a towel and let rest 10 minutes. Roll dough out into a 24 x 15-inch rectangle.

Combine brown sugar, butter, and cinnamon in small bowl and stir well. Spread out onto dough to within 1 inch of the edges. Roll up tightly lengthwise, pinching edges together to seal. Cut into 16 slices with a serrated bread knife. Place

When Is Bread Baked?

To test muffins and quick breads to see if they are done, insert a toothpick into the middle. If it comes out clean, the bread is done.

To test traditional yeast breads, tap the crust with your knuckle. If the loaf sounds hollow, it is done.

rolls onto two greased 13 x 9-inch baking pans. Cover with a towel and let rise until doubled, about 15 minutes.

Heat oven to 375°F. Bake until golden brown, 20 to 25 minutes. Let cool slightly. For frosting stir together confectioners' sugar, milk, and vanilla in a small bowl. Mix until smooth. Drizzle over rolls.

Variations: Raisins that have been softened by boiling for three minutes (drain thoroughly) can be added to the filling. For caramel-nut rolls, spread 1/2 cup brown sugar and 1/2 cup coarsely chopped pecans or walnuts in the baking pan prior to placing roll slices on top to rise for the last time.

Basic Biscuits

Yield: 12 biscuits

> 2 cups flour
> 1 tablespoon baking powder
> 1/2 teaspoon salt
> 1 tablespoon sugar
> 1/3 cup butter or shortening
> 3/4 cup milk

Preheat oven to 425°F. Sift together the flour, baking powder, and salt. Stir in the sugar. Cut the butter or shortening into the dry ingredients until the mixture resembles coarse crumbs. Add the milk all at once and mix quickly with a fork just until a dough forms.

Turn onto a floured board and knead gently about 10 times. Roll or pat the dough to a 3/4-inch thickness and cut with a biscuit cutter or 2 1/2-inch round cutter. Place on an ungreased cookie sheet and bake 12 to 15 minutes, or until golden brown.

Buttermilk Biscuits: Add 1/4 teaspoon baking soda and omit sugar. Substitute buttermilk for whole milk.

Drop Biscuits: Increase milk to 1 cup. Combine ingredients well but do not knead. Drop by tablespoons onto a greased cookie sheet.

Raspberry Cream Cheese Breakfast Biscuits

Yield: 15 biscuits

> 3 cups flour
> 2 tablespoons baking powder
> 3/4 teaspoon salt
> 3 tablespoons shortening
> 3/4 cup orange juice or milk
> 3-ounce package cream cheese
> 2 tablespoons raspberry all-fruit spread
>   or jam

Preheat oven to 450°F. Sift together the flour, baking powder, and salt. Cut in the shortening until the mixture resembles coarse crumbs. Add the orange juice and beat to form a soft dough. Turn dough onto a surface well dusted with flour and knead

(continued)

10 times. Roll or pat the dough till it's ¹/₂ inch thick. Cut rounds with a biscuit cutter or a 2¹/₂ inch round cutter (a drinking glass can be used). Place the rounds on an ungreased cookie sheet.

Soften the cream cheese. Add the jam and mix until marbled but not thoroughly combined. Spoon about 1 teaspoon onto the center of each round. Sprinkle with sugar. Bake 8 to 10 minutes, or until golden brown.

Note: You can replace the flour, baking powder, salt, and shortening by substituting 3 cups of prepared biscuit mix, such as Bisquick.

Popovers

Yield: 6 popovers

1 cup flour
¹/₂ teaspoon salt
2 eggs
1 cup milk
1 tablespoon melted shortening or oil

Preheat oven to 475°F. Grease *well* a popover pan or 6 6-ounce custard cups.

In a separate bowl, sift together the flour and salt, beat the eggs well and add the milk to them. Add the flour mixture and beat with an electric mixer on medium for 1 minute. Add the melted shortening and beat 1 minute more.

Fill the prepared cups half full. Bake at 475°F for 15 minutes, then reduce heat to 350°F and continue baking 25 to 30 minutes longer, until well browned. A few minutes before they are to be removed from the oven, carefully prick each popover with a fork to allow steam to escape. Remove immediately from the pans.

Popover tip: Bake alone in the oven for best results. Serve immediately and hot!

English Muffins

Yield: 10 to 12 muffins

³/₄ cup milk
¹/₄ cup lukewarm water
1 tablespoon sugar
¹/₂ package active dry yeast (1¹/₈ teaspoons)
¹/₂ teaspoon salt
2 tablespoons melted butter or shortening
3 cups flour
cornmeal for dipping

Scald the milk and allow it to cool to lukewarm. In the warm water, dissolve the sugar and the yeast. Add the cooled milk. Stir in the salt, butter, and half the flour, and beat until smooth. Mix in the remaining flour.

Turn onto a lightly floured work surface and knead until smooth and elastic, about 6 to 8 minutes. Put in a greased bowl, cover

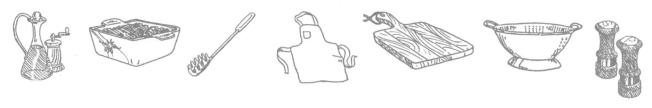

with a damp cloth, and allow to rise until double, about 1 hour.

Punch down the dough and return to the work surface. Pat or roll the dough to a thickness of about ³/₄ inch. Cut the muffins with a 4-inch circular cutter dipped in flour. Dip each cut round in cornmeal to coat both the top and bottom. Cover and let rise until light, about 30 minutes.

Cook the muffins on a lightly buttered or greased griddle or skillet over medium-high heat. Turn every 5 minutes until they are done, using a spatula. Total cooking time will be 15 minutes or more. Cool slightly on a rack before serving.

To serve, split open with a fork horizontally and toast.

Muffin rings: Special English muffin rings are available in cooking supply stores, or you can make your own from tuna or similar cans by removing the top and bottom and cleaning thoroughly. Grease the rings well. Allow the dough to rise once, then punch it down as directed above. After it has been punched down, divide it equally among 10 to 12 rings. (If desired, you can flatten the dough slightly by patting to make it easier to divide, but do not roll it.) If using cans for rings: cover the rings and allow the dough to rise in them until even with the top edges. Do not remove the dough from the rings before cooking as directed above. If using purchased rings: follow manufacturer's directions.

Scones

Yield: 12 scones

> 2¹/₄ cups cake flour
> 1 tablespoon baking powder
> ¹/₂ teaspoon salt
> 2 tablespoons sugar
> 5 tablespoons butter
> 1 egg
> ¹/₂ cup light or heavy cream*

Preheat oven to 425°F. Sift the flour, baking powder, salt, and sugar together. Cut in the butter until the mixture is the size of small peas. Make a well in the mixture. Beat the egg lightly and combine with the cream. Pour the liquids into the dry ingredient well and combine quickly but thoroughly.

Turn onto a lightly floured work surface. Pat or roll the dough to a thickness of about ³/₄ inch. With a sharp knife, cut into diamond shapes. Brush the tops with cream and sprinkle with sugar. Bake 12 to 15 minutes on an ungreased cookie sheet.

Variation: Add ¹/₂ cup raisins or currants when adding the egg-cream mixture to the dry ingredients. Or use ¹/₃ cup dried cherries or dried mixed fruits that have been steamed briefly to plump.

Note: If substituting all-purpose flour for the cake flour, reduce the amount to 2 cups and knead 10 times before shaping and cutting.

*Cream gives scones their characteristic richness; do not substitute milk.

Best Banana Bread

Yield: 2 loaves

2²/₃ cups flour
1 teaspoon baking powder
1 teaspoon baking soda
¹/₂ teaspoon salt
²/₃ cup butter
1¹/₃ cups sugar
2 eggs
1¹/₂ cups mashed banana
¹/₂ cup sour cream
1 cup chopped nuts, optional

Preheat oven to 350°F. Grease two loaf pans and flour the bottom of the pans.

Sift together the flour, baking powder, baking soda, and salt. Set aside.

Cream the butter and sugar until light. Add the eggs, mixing well after each. Add the mashed banana. Add the flour mixture in thirds, alternately with the sour cream, ending with flour. Blend quickly but thoroughly. Stir in the nuts. Pour into prepared pans and bake 45 minutes, or until the center tests done.

Mashed Banana Tips

When using bananas in baked goods, allow them to ripen until the skins are heavily speckled with brown. When bananas are very ripe, their starch turns to sugar—they will be sweeter than less ripe bananas.

A medium banana, mashed, equals about ¹/₃ cup.

Pumpkin Tea Bread

Yield: 1 loaf

²/₃ cup soft vegetable shortening
2²/₃ cups sugar
4 eggs
2 cups canned pumpkin
²/₃ cup water
2¹/₂ cups flour
1 cup whole wheat flour
2 teaspoons baking soda
¹/₂ teaspoon baking powder
1¹/₂ teaspoons salt
1 teaspoon cinnamon
1 teaspoon cloves
1 cup chopped pecans or walnuts

Preheat oven to 350°F. Grease and flour a bundt pan or 2 5 x 9-inch loaf pans.

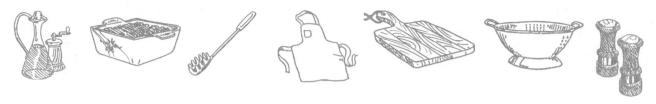

In a mixing bowl, cream together shortening and sugar. Beat in eggs. Add pumpkin and water, stirring until blended. Sift together dry ingredients and spices. Stir into pumpkin mixture with a wooden spoon just until blended. Fold in nuts. Pour into prepared pan(s). Bake 1 hour or until a toothpick inserted comes out clean.

Let cool 10 minutes in pan, then turn out on rack to cool completely.

Apple Date Bread

Yield: 1 loaf

Topping:
³/₄ cup firmly packed brown sugar
³/₄ cup chopped nuts
2 tablespoons butter, softened
¹/₄ cup all-purpose flour
¹/₄ teaspoon ground cinnamon
¹/₄ teaspoon salt

Bread:
1¹/₂ cups all-purpose flour
1¹/₂ cups whole-wheat flour
1 cup sugar
1 tablespoon baking powder
1¹/₂ teaspoons salt
1 cup flaked dried coconut
1¹/₂ cups 1 percent milk
1 egg, lightly beaten
1 cup pitted and sliced dates
1 cup peeled, cored, and finely chopped apples

Preheat oven to 350°F. Spray a 9 x 3-inch loaf pan with nonstick cooking spray. To make the topping, combine all the ingredients in a bowl, mixing well. Set aside.

In a larger bowl, stir together the flours, sugar, baking powder, and salt. Stir in the coconut. In another bowl, stir together the milk and egg. Add the milk mixture to the flour mixture, blending well. Stir in the dates and apples, mixing well. Turn into the prepared loaf pan. Sprinkle with the topping. Bake until a knife comes out clean, about 1¹/₄ hours.

Cool on a rack, then turn out of the pan and slice to serve.

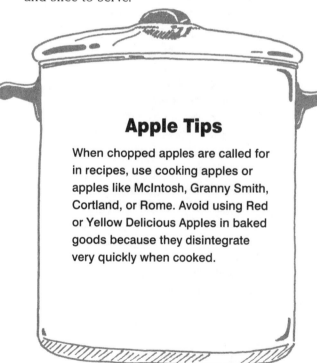

Apple Tips

When chopped apples are called for in recipes, use cooking apples or apples like McIntosh, Granny Smith, Cortland, or Rome. Avoid using Red or Yellow Delicious Apples in baked goods because they disintegrate very quickly when cooked.

Zucchini Bread

Yield: 2 loaves

> 3 eggs
> 1½ cups sugar
> 1 cup salad oil
> 1 tablespoon vanilla
> 2 cups grated, unpeeled zucchini, loosely
>   packed
> 2 cups flour
> 2 teaspoons baking soda
> ½ teaspoon baking powder
> 1 teaspoon salt
> 1½ teaspoons cinnamon
> 1 cup chopped walnuts

Preheat oven to 350°F. Oil two 9-inch loaf pans.

In a large bowl, beat eggs until frothy. Beat in sugar, oil, and vanilla until thick and lemon-colored. Stir in zucchini. Sift together flour, baking soda, baking powder, salt, and cinnamon. Stir into zucchini batter. Fold in nuts. Pour mixture into prepared pans. Bake 40 minutes or until center springs back when lightly touched.

Let cool 10 minutes before turning out on a wire rack.

Quick Breads and Gluten

Gluten is the protein in wheat flour that gives dough its elasticity and baked goods their substance. It can only develop, however, when liquid is present or when the grain is worked, as in stirring or kneading. Soft flours have less gluten and are said to be less elastic and more delicate—one reason a slice of cake crumbles more easily than a slice of bread.

When making quick breads and muffins, combine dry and liquid ingredients quickly and keep mixing to a minimum. If the batter is mixed too long, the gluten in the flour will begin to develop and the bread will be tough. The properly mixed batter will be a little lumpy.

Cranberry Nut Bread

Yield: 1 loaf

2 cups fresh cranberries
½ cup sugar
zest of 1 orange
2 tablespoons orange juice
6 tablespoons butter
¾ cup light brown sugar
2 eggs at room temperature
1 cup sour cream
2½ cups all-purpose flour
⅛ teaspoon cloves
1 teaspoon baking soda
1½ teaspoons baking powder
½ teaspoon salt
1 cup pecans or walnuts, finely chopped

Preheat oven to 375°F. In a small saucepan, cook the cranberries, sugar, orange zest, and orange juice over high heat, stirring frequently, until most berries burst and the sugar is dissolved, about 4 to 5 minutes.

In a large mixing bowl, cream the butter and brown sugar until light and fluffy, then add eggs one at a time and beat until smooth. Add sour cream. In a separate bowl, combine flour, cloves, baking soda, baking powder, and salt; stir half into the batter. Add the cranberries and remaining flour mixture and then fold in the nuts.

Butter and flour a medium-sized loaf pan. Spoon batter into the pan and bake in the center of the oven until well browned on top and a toothpick inserted in the center comes out clean, about 65 to 70 minutes. Cool in the pan for 10 minutes, then turn out on a wire rack to cool completely. Slice and serve.

Basic Muffins

Yield: 12 muffins

2 cups all-purpose flour
¼ cup sugar
1 tablespoon baking powder
½ teaspoon salt
1 large egg
1 cup milk
⅓ cup vegetable oil

Preheat oven to 400°F. Grease well a 12-cup muffin tin, or line with paper cups.

Sift together the flour, sugar, baking powder, and salt. Place the sifted dry ingredients into a bowl and make a well in the center.

In a second bowl, beat the egg lightly. Add the milk and oil and combine.

Pour the egg mixture into the well in the dry ingredients and combine quickly, until dry ingredients are just moistened. Some lumps will remain in the batter.

Fill the muffin cups about ⅔ full. Bake about 20 minutes, or until the center tests done.

(continued)

If desired, try one of the following variations.

Banana Muffins: Mash ³/₄ cup banana and combine with the liquid ingredients.

Blueberry Muffins: To the prepared batter, quickly fold in ³/₄ cup fresh or thawed and drained frozen blueberries.

Cherry or Cranberry Nut Muffins: To the prepared batter, quickly stir in ¹/₂ cup dried cherries or dried cranberries (called "Craisins") and ¹/₂ cup chopped pecans or walnuts.

Cinnamon Raisin Muffins: To the dry ingredients, add ³/₄ teaspoon cinnamon. Before combining dry and liquid ingredients, add ³/₄ cup raisins to the batter.

Buttermilk Muffins: Reduce baking powder to 2 teaspoons and add ¹/₂ teaspoon soda. Substitute 1 cup buttermilk for the whole milk.

Breakfast Muffins

Yield: 12 muffins

> 2 cups shredded unpeeled apples
> 1¹/₃ cups sugar
> 1 cup cranberries, chopped (soaked raisins can be substituted)
> 1 cup walnuts or pecans, chopped finely
> 1 cup shredded carrots
> 2¹/₂ cups unbleached flour
> 1 tablespoon baking powder

> 2 teaspoons baking soda
> ¹/₂ teaspoon salt
> 2 teaspoons cinnamon
> 2 large eggs, beaten well
> ¹/₂ cup canola or vegetable oil

In a large bowl, mix the apples and the sugar. Set aside. Grease a muffin tin and preheat oven to 350°F. Add cranberries, nuts, and carrots to apple mixture and stir gently.

Mix dry ingredients and add to the apple mixture. Mix well. Stir in eggs and oil gently but thoroughly. Put batter in muffin tin and bake 25 to 30 minutes. Cool for 5 minutes and remove to wire rack.

Blueberry Muffins

Yield:

> 1³/₄ cups sifted flour
> 2¹/₂ teaspoons baking powder
> ¹/₂ teaspoon salt
> 1 egg
> about ³/₄ cup milk
> ¹/₄ cup butter, softened
> ¹/₂ cup sugar
> 1 cup fresh blueberries

Preheat oven to 400°F. Oil muffin tins. Sift together dry ingredients. Break egg into a glass measuring cup, and then add enough milk to measure 1 cup. In a large mixing bowl, cream together butter and sugar. Beat in egg-milk mixture.

(continued)

Muffin Tips

Muffin tins are now widely available in mini and jumbo sizes as well as the standard 2½ inch size. You will need to subtract about 10 minutes from baking time if making mini muffins, and add at least 8 minutes if making jumbo muffins.

If using either insulated muffin tins (which sometimes bake more slowly) or dark nonstick tins (which sometimes brown foods more quickly), check the manufacturer's directions or watch carefully.

Grease only the bottom and halfway up the sides of muffin cups to prevent a lip from forming around the edge of the muffin. Paper baking cups may be used instead; they are placed inside the cups in a muffin tin.

Unless directed otherwise by a recipe, fill muffin cups only ⅔ full.

If you do not have enough batter to fill all the cups in the muffin tin, fill the empty ones about a quarter full of water to protect the pan.

Allow muffins to cool in the pan for no more than 2 minutes before removing, unless directed otherwise by a recipe. Muffins left to cool in the pan become soggy. Run a knife around the muffins to loosen if necessary, then cool them on a wire rack.

Stir in dry ingredients only until blended. Do not beat. Gently stir in blueberries. Fill prepared muffin tin about ²/₃ full. Bake 20 to 25 minutes.

These muffins keep well if made a day ahead or frozen. If frozen, wrap each in aluminum foil and warm in conventional oven before serving.

Rhubarb Muffins

Yield: 12 muffins

2 cups finely chopped rhubarb
³/₄ cup sugar
1 teaspoon grated orange zest
2¹/₂ cups all-purpose flour
¹/₂ teaspoon baking powder
1 teaspoon baking soda
1 teaspoon salt
2 eggs, beaten
³/₄ cup nonfat buttermilk
3 tablespoons butter or reduced-fat margarine

Preheat oven to 375°F. Grease a 12-cup muffin tin. In a bowl, combine the rhubarb, ¹/₄ cup of the sugar, and the orange zest. Stir well and let stand for 5 minutes.

In another bowl, stir together the flour, the remaining ¹/₂ cup sugar, the baking powder, baking soda, and salt. Make a well in the center. In another bowl, stir together the eggs, buttermilk, and butter or margarine. Add all at once to the flour

mixture, stirring just until moistened. The batter should be lumpy. Gently fold in the rhubarb mixture.

Spoon into the prepared muffin tin, filling each cup ²/₃ full. Bake until a knife comes out clean, 20 to 25 minutes. Remove from the oven and cool no a rack for 15 minutes before serving.

Apple Muffins

Yield: 12 muffins

2 cups flour
1 tablespoon baking powder
¹/₂ teaspoon salt
¹/₂ cup sugar
1 teaspoon cinnamon
1 cup finely chopped cooking apples
¹/₄ cup raisins
¹/₄ cup butter or shortening
1 egg
³/₄ cup milk

Preheat oven to 400°F. Grease a muffin tin well. Sift flour, baking powder, and salt together. Stir in sugar and cinnamon. Toss chopped apples and raisins in the flour mixture until well combined. Make a well in the center of the mixture.

Melt butter or shortening. Beat egg lightly, then combine with butter and milk. Add the liquid ingredients to the dry ingredients, and stir until just moistened. Fill muffin cups ²/₃ full and bake for 20 to 25 minutes.

Lemon Chocolate Chip Muffins

Yield:

8 tablespoons (1 stick) unsalted butter
1 cup sugar
2 large eggs
zest of 1 lemon
1 teaspoon baking soda
2 cups flour
1 cup buttermilk
3/4 cup (5 ounces) semisweet
    chocolate chips
1/4 cup fresh lemon juice

Preheat oven to 375°F. Grease muffin tin. Mix butter and sugar together well, beating with mixer until pale and creamy. Beat in eggs one at a time. Stir in lemon zest and baking soda. Fold in 1 cup flour, then 1/2 cup buttermilk, then repeat. Fold in chocolate chips. Put batter in muffin tins and bake 25 minutes or until browned.

Remove from the oven and brush lemon juice over the tops of the muffins. Let stand for 5 minutes before removing from the muffin tins.

Rich Date Loaf

Yield: 1 loaf

8 ounces dates, chopped'
8 ounces walnuts, chopped
1/2 cup sugar
1/2 teaspoon salt
2 egg yolks
2 egg whites
1/2 cup flour
1 teaspoon baking powder
1/2 teaspoon vanilla

Preheat oven to 325°F. Grease a loaf pan and cover the bottom with waxed paper cut to fit.

Mix together the dates, nuts, sugar, and salt. Beat the egg yolks lightly and stir into the date mixture. Beat the egg whites until soft peaks form.

Add the flour and baking powder to the date-egg mixture and combine quickly but thoroughly. Stir in the vanilla. Fold in the beaten egg whites. Pour into the prepared pan and bake for 1 hour. Allow to stand 10 minutes before removing from pan.

Lemon Loaf

Yield: 2 loaves

2 cups cake flour
1 teaspoon baking powder
½ teaspoon salt
½ cup butter
1 cup sugar
2 eggs
grated peel of 1 lemon
½ cup milk
juice of 1 lemon into which ¼ cup sugar
    has been dissolved

Preheat oven to 350°F. Grease two loaf pans on the bottom only.

Sift the dry ingredients together and set aside. Cream together the butter and sugar. Beat in the eggs one at a time. Mix in grated lemon rind. Add the dry ingredients half at a time, alternately with the milk.

Pour the batter into pans and bake for 50 to 60 minutes. Remove loaves to a wire rack that has been placed over a sheet of foil or waxed paper. Drizzle the lemon juice-sugar mixture over the loaves and allow to cool.

Bread Rising

The dough of a yeast bread rises because it contains yeast. Quick breads, muffins, and coffeecakes rise because they contain baking powder and/or baking soda, which works more quickly than yeast. Standard double-acting baking powder works once when it meets liquids in the mixing process, and a second time during baking.

Yeast breads can be either batter doughs or kneaded doughs. Batter doughs are well stirred, usually with an electric mixer, and usually rise once in the pan in which they are to be baked.

Orange Coconut Loaf

Yield: 2 loaves

Topping:
½ cup flaked coconut
⅓ cup sugar
1½ tablespoons butter, softened
2 teaspoons grated orange zest

Loaf:
1¾ cups flour
1 teaspoon baking soda
1 cup sugar
½ cup butter
2 eggs
1 cup creamy orange-flavored yogurt
1 tablespoon grated orange zest

Preheat oven to 350°F. Grease the bottom only of two bread pans.

To make the topping: Combine all topping ingredients in a small bowl.
Set aside.

Sift the flour and soda together; set aside. Cream the sugar and butter. Beat in the eggs, yogurt, and orange zest. Add the dry ingredients and stir until just mixed.

Pour batter into the loaf pans and sprinkle the topping evenly on top. Bake for 50 minutes or until the loaf tests done. Cool the bread 10 minutes in the pan, then transfer loaves onto a wire rack.

Variation: Omit the topping. Immediately after removing the bread from the oven but before removing it from the pans, drizzle ¹⁄₂ cup orange juice over the hot loaves.

"Wilma's" Cinnamon Sour Cream Coffeecake

This classic recipe is still one of the best available.

Yield: 10-inch diameter cake

Streusel
6 tablespoons butter
1 cup brown sugar
2 teaspoons cinnamon
1 cup chopped nuts

Cake:
2 cups flour
1 teaspoon baking powder
1 teaspoon baking soda

¹⁄₂ cup butter
³⁄₄ cup sugar
3 eggs
1 teaspoon vanilla
8 ounces sour cream

Preheat oven to 350°F. Prepare a 10-inch tube pan by greasing well and fitting a cut waxed paper insert to the bottom.

Prepare the streusel: Soften the butter and cut in the brown sugar and cinnamon with a fork. Mix the nuts in well. Set aside.

Prepare the cake: Sift together flour, baking powder, and baking soda. Set aside.

Cream the butter and sugar until light and fluffy. Add eggs, one at a time, beating well after each. Add vanilla. Add flour mixture alternately with the sour cream, combining quickly but thoroughly on low speed.

Spread half the batter in the prepared tube pan. Sprinkle with half the streusel mixture. Spread the remaining batter and sprinkle with the remaining streusel. With a table knife, make about 8 cuts through the batter to distribute the streusel. Bake for 50 minutes.

To cool, remove the cake with the tube and bottom of the pan still attached by pulling up on the tube. Allow to cool for a few minutes on a wire rack. Reinsert into the pan and invert onto a second rack or plate, loosening cake around the tube first if necessary. Peel the waxed paper from the cake's bottom. Turn the cake right side (streusel side) up onto a rack to finish cooling.

Sweet Cherry Coffeecake

Yield: 10-inch diameter cake

Streusel:

3 tablespoons butter
1/4 cup flour
1 cup brown sugar
1 teaspoon cinnamon
1 cup chopped pecans or almonds, optional
*1 cup sweet Bing cherries, pitted and
    quartered*

Cake:

2 cups flour
1 teaspoon baking soda
1 teaspoon baking powder
1/2 cup butter
1/2 cup sugar
3 large eggs
1/2 teaspoon vanilla extract
1/3 cup apple juice

Glaze:

1/2 cup powdered sugar
2 or more teaspoons apple juice

Preheat oven to 350°F. Prepare a 10-inch tube pan by greasing well and fitting a cut waxed paper insert to the bottom.

Prepare the streusel: Soften the butter well. Combine the flour, brown sugar, and cinnamon; cut in the softened butter with a fork. Mix in the nuts, if using, and toss the cherries in the mixture until well distributed. Set aside.

Spoon and spread half the batter into the tube pan. Sprinkle with half the streusel mixture. Spoon and spread the remaining batter and top with the remaining streusel. Using a table knife, carefully cut through the batter in a large zigzag pattern around the tube to distribute the streusel. Do not drag the knife; raise and lower it.

Bake 45 to 50 minutes. To cool, remove the cake, with the tube and bottom of the pan still attached, by pulling up on the tube. Allow to cool for a few minutes on a wire rack. Reinsert the cake into the pan and invert onto a second rack or plate, loosening cake around the tube first if necessary. Turn the cake right side (streusel side) up onto the rack to finish cooling.

When the cake is cool, combine the glaze ingredients, mixing well, and drizzle over the top.

Variation: If Bing cherries are not available, substitute 1 cup chopped apples and 1/2 cup raisins for the cherries; reduce the nuts to 1/2 cup, and substitute walnuts for the pecans.

"Healthy" Coffeecake

Yield: 8-inch square cake

Topping:

1/4 cup butter
2/3 cup brown sugar
2/3 cup rolled oats
1/2 teaspoon cinnamon
1/2 cup chopped nuts, optional

Cake:

2 cups low-fat biscuit mix such as Bisquick
²⁄₃ cup skim milk
¹⁄₂ cup rolled oats
¹⁄₄ cup liquid egg substitute (equivalent to 1 egg)
2 tablespoons brown sugar
¹⁄₂ teaspoon cinnamon

Preheat oven to 375°F. Grease an 8-inch-square cake pan.

Prepare the topping: Combine the butter and brown sugar with a fork; add the remaining topping ingredients, combining well. Set aside.

Make the cake: Combine all cake ingredients and mix just until the dry ingredients are moistened. Spread half the batter in the pan and top with half the topping mix. Spread the remaining batter and add remaining topping.

Bake 35 to 40 minutes, or until coffeecake tests done.

At the Lake Cake

Yield: 2 coffeecakes

This is a quick and easy coffeecake.
1 loaf unsliced bread
¹⁄₃ cup butter, softened
²⁄₃ cup brown sugar
1 teaspoon cinnamon
2 tablespoons half-and-half or cream

Preheat oven to 425°F. Trim all crusts from the bread. Slice in half horizontally. In the top of each half, make one lengthwise cut and six crosswise cuts about halfway through the thickness of the bread.

Mix together the butter, brown sugar, cinnamon, and half and half. Spread the mixture in the cuts and on the top of each half. Wrap loosely in foil (cakes can be frozen for future use at this point if desired) and place each half in a loaf pan. Bake for 20 minutes.

Size of Your Eggs

Recipes are based on *large* eggs unless otherwise specified. However:

For 1 large egg, you can substitute 1 extra large, medium, or small

For 2 large eggs, substitute 2 extra-large or medium, but 3 small

For 3 large eggs, substitute 3 extra-large or medium, but 4 small

For 4 large eggs, substitute 4 extra-large, but 5 medium or small

Butter Coffeecake

Yield: 9-inch square cake

Crust:

1 cup all-purpose flour
3 tablespoons granulated sugar
5 tablespoons unsalted butter, softened
1 tablespoon ice water, if needed

Filling:

1¼ cups granulated sugar
¾ cup (1½ sticks) unsalted butter, softened
1 egg
1 cup all-purpose flour
⅔ cup evaporated milk
¼ cup light corn syrup
1 teaspoon vanilla extract
powdered sugar for garnish

Preheat oven to 350°F. Lightly butter or oil a 9-inch-square baking pan.

To make the crust, mix the flour and sugar in a food processor.* By pulsing on and off, cut in the butter until the mixture resembles coarse crumbs. If necessary to make the dough hold together, add the ice water and blend a few seconds until the mixture holds. Pat the crust dough into the bottom and onto the sides of the baking pan.

To make the filling cream together the sugar and the butter with an electric mixer until light and fluffy. Beat in the egg until well blended. Alternate mixing in a little of the flour and a little of the evaporated milk until both are incorporated. Add the corn syrup and vanilla extract, and blend one last time.

Pour the batter into the prepared crust, and bake for 25 to 35 minutes, or until the cake is nearly set. Do not overbake. The top should remain moist. Let the cake cool slightly in the pan and garnish with powdered sugar before serving.

*If you do not have a food processor to make the crust, use a pastry cutter.

Coffeecake

This old favorite is often called "Cowboy Cake"

Yield: 1 8-inch cake

1¼ cups flour
¼ teaspoon salt
1 cup brown sugar
⅓ cup shortening
1 teaspoon baking powder
¼ teaspoon baking soda
¼ teaspoon cinnamon
⅛ teaspoon nutmeg
1 egg
½ cup soured milk or buttermilk

Preheat the oven to 375°F. Grease and flour an 8-inch square or round cake pan.

Combine flour, salt, sugar; cut in the shortening until the mixture has a crumb like texture. Remove and reserve ¼ cup of the mixture. To the remaining mixture, stir in the baking powder, baking soda, and spices. Beat the egg well; mix with the milk. Add to the dry ingredients and mix quickly but thoroughly.

Pour into the baking pan and top with the reserved crumb mixture. Bake 25 to 30 minutes.

Chapter 4

Breakfast and Brunch Dishes

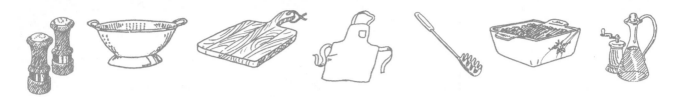

E veryone knows that breakfast is the most important meal of the day. Start yours off right with easy tips for perfect eggs cooked every-which way, and delicious pancakes and skillet-bakes. Or try a quiche for a quick and filling lunch or dinner. From the everyday to the exotic, these recipes will get you out of bed on the right side.

Poached Eggs

Poached eggs are removed from the shell and cooked directly in boiling water. The pan should be large enough so that the eggs do not touch during cooking. Use a saucepan to poach one or two eggs at a time, or a medium skillet to poach up to four at a time.

Fill the pan up to half full with water, but no more than 3 inches deep. Bring the water to boiling, then reduce to a simmer. Break one egg into a small bowl and, holding the bowl close to the surface of the simmering water, slide the egg carefully in. Repeat for each egg to be poached.

Cook eggs until the whites are firm and the yolks thicken but are not hard—no more than 5 minutes. Remove with a slotted spoon and season with salt and pepper.

Soft-Boiled Eggs

Soft-boiled eggs are cooked in the shell. Traditionally, they are called "3-minute eggs" because that is the perfect timing to cook them. Place up to four eggs in a medium saucepan and cover with cold water at least an inch deeper than the eggs.

To use the 3-minute method, bring to a boil, then immediately remove from the heat and cover. Let stand exactly 3 minutes, then drain and fill the pan with cold water to stop further cooking.

Or, you can bring the eggs to a boil; reduce the heat to a low simmer, cover, and cook 3 to 5 minutes. Drain and fill the pan with cold water to stop further cooking.

The cooked eggs can be cut in half, and a spoon used to scoop out the contents. Chop slightly if desired and season. Or, if you have egg cups, cut off the tops of the eggs and place the eggs still in the shell into the cup to serve.

Hard-Boiled Eggs

Place up to four eggs in a medium saucepan and cover with cold water at least an inch deeper than the eggs. If you want to cook more eggs at one time, use a larger saucepan or pot. Bring the water to a boil, reduce to a low simmer, cover, and cook 15 minutes.

Poached Eggs

Over Easy or Fried Hard Eggs

Shirred (Baked) Eggs

Scrambled Eggs

Or, bring the water to a boil, cover, and remove from heat. Let stand exactly 18 minutes.

Then drain the pan and refill with cold water to stop further cooking. Crack the shells and peel immediately if desired, or add ice to the water in the pan and allow the eggs to cool further.

Fried Eggs

Over Easy or Fried Hard: Melt about 1 teaspoon of butter for each egg to be cooked, over medium heat, or spray a cold skillet with cooking oil then preheat. Add eggs carefully, one at a time, from the bowl into which they have been cracked. Reduce heat to low, and cook until a film forms over the yolk and the whites are set (about 3 minutes). Carefully turn over and cook an additional 1 minute for over easy eggs, or 2 to 3 minutes for fried hard eggs.

Sunny-Side Up: Melt about 1 teaspoon of butter for each egg to be cooked, over medium heat, or spray a cold skillet with cooking oil then preheat. Add eggs care-fully, one at a time, from the bowl into which they have been cracked. After the whites have begun to set, add 2 to 4 table-spoons water to the skillet, reduce heat to low, and cover loosely. Cook until whites are set and a film has formed over the yolk but it is still not solid, about 3 or 4 minutes.

Classic Shirred (Baked) Eggs

Say "shurd" eggs.

Preheat oven to 325°F. Grease one small oven-proof glass custard cup with butter for each egg to be cooked. Break one egg into each cup. Season with salt and pepper, drizzle 1 tablespoon light cream or half-and-half over each, and dot with butter. Place the cups in an appropriately sized baking dish (they should not touch) and place the dish on a partially pulled out rack of the oven. Pour hot water into the baking dish to a depth of 1 inch. Carefully push in the rack and bake 15 to 20 minutes or until firm.

Scrambled Eggs

Servings: 2 or 3

> 6 eggs
> 1/3 cup milk or cream
> salt and pepper to taste
> 1 tablespoon butter

Beat the eggs, milk, and seasonings together lightly (with white and yellow streaks still visible) or well (until a uniform color) as preferred, using a fork or whisk. Heat the butter in a skillet and pour the egg mixture in. After the eggs begin to thicken, stir *gently* with a wooden spoon until eggs are thick but still moist. **OR**, **instead of stirring,** after the eggs begin to thicken, lift portions to allow the uncooked egg to flow to the bottom until the eggs are uniformly thickened. Total cooking time after the eggs begin to thicken will be 2 to 4 minutes.

Denver Eggs: Before adding eggs to skillet, cook 1/3 cup chopped onion, 1/3 cup diced green pepper, and 1/3 cup diced ham in the melted butter.

Cheesy Eggs: Add 1/2 cup shredded American or other process cheese to the eggs after they have begun to thicken.

Sausage Eggs: Cook 1/2 pound of bulk sausage until no longer pink; drain well. Add to the eggs after they begin to thicken.

Basic Omelet

Servings: 1

> 2 eggs per omelet if using 8-inch omelet
>   pan or skillet
> 3 eggs per omelet if using 10-inch omelet
>   pan or skillet
> spray cooking oil if using nonstick skillet
> 1 teaspoon butter for each egg if using
>   traditional noncoated omelet pan or
>   skillet

Beat the eggs well in a bowl, but do not allow them to become frothy.

If using an uncoated omelet pan or skillet: Melt the butter over medium to medium-high heat, tilting the skillet to coat the bottom, until the butter just begins to turn brown. Pour in the eggs; stir gently with a fork while they thicken to distribute the eggs from top to bottom. Stop stirring when eggs begin to set.

If using a nonstick pan or skillet: Coat well with cooking oil spray. Preheat the skillet for a minute or so but do not allow the spray to begin to brown. Add the eggs. As they thicken, lift the edges of the omelet and allow the uncooked eggs to flow underneath.

Allow to cook until the bottom is golden and the top is set but shiny. With a long turner, gently loosen the edge of the omelet and fold the omelet in half toward you. With the help of the turner, slide it out of the pan and onto the plate.

If making multiple omelets: Cover with foil to keep warm.

To add additional ingredients like cheese, meat, or vegetables, distribute them down the center of the omelet when the top is set but still shiny, and before folding the omelet.

Good omelet additions: Use ⅓ to ½ cup if adding one ingredient; reduce amounts accordingly if multiple ingredients are used.

Meats: Diced ham or turkey or crumbled bacon

Vegetables: Onion or bell peppers (sautéed briefly in a small amount of butter if desired). You can also include: Chopped broccoli, chopped or shredded carrots, steamed briefly. Mushrooms, sautéed briefly if desired (if using fresh rather than canned, they should be sautéed until done). Fresh tomatoes, seeded and chopped.

Cheeses: Shredded Cheddar, Swiss, Monterey Jack, or other cheese of your choice

Omelet troubleshooting: If the bottom of the eggs browns too quickly before the top fully sets, reduce the heat.

Cheesy Golden Apple Omelet

Servings: 2

1 Golden Delicious apple, pared, cored, and sliced
2 tablespoons butter, divided
4 eggs
1 tablespoon water
¼ teaspoon salt
dash pepper
2 tablespoons crumbled blue cheese
2 tablespoons grated Parmesan cheese

(continued)

Break an Egg!

Always break eggs one at a time into a small bowl, then add them one at a time to the skillet or pan. If you break them directly into the pan, and you accidently break the yolk of the sixth egg, the first five will be spoiled as well! The same holds true for any recipe calling for eggs. Also, bits of egg shell might fall into the skillet or pan.

Sauté apple in 1 tablespoon butter until barely tender; remove from pan. Combine eggs, water, salt, and pepper until blended. Heat remaining butter in an omelet pan; add egg mixture. Cook slowly, lifting edges to allow the uncooked portion to flow under. Arrange apple slices on half of the omelet. Sprinkle with cheeses; fold in half.

Basic Frittata

Servings: 4

1 tablespoon olive oil
1 clove garlic, minced
¼ cup chopped onion
¾ cup packaged broccoli slaw or shredded broccoli or other shredded or diced vegetables
4 eggs
Salt and pepper to taste
¼ cup sliced black olives
½ cup shredded packaged Italian-blend cheeses or other shredded cheese

In a 10-inch skillet heat the oil and sauté the garlic, onion, and broccoli or other vegetables until crisp-tender (no more than 5 minutes.) Beat the eggs well and add salt and pepper to taste. When vegetables are done, distribute them evenly in the skillet with a spatula. Sprinkle the olives over top and pour the eggs over. Sprinkle cheese on the eggs. Reduce heat to medium-low. As the eggs thicken, lift the edges with a spatula and allow the liquid on top to run underneath.

Traditionally, frittatas are placed under the broiler to finish cooking the top when eggs are set. Or, you can cover the skillet after adding the cheese (do not cover tightly) and allow to cook until eggs are completely done, up to 10 minutes.

A frittata is an Italian-style omelet. Omelets have ingredients folded inside them after they are cooked. Frittatas have ingredients cooked with the eggs. In some frittata recipes, eggs are poured over the other ingredients in the pan; in some they are mixed together before adding to the cooking pan.

Eggs and Lox

Servings: 4 to 5

3 ounces lox or smoked salmon
3-ounce package cream cheese
6 eggs
½ cup milk or water
½ teaspoon dill
salt and pepper to taste
1 tablespoon butter

Chop the lox. Soften the cream cheese well. With a whisk, beat the eggs and milk lightly. Add the cream cheese and combine thoroughly. Stir in the dill, salt and pepper, and lox.

Melt the butter in a 10- or 12-inch skillet. Scramble the egg mixture until thickened but still moist.

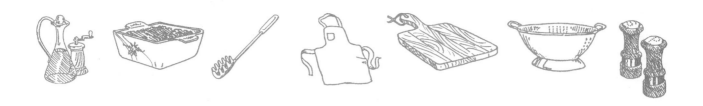

Egg Safety:
Buying and Storing Fresh Eggs

Due to salmonella outbreaks in recent years, the USDA has detailed instructions on egg safety (call 800-535-4555 for more information.) To reduce the chance of bacterial contamination:

- At the grocery store, open egg cartons and check to see that eggs are not cracked. Commercially processed eggs are washed; avoid buying eggs that appear dirty.
- When removing from the carton, discard any egg that is cracked or sticks to the carton. If *you* accidentally break an egg, discard it or cook it immediately
- Eggs can be refrigerated for up to 5 weeks from the date stamped on the carton.
- Leftover egg whites can be stored, tightly covered, for up to 4 days. Yolks can be stored 2 days; store in water for best results.
- Store whole eggs with the larger end up. The yolks will center and boiled or fried eggs will have a more attractive appearance.

Eggs Benedict

Servings: 4

> *Hollandaise Sauce (see page 119)*
> *2 English muffins*
> *butter*
> *4 eggs*
> *4 slices Canadian bacon*

Prepare the Hollandaise Sauce; set aside but keep warm. Split the English muffins, butter one side of each muffin, and place on a baking sheet. Poach the eggs (see page 74).

While the eggs are cooking, brown the muffins lightly under the broiler. Top each with a slice of Canadian bacon, and broil about 1 to 2 minutes more until warmed. To serve, place a muffin on the serving plate, top with an egg, and spoon Hollandaise Sauce over each.

Crab or Seafood Benedict: Preheat 1 cup of cooked and chopped crabmeat or other seafood such as shrimp or lobster in the microwave or in a skillet with a small amount of butter. Substitute for the Canadian bacon.

Eggs Benedict were invented at Delmonico's Restaurant in New York. They were named for frequent patrons, the Benedicts, who complained about the lack of variety on the lunchtime menu.

Huevos Rancheros

Say "WAVE-os ron-CHAIR-os"

Servings: 6

> *½ pound bulk chorizo* or pork sausage*
> *6 corn tortillas*
> *cooking oil*
> *1 cup tomato salsa (see page 116) or commercial salsa*
> *6 eggs*
> *1 cup shredded Cheddar cheese*

Break up and cook the sausage in a skillet until browned. Drain the fat and keep the sausage warm. In a skillet just slightly larger than the tortillas, cook the tortillas one at a time in a small amount of oil, turning once. Cook until crisp, about 1 minute. Keep the tortillas warm.

Heat the salsa until hot in a saucepan. Meanwhile, fry the eggs over easy. (see page 75)

To assemble, spread a spoonful of salsa on each tortilla. Top with an egg, sausage, salsa, and cheese. Serve with additional salsa.

*Chorizo (say "chor-REE-zo") is a spicy Mexican pork sausage available in some grocery stores and ethnic food shops.

Vegetable Egg Scramble

Servings: 6

> 1 teaspoon olive oil
> 3 scallions, minced
> 2 cloves garlic, minced
> 1/2 pound fresh mushrooms, sliced
> 1 green bell pepper, chopped
> 8-ounce can corn, drained
> 6 eggs
> salt and pepper to taste

In a large skillet, heat the oil over medium heat. Add the scallions, garlic, mushrooms, bell pepper, and corn. Sauté, stirring occasionally, until vegetables are tender, about 5 minutes.

Meanwhile, beat the eggs lightly in a bowl. Add the eggs to the vegetables, season with salt and pepper, and scramble until thoroughly cooked. Serve at once.

Eggs in Tomato Broth

Servings: 2

> 1 tablespoon olive oil
> 1 clove garlic
> 16-ounce can crushed tomatoes
> 1/2 cup water
> 1 1/2 teaspoons chopped thyme
> 1 1/2 teaspoons basil
> 1/4 teaspoon salt
> 1/4 teaspoon sugar
> 4 large eggs

Heat oil in a large skillet over medium heat. Add garlic and stir 3 to 4 minutes, until garlic is tender and golden. Discard garlic. Stir in remaining ingredients except for the eggs. Bring slowly to a boil. Reduce heat and simmer uncovered for 7 minutes, stirring occasionally.

Break eggs one at a time into a cup and gently slide them into the sauce. Cover and simmer for 5 to 6 minutes, or until eggs are set.

Egg Facts

- The yolk contains protein and all of the vitamins and minerals in an egg. Unfortunately, it also contains all of the fat and cholesterol. The white contains protein and water, but no other nutrients—or fat or cholesterol.
- Usually, *2 egg whites* can be substituted for *1 whole egg*. However, in a recipe calling for many eggs, this substitution will not be satisfactory.
- Eggs of different grades (AA or A) do not differ in nutritive value.
- Brown and white eggs do not differ in nutritive value, although some people believe they differ in taste.

Sausage Skillet

Servings: 4 to 6

> 1 tablespoon oil
> 2 cups frozen shredded hash
>   brown potatoes
> ¹/₂ pound sausage
> 2 tablespoons diced red or green
>   bell pepper
> 6 eggs
> salt and pepper to taste
> ¹/₃ cup shredded Cheddar cheese

Heat the oil in a medium skillet on medium-high heat. Add the hash browns and cook 8 to 10 minutes, stirring occasionally.

Meanwhile, brown the sausage in another skillet. The last minute of cooking, add the peppers and stir. Remove from heat and drain well. In a bowl, beat the eggs well, then add the sausage and pepper mixture. Season with salt and pepper.

When the hash browns are cooked, spread to cover the bottom of the skillet evenly. Pour the egg mixture over the hash browns. Reduce heat to medium-low and cover. Cook 10 minutes or until eggs are set. Remove from heat and sprinkle with cheese.

Rosemary Potato Skillet

Servings: 4 to 6

> 2 cups quartered small, unpeeled new
>   (red) potatoes
> 1 tablespoon oil
> 6 eggs
> ¹/₂ cup chopped cooked chicken or turkey
> 1 tablespoon fresh snipped chives
> 1 tablespoon fresh chopped parsley
> 1 teaspoon rosemary
> salt and pepper to taste
> ¹/₃ cup shredded Muenster, Monterey Jack,
>   or other mild white cheese

Steam or boil the potatoes *whole* until partially cooked (a fork can be inserted with pressure). Drain. When cool enough to handle, cut into quarters. In a medium skillet heat the oil over medium-high heat; add the potatoes and sauté 4 to 5 minutes, stirring occasionally.

Meanwhile, in a bowl, beat the eggs well. Stir in the chicken, herbs, and salt and pepper. When the potatoes are done, spread to cover the bottom of the skillet evenly and pour the egg mixture over the potatoes. Cover and cook 5 minutes; sprinkle with cheese, recover, and cook 5 minutes more or until eggs are set.

Skillet (Crustless) Quiche Lorraine

Servings: 4 to 6

6 slices bacon
1 medium onion
1½ tablespoons cooking oil
6 eggs
1½ cups shredded Swiss cheese or a
*   mixture of Swiss and Gruyère cheese*
dash nutmeg
salt and pepper to taste

Preheat the broiler. Cook the bacon in a skillet until hard. Drain well, crumble, and reserve. Slice the onion very thinly. In a 10-inch ovenproof skillet, heat the oil and sauté the onion for about 2 minutes.

Beat the eggs well. Stir in the cheese, nutmeg, salt and pepper, and bacon. When the onions have finished cooking, stir to distribute evenly (do not drain), and pour the egg mixture over them. Reduce the heat to medium-low and cook until set but still moist on top, about 8 minutes. Immediately put the skillet in the broiler, about 5 inches from the flame or element, and cook until the top is done but not browned.

Egg Safety

- When bringing an egg or egg white to room temperature, do not allow it to stand for more than a half-hour.

- To separate whites and yolks, use an inexpensive kitchen tool called an egg separator, available at any variety or cooking store. **Do not** use the traditional method of pouring the egg from one half of the egg shell to the other, which increases the chances that the egg might come in contact with a contaminated outer shell.

- When finished working with eggs, wash the work surface, dishes, and utensils with hot soapy water. Wash your hands before and after.

83

Skillet (Crustless) Broccoli Quiche

Servings: 6

6 slices bacon
3 cups chopped broccoli, fresh or frozen
1½ tablespoons cooking oil
½ cup chopped onion
6 eggs
¾ cup shredded Swiss cheese
¾ cup shredded Cheddar cheese
salt and pepper to taste

Preheat the broiler. Cook the bacon in a skillet until hard. Drain well, crumble, and reserve. Bring a large saucepan about one half full of water to a boil, then add the broccoli and cook 1 minute. (Broccoli can also be steamed or microwaved.) Drain well and reserve. In a 12-inch oven-proof skillet, heat the oil and sauté the onion for about 2 minutes.

Beat the eggs well. Stir in the cheeses, broccoli, salt and pepper, and bacon. When the onions have finished cooking, stir to distribute evenly (do not drain), and pour the egg mixture over them. Reduce the heat to medium and cook until set but still moist on top, about 8 minutes. Immediately put the skillet in the broiler, about 5 inches from the flame or element, and cook until the top is done but not browned.

Low-Fat Substitutions

To reduce the fat and cholesterol in breakfast and brunch recipes:

- Use liquid egg substitute. Made from egg whites, it has no cholesterol. Substitute ¼ cup for each whole egg.
- Use reduced or low-fat shredded cheeses, cream cheese, or sour cream. Substitute with no change in measurements. These products contain more moisture, and some dishes will be more moist.
- *Do not* substitute fat-free cheeses or sour cream in recipes. The resulting dish will be unsatisfactory. Use *fat-free products* only in recipes designed for them.

Crustless Spinach Quiche

Our favorite brunch accompaniment

Servings: 6 to 8

10-ounce package frozen chopped spinach
3 eggs
1 cup creamy cottage cheese
2 tablespoons minced onion
$^1\!/_2$ cup grated Parmesan cheese
$^1\!/_8$ teaspoon nutmeg
1 teaspoon seasoned salt
pepper to taste
paprika

Preheat oven to 350°F. Grease a 9-inch pie pan or an 8-inch-square baking dish.

Thaw the spinach, drain in a colander, then squeeze in paper towels to remove excess moisture. In a blender, combine the eggs and cottage cheese on medium speed until well blended. Or, you can beat the eggs well by hand with a wire whisk, then beat in the cottage cheese well. Stir in the Parmesan cheese, nutmeg, salt, and pepper, then stir in the spinach until evenly distributed. Sprinkle with paprika. Bake 25 to 30 minutes, until the center is set.

Fettuccine Frittata à la Pesto

Servings: 4

3-ounce package dried tomato halves, halved or quartered
9-ounce package fresh (refrigerated) spinach or fettuccini noodles, or substitute 8 ounces dry spinach or egg noodles
3 tablespoons prepared pesto
4 eggs, lightly beaten
$^1\!/_4$ cup milk
grated Parmesan cheese (optional)
extra pesto (optional)
fresh basil leaves for garnish (optional)

Bring a large pot of water to boiling. Add the dried tomatoes and noodles and cook until al dente, about 8 to 10 minutes. Drain well. Return to the pot. Add pesto and toss until noodles are evenly coated. In a small bowl, beat together eggs and milk until blended. Pour over noodle mixture. Cook over medium heat, gently turning with a pancake turner, until eggs are thickened and no visible liquid egg remains. Serve immediately with Parmesan cheese and additional pesto, if desired. Garnish with basil if desired.

Shirred Egg Brunch

Servings: 12

> 4 slices soft bread
> 1 tablespoon butter
> 12 slices Canadian bacon
> 12 slices (about 3½ x 3½) pepper cheese
>   (white cheese with pepper bits)
> 12 eggs
> salt to taste
> 1 cup half-and-half or light cream

Preheat oven to 450°F. Crumb the bread into medium crumbs by hand or in an electric chopper. Melt the butter in a medium skillet; remove from heat and toss the bread crumbs in the skillet to absorb the butter. Set aside.

Line the bottom of a 9 x 13-inch ungreased baking dish with the Canadian bacon. Cover with the cheese slices. Break one egg into a bowl; do not stir it or break the yolk. Pour the egg on top of the cheese slices. Repeat with each remaining egg. As you add each egg to the pan, pour it in a different place to distribute the yolks as evenly as possible. The whites will spread out. Sprinkle with salt to taste. Carefully pour the cream on the whites of the eggs but not on the yolks. Bake for 10 minutes. Sprinkle bread crumbs on top of the whites of the eggs only; the yolks should "peak through." Return to oven and bake 8 to 10 minutes longer. To serve, cut into squares.

Southwestern Brunch

Servings: 8

> 8 ounces southwestern-style refrigerated
>   hash browns, or frozen southwestern-
>   flavored hash browns, thawed
> ¼ cup sliced green onions
>   (whites and some green tops)
> 1 cup taco- or nacho-flavored
>   shredded cheese
> 2 16-ounce cans Mexican-style corn,
>   drained
> 6 eggs
> 1 cup milk
> ½ teaspoon seasoned salt
> ½ teaspoon Spike seasoning
> ¼ teaspoon pepper

Preheat oven to 350°F. Lightly grease an 8 x 11-inch baking dish.

Spread the potatoes in the prepared dish. Sprinkle the onions over the potatoes, then the cheese, then the corn. Beat the eggs together with the milk until well blended; add the seasonings. Pour carefully over the mixture in the baking dish.

Bake 40 to 50 minutes, or until the center is set.

Bacon and Egg Brunch Dish

Servings: 6 to 8

> 8 slices bacon
> 1 medium tomato
> 8 ounces refrigerated hash browns with
>   onions, or frozen chunky hash browns
>   with onions, thawed
> 1 cup shredded Cheddar cheese
> 6 eggs
> 1 cup milk
> 1 teaspoon seasoned salt
> ¼ teaspoon pepper

Preheat oven to 350°F. Lightly grease an 8 x 11-inch baking dish.

Cook the bacon well; drain and crumble. Seed and chop the tomato, draining on paper towels if necessary. Spread the potatoes in the prepared dish. Sprinkle the cheese over the potatoes, then the bacon and tomatoes. Beat the eggs together with the milk until well blended; add seasoned salt and pepper. Pour carefully over the mixture in the baking dish.

Bake 40 to 50 minutes, or until the center is set.

Sausage Strata

A make-ahead dish for brunch

Servings: 4

> 5 or 6 slices stale French bread
> 6 eggs
> 1 cup milk
> ¼ teaspoon dry mustard
> salt and pepper to taste
> ⅓ pound sausage
> 1 cup shredded Cheddar cheese

(continued)

How to Seed Tomatoes

- Work over a plate or paper towels.
- Cut the tomato in half. If using Roma tomatoes, cut lengthwise.
- Using a small spoon, scoop out the seeds.
- Invert and drain on paper towels for a few minutes.

Arrange the bread slices in a square or oblong 2-quart baking dish. In a bowl, beat the eggs well with the milk, mustard, salt, and pepper. Pour over the bread.

In a skillet, cook the sausage, breaking it into bite-sized pieces until browned, about 5 minutes. Drain well in a sieve or on paper towels. Sprinkle sausage and cheese on top of egg mixture. Cover and refrigerate overnight.

Preheat the oven to 350°F. Bake about 30 minutes, or until a knife inserted in the center comes out clean. Cut into squares and serve immediately.

Swiss Eggs

Servings: 4

1 tablespoon butter
$^1/_4$ pound Gruyère cheese, sliced thin
4 eggs
1 teaspoon salt
$^1/_2$ teaspoon black pepper
$^1/_4$ cup heavy cream
$^1/_2$ cup grated Parmesan cheese

Preheat oven to 350°F. Melt butter in a shallow casserole dish. Line dish with thin cheese slices. One at a time, break the eggs into a small bowl, then carefully pour them into the cheese-lined dish, keeping the yolks whole. Add the salt and pepper to the cream, and carefully pour over the eggs. Sprinkle with Parmesan cheese and bake for 10 minutes. If necessary, brown the cheese topping under the broiler for a few minutes.

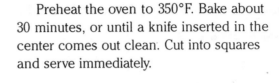

Egg Safety

- Cook egg dishes promptly! If dishes must stand for a while before cooking or baking, refrigerate them.
- When making a "do-ahead" egg dish, do not store for more than 24 hours before cooking.
- Serve egg dishes soon after cooking and refrigerate leftovers quickly. Discard them after two days if they have not been eaten.
- Hard-boiled eggs can be stored for up to a week in the refrigerator.

Brunch for Two

Servings: 2

>1 medium potato
>1 medium tomato
>2 green onions
>2 slices bacon
>2 eggs
>1/4 cup shredded Swiss cheese
>1 tablespoon chopped fresh parsley
>dash garlic powder, optional
>salt and pepper to taste

Preheat oven to 350°F. Grease a small baking dish, about 6 inches square.

Peel the potato, cut into ½-inch cubes, and cook until just tender in boiling water or by steaming. Meanwhile, seed and chop the tomato, draining on paper towels if necessary. Chop the green onions, using the whites and about 3 inches of the green tops. In a small skillet, fry the bacon until crisp. Drain, reserving a small amount of fat in the skillet. Cook the chopped tomato and green onion in the skillet about 1 minute. Crumble the bacon. Beat the eggs lightly and combine with the cheese, parsley, and seasonings. Stir in the crumbled bacon and the tomato mixture.

Pour into the prepared baking dish and **place it in a second, larger pan** that has been filled with about 1 inch of water. Bake until set, about 25 minutes.

California Rarebit

Rarebit is pronounced "rabbit" and is an open-faced sandwich with a tangy cheese sauce.

Servings: 4

>3 tablespoons butter, divided
>½ cup dry white wine
>2½ cups cubed Jack cheese, divided
>1 large egg, lightly beaten
>1 teaspoon Worcestershire sauce
>½ teaspoon crushed basil
>2 cups sliced mushrooms
>½ teaspoon garlic powder
>toast points or triangles

Melt 1 tablespoon of the butter in the top of a double boiler. Add the wine and heat, then stir in 2 cups of the cheese. Heat until melted. Add a little of the cheese mixture to the beaten egg and then add the egg mixture back into the cheese. Cook and stir about 1 minute. Add the Worcestershire sauce and basil; set aside, keeping the sauce warm.

Sauté the mushrooms in the remaining butter until just tender, then sprinkle with the garlic powder. Remove from the heat.

Arrange toast points or triangles on individual heat-proof plates. Spoon the sauce over the toast, then top with the sautéed mushrooms. Sprinkle with the remaining cheese and broil until bubbly.

Cheese Rarebit

Servings: 6

> 2 tablespoons butter
> 1 pound sharp Cheddar cheese, shredded
> 1 cup beer
> 6 eggs, poached (see page 74)
> 1 teaspoon dry mustard
> 1 teaspoon paprika
> 6 slides Canadian bacon, warmed
> 6 English muffins or 6 slices toast

Melt butter in the top of double broiler; add the cheese. Stir until the cheese begins to melt. Add the beer gradually, stirring constantly until the cheese is melted and the mixture is smooth. Stir in egg, mustard, and paprika. To serve, place one slice Canadian bacon and one egg on each slice of toast and pour sauce over.

Apple Accompaniment

Yield: about 2 cups

> 3 tablespoons butter
> 2 cups sliced, chunked, or coarsely
>   chopped apple
> 2 tablespoons packed brown sugar
> 1/2 teaspoon cinnamon
> 1/4 cup water

In a medium skillet, melt the butter over medium-high heat (do not allow to brown)

and sauté the apples 2 to 3 minutes. In a small bowl, mix the brown sugar, cinnamon, and water. Add to the apples, reduce heat to low, and continue cooking an additional 2 or 3 minutes. Apples should be tender but remain firm. Use as a topping for pancakes or an accompaniment to eggs or ham. Also a great ice cream topping!

Seasoning variation: Add 1/4 teaspoon pumpkin pie spice to the cinnamon.

Basic French Toast

Servings: 3 or 4

> 2 eggs
> 1/2 cup milk
> 2 teaspoons sugar
> 1/4 teaspoon vanilla
> 1/2 teaspoon cinnamon
> 1/4 teaspoon salt
> 5 or 6 slices day-old French or
>   other bread*
> cooking oil

Beat the eggs lightly, then combine with the milk, sugar, vanilla, cinnamon, and salt. Pour into a flat-bottomed dish somewhat larger than the slices of bread. Dip the bread into the mixture on both sides, one slice at a time, restirring the mixture after each. Do not soak. Place bread on a plate and allow to stand for a few minutes.

In a medium skillet, heat about 1 tablespoon of oil over medium-high heat. Cook bread for 2 to 3 minutes on each side. Add more oil if needed for the second batch. Serve with syrup.

*French bread should be sliced about 1 inch thick. If bread is fresh, it can be dried slightly in an oven set at 300°F; watch carefully.

French Toast Casserole

Servings: 3 or 4

6 slices cinnamon bread without icing, standard loaf size
2 tablespoons butter
2 eggs
1 cup light cream
1 tablespoon brown sugar
1 teaspoon vanilla

Preheat over to 350°F. Lightly grease an 8- or 9-inch square baking dish.

Place the bread in the dish in two overlapping layers. Melt the butter. In a bowl, beat the eggs well together with the cream; add the melted butter, brown sugar, and vanilla, stirring to combine. Pour slowly over the bread slices; if they begin to float, press down lightly with fingertips until they absorb the liquid. Bake 45 minutes. Cut in squares to serve.

Toast 'n' Eggs

A do-ahead brunch recipe

Servings: 10

1 standard size loaf cinnamon bread without icing*
2 cups Apple Accompaniment (see page 90)
¼ cup raisins (can be omitted if using cinnamon raisin bread)
8 eggs**
2¼ cups milk
1 tablespoon sugar
1 tablespoon vanilla

Grease a 9 x 13-inch baking dish. Cut the bread into 1-inch cubes and spread in the prepared pan. Spread the Apple Accompaniment evenly over the bread and sprinkle with raisins. In a bowl, beat the eggs well and combine with the milk, sugar, and vanilla, mixing well. Pour evenly over the bread, stirring slightly if necessary to distribute the eggs evenly. Cover and refrigerate overnight.

To bake, preheat the oven to 350°F. Remove pan from the refrigerator and bake about 45 minutes, or until set in the middle. Allow to stand 5 minutes before serving with syrup.

*If using a small circular loaf (3 to 4 inches diameter), increase to 10 slices.

**If using liquid egg substitute (2 cups equivalent), reduce the milk to 2 cups.

Basic Pancakes

Yield: 8 to 10 4-inch cakes

1 cup flour
1 tablespoon sugar (granulated or brown)
2½ teaspoons baking powder
¼ teaspoon salt
1 egg
1 cup milk
2 tablespoons cooking oil

Combine the flour, sugar, baking powder, and salt in a bowl by stirring, then make a well. In a different bowl, beat the egg well and thoroughly combine with the milk and oil. Add the liquid to the flour mixture and stir quickly until moistened; batter will have some lumps.

Preheat a greased or buttered griddle or skillet over medium-high heat. Cook pancakes on the hot griddle, using about ¼ cup batter per cake. Cook about 2 or 3 minutes on each side; pancakes are ready to turn when the tops have broken bubbles on the surface and the edges appear dry.

Whole-Wheat Pancakes: Use brown sugar and substitute whole-wheat for all-purpose flour.

Buckwheat Pancakes: Use brown sugar and replace ½ cup of the all-purpose flour with buckwheat flour.

Blueberry Pancakes: Add ½ cup fresh or frozen (thawed and drained) berries to the batter.

Apple Blender Pancakes: Peel and slice one medium apple. Place the apples, egg, milk, and oil in a blender and blend on low until liquids are combined and apples are chopped. Proceed as directed.

Buttermilk Pancakes

Yield: 8 to 10 4-inch cakes

1 cup flour
1 tablespoon sugar
1 teaspoon baking powder
½ teaspoon baking soda
¼ teaspoon salt
1 egg
1 cup buttermilk or sour milk
2 tablespoons cooking oil

Combine the flour, sugar, baking powder, baking soda, and salt in a bowl by stirring, then make a well. In a different bowl, beat the eggs well and thoroughly combine with the milk and oil. Add the liquid to the flour mixture and stir quickly until moistened; batter will have some lumps.

Preheat a greased or buttered griddle or skillet over medium-high heat. Cook pancakes on the hot griddle, using about ¼ cup batter per cake. Cook about 2 or 3 minutes on each side; pancakes are ready to turn when the tops have broken bubbles on the surface and the edges appear dry.

Cornmeal Pancakes

Yield: about 6 cakes

³/₄ cup flour
¹/₂ cup cornmeal
1 tablespoon baking powder
¹/₂ teaspoon salt
1 egg
1¹/₄ cups milk
2 tablespoons vegetable oil

Combine the flour, cornmeal, baking powder, and salt in a bowl by stirring, then make a well. In a different bowl, beat the egg well and thoroughly combine with the milk and oil. Add the liquid to the flour mixture and stir quickly but thoroughly; batter will have some lumps.

Preheat a greased or buttered griddle or skillet over medium-high heat. Cook on the hot griddle, using about ¹/₄ cup batter per cake. Cook about 2 or 3 minutes on each side; pancakes are ready to turn when the tops have broken bubbles on the surface and the edges appear dry.

Weekend Pancakes

Yield: 8 cakes

1 cup flour
³/₄ teaspoon baking powder
¹/₄ teaspoon salt
2 egg yolks
1¹/₄ cups buttermilk
¹/₂ teaspoon baking soda
2 egg whites
2 tablespoons vegetable oil
fresh berries or fruit sauces, optional

(*continued*)

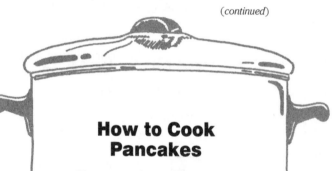

How to Cook Pancakes

- Most pancakes will need to cook about 2 or 3 minutes on each side.

- Pancakes are ready to turn when the tops have broken bubbles on the surface and the edges appear dry.

Combine the flour, baking powder, and salt; set aside. Beat the egg yolks lightly and combine with the buttermilk and baking soda and set aside. Beat the egg whites until stiff peaks form. Quickly combine the dry ingredients and the egg yolk mixture and stir in the oil. Fold in the egg whites.

Cook immediately on a hot greased griddle or skillet. Cook about 2 or 3 minutes on each side; pancakes are ready to turn when the tops have broken bubbles on the surface and the edges appear dry. Serve with berries or fruit sauces if desired.

High Protein Pancakes

Yield: about 9 4-inch cakes

3 eggs, separated
³/₄ cup cottage cheese, small curd
   preferable
¹/₂ teaspoon salt
¹/₂ cup flour
1 tablespoon sugar

Combine eggs, cottage cheese, and salt in a blender and blend well until smoother. Add the flour and sugar and blend again. Pour onto a hot, well-greased griddle, keeping cakes no larger than 4 inches in diameter. Cook until golden brown, turning once. These cakes will take longer to cook through than ordinary pancakes. Serve with Apple Accompaniment, page 90, or with fruit syrups or sauces.

Baked Apple Pancake

Servings: 6

1 tablespoon butter
4 medium apples, peeled, cored, and thinly
   sliced
3 tablespoons granulated sugar, divided
2 teaspoons vanilla extract
¹/₄ teaspoon cinnamon
3 eggs
1 cup flour
1 cup milk
3 tablespoons confectioners' sugar

Preheat oven to 425°F. In an ovenproof skillet, melt the butter over medium heat. Add the apple slices to the skillet, and sprinkle 2 tablespoons of the sugar over them. Cook over medium heat until the apples have softened, about 15 minutes. Arrange the apples evenly in the skillet and sprinkle with the vanilla and cinnamon. Remove from the heat.

In a bowl, beat the eggs lightly and blend in the flour, milk, and remaining 1 table-spoon sugar. Pour the batter over the apples.

Bake for 20 minutes at 425°F, then reduce the heat to 350°F and bake about 15 minutes longer, or until the top browns. Remove from the oven, and sprinkle with confectioners' sugar. Cut into wedges and serve immediately.

Basic Waffles

Yield: about 6 waffles

2 cups flour
4 teaspoons baking powder
$\frac{1}{4}$ teaspoon salt
2 eggs
$1\frac{3}{4}$ cups milk
$\frac{1}{2}$ cup vegetable oil

Preheat waffle iron following manufacturer's instructions.

Stir together the flour, baking powder, and salt, and make a well in the middle. Beat the eggs lightly, then beat in the milk and oil until well combined. Add all at once to the dry ingredients and combine until just moistened. Batter will have a few lumps.

Use manufacturer's directions to determine how much batter to use per waffle; use about 1 cup for a standard 7-inch circular waffle. Do not open the iron while the waffle is cooking! Remove with a fork.

Fruity Granola

Yield: about 6 cups

$\frac{1}{4}$ cup butter
$\frac{1}{4}$ cup honey
$1\frac{1}{2}$ teaspoons cinnamon
$\frac{1}{2}$ teaspoon salt

3 cups rolled oats, quick cooking or regular
1 cup chopped almonds or other nuts
1 cup dried fruit: apples, peaches, pears, apricots, cherries, cranberries ("Craisins") or a mixture
$\frac{2}{3}$ cup raisins
$1\frac{1}{2}$ teaspoons cinnamon
$\frac{1}{2}$ teaspoon salt

(continued)

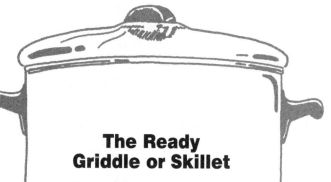

The Ready Griddle or Skillet

- When using a greased griddle or skillet, it is hot enough for cooking when a drop of water "skitters" across it.

- When using a small amount of oil or butter in the skillet, it is ready just before it begins to sizzle. Do not allow it to brown!

Preheat oven to 350°F.

Melt butter in a large saucepan; remove from heat and stir in honey. Stir in the cinnamon and salt. Add the oats and nuts; toss to coat evenly. Spread in an ungreased 13 x 9-inch baking pan and bake 30 minutes or until golden brown, stirring occasionally. Pour into a large bowl and toss in the dried fruit and raisins.

Cool thoroughly and store in a tightly covered container in a cool dry place, or in the refrigerator. Serve as a snack or as a cereal with milk.

Cold Swiss Oatmeal (Muesli)

A do-ahead cold cereal

Servings: 6

> 2 cups quick-cooking rolled oats
> $1/2$ cup orange or apple juice
> $3/4$ cup chopped prunes, raisins, or currants
> $1/3$ cup chopped nuts or wheat germ
> $1/4$ teaspoon salt
> $1/4$ cup honey
> $1^1/4$ cups milk

Place the oats in a bowl and pour the juice over them; toss till it is evenly absorbed. Stir in the fruit, nuts, and salt. Pour the honey over the mixture and toss until evenly combined. Stir in the milk. Cover and refrigerate at least 8 hours.

Do not cook; serve cold with brown sugar and additional milk or cream if desired.

Egg Safety

- Raw eggs can be harmful to some people. Pregnant women, infants and young children, the elderly, and those who are already ill (especially with immune disorders) should not eat them unless on a doctor's advice.

- Raw eggs are an ingredient in *homemade* mayonnaise, ice cream, eggnog, and some salad dressing. Commercially prepared varieties of these foods are pasteurized and do not pose a risk.

- If preparing a recipe that uses raw eggs as an ingredient, use pasteurized eggs, available at most groceries.

Blender Crepes

Yield: 12 crepes

1 cup flour
2 tablespoon butter
½ cup cold milk
½ cup cold water
2 eggs
¼ teaspoon salt

Sift the flour. Melt the butter. Put the butter, milk, water, eggs, and salt in the blender and combine well. With the blender still running on a low speed, gradually add the flour until well combined. Refrigerate in the blender container for at least 2 hours.

To cook crepes, grease a 6-inch skillet or crepe pan and heat. Remove from the heat and add about 3 tablespoons crepe mix, tilting the pan to spread the batter. Cook on one side only, then invert onto a paper towel. Crepes can be stacked as they are made if waxed paper is placed between them.

Sweet or Dessert Crepes: add ¼ cup sugar and omit the salt.

Boiled Egg Tips

Soft boiled: Pierce the ends of eggs with a straight pin to prevent them from cracking while being soft boiled. If the eggs do crack while boiling, however, they are still perfectly fine to eat.

Hard boiled: If the egg is too hot to handle, roll and peel under cold running water. To peel hard-boiled eggs easily, roll the egg between your hands after cracking and before peeling.

If hard-boiled eggs have a greenish ring around the outside of the yolk, it is probably because they have been cooked too long. However, they are still perfectly fine to eat.

Chapter 5

Salads, Dressings, Sauces, Salsas, and Condiments

S alad greens include lettuce, herbs, spinach, and cabbages. A wonderful variety of greens is available at most well-stocked supermarkets and food cooperatives. Dark greens have the most beta-carotene or vitamin A—an important cancer preventer. Just one cup of chard, spinach, or dandelion or mustard greens provides 100 percent of the recommended daily requirement of vitamin A. Fresh green salads can be tossed or carefully arranged on a large platter with dressing served on the side.

Lexicon of Salad Greens

Crispheads

These are lettuces, like iceberg, that offer texture and can support a heavy dressing.

Romaine or Cos Lettuces

Romaine has long crisp and nutty-flavored leaves and is the most nutritious of the lettuces. Its dark green leaves indicate its high beta-carotene content. It is also a good lettuce to use with heavier dressings such as avocado, bleu cheese or Caesar.

Looseleaf Lettuces

The young soft red or green oakleaf lettuces are the sweetest. They require lighter dressings than iceberg and romaine.

Butterheads

These soft loose-headed lettuces like Boston, Bibb, and butter have curvaceous leaf patterns that do taste buttery. Some more exotic varieties have red-edged leaves.

Gourmet Salad Mix or Mesclun

This mixture of young and tender greens often includes arugula, nasturtium, chervil, and baby spinach. Mesclun is a French word for a fairly specific mixture, although American farmers often design their own combinations. Mesclun is a collection of a dozen or more wild greens, herbs, and edible flowers.

Chicories

Greens in this category include those with curly leaves and a pale center. The level of bitterness varies in these greens, which include endive, dandelion, radicchio, and escarole.

Cabbage

Cabbages such as green Chinese, which has very light crinkly leaves, make excellent salads. Dutch, Savoy, and Napa cabbage may be wilted in boiling water to make them more appealing to some tastes.

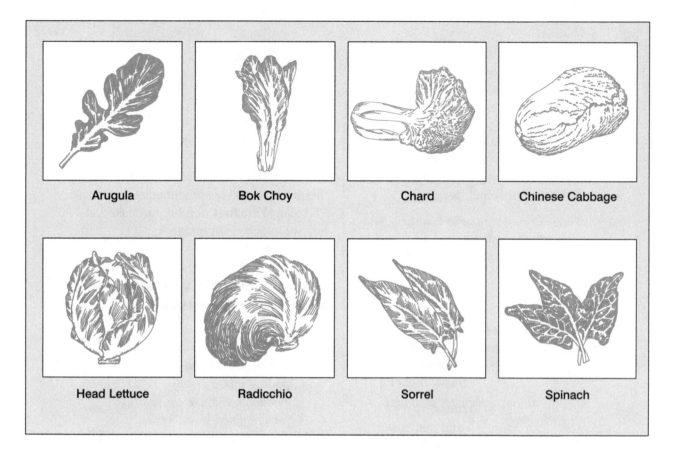

Arugula   Bok Choy   Chard   Chinese Cabbage

Head Lettuce   Radicchio   Sorrel   Spinach

Herbs

A wide variety of herbs can be used to make very tasty salads. Arugula, parsley, watercress, basil, and sorrel are just a few. A salad composed totally of herbs requires only a light dressing of lemon juice and olive oil to enhance the flavors of these plants.

Wild Greens

Common greens found growing in many places can be used in salads. Lamb's quarters, miner's lettuce, and purslane are examples.

Red-Leafed Greek Salad

Servings: 4

4 to 6 handfuls red-leafed salad greens
1 large tomato cut into wedges
1 large red onion, sliced thinly
4 ounces feta cheese, crumbled
2 tablespoons balsamic vinegar
2 cloves garlic, pressed
5 tablespoons extra virgin olive oil
salt and freshly ground pepper to taste

Carefully sort through the greens and then wash and dry them well. Toss the greens with the tomato wedges, onion

(continued)

slices, and feta cheese. Mix the vinegar, garlic, olive oil, and salt and pepper well, whisking in a small bowl. Pour over the greens mixture and toss. Serve immediately with a fresh loaf of French bread.

 If edible flowers are used in a salad, add them after the salad is dressed so they won't wilt. They can be scattered over the top of the salad just before serving.

Spinach Salad with Mango Chutney Dressing

Servings: 4

> 1 large bunch of spinach, washed and
>   carefully dried
> 1 tart green apple, chopped coarsely
> $^1/_4$ cup chopped green onion
> 1 cup whole roasted peanuts

Dressing:
> $^1/_4$ cup lemon juice
> 2 tablespoons red wine vinegar
> $^1/_4$ cup mango chutney*
> 1 teaspoon curry powder
> $^1/_8$ teaspoon cayenne pepper
> $^1/_4$ teaspoon turmeric
> $^1/_2$ teaspoon sugar
> $^1/_2$ teaspoon salt
> $^3/_4$ cup light olive oil

Toss together the spinach, apple, green onion, and peanuts. In a blender, combine the lemon juice, red wine vinegar, mango chutney, curry powder, cayenne, turmeric, sugar, and salt, and blend for 2 minutes. Gradually add the olive oil and blend until mixture is smooth. Toss the spinach with the dressing and serve immediately.

*Mango chutney can be purchased at any well-stocked supermarket.

Endive Salad with Apples and Blue Cheese

Servings: 6–8

> 2 large heads Belgian endive
> 4 handfuls mixed greens
> $^1/_2$ medium red apple cut in strips
> $^1/_4$ cup crumbled blue cheese
> $^1/_4$ cup walnuts, toasted and chopped*
> 3 tablespoons extra-virgin olive oil
> 1 tablespoon white wine vinegar
> salt and freshly ground pepper to taste

Trim the core from the endive and cut in half lengthwise; then cut crosswise in $^1/_2$-inch slices. Combine endive in a salad bowl with the greens, apple, blue cheese, and nuts.

Combine the oil, vinegar, salt, and pepper in a small bowl, mixing well. Toss with the salad.

*Toast walnuts by heating a skillet to medium heat and adding the walnuts, stirring until slightly browned.

 Raw vegetables and fruits may contain a variety of parasites. Soak all greens,

roots, and fruit to be eaten raw in a mild solution of apple cider vinegar. Use 1 tablespoon of vinegar per gallon of soaking water or ¼ cup for a sinkful. Hydrogen peroxide, which also removes parasites, can also effectively denature the poison sprays found on nonorganic produce.

Spicy Herb Salad

Servings: 4

> 5 handfuls romaine leaves, chopped into bite-sized pieces
> 1 handful loosely packed whole mint leaves
> ¼ cup whole green basil leaves
> ½ cup whole oregano leaves
> ¼ cup finely chopped green onions
> salt to taste

Vinaigrette:

¼ cup olive oil
2 teaspoons red wine vinegar
2 tablespoons water
½ teaspoon salt
1 teaspoon Dijon mustard

Just before serving, combine the romaine with the mint, basil, oregano, and green onions in a large bowl. Lightly salt and toss to mix well.

In a jar with a lid, mix the olive oil, red wine vinegar, water, salt, and mustard. Shake well until completely blended. Drizzle half the vinaigrette over the salad and gently toss to mix well. Add more vinaigrette if needed.

Green Salad Tips

- Tear greens into bite-sized pieces by hand rather than using a knife. Lettuce cut with a knife browns much more quickly, so if you must cut, do so a short time before serving.
- Use a variety of greens, including the "reds" of cabbage and radicchio (say ra-DEE-keyo). But taste greens first, because some are more bitter than others.
- Greens should be thoroughly dry before adding dressing, to enable it to stick to the leaves.
- Don't dress a salad until you are ready to serve it. Use only enough to coat the greens lightly. If desired, you can serve additional dressing at the table.

Wilted Amaretto Spinach Salad

Servings: 6

5 cloves garlic
2 tablespoons olive oil
1 tablespoon lemon juice
2 teaspoons Dijon or other spicy mustard
1½ cups sliced fresh mushrooms
1 tablespoon amaretto liqueur
1 pound fresh spinach
3 tablespoons grated Parmesan cheese

Slice the garlic thinly. In a large, deep skillet with a lid, heat the oil over medium heat and sauté the garlic for about 1 minute. Add the lemon juice and mustard, quickly mixing it directly in the skillet. Add the mushrooms and spread them thinly in the skillet. Add the amaretto, and mix. Let the mixture simmer for 3 to 4 minutes, stirring frequently, until the mushrooms are covered with sauce and soft.

Place the spinach on top of the mixture, but do not stir. Cover tightly. The steam will wilt the spinach in about 3 minutes. Remove from the heat. In a serving dish, lightly toss the salad, and sprinkle with Parmesan cheese. Serve immediately.

Storing Greens

- Iceberg and Romaine lettuce and cabbage will keep up to a week with proper refrigerator storage, but most other lettuces and greens will wilt within 2 or 3 days. Bibb, leaf lettuce, and radicchio will keep up to 5 days.
- Greens can be refrigeratored unwashed in their original plastic bag, then washed just before use. Greens washed earlier must be well dried and stored in an airtight plastic bag or container.
- Dressed leftover salad can be safely refrigerated and saved, but the greens will become very limp quickly.

Easy Greens with Spicy Lemon Dressing

Servings: 4

¼ cup olive oil
2 tablespoons lemon juice
2 cloves garlic, minced or pressed
1 tablespoon Dijon or other spicy mustard
10–12 ounces mixed greens
grated Parmesan cheese
salt and freshly ground black pepper

In a large salad serving bowl (not wooden), whisk together the first 4 ingredients. Add the fresh greens; sprinkle with Parmesan cheese and salt and pepper to taste. Toss until the dressing thoroughly coats the greens.

Strawberry Garden Salad

Servings: 8

3 strips bacon
1 large orange
12 ounces fresh spinach
1 head Boston lettuce
1 red onion
1 pint strawberries, cleaned and halved
¼ cup chopped fresh mint

Dressing:
1 teaspoon Dijon mustard
½ cup oil
juice of 1 lemon

Cook the bacon until crisp; drain, and crumble. To make the dressing, whisk together the mustard and the oil, then add the lemon juice slowly, whisking to combine.

Section the orange and cut sections into three pieces. Wash the greens and tear into bite-sized pieces. Slice the onion very thinly. To assemble the salad, toss the greens, fruits, onion, bacon, and mint with the dressing.

The Best Coleslaw

Servings: 6 to 8

2 pounds green cabbage, shredded
(1 good-sized head)
1 green pepper, chopped

½ medium white onion, chopped
1 small jar pimiento (2–3 ounces),
chopped
¾ cup sugar
½ cup vegetable oil
½ cup cider vinegar
salt and celery seed to taste

Mix the shredded cabbage with the chopped green pepper and onion. Add the pimiento.

Blend the sugar, oil, vinegar, salt, and celery seed in a blender on high speed for several minutes. Pour over the chopped vegetables and stir. Place in a sealed container and refrigerate overnight before serving.

Marinated Cucumbers

Servings: 4 to 6

5 medium to large cucumbers
1 pint sour cream
2 packages Hidden Valley ranch dressing
mix (original)
1 cup mayonnaise

Slice cucumbers and set aside. Mix the sour cream, dressing mix, and mayonnaise. Pour over sliced cucumbers; stir. Place in a sealed container and marinate overnight in the refrigerator before serving.

Mushroom Salad

Servings: 6

>1 pound fresh mushrooms
>1 cup snipped fresh parsley
>1 clove garlic
>½ cup salad oil
>3 tablespoons white wine vinegar
>1½ tablespoons mayonnaise
>1 teaspoon salt
>½ teaspoon white pepper
>½ teaspoon dry mustard

Wash and slice the mushrooms, and combine with the parsley; set aside. Peel the garlic clove and place in the blender with the remaining ingredients. Blend until smooth. Just before serving, toss the mushrooms with the dressing.

Tricolor Pepper Salad

Servings: 8

Dressing:

>3 tablespoons lime juice
>1 tablespoon lemon juice
>2 tablespoons white wine vinegar
>1 tablespoon olive oil
>4 cloves garlic, minced
>½ teaspoon salt
>⅛ teaspoon cayenne pepper, or to taste

Salad:

>2 red bell peppers, chopped
>2 yellow bell peppers, chopped
>2 green bell peppers, chopped
>2 celery stalks, diced
>2 large cucumbers, diced
>2 cups cherry tomatoes, halved
>¼ cup fresh snipped parsley

In a small bowl, whisk together the lime and lemon juice, vinegar, olive oil, garlic, salt, and pepper. Allow to stand for 15 minutes.

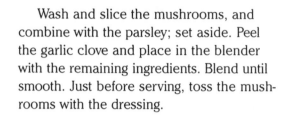

How to Seed and Chop a Bell Pepper

1. About ¾ inch out from the stem of the pepper, make a circular cut with a sharp paring knife. Grasp the stem and pull up to remove the core.
2. Slice the pepper in half lengthwise. With the knife, cut away the remaining white membranes and seeds.
3. Slice the halves horizontally into strips the width of the dice you want. Holding several strips together, cut across them to make the dice.

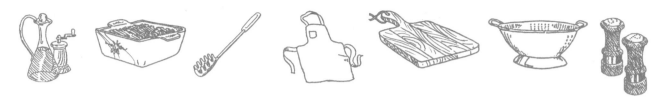

In a large bowl, toss together the peppers, celery, cucumbers, tomatoes, and parsley. Add the dressing to the salad; toss well to combine. Cover and chill for 1 hour, tossing occasionally, before serving.

Garden Tomato Salad

Servings: 6

> *4 large vine-ripened tomatoes, thinly sliced*
> *1 tablespoon chopped fresh basil*
> *2 teaspoons olive oil*
> *1 tablespoon red wine vinegar*
> *2 cloves garlic, minced*
> *salt and pepper to taste*
> *1 red salad onion, thinly sliced*

In a shallow serving dish, layer about a third of the tomatoes. Sprinkle with about a third of the basil, olive oil, vinegar, and garlic. Sprinkle with salt and pepper. Cover with about half of the onion. Repeat, then top with the remaining tomatoes and seasonings. Chill before serving.

Fresh Summer Potato Salad

Servings: 6

> *5 pounds small red potatoes*
> *1 dozen eggs*
> *4 bunches fresh green onions, chopped*

(continued)

How to Seed and Chop a Cucumber

To remove the seeds:

1. Slice the cucumber in half lengthwise, then run a melon ball maker or a small round metal spoon down the middle of each half to remove the seeds.
2. Place the halves side by side and cut each into lengthwise strips the width of the desired dice.
3. Hold the strips together, and cut crosswise to make the dice.

To add color interest to your salads, peel cucumbers only *partially* by using a potato parer to remove lengthwise strips of skin about 1/3 inch wide from the cuke before cutting it, leaving strips of unpeeled skin about the same width in between the peeled strips.

1 teaspoon mustard
¼ cup half-and-half
¾ cup mayonnaise
¼ teaspoon freshly ground pepper
salt to taste

Scrub and cut the potatoes in half or slightly smaller; boil until soft, testing by piercing them with a fork. Drain and "fluff" them in a colander. (Shake the potatoes up and down a bit in the colander, until they detach from the colander and the outside layer of the potatoes appear fluffy. This strategy also works well when you are making mashed potatoes, as they have a better texture for some reason). Slice the potatoes into bite-size pieces and set aside.

Hard-boil the eggs, then cool and slice them. Add the sliced eggs and the chopped onions to the potatoes. Mix the mustard, half-and-half, mayonnaise, and pepper together; add to the potato mixture. Add salt to taste and extra mayonnaise if the salad appears too dry.

This potato salad is best in summer with fresh garden potatoes and green onions. The secret here is the use of a rich mayonnaise like Hellmann's and fresh cream or half-and-half for the dressing. This recipe is not low calorie or low fat, but it *is* simply the best potato salad you will ever eat. A little fresh red pepper can also be added to enhance both the color and the texture.

Quick Low-Fat Potato Salad

Servings: 8

Dressing:
1 cup plain low-fat yogurt
½ teaspoon celery seed
½ teaspoon dry mustard
½ teaspoon white pepper

Salad:
2 pounds potatoes, boiled, skinned, and cut into chunks
1 large onion, thinly sliced
2 tablespoons snipped fresh parsley
paprika

Whisk together the dressing ingredients in a serving bowl. Add the potatoes and toss them gently to coat. Place the onion rings on top and sprinkle with parsley and paprika.

Minnesota Wild Rice Salad

Servings: 8 to 10

2 12-ounce packages frozen cooked diced chicken*
6 bay leaves
1 small jar artichoke hearts
3 cups cooked wild rice (1 cup raw)
3 cups halved red grapes
½ to 1 cup mayonnaise
salt and pepper to taste

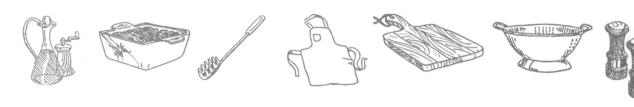

Thaw the chicken in a bowl with the bay leaves, stirring occasionally. Drain the artichokes well and quarter. Combine the rice with the thawed chicken (discard the bay leaves), artichokes, and grapes. Season to taste. Add the mayonnaise, beginning with ¹/₂ cup, and adding more if needed; combine well. Salad should remain moderately dry rather than creamy. Chill thoroughly before serving.

*3 cups cooked, cubed chicken can be substituted.

Fresh Tomato and Wild Rice Salad

Servings: 4

3 large vine-ripened tomatoes
1 clove garlic
2 cups cooked wild rice
3 green onions, chopped
3 tablespoons chopped fresh basil
2 tablespoons olive oil

Peel, seed, and chop the tomatoes. Peel and cut the garlic; rub the salad bowl well with it and discard. Place the rice, tomatoes, onion, and basil in the bowl; drizzle the olive oil over all and toss well to combine. Let stand at room temperature about 20 minutes before serving, to combine the flavors.

Tomato Cups

Egg, tuna, chicken, and seafood salads are often served in tomato cups. To make a tomato cup, slice about ¹/₄ inch off the top and about ¹/₈ inch off the bottom of a large washed tomato. (The slice off the bottom enables it to sit flat.) The tomato can be peeled or unpeeled, depending on your preference. With a spoon, scoop out all the pulp, leaving only the shell, which will usually be ¹/₄ to ¹/₂ inch thick.

As an alternative, remove the tomato stem and slice into 6 wedges, but do not slice all the way through to the bottom. Gently spread the sections and scoop the salad on top.

Easy Four-Bean Salad

Servings: 8 to 10

16-ounce can garbanzo beans
16-ounce can red kidney beans
16-ounce can white kidney beans
16-ounce can black beans
1 onion, diced
1 green bell pepper, diced
1 cup Italian salad dressing
salt and pepper to taste
1 tablespoon snipped fresh parsley

Drain the beans and rinse well. In a bowl, combine the beans, onion, pepper, and salad dressing, mixing well. Season with salt and pepper, and sprinkle with parsley. Cover and refrigerate for at least 2 hours before serving.

Traditional Three-Bean Salad

Servings: 6 to 8

16-ounce can French-cut green beans
16-ounce can yellow (wax) beans
16-ounce can red kidney beans
1 onion
$\frac{1}{2}$ cup sugar
$\frac{2}{3}$ cup vinegar
$\frac{1}{3}$ cup vegetable oil
$\frac{1}{2}$ teaspoon salt
$\frac{1}{8}$ teaspoon pepper

Drain the beans. Slice the onion thinly, then cut the slices in quarters. Whisk together the sugar, vinegar, oil, and salt and pepper. Combine the beans, onions, and dressing, mixing well. Chill at least 4 hours or overnight, stirring occasionally. If desired, the salad can be drained before serving.

Tabbouleh

Say "ta-BOO-ly"

Servings: 4 to 6

1 cup bulgur wheat, uncooked
2 cups boiling water
$\frac{1}{2}$ cup vegetable oil
$\frac{1}{2}$ cup lemon juice
2 teaspoons salt
1 teaspoon pepper
$\frac{1}{3}$ cup chopped fresh parsley
3 tablespoons chopped fresh mint
6 green onions, finely chopped (whites and 4 inches of greens)
2 tomatoes, seeded and finely chopped

Place the bulgur in a bowl, pour the boiling water over it, and let it stand for an hour.

Drain the bulgur well. Toss the remaining ingredients with the bulgur. Chill thoroughly before serving.

Basic Egg Salad

Servings: 4

>1 tablespoon cream cheese
>$\frac{1}{4}$ cup salad dressing or mayonnaise
>1 teaspoon finely minced onion
>4 hard-boiled eggs, chopped
>1 tablespoon sweet pickle relish, slightly drained, or 1 tablespoon chopped sweet pickles
>salt and pepper to taste

Soften the cream cheese and combine well with the salad dressing and onion. Combine dressing with the chopped egg and relish. Add salt and pepper. Chill before serving.

Basic Seafood Salad (Tuna, Shrimp, or Crab)

Servings: 6

>2 6-ounce cans white tuna, or 2 cups cooked cleaned shrimp, crabmeat, or imitation crabmeat
>$\frac{1}{2}$ cup peeled, diced cucumber
>$\frac{1}{2}$ cup chopped celery
>$\frac{1}{2}$ cup diced green bell pepper
>2 hard-boiled eggs, chopped
>$\frac{1}{4}$ teaspoon salt
>$\frac{1}{8}$ teaspoon white pepper
>juice of 1 lemon
>salad dressing or mayonnaise

Chop the shrimp or flake the tuna or crabmeat. Toss with all other ingredients except the lemon juice and salad dressing. Sprinkle the lemon juice over the mixture and mix again. Add just enough salad dressing to moisten, about $\frac{1}{4}$ cup or to taste. Chill before serving.

Chicken Almond Salad

Servings: 4

Dressing:

>$\frac{1}{2}$ cup sour cream
>1 tablespoon minced onion
>$1\frac{1}{2}$ tablespoons white wine vinegar
>1 tablespoon sugar
>$\frac{1}{2}$ teaspoon salt
>$\frac{1}{4}$ teaspoon dry mustard
>dash pepper
>dash hot pepper sauce

Salad:

>$1\frac{1}{2}$ cups diced cooked chicken breast
>$\frac{1}{2}$ cup diced celery
>$\frac{1}{2}$ cup slivered, toasted almonds
>1 small can pineapple tidbits, well drained

Combine dressing ingredients in blender and process until well blended. Chill at least 1 hour. You will have about $\frac{2}{3}$ cup dressing.

Combine the chicken with the celery, almonds, and pineapple. Add about $\frac{1}{2}$ cup dressing and toss until blended. Refrigerate remaining dressing for later use.

Cuban Shrimp Salad

Servings: 6–8 side dish

> 2 tablespoons oil
> 1 pound medium shrimp, peeled and
>   deveined
> 2 cloves garlic, minced
> 10-ounce can black beans, rinsed
>   and drained
> 16-ounce can corn, drained
> 1 can diced green chilies
> 6 green onions, chopped
> 1/4 cup mayonnaise
> 1/4 cup tomato salsa
> 2 tablespoons lime juice
> 1 teaspoon salt
> 1/4 teaspoon pepper
> 1/4 cup chopped fresh cilantro
> 1 orange

In a large skillet, heat the oil. Cook the shrimp and garlic until the shrimp are pink and thoroughly cooked. Drain and chill at least 2 hours.

When the shrimp is chilled, add the beans, corn, chilies, and onions; mix well. In a small bowl, combine the mayonnaise, salsa, lime juice, salt, and pepper. Add to the shrimp mixture and combine thoroughly. Chill at least 1 hour.

To serve, place the salad in a serving bowl and sprinkle cilantro on top. Cut the unpeeled orange in wedges and use as a garnish.

Tuna Macaroni Salad

Servings: 10 to 12

> 1 cup mayonnaise
> 1/2 cup chopped onion
> 1 teaspoon salt
> 1/2 teaspoon pepper
> 8 ounces wagon wheel, elbow, or other
>   macaroni
> 4 6-ounce cans tuna, drained
> 2 cups shredded carrot
> 2 cups thinly sliced celery
> 4 hard-boiled eggs, chopped

In a small bowl, combine the mayonnaise, onion, salt, and pepper. Prepare the macaroni according to package instructions; drain and cool. Stir about half the mayonnaise into the macaroni, then add the remaining ingredients along with the remaining mayonnaise, combining well.

Tuna Rice Salad

Servings: 4

> **Salad:**
> 6-ounce can chunk tuna
> 2 cups cooked white rice
> 1 cup cooked green beans
> 1 medium tomato, seeded and chopped
> 1/2 cucumber, peeled and chopped
> 1 tablespoon chopped fresh mint
> 2 tablespoons black olives, sliced

Dressing:
2 tablespoons lemon juice
1 tablespoon water
1 tablespoon olive oil

Drain the tuna well. In a large bowl, toss all the salad ingredients to combine. In a separate bowl, combine the lemon juice and water; drizzle the oil into the mixture while whisking to combine. Pour over the salad and toss well.

Classic Waldorf Salad

Servings: 6

¹/₂ cup mayonnaise
1 tablespoon sugar
1 teaspoon lemon juice
salt to taste
2 cups diced red-skinned apples
1 cup finely sliced celery
¹/₂ cup coarsely chopped walnuts

Blend the mayonnaise with the sugar, lemon juice, and salt. Combine the apples, celery, and nuts, and fold in the dressing mixture. Chill before serving.

Waldorf-Style Fruit Salad

Servings: 6

*2 unpeeled Red Delicious apples cored
    and cubed*
24 red grapes
24 green grapes
2 oranges, sectioned
1 cup plain yogurt
1 tablespoon honey
lettuce leaves
2 bananas, sliced
¹/₄ cup walnuts, chopped

In a bowl, toss together the apples, grapes, and oranges. In a small bowl, stir together the yogurt and honey. Mix into the fruit, tossing to coat evenly. To serve, place lettuce leaves on each plate and place the fruit mixture on the lettuce. Place the bananas around the edge of the plates, and sprinkle the walnuts over all.

Five Cup Salad

Servings: 8

1 cup drained mandarin oranges
1 cup drained crushed pineapple
1 cup coconut
1 cup miniature marshmallows
1 cup sour cream

Combine all ingredients and refrigerate overnight.

Strawberry Gelatin Salad

Servings: 10 to 12

10-ounce package frozen strawberries
2 3-ounce packages strawberry
    flavored gelatin
2 cups water
2 firm bananas
4 ounces sour cream
8-ounce can crushed pineapple

J·E·L·L·O!

Jello, the first fruit-flavored gelatin dessert, was invented in 1897 by a cough-syrup manufacturer from New York. By the 1930s, more than a third of all recipes in most cookbooks were gelatin based! Many used lime flavor, introduced in 1930, and combined it with incongruous ingredients like cabbage, onion, Tabasco sauce, and pimiento. Today over a million packages are sold daily, and about three quarters of all American households have a package in the pantry.

Allow the strawberries to thaw partially. In a bowl, dissolve one package of the gelatin in 1 cup boiling water. Add the strawberries (do not drain) plus $\frac{1}{3}$ cup cold water. Stir until the strawberries are completely thawed and well distributed, then turn into an 8 x 11-inch dish. Slice the bananas on top, pressing lightly to cover in the liquid. Chill until firm.

When the mixture is firm, bring the sour cream to room temperature. Spread it evenly over the gelatin, then return to the refrigerator until the sour cream is thoroughly chilled.

In a bowl, dissolve the second package of gelatin in 1 cup boiling water. Add the pineapple (do not drain) plus 6 ice cubes. Stir until the ice cubes are dissolved. Refrigerate for no longer than $\frac{1}{2}$ hour, or until the mixture has began to gel slightly but can still be easily stirred. Carefully pour over the sour cream and chill until firm.

Holiday Gelatin Salad

Servings: 8 to 10

3-ounce package orange flavored gelatin
3-ounce package cranberry flavored gelatin
$1\frac{1}{2}$ cups boiling water
8-ounce can crushed pineapple
1 cup cranberry-orange sauce (can be
    purchased refrigerated or canned)
1 cup lemon-lime soda (such as 7-Up
    or Sprite)

In a bowl, dissolve both packages of gelatin in the boiling water. Add the pineapple (do not drain) and stir in the cranberry-orange sauce. Chill until thick but not set.

Slowly stir in the soda and pour into a mold or an 8 x 11-inch glass dish. Chill until set.

Serve on lettuce leaves.

Mango Cilantro Salsa

Yield: 2 cups

1 mango, peeled and sliced
$^1/_2$ cup minced red onion
$^1/_4$ cup chopped green onion
$^1/_4$ cup minced cilantro leaves
4 teaspoons fresh lime juice
$^1/_2$ jalapeño or serrano chili, seeded and minced
cayenne pepper

Mix mango, red and green onion, cilantro, lime juice, and chili in a small bowl; add a pinch of cayenne pepper to taste. Cover and chill in the refrigerator for at least 3 hours before serving.

Pumpkin Salsa

Yield: 4 cups

$2^1/_2$ pound pumpkin
4 cloves garlic, skin on
2 tablespoons olive oil
1 large yellow onion, chopped
1 poblano pepper, seeded and chopped
$^3/_4$ cup cooked black beans
$^1/_4$ cup chopped fresh cilantro
1 tablespoon brown sugar
$^1/_2$ teaspoon ground nutmeg
juice of 1 lime
$^1/_2$ teaspoon salt
$^1/_8$ teaspoon freshly ground pepper
$^1/_2$ cup toasted pumpkinseeds
tortilla chips

Heat oven to 350°F. Cut pumpkin into quarters; remove seeds and fibers. Set seeds aside. Cut the flesh from the rind and cut the flesh into ¾-inch diced pieces. Place in a bowl and add garlic. Toss with oil. Spread mixture on a baking sheet and bake about 35 minutes, turning mixture occasionally with a spatula. Bake until pumpkin is softened and golden. Let cool.

Put pumpkin mixture into a large bowl and remove garlic cloves. Squeeze garlic from the skins and add it to pumpkin in bowl. Add the onion, poblano pepper, black beans, cilantro, brown sugar, nutmeg, lime juice, salt, and pepper. Cover and refrigerate 1 hour or overnight.

Stir in toasted pumpkinseeds just before serving with tortilla chips.

Tomato Avocado Salsa

Yield: 2–3 cups

> 2 cups chopped tomatoes
> 1 small red onion, chopped
> 2 tablespoons chopped fresh coriander
> 1 poblano pepper, chopped finely
> 1 clove garlic, chopped
> 1/2 teaspoon fresh thyme
> 2 avocados
> ground red pepper to taste
> salt to taste

In a bowl combine tomatoes, onion, coriander, pepper, garlic, and thyme. *Salsa can be prepared to this point and refrigerated for up to 3 hours.*

Peel, pit, and chop the avocados into small pieces; toss with the tomato mixture. Season with ground red pepper and salt to taste.

This salsa can be served with tacos or served over grilled, steamed, or pan-fried fish.

Green Salsa

Yield: 2 cups

> 3/4 pound husked tomatillos*, husked and quartered
> 2 serrano chili peppers, chopped
> 1/4 small yellow onion, sliced
> 1/4 cup chopped green onion
> 1/3 cup water

> 1 teaspoon salt
> 1/4 cup coarsely chopped cilantro

In a blender or food processor fitted with a metal blade, combine tomatillos, chilies, onions and water. Process briefly until chunky. Add the salt and the cilantro and purée until no large chunks remain, about 2 minutes. Taste and add more salt if needed. Pour into a bowl, cover, and refrigerate for up to 3 days.

*Tomatillos can be purchased in any well-stocked supermarket. Look in the section where chili peppers are displayed.

Bottled green salsa can't compare to freshly made. Green salsa can be served as a dip, on tacos, or cooked in soups or stews. Its flavor perks up already rich flavors of a variety of dishes.

Fresh Tomato Salsa

Yield: 2 cups

> 2 large ripe seeded tomatoes, diced
> 1/4 red onion, finely diced
> 1 bunch green onions, chopped
> 1 fresh jalapeño or serrano chili pepper, stemmed, seeded, and finely diced
> 2 tablespoons coarsely chipped fresh cilantro
> juice of 1 lime
> 1/2 teaspoon salt
> freshly ground black pepper to taste

In a bowl, stir all ingredients together.

Quick Tomato Sauce

This sauce can be served over polenta, baked into lasagna, or poured over cooked pasta and served with a little Parmesan cheese.

Servings: 6 to 8

> 2 pounds very ripe tomatoes
> 2 tablespoons extra-virgin olive oil
> 2 cloves garlic, minced
> 2 large fresh thyme sprigs or
>   ½ teaspoon dried thyme
> ½ teaspoon ground cumin
> 1 bay leaf
> salt and freshly ground pepper to taste
> 3 tablespoons chopped basil, tarragon,
>   parsley, or cilantro

Peel and seed tomatoes, and chop them with a knife or food processor. Heat the olive oil in a large skillet. Add the garlic and sauté over low heat about 10 seconds. Add the tomatoes, thyme, cumin, bay leaf, and salt and pepper to taste. Cook uncovered over medium-high heat, stirring often, 8 to 10 minutes, until tomatoes are soft and sauce is thick. Reduce heat toward end of cooking time.

Discard bay leaf and thyme sprigs. Taste and adjust seasoning. Just before serving sauce, stir in fresh herbs. Serve hot or cold.

To seed tomatoes, cut each tomato (peeled or unpeeled) in half. Hold it, cut side down, over a bowl and squeeze to remove most of the seeds and juice.

Basic Tomato Sauce

Yield: about 5 cups

Tomato sauce is the basis for innumerable pasta, polenta, and vegetable main dishes. It can be made with canned Italian plum tomatoes or with fresh garden tomatoes in the summer. This sweet sauce is wonderful with either canned or fresh tomatoes.

> ¼ cup olive oil
> 2 cups coarsely chopped yellow onions
> ½ cup sliced carrots
> 2 cloves garlic, minced
> 4 cups canned Italian plum tomatoes
> salt and freshly ground black pepper to taste
> 2 tablespoons butter or extra virgin olive oil
> 1 teaspoon dried oregano
> 1 tablespoon chopped fresh basil, or 1
>   teaspoon dried basil
> ¼ teaspoon sugar
> dash of ground anise seed

Heat the oil in a large skillet; add the onions, carrots, and garlic. Sauté until golden brown. Purée the tomatoes in a food processor or blender. Add the puréed tomatoes to the skillet and add salt and pepper to taste. Simmer 15 minutes, partially covered.

Purée the sauce in a food processor or blender. Add the butter or oil, oregano, basil, sugar, and ground anise seed. Simmer an additional 30 minutes.

117

Taco Sauce

Yield: 8 cups

16 cups coarsely chopped fresh tomatoes
1 cup chopped onions
1 cup cider vinegar
2 cloves garlic, minced
¼ cup sugar
2 tablespoons chili powder
1 teaspoon salt
1 teaspoon ground cumin
½ teaspoon cayenne pepper

In a large saucepan, combine tomatoes, onions, vinegar, and garlic. Bring to a boil; reduce heat, cover, and simmer for about an hour.

Cool sauce, then puree in a blender for about 1 minute. Stir in sugar, chili powder, salt, cumin, and cayenne pepper. Bring to a boil in a saucepan. Reduce heat and simmer, stirring often, for about 25 minutes or until thick enough to coat a spoon.

Cool and pour into a sealable container. Sauce can be kept refrigerated for up to a week.

Choose fresh garlic by weight and size; the heavier it is, the fresher it is likely to be. Large heads have bigger cloves that take longer to dry out.

Creamy Low-Fat Clam Sauce

Servings: 4

1 cup ricotta cheese
2 tablespoons 1% milk
2 5-ounce cans baby clams
1 tablespoon olive oil
1 yellow onion, chopped
1 stalk celery, diced
2 cloves garlic, minced
2 tablespoons all-purpose flour
½ teaspoon dried thyme
pinch of red pepper flakes
½ teaspoon freshly ground pepper
¼ teaspoon salt
1 small bottle clam juice
2 teaspoons lemon juice
2 tomatoes, diced
¼ cup chopped fresh parsley

In a food processor, purée ricotta with the milk and set aside. Drain clams, reserving juice, and set aside. In a large heavy saucepan, heat oil over medium heat. Sauté onion, celery, and garlic for 3 minutes or until softened.

Sprinkle vegetables with flour, thyme, pepper flakes, pepper, and salt. Cook and stir for another minute. Pour in reserved and bottled clam juice and bring to a boil. Reduce heat to medium-low and cook for another 5 minutes or until thickened. Add clams, ricotta mixture, lemon juice, and tomatoes. Cook until heated through.

Sauce can be served on freshly cooked pasta and garnished with parsley.

Hollandaise Sauce

Yield: about 1 cup

3 egg yolks
2 tablespoons fresh lemon juice
¼ teaspoon salt
¼ teaspoon ground white pepper
½ cup butter

Combine the egg yolks, lemon juice, salt, and white pepper well in the blender. In a small saucepan, heat butter until foamy. Skim off the white solids. Turn the blender to the highest speed and pour the hot butter into the egg yolk mixture, at first, just a few droplets at a time. Then pour in a slow, steady stream until it is a thick cream.

This version of Hollandaise sauce is very easy to make. Serve it on steamed vegetables or over a toasted English muffin topped with Canadian bacon and a poached egg to make the popular Eggs Benedict.

Boiled Bacon Dressing

Yield: about 1½ cups

4 slices bacon
½ cup sugar
2 teaspoons salt

1 tablespoon cornstarch
1 beaten egg
¼ cup vinegar
1 cup cream

Fry the bacon until it's crisp, then crumble it. Reserve the bacon fat. In a saucepan, combine the sugar, salt, and cornstarch. Mix thoroughly; add the beaten egg and vinegar. Mix well again. Add the cream, bacon, and fat. Cook to the desired thickness (boiling slightly), watching closely.

Serve warm over washed and dried spinach leaves with sliced hard-boiled eggs.

Simple Vinaigrette Dressing

(French Dressing)

Yield: ¾ cup

¼ cup red wine vinegar
1 tablespoon fresh lemon juice
1 teaspoon prepared Dijon mustard
salt and freshly ground pepper to taste
½ cup extra-virgin olive oil

Mix together the vinegar, lemon juice, mustard, salt, and pepper. Add the olive oil a little at a time, beating with a whisk until the mixture emulsifies.

This dressing can also be made in the blender. Put all ingredients into the blender and blend at high speed for a very short time.

Buttermilk Salad Dressing

Yield: 1 cup

½ cup buttermilk
½ cup low-fat mayonnaise
3 tablespoons minced fresh parsley
3 tablespoons minced fresh chives
1 clove garlic, minced
1 tablespoon minced fresh tarragon
1 tablespoon lemon juice
dash of Worcestershire sauce
salt and freshly ground pepper to taste

In a bowl, gently fold all of the ingredients together. Cover and refrigerate until serving time. Spoon over torn lettuce or mixed salad greens.

Creamy Dill Parsley Dressing

Yield: 1 cup

1 cup plain nonfat yogurt
1 teaspoon crumbled dried dill
½ teaspoon lemon juice
1 teaspoon chopped parsley

In a bowl, mix ingredients well. Serve with mixed fresh greens.

Garlic Vinaigrette

Yield: about ¾ cup

¼ cup red wine or tarragon vinegar
2 tablespoons Dijon mustard
¼ teaspoon salt
freshly ground black pepper
2 to 3 large cloves garlic, minced
½ cup olive oil

Combine the vinegar, mustard, salt, pepper, and garlic. Beat in the olive oil gradually with a fork or whisk until the mixture emulsifies. To make this dressing in a blender, mix all the ingredients together and blend at high speed for several minutes.

Note: Only whole fresh garlic cloves will create the desired intensity in this dressing.

Hot Pepper Paste

Yield: ½ cup

30 dried red chili peppers
hot water
¼ cup or more white vinegar
2 teaspoons salt

Place the chili peppers in a small bowl and cover with hot water. Let soak for 10 minutes. Remove and drain, then place them along with the vinegar in a blender. Blend to a rough paste, adding as much vinegar as necessary to achieve a paste. Add the salt and blend 5 seconds more. Transfer to a sterilized jar and cap tightly.

Indian Yogurt Salad
Servings: 4

Yogurt Dressing:
$\frac{1}{2}$ teaspoon ground cumin
2 cups plain unsweetened yogurt
$\frac{1}{2}$ cup whipping cream
$\frac{1}{4}$ teaspoon ground cardamom
$\frac{1}{4}$–$\frac{1}{2}$ teaspoon salt
$\frac{1}{4}$ teaspoon ground white pepper
$\frac{1}{4}$ teaspoon cayenne pepper

Salad:
12 or more pistachio nuts or blanched
    almonds, hulls removed
1 large crisp apple, peeled, cored,
    and quartered
sprig of fresh mint

Heat the ground cumin in a small frying pan over medium heat until it thickens and begins to darken. Immediately pour it into a mixing bowl and cool. Combine the yogurt and cream with the cumin, and then stir in the remaining dressing ingredients. Blend well, set aside.

In a food processor, grind the nuts to a coarse powder. Add the apple and blend until the contents are a rough purée, about 1 minute. Do not grind too fine. Transfer the mixture to a bowl and stir in the yogurt dressing. Mix thoroughly, then transfer to serving bowls. Chill until ready to serve, and garnish with fresh mint.

Indian yogurt salads are used as side dishes to accompany often highly spiced hot Indian dishes. The Indian salad is usually a selection of vegetables, cooked or raw, or marinated fruit in a thick, creamy, spiced yogurt dressing.

Parsley Hints

Lots of fruit and vegetable salads benefit from a couple of sprigs of parsley. The problem is that you need to buy a whole bunch to get those few sprigs. Parsley, however, will stay crisp and fresh for up to a week if you store it standing in a glass of ice water in the refrigerator. Change the water every couple of days, and give some parsley to the dog to freshen his breath.

Chapter 6

Beef, Veal, Pork, and Lamb Dishes

eat is the staple of many of our favorite meals. It is an important source of protein, and can be cooked a thousand different ways. Every chef should know how to trim and prepare various cuts of beef, veal, lamb, and pork. Armed with recipes for everything from tenderizers and marinades to old-fashioned pot roasts and exotic pork loins, you'll have everything you need to create a fabulous family dinner.

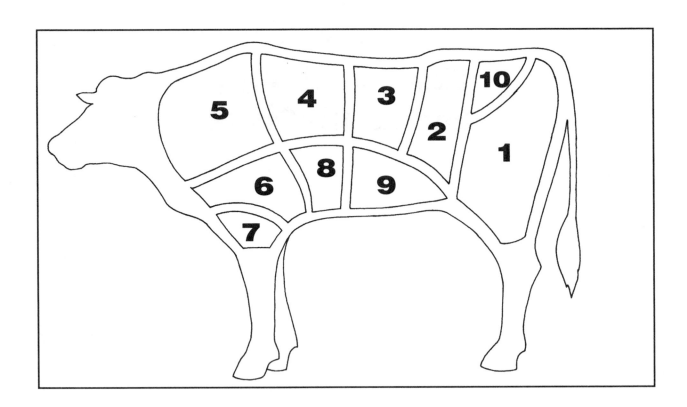

Beef Cuts and How to Cook Them

SOURCE	CUT	HOW TO COOK
1 The Round	Round Steak	Braise or pan-fry
	Top Round	Broil, pan-broil or pan-fry, stir-fry
	Bottom Round	Braise or pan-fry
	Eye of Round Steak	Broil, pan-broil or pan-fry, stir-fry*
	Tip Steak	Broil, pan-broil or pan-fry, stir-fry
	Top Round Roast	Roast
	Bottom Round Roast	Braise or roast
	Eye of Round Roast	Braise or roast
	Rump Roast	Braise or roast
2 The Sirloin	Sirloin Steak	Broil, pan-broil or pan-fry, stir-fry*
	Top Sirloin Steak	Broil, pan-broil, or pan-fry*
	Bottom Sirloin Steak	Broil, pan-broil, or pan-fry*
	Sirloin Roast	Roast
3 The Short Loin	T-Bone Steak	Broil, pan-broil, or pan-fry*
	Porterhouse Steak	Broil, pan-broil, or pan-fry*
	Top Loin (Strip) Steak	Broil, pan-broil, or pan-fry*
	Tenderloin Steak (ex. Filet Mignon)	Broil, pan-broil, or pan-fry*
	Beef Tenderloin (Roast)	Roast*
4 The Rib	Rib Eye Steak	Broil, pan-broil or pan-fry*
	Rib Eye Roast, Rib Roast	Roast
	Back Ribs	Braise or cook in liquid
5 The Chuck	Chuck Steak	Braise, pan-fry, stir-fry
	Chuck Roast	Braise
	(including Pot Roast, Arm Roast, 7-Bone, and Blade Roast)	
	Short Ribs	Braise or cook in liquid
6 The Brisket	Brisket (including Corned Beef Brisket)	Braise or cook in liquid
7 Foreshank	Shanks	Braise or cook in liquid
8 The Short Plate	Flank Steak	Broil, braise, pan-fry, stir-fry*
9 Flank	Skirt Steak	Broil, braise, pan-fry, stir-fry*
10 Rump	Rump Roast	Braise or roast

*Cut is suitable for cooking on the grill

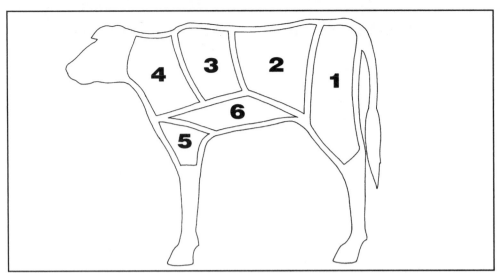

Veal Cuts and How to Cook Them

SOURCE	CUT	HOW TO COOK
1 The Sirloin/Round	Top Round Steak	Braise or pan-fry
	Cutlets	Braise or pan-fry
	Sirloin Steak	Broil or pan-fry*
2 The Loin	Loin Chop	Broil or pan-fry*
	Loin Roast	Roast
3 The Rib	Rib Chop	Broil or pan-fry*
	Rib Roast	Roast
4 The Shoulder	Blade Steak	Braise, broil, or pan-broil*
	Shoulder Steak	Braise, broil, or pan-broil*
	Shoulder Roast	Braise or roast
5 The Foreshank	Breast Roast	Braise or roast
6 Breast	Shank	Braise or cook in liquid
	Ribs	Braise or cook in liquid

*Cut is suitable for cooking on the grill

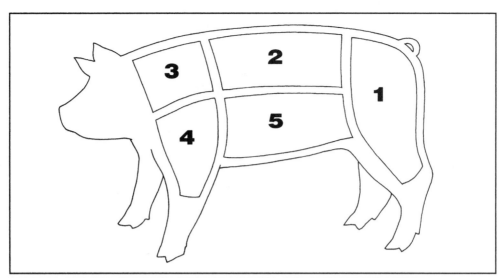

Pork Cuts and How to Cook Them

SOURCE	CUT	HOW TO COOK
1 The Leg or Ham	Hams (whole, half, or boneless)	Roast
	Ham Slice	Broil, pan-broil, or pan-fry*
2 The Loin	Pork Roast	Roast
	Rib or Crown Roast	Roast
	Tenderloin	Roast or braise
	Pork Chops (all kinds)	Broil, pan-broil, or pan-fry (stir-fry if boneless)*
	Ribs (back or country style)	Braise, cook in liquid, broil, roast*
	Canadian Bacon	Broil, pan-broil, pan-fry
3 The Shoulder or Butt	Blade Steaks	Braise, broil, pan-broil, or pan-fry*
4 Picnic	Blade Roast	Braise or roast
	Shoulder or Picnic Ham	Roast or cook in liquid
	Ham Hocks	Braise or cook in liquid
5 The Side	Spareribs	Braise or cook in liquid, broil, roast*
	Bacon	Broil or pan-fry, microwave

*Cut is suitable for cooking on the grill

127

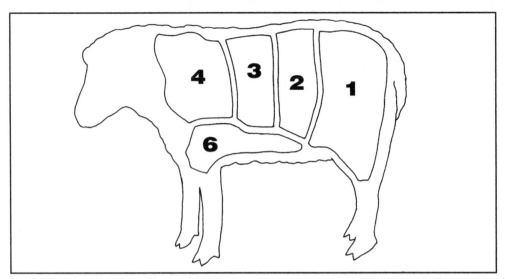

Lamb Cuts and How to Cook Them

SOURCE	CUT	HOW TO COOK
1 The Leg	Leg of Lamb	Roast
	Roast or Sirloin Roast	Roast
	Sirloin Chop	Broil, pan-broil, or pan-fry*
2 The Loin	Loin Roast	Roast
	Loin Chop	Broil, pan-broil, or pan-fry*
3 The Rib	Rib Roast	Roast
	Crown Rib Roast	Roast
	Rib Chop	Broil, pan-broil, or pan-fry*
4 The Shoulder	Shoulder Roast	Braise or roast
	Arm Chop	Broil, pan-broil, or pan-fry*
	Blade Chop	Broil, pan-broil, or pan-fry*
5 The Brisket	Shanks	Braise or cook in liquid
6 Foreshank	Riblets	Braise or cook in liquid

*Cut is suitable for cooking on the grill

128

Using a Meat Thermometer

Home economists recommend the use of a meat thermometer as the most foolproof way to test the doneness of meats.

A *standard meat thermometer* is inserted into meat or poultry and left in place during cooking. It is inserted into the center of the thickest part of the meat, usually at a slight angle. To provide an accurate reading it should not touch bone or fat or the pan.

An *instant* or *rapid response thermometer* is a more expensive tool that takes a temperature reading within one minute. *It should not be left in the meat or in the oven.* It is easier to use than a standard thermometer for meat that is grilled or broiled, and it is particularly useful to gauge doneness when cooking steaks thicker than 1½ inches.

Marinades and Rubs

A *marinade* is a seasoned liquid mixture used to add flavor to meat and in some cases to help tenderize it. To tenderize meat, a marinade must contain an acidic ingredient or a natural tenderizing enzyme, like those found in ginger and pineapple. Commonly used acidic ingredients are fruit juices, vinegar, wine, Italian dressing, and salsa. Generally, a tenderizing marinade should penetrate about ¼ inch into the meat.

A *rub* is a blend of seasonings rubbed onto the surface of meat for flavor. It can be a dry rub, made from fresh or dry herbs and spices, or a paste rub containing oil or mustard. Rubs combine with the juices drawn from the meat to flavor it, but they do not tenderize.

To use a rub, moisten the meat with water or rub it lightly with vegetable oil, then rub the mix onto the surface with your hands. Cook immediately, or allow to stand for up to 12 hours, covered and refrigerated, for a more intense flavor. Wear plastic gloves when rubbing meat for easy cleanup. Inexpensive disposable plastic gloves are available at paint and hardware stores.

- Always marinate meat in the refrigerator. Use a sealed plastic food bag or a glass container. (Some marinades react with and discolor metal pans.) Allow about ¼ to ½ cup marinade per pound of meat. Stir or turn occasionally.
- Marinate tender cuts for flavor only, 15 minutes to 2 hours.
- Marinate less tender cuts from 6 hours to overnight. Use a marinade containing an acidic ingredient or enzyme.
- Do not marinate longer than 24 hours; meat will become mushy.
- Before adding the raw meat, reserve a portion of the marinade for use in basting or as a sauce If you cannot do so, bring the marinade to a full boil after removing the raw meat and before using it to baste.
- Do not save and reuse marinades!

Tenderizing South-of-the Border Marinade

Yield: 1/2 cup

1/3 cup tomato salsa
2 tablespoons fresh lime juice
1 clove garlic, crushed or minced
1 teaspoon dried oregano
1/4 teaspoon ground cumin

Mix all ingredients together well. This marinade will tenderize meat.

Tenderizing Southwestern-Style Marinade

Yield: 1 1/3 cups

1 cup orange juice
1/4 cup lime juice
3 cloves garlic, crushed
2 chipotle peppers, seeded and chopped
2 teaspoons oregano
1 teaspoon cumin

Mix all ingredients together well.

Asian-Style Flavoring Marinade

Yield: 1/3 cup

2 tablespoons soy sauce
2 tablespoons water
1 tablespoon dark sesame oil
2 cloves garlic, crushed
2 teaspoons sugar

Mix all ingredients together well.

Asian-Style Tenderizing Marinade

Yield: 1 cup

1/4 cup soy sauce
1/4 cup sherry
1/2 cup minced onion
2 tablespoons fresh grated gingerroot
2 teaspoons five-spice powder
2 teaspoons sesame oil

Mix all ingredients together well.

Tenderizing Honey Marinade

Yield: 1 cup

½ cup lemon juice
¼ cup honey
2 tablespoons soy sauce
1 tablespoon sherry
2 cloves garlic, crushed

Mix all ingredients together well.

Tenderizing Red Wine Marinade

Yield: 1½ cups

¼ cup tarragon vinegar
½ cup Burgundy or other red wine
¼ cup lemon juice
½ cup cooking oil
½ teaspoon dry mustard
1 bay leaf
6 peppercorns
1 teaspoon salt
1 large onion, sliced ¼-inch thick

Mix all ingredients together well.

Regional Flavorings

Asian soy sauce, ginger, sesame, garlic

Cajun red, black, and white ground pepper, paprika, garlic, onion

Caribbean lime, allspice, ginger, rum

French white wine, mustard, tarragon, thyme

Greek lemon, mint, rosemary, garlic

Indian curry powder, chili powder, cinnamon, garlic

Indonesian peanut, lime, ginger

Italian oregano, garlic, basil, and often tomatoes

Mexican chilies, chili powder, cilantro, cumin, oregano

Russian paprika, sour cream

Southwestern peppers, lime, cilantro, cumin

Basting

Meat can be basted with its own drippings, with broth, or with a flavorful sauce both before and during cooking.

When you **roast** meat you can baste it by using a:

- **Long-handled large spoon** Spoon the gathered drippings or the sauce over the surface of the meat. If basting with drippings, tip the roasting pan slightly to obtain them.
- **Bulb-type baster** This inexpensive gadget, available at grocery or discount stores, allows you to suction the drippings or sauce out of the pan or container, then squirt the liquid on to the meat.
- **Basting brush** This special brush, available at grocery or discount stores, allows you to brush a sauce over the meat, either before or during cooking.

Basic Herb Rub

Yield: ¹/₂ **cup**

> 2 tablespoons onion powder
> 2 tablespoons lemon pepper
> 2 tablespoons basil
> 2 tablespoons Italian seasoning
> 2 teaspoons sage

Mix together well and store in a tightly closed container. Use on tender cuts of meat.

Cajun Rub

Yield: ¹/₂ **cup**

> 2 teaspoons cayenne pepper
> 1¹/₂ teaspoons ground white pepper
> 1 teaspoon ground black pepper
> 2 teaspoons garlic powder
> 2 teaspoons onion powder
> 2 tablespoons paprika
> ¹/₂ teaspoon thyme
> ¹/₂ teaspoon oregano
> 1 teaspoon salt

Mix together well and store in a tightly closed container. Use on tender cuts of meat.

Caribbean Rub

Yield: ½ cup

>   2 teaspoons allspice
>   ½ teaspoon cinnamon
>   ½ teaspoon nutmeg
>   2 teaspoons black pepper
>   1 teaspoon cayenne pepper
>   2 teaspoons thyme
>   1 tablespoon onion powder
>   1 tablespoon garlic powder
>   1 tablespoon sugar

Mix together well and store in a tightly closed container. Use on tender cuts of meat.

South-of-the-Border Rub

Yield: ½ cup

>   2 tablespoons chili powder
>   2 tablespoons cumin powder
>   1 tablespoon ground coriander
>   1½ teaspoons cinnamon
>   1 tablespoon ground black pepper
>   1 teaspoon ground red pepper
>   1 tablespoon brown sugar, not packed
>   ½ teaspoon salt

Mix together well and store in a tightly closed container. Use on tender cuts of meat.

Basic Roasting: Beef, Veal, Pork, and Lamb

Meat is roasted by placing the meat on a wire rack in a shallow roasting pan. The rack holds the meat above the fat drippings; rib roasts make their own rack and do not need a wire one. The fat side of the meat (if there is one) is placed up, and the fat bastes the meat while it cooks. Do not trim the fat before cooking.

Preheat the oven to 325°F or the specified temperature. If desired, line the roasting pan with aluminum foil to make cleaning it easier. Place the meat on the rack. Do not cover it or add liquid to the pan. Salt the meat before roasting; other seasonings can be added before or after cooking. If using a meat thermometer, place it in the thickest part of the roast.

Roast for the specified amount of time or until the thermometer registers the correct temperature. (See the Recommended Doneness Chart on page 134.) Remove the roast from the oven, cover loosely with aluminum foil, and allow to stand at least 10 minutes before carving. If using a meat thermometer, you will notice that the temperature will continue to rise; the meat continues to cook after removal from the oven.

Internal Meat Temperature When Roasting

Home economists recommend the use of a meat thermometer as the most foolproof way to test the doneness of meats.

A standard meat thermometer is inserted into meat or poultry and left in place during cooking. It is inserted into the center of thickest part of the meat, usually at a slight angle. To provide an accurate reading, it should not touch bone or fat or the pan

An instant or rapid response thermometer is a more expensive tool, which takes a temperature reading within one minute. It should not be left in the meat or in the oven. It is easier to use than a standard thermometer for meat that is grilled or broiled, and it is particularly useful to gauge doneness when cooking steaks thicker than 1½ inches.

MEAT	INTERNAL TEMPERATURE
Beef Roasts	145°F medium rare
	160°F medium
Other Beef Cuts	145°F medium rare
	160°F medium
	170°F well done
Veal Roasts	160°F medium
Pork Roasts	160°F medium
	170°F well done
Other Pork Cuts	160°F medium
	170°F well done
Ham (fully cooked)	140°F heated through
Lamb Roasts	145°F medium rare
	160°F medium
	170°F well done
Other Lamb Cuts	145°F medium rare
	160°F medium

Braising Time Chart

CUT OF MEAT	SIZE OR WEIGHT	APPROXIMATE TIME IN HOURS
Boneless Roast	3 to 4 pounds	2 to $2\frac{1}{2}$ hours
Chops or Steaks, bone in	$\frac{3}{4}$ to 1 inch thick	45 to 60 minutes
Round Steak, beef	$1\frac{1}{2}$ pounds	$1\frac{1}{2}$ hours
Round Steak, veal	$\frac{1}{4}$ inch	30 minutes
Shanks or Riblets	4 pounds	2 or more hours
Stew Meat	1/1 to 1 inch cubes	45 to 60 minutes

Basic Roasting: Hams

This method of cooking is often referred to as "baking a ham."

For fully cooked hams, bone in: If desired, line a shallow roasting pan, or a large roaster with a cover, with aluminum foil to make cleaning it easier. Place the ham on a rack in the pan. Place the fat side of the meat (if there is one) up, so the fat bastes the meat while it cooks. Do not trim the fat before cooking. Preheat the oven to 325°F. If using a meat thermometer, place it in the thickest part of the roast. Cover the roasting pan with its lid or an aluminum foil tent.

Roast for the specified amount of time or until the thermometer registers the correct temperature. Remove from the oven, cover loosely with aluminum foil, and allow to stand at least 10 minutes before carving. If using a meat thermometer, you will notice that the temperature will continue to rise; the meat continues to cook after removal from the oven.

For fully cooked hams, boneless: Follow the instructions for bone-in hams, but add $\frac{1}{2}$ to 1 cup of water to the roasting pan before covering.

For canned hams: Follow the instructions for bone-in hams, but add the can juices to the roasting pan, and do not cover.

Basic Braising: Beef, Veal, Pork, and Lamb

Braising, a method of cooking slowly in a small amount of liquid, tenderizes less tender cuts of meat. It is the classic method of making a pot roast or a Swiss steak. Braising can be done on the stovetop in a Dutch oven or heavy skillet with a tight-fitting lid, or in the oven. Water can be used as the liquid, but flavorful additions like wine, Worcestershire sauce, or tomato juice are often used.

To braise meat, heat about 2 tablespoons of oil to medium in a Dutch oven or skillet. If desired, the meat may be dredged or coated in flour. Place the meat in the pan and brown on all sides. Browning time will vary with the thickness of the cut, but will usually take about 15 or 20 minutes.

When the meat is well browned, you can transfer it to a roaster or baking dish to be cooked in the oven. Deglaze the skillet with at

Approximate Broiling Times

All times are for cuts about 1 inch thick, broiled 3 to 4 inches from the heating element, unless otherwise indicated. If using thinner or thicker cuts, adjust times accordingly.

MEAT	DONENESS	MINUTES
Beef Chuck or Round Steaks	medium rare	14 to 16
	medium	16 to 20
Beef Sirloin, Tenderloin, T-bone,	medium rare	10 to 12
Porterhouse, Rib	medium	13 to 15
Beef, Ground—about ¹/₂ inch thick	medium to well	10 to 12
Veal Chops, 4 inches from heat	medium well	14 to 17
Veal, Ground—about ¹/₂ inch thick	medium well	10 to 12
Lamp Chops, Loin or Rib	medium	7 to 11
Lamb Chops, Sirloin	medium	12 to 15
Lamb, Ground—about ¹/₂ inch thick	medium to well	10 to 12
Pork Chops, boneless	medium	6 to 8
Pork Chops, bone in	medium	8 to 10
Ham Slices	well heated	14 to 16

least 1 cup of water or other liquid, then add this liquid to the meat, season it, and cover well. (Vegetables may also be added at this time.) Bake at 325°F until fork-tender.

Or, if you prefer, you can continue cooking the meat on the stovetop in the pan in which it was browned. Add the water or other liquid, heat to just boiling, then reduce to a simmer until fork-tender.

With either method, cooking time will vary with the type and thickness of the cut. Check occasionally during cooking to make sure that the liquid has not evaporated. After cooking, the liquid can be reduced or thickened for a sauce, if desired.

Basic Broiling: Beef, Veal, Pork, and Lamb

Broiling is a low-fat cooking method; no fat is added and some fat from the meat will drain into the broiler pan. It is used for tender cuts of meat. Less tender cuts can be marinated before broiling. Refer to the

Pan-Broiling Time Chart

BEEF	THICKNESS	APPROXIMATE TOTAL MINUTES
Ground Beef patties	½ inch	8
Sirloin Steak	¾ to 1 inch	11
Rib Eye	½ to ¾	5
Porterhouse, T-Bone	¾ to 1 inch	9

VEAL	THICKNESS	APPROXIMATE TOTAL MINUTES
Veal Chops	¾ to 1 inch	10 to 14
Steaks	¾ inch	13 to 15
Cutlets	less than ½ inch	6
Ground Veal patties	½ inch	6 to 9

PORK	THICKNESS	APPROXIMATE TOTAL MINUTES
Pork Chops, bone in or boneless	¾ inch	8 to 10
Ground Pork	½ inch	7 to 9
Ham slices	½ inch	5 to 6

charts on page 125–128 to determine if a cut of meat can be broiled.

Preheat the broiler at least 10 minutes. Pat meat dry with paper towels so it will brown well. If there is fat around the edge of the meat, make small slashes every inch to prevent curling. Do not trim off the fat before cooking, however, to preserve juiciness. (If desired, fat can be trimmed after cooking and before serving.)

If desired, line the broiler pan with aluminum foil to make cleaning it easier. Place the meat on the rack of the broiler pan and place in the preheated broiler. Broil for approximately half the total time;

turn the meat, and continue broiling until done. Check doneness by making a small cut in the center of the meat. Salt each side of the meat *after* it has cooked; salt draws moisture out of meat when it is added before cooking. It also inhibits browning.

Basic Pan-Broiling: Beef, Veal, and Pork

Pan-broiling is a lower-fat cooking method that uses little extra fat. It is used for tender cuts of meat. Less tender cuts can be marinated before pan-broiling. Refer to the charts on page 125–128 to determine if a cut of meat can be pan-broiled.

Sautéing Time Chart

Meat	Thickness	Approximate Total Minutes
Veal Cutlets	⅛ to ¼ inch	3 to 4
Cubed Steaks, veal or beef	¼ to ½ inch	5 to 6
Ground Veal patties	½ inch	5 to 7
Ham slices	¼ to ½ inch	4 to 6

Use a heavy skillet or a broiling/grilling pan with raised ridges designed for the stovetop. If the meat is lean, spray the pan with cooking spray or wipe with a small amount of cooking oil. Preheat the pan to medium-low for meats thicker than ½ inch, or medium-high for meats thinner than ½ inch. Add the meat, but do not add oil or water. Thin cuts should be turned once, but cuts thicker than ½ inch can be turned several times until the desired degree of doneness. If desired, excess fat can be skimmed or poured from the pan as it accumulates during cooking. Check doneness by making a small cut in the center of the meat. Herbs and spices may be added before cooking, but add salt *after* cooking.

Sautéing Veal, Beef, and Ham Slices

Veal cutlets, ground veal patties, cubed steaks (veal or beef), and ham slices can be sautéed in a small amount of vegetable oil or butter. (Use as little as needed, but usually not more than 1 tablespoon.) Put the oil in the pan, preheat the skillet to medium-high heat, then add the meat to the skillet. Do not add water or cover. Turn once during cooking. Herbs and spices may be added before cooking, but always salt *after* cooking.

The Perfect Basic Burger

Allow ¼ pound ground meat per burger. Thaw meat in the refrigerator, if frozen; make sure it is completely thawed in the middle as well as on the surface. Gently shape into patties that are about 4 inches in diameter and ½ inch thick. If patties are not to be cooked immediately, separate with waxed paper and refrigerate.

If using ground beef that is 90 percent or more lean, spray the skillet lightly with cooking spray or wipe lightly with oil. Do not add additional fat or water. Preheat the skillet over medium heat for about 5 minutes. Add the burgers and cook 10 to 12 minutes, until the juices run clear and the center is no longer pink or is very slightly pink. Turn once during cooking, but to preserve the juiciness do not press to flatten with a spatula. Season after cooking is completed.

Cheeseburgers: Top with a slice of cheese after turning.

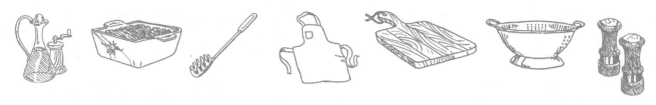

Basic Burger Mix: To 1 pound of ground beef add $\frac{1}{3}$ cup fine bread crumbs, $\frac{1}{4}$ cup finely chopped onion, 1 tablespoon Worcestershire sauce, and $\frac{1}{2}$ teaspoon pepper. Mix before shaping into patties. Do not overmix or the texture will become too compact.

Burger Dress-Ups

Pinwheel Burger: Cut four slices of different kinds and colors of cheese into diagonal quarters. After turning burgers, top each with four quarters of different cheeses in a pinwheel shape.

Pepper Burger: Before shaping into patties, mix 2 tablespoons chopped jalapeño peppers and $\frac{1}{4}$ cup chopped onion into the ground beef. Top with Jack cheese.

Blue Burger: Before shaping into patties, mix $\frac{1}{4}$ cup chopped, well-drained canned mushrooms and $\frac{1}{4}$ teaspoon pepper into the ground meat. After removing from the skillet, top with crumbled bleu cheese.

Earth 'n' Turf Burger: After cooking, top burger with a slice of cheese, sliced tomatoes, sliced cucumbers, and sprouts; spread the bun with creamy Italian salad dressing.

Ground beef and cubed beef (or stew meat) can come from just about any cut of beef. Ground or cubed *chuck* is from the chuck and is about 80 percent lean. Ground or cubed *round* is from the round and is about 85 to 90 percent lean. Ground and cubed beef can also come from the sirloin. The USDA recommends that ground beef always be cooked to at least 160°F, or until the middle is light pink and the juices are clear.

To Preserve Juiciness

When broiling or pan-broiling meat, salt each side after it has cooked, not before. Salt draws moisture out of meat when it is added before cooking. It also inhibits browning.

Use tongs to turn steaks; do not pierce them with a fork. Use a spatula to turn ground beef patties and do not flatten them, which will cause the flavorful juices to run out.

Cost per Serving

To get the most for your money, pay attention to the *cost per serving* rather than the cost per pound. To calculate the cost per serving, divide the cost per pound by the number of servings per pound.

BEEF	AVERAGE SERVINGS PER POUND
Brisket	2½ to 3
Pot Roast	2½ to 3
Rib Roast	2½
Round or Rump Roast	4
Tenderloin Roast	4
Chuck Steak	3 to 3½
Flank Steak	4
Porterhouse or T-bone Steak	2½
Rib-Eye Steak	3
Round Steak	4
Sirloin Steak, boneless	3
Shanks and Short Ribs	1½ to 2½
Stew Beef	3
Ground Beef	4

PORK	AVERAGE SERVINGS PER POUND
Bacon	6
Bacon, Canadian	5
Chops, boneless	4
Chops, bone in	2½
Hams, leg	4
Hams, picnic	3½
Country-Style Ribs	2
Back Ribs	1½
Spare ribs	1¼
Roast, boneless	3½ to 4
Roast, bone in	3
Sausage and Ground Pork	4
Tenderloin	4

VEAL	AVERAGE SERVINGS PER POUND
Chops, bone in	2
Chops, boneless	3
Cutlets or Steaks, boneless	4
Roasts, bone in	2½
Roasts, boneless	4
Shanks and Ribs	1½
Stew Cubes	3½
Ground Veal or Cubed Steak	4

Classic Beef Pot Roast

Servings: 8

> vegetable oil
> 3½ to 4 pound beef chuck roast
> 1 teaspoon salt
> ½ teaspoon pepper
> 1½ cups tomato or vegetable juice
>   or water
> 1 tablespoon Worcestershire sauce,
>   optional
> 8 small potatoes or 12 very small new
>   potatoes
> 8 medium carrots
> 2 medium onions or 8 small boiling
>   onions
> 3 stalks celery

In a Dutch oven, heat a small amount of oil over medium heat. Add the beef and brown well on all sides. Season the meat with salt and pepper. Mix together the juice and Worcestershire sauce and pour over the meat. Bring to a boil, then reduce the heat to low. At this point you can: Cover and simmer for 2 hours on the stovetop, or cover and bake in a preheated 325°F oven for 2 hours before adding the vegetables.

Peel the potatoes; if using new potatoes, cut them in half. Peel the carrots and cut each into 4 chunks. Peel the onions; if using medium size, cut into quarters. Wash the celery stalks and cut into 2-inch chunks. Add all vegetables to the Dutch oven. Recover and simmer an additional 1½

hours, or until meat is fork-tender and vegetables are done.

When the dish is done, serve with natural juices, or if preferred, remove the meat and vegetables to a platter to keep warm and make gravy. *To make gravy:* In a jar or gravy shaker, combine 1 cup cold water and ¼ cup instant flour*. Skim excess fat from the juices in the pot, then add water if juices do not equal 1½ cups. Slowly stir in the flour mixture, then bring to a boil for 1 minute, stirring constantly.

*Instant flour is finely ground for sauces and gravies. It usually is packaged in a small canister and located with other flours at the grocery. If it is not available, all-purpose flour an be substituted.

Unless a specific recipe states otherwise, all cooking times for meats assume that the meat will be cooked immediately after being removed from the refrigerator, without being brought to room temperature.

Rosemary Red Wine Pot Roast

Servings: 6 to 8

> vegetable oil
> 4 cloves garlic, crushed
> 3 to 3½ pound boneless beef chuck roast
> ½ cup water
> ½ cup dry red wine
> ½ teaspoon pepper

(continued)

141

1 teaspoon salt
1 teaspoon dried rosemary
6 medium carrots
8 small new red potatoes
1 tablespoon dried parsley flakes
2 tablespoons cornstarch

In a Dutch oven, heat a small amount of vegetable oil over medium heat. Cook the garlic briefly, then push to the sides. Add the beef and brown well on all sides. Mix together the water and wine and pour over the meat; sprinkle the pepper, salt, and rosemary over the meat. Bring to a boil, then reduce the heat to low. Now you can: Cover and simmer for 1½ hours on the stovetop, or cover and bake in a preheated 325°F oven for 1½ hours before adding the vegetables.

Peel the carrots and cut each into 4 chunks. Add the carrots and unpeeled potatoes to the Dutch oven and sprinkle with the parsley. Re-cover and simmer an additional 1¼ hours, or until meat is fork-tender and vegetables are done.

Remove the meat and vegetables to a platter to keep warm. Skim excess fat from the juices in the pot, then add water if juices do not equal about 2 cups. Dissolve the cornstarch in about ¼ cup of cold water and add to the juices. Bring to a boil for 1 minute, stirring constantly. Arrange the roast on the serving platter and carve across the grain into diagonal slices.

Arrange the vegetables around it. Drizzle gravy over all and serve the additional gravy on the side.

Herb-Rubbed Braised Roast

Servings: 6

1 teaspoon each: garlic salt and
    celery salt
½ teaspoon each: onion powder, paprika,
    and pepper
¼ teaspoon each: dill, sage, and rosemary
3 to 3½ pound bottom round rump or
    tip roast
1 tablespoon olive oil
1 cup water
1 tablespoon cornstarch

Combine the herbs and seasonings. Reserve ½ teaspoon of the mixture and rub the remainder evenly into the surface of the beef. Allow to sit in the refrigerator for 1 hour.

Heat the oil in a Dutch oven over medium heat. Brown beef well on all sides. Add the water and bring to a boil. Reduce the heat to low. At this point you can: Cover and simmer for 2½ to 2¾ hours on the stovetop, or cover and bake in a preheated 325°F oven for 2½ to 2¾ hours, or until meat is fork-tender.

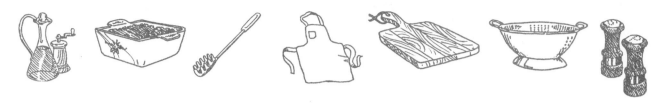

Remove the beef and keep warm. Skim excess fat from the cooking liquid. Dissolve the cornstarch in about ¼ cup cold water, and add the ½ teaspoon reserved herbs. Add the cornstarch mixture to the cooking liquid. Bring to a boil and boil for 1 minute or until thickened, stirring constantly. Serve the roast with sauce on the side.

Pot Roast Olé

Servings: 6

1½ teaspoons chili powder
¼ teaspoon cumin
¼ teaspoon oregano
3 to 3½ pound bottom round roast or
    boneless chuck roast
vegetable oil
½ teaspoon salt
¼ teaspoon pepper
1 cup tomato salsa
½ cup water
2 medium yellow squash
2 tablespoons cornstarch
2 medium zucchini

Mix the chili powder, cumin, and oregano and rub the roast evenly with the mixture. In a Dutch oven, heat a small amount of oil over medium heat. Add the roast and brown on all sides. Pour off the drippings.

Sprinkle the meat with salt and pepper. Mix the salsa and water and add to the pot.

Bring to a boil. Reduce the heat to low. Now you can: Cover and simmer for 2½ hours on the stovetop, or cover and bake in a preheated 325°F oven for 2½ hours before adding vegetables.

To prepare the vegetables, cut them lengthwise into quarters, then crosswise into strips about 2 inches long. Add them to the pot, re-cover it, and continue cooking for at least 15 minutes, or until the vegetables are done and the meat is fork-tender.

(continued)

How Done Is It?

Braised meats are cooked until they are "fork-tender," or until they can be sectioned or torn apart with two forks, without the aid of a knife.

Remove the meat and vegetables to a platter and keep warm. Skim excess fat from the top of the liquid in the pot. Dissolve the cornstarch in about ¼ cup cold water and add to the liquid in the pot. Bring to a boil and boil about 1 minute, or until thickened.

To serve, slice the meat and pour about 1 cup of the sauce over the meat. Surround with the vegetables and serve the remaining sauce on the side.

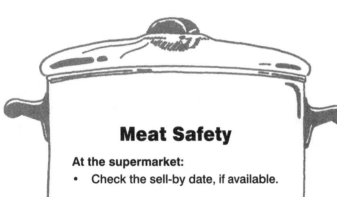

Meat Safety

At the supermarket:

- Check the sell-by date, if available.

- Select meat that feels firm, not soft.

- Avoid packages with holes or tears, or with excessive liquid, which indicates that the correct temperature and storage procedures have not been maintained.

Old-Fashioned Roast

Servings: 4

> cooking oil
> 1½ to 1¾ pound bottom round or boneless rump roast
> 16-ounce can crushed tomatoes
> 1 cup beef broth, fresh, canned, or prepared with beef bouillon
> ⅓ cup diced carrot
> ⅓ cup diced turnip
> ⅓ cup diced parsnips
> 3 small leeks, chopped (whites and light green)
> 2 tablespoons chopped fresh parsley
> ¼ teaspoon thyme
> 4 black peppercorns
> 1 bay leaf

In a Dutch oven, heat a small amount of oil over medium heat. Add the beef and brown well on all sides. Reduce the heat and add the tomatoes (undrained) and broth, then all remaining ingredients. Bring to a boil, then reduce the heat to low. At this point you can: Cover and simmer for about 3 hours on the stovetop, or cover and bake in a preheated 325°F oven for about 3 hours, or until fork-tender.

Remove the roast to a serving platter and keep warm. Increase the heat to medium-high and cook the vegetable mixture until it is reduced to no more than 2 cups. Remove the bay leaf and peppercorns. Slice the roast, pour about half the sauce over the roast, and serve the remaining sauce on the side.

Brisket Teriyaki

Servings: 10 to 12

1 large orange
1 cup thick bottled teriyaki baste or glaze
1 cup water
2 cloves garlic, crushed
½ teaspoon pepper
3 to 3½ pound fresh beef brisket
1½ teaspoons dark sesame oil
1 tablespoon cornstarch
¼ cup toasted sesame seeds

Preheat the oven to 325°F.

Using a vegetable peeler, make strips of orange zest from the peel of the orange, then set the orange aside. Combine the orange zest, teriyaki sauce, water, garlic, and pepper.

Place the meat in a 9 x 13-inch baking dish. Pour the teriyaki mixture over it and cover tightly with foil. Bake about 3 hours, or until the meat is tender. Turn the meat once about halfway through cooking.

When the meat is done, remove it from the baking dish and keep warm. Squeeze the orange to make about ½ cup juice. Skim the fat from the liquid in the baking dish; strain the liquid to remove garlic and orange zest. In a saucepan, combine 1¼ cups of the liquid, ½ cup orange juice, and sesame oil. Dissolve the cornstarch in about ¼ cup cold water. Add to the saucepan and bring to a boil; cook and stir 1 minute or until thickened and bubbly. Slice the brisket and pour the glaze over all. Sprinkle with sesame seeds. Serve with rice.

Corned Beef and Cabbage

Servings: 6

2½ to 3 pound corned beef brisket
1 onion, chopped
2 cloves garlic, crushed
4 whole cloves
1 bay leaf
3 medium potatoes
3 medium carrots
1 small head of cabbage

Rinse the corned beef in cold water. Place in a large Dutch oven and cover with water. Add the chopped onion, garlic, cloves, and bay leaf. Heat to boiling, then reduce heat to low, cover well, and simmer about 2½ hours, or until the meat is tender.

Peel and dice the potatoes. Scrape and dice the carrots. Core the cabbage and cut into 6 wedges. Remove the meat from the broth and keep warm. Add the vegetables to the broth, bring to a boil, cover, and reduce to a simmer. Cook for 20 minutes or until tender.

To serve, slice the corned beef thinly across the grain. Drain the vegetables and serve with the meat.

New England Boiled Dinner

Servings: 6

>2 to 2¹/₂ pound corned beef brisket
>1 bay leaf
>3 medium potatoes
>3 medium carrots
>3 turnips
>¹/₂ cup maple syrup*
>12 small boiling onions or 3 medium onions,
>   quartered

Rinse the corned beef in cold water. Place in a large Dutch oven, cover with water, and add the bay leaf. Heat to boiling, then reduce heat to low, cover well, and simmer 1¹/₂ hours.

Preheat the oven to 400°F. Peel and halve the potatoes. Scrape the carrots and cut into 4 pieces. Peel and cube the turnips. Remove the meat from the broth, place in a baking dish, and drizzle with maple syrup. Bake uncovered for 20 minutes. Meanwhile, add the onions, potatoes, carrots, and turnips to the broth, bring to a boil, cover, and reduce to a simmer. Cook for 20 minutes or until tender. To serve, slice the corned beef thinly across the grain and drizzle with the drippings from the pan. Drain the vegetables and serve with the meat.

*Or substitute a mixture of ¹/₃ cup dark brown sugar, 1 tablespoon prepared mustard, and enough broth to make a thick paste. Spread over the brisket.

Apple-of-My-Eye Short Ribs

Servings: 4

>2¹/₂ to 2³/₄ pounds boneless or 3³/₄ to 4
>   pounds bone-in beef short ribs
>1 medium onion
>1 clove garlic
>8 whole cloves
>1 teaspoon salt
>10-ounce jar apple jelly
>¹/₃ cup dry white wine
>2 tablespoons Dijon mustard
>¹/₄ cup chopped green onions (whites and 3
>   inches of greens)
>¹/₂ teaspoon salt
>¹/₄ teaspoon pepper

Trim the fat from the ribs and cut them into serving-sized pieces. Place in a large pot and cover with water. Add the onion, peeled and quartered; the garlic clove, cut in half; the whole cloves; and 1 teaspoon of salt. Bring to a boil, reduce heat to a simmer, and cover. Cook about 1¹/₂ hours or until tender. Drain.

Preheat the broiler and adjust the rack so that the ribs will cook about 4 to 5 inches from the heat element.

Prepare the glaze: Combine the apple jelly, wine, mustard, green onions, ¹/₂ teaspoon salt, and pepper in a saucepan. Heat and stir until the jelly melts. Place the ribs on the broiler pan and brush with the glaze. Broil for a total of about 15 minutes, turning often and brushing with glaze each time you turn. Serve the remaining warm glaze on the side.

Herbed Beef Rib-Eye Roast with Potatoes

Servings: 8 to 10

2 teaspoons rosemary
4 cloves garlic, crushed
1 teaspoon dry mustard
1 teaspoon salt
1 teaspoon cracked black pepper
4-pound beef rib-eye roast (boneless)
2 tablespoons vegetable oil
2 large sweet potatoes
2 medium Yukon gold potatoes
4 small red potatoes

Preheat the oven to 350°F.

Combine the rosemary, garlic, mustard, salt, and pepper, and divide in half. Rub or press half the mixture into the surface of the meat. Place the meat on a rack in a shallow roasting pan and place the meat thermometer, if using, into the thickest part of the meat. Total roasting time will be about 1³/₄ to 2 hours for medium-rare (or until meat thermometer reads 135°F) or about 2¹/₄ to 2³/₄ hours for medium (or until meat thermometer reads 150°F).

Meanwhile, mix the remaining seasonings with the oil in a large bowl. Peel all the potatoes and cut them into pieces that are roughly the same size, about 8 pieces for the sweet potatoes, 4 pieces for the Yukons, and 2 to 4 pieces for the red potatoes. Add the potatoes to the oil and herb mixture and toss well to coat. About 1 hour before the roast will be done, place the potatoes in the roasting pan around the rack.

Filet Southwestern

Filet mignon is very tender but must be cooked with fat because it is so lean.

Servings: 4

$\frac{1}{4}$ cup butter
1 tablespoon lime juice
3 tablespoons minced shallots
1 tablespoon minced fresh cilantro
2 teaspoons puréed chipotle peppers in adobo sauce*
4 1-inch tenderloin steaks or filet mignons (if cut to order, have the butcher flatten them)
vegetable oil

Preheat the broiler and adjust the rack so the filets will be 4 inches from the heating element.

Soften the butter and beat the butter and lime juice with an electric mixer until light and fluffy. Mix in the shallots, cilantro, and peppers. Remove the filets from the refrigerator about 15 minutes before you are ready to begin cooking them. If the butcher did not flatten the filets, flatten them slightly by pressing with a plate. Oil one side of the filets lightly and place on the broiler pan oiled side down. On the top of each, spread about 1 teaspoon of the butter mixture. Broil 4 minutes (for rare) or 6 minutes (for medium).

Turn the filets; top each with another teaspoon of the butter mixture, and broil an additional 4 to 6 minutes. To serve, top each filet with a quarter of the remaining butter mixture.

*Chipotle peppers canned in adobo sauce are available at many groceries. Purée the entire contents in the blender, and store what you do not use in this recipe tightly covered in the refrigerator for seasoning other Southwestern dishes.

Classic Swiss Steak

Servings: 4

2 tablespoons flour
$\frac{1}{2}$ teaspoon salt
$\frac{1}{4}$ teaspoon pepper
1 pound boneless round steak
vegetable oil
2 medium carrots
1 medium onion
1 stalk celery
1 medium green bell pepper
16-ounce can whole or wedge-cut tomatoes

Mix the flour, salt, and pepper. Place the meat on a wooden board or other working surface. (To make cleanup easier, cover the board with waxed paper first if desired.) Sprinkle half the flour mixture onto the meat, and with a meat mallet, pound the mixture into the meat. Turn the meat over and repeat. Cut into serving size pieces and trim any excess fat.

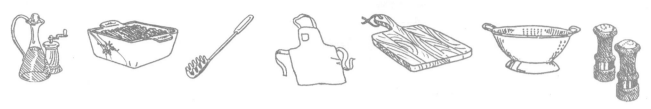

In a large skillet with a tight-fitting lid, heat about 1 tablespoon of oil over medium-high heat. Add the beef and brown well on both sides. Now you can: Reduce the heat to low and proceed with stovetop preparation, or place the meat in a 2 or 2½ quart square or oblong baking dish and preheat the oven to 325°F.

Peel the carrots and cut each into 4 chunks. Peel the onion and cut into quarters. Cut the celery stalk into 2-inch chunks. Seed the green pepper and cut into rings. Pour the tomatoes, undrained, over the meat. Place the carrot, onion, and celery chunks around the meat and lay the pepper rings over all. Cover tightly and simmer on the stovetop or bake in the preheated oven about 1¼ hours, or until meat is fork-tender.

Baked Steak 'n' Gravy

Servings: 6

> 6 tablespoons flour
> ½ teaspoon salt
> ¼ teaspoon pepper
> 1½ pounds boneless round steak
> vegetable oil
> 1 clove garlic, crushed
> 4-ounce can mushroom pieces
> 13- to 16-ounce can beef broth

Mix the flour, salt, and pepper. Cut the meat into serving pieces and remove any excess fat. Place on a wooden board or other working surface. (To make cleanup easier, cover the board with waxed paper first if desired.) Sprinkle half the flour mixture onto the meat, and with a meat mallet, pound the mixture into the meat. Turn the meat over and repeat. Pound until the pieces have been about doubled in diameter and all of the flour mixture has been used.

(continued)

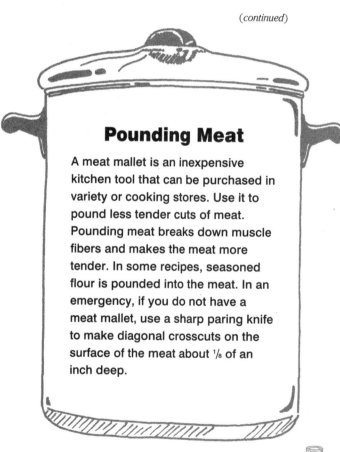

Pounding Meat

A meat mallet is an inexpensive kitchen tool that can be purchased in variety or cooking stores. Use it to pound less tender cuts of meat. Pounding meat breaks down muscle fibers and makes the meat more tender. In some recipes, seasoned flour is pounded into the meat. In an emergency, if you do not have a meat mallet, use a sharp paring knife to make diagonal crosscuts on the surface of the meat about ⅛ of an inch deep.

Steak Broiling Chart: Total Minutes

Steaks 1½ inch and thicker should be broiled 5 inches from the source of heat.

Steaks 1 inch thick should be broiled 4 inches from the source of heat.

THICKNESS	RARE	MEDIUM	WELL DONE
1 inch	8 to 10	12 to 14	17 to 19
1½ inches	14 to 16	18 to 20	23 to 28
2 inches	20 to 25	27 to 32	35 to 40

In a large skillet with a tight-fitting lid, heat 1 tablespoon or more of oil over medium-high heat. Add the beef and brown well on both sides. The last few minutes of browning, add the garlic and cook until softened. Preheat the oven to 325°F and place the meat in a 2- or 2½-quart square or oblong baking dish. Add the mushrooms and liquid (do not drain) to the dish. Use about ¼ cup of the beef broth to deglaze the skillet, then add the remaining broth and bring to a boil. Pour over the meat, cover tightly, and bake for about 1¼ hours or until meat is fork-tender. Check occasionally and add water if the liquid in the pan is too reduced.

Garlicky London Broil

Servings: 4

1½ pound beef flank steak
¾ teaspoon cracked black pepper
2 cloves garlic, crushed separately
¼ cup olive oil
3 tablespoons lemon juice
salt and pepper

Score the flank steak on both sides in a diamond-shaped pattern with cuts about ¼-inch deep. Combine the pepper and 1 clove crushed garlic; rub into the surface of the meat. Make the marinade by combining the remaining crushed garlic with the olive oil and lemon juice. In a glass dish or plastic food bag, place the meat and marinade, turning to coat. Marinate in the refrigerator about 1 hour, turning several times.

Preheat the broiler and adjust the rack so that the top of the steak will be 3 inches from the heating element. Place the steak on the broiler pan, broil about 5 minutes, season the top with salt and pepper, then turn. Broil 5 minutes more for medium-rare, or a few minutes longer if medium is desired. Remove, season, and slice very thinly diagonally across the grain to serve.

Sirloin Italiano

Servings: 4 to 6

> 2 tablespoons chopped sun-dried tomatoes,
>   rehydrated in ¹/₂ cup hot water
> 2 16-ounce cans diced tomatoes
> ¹/₃ cup red wine
> ¹/₄ cup chopped fresh basil
> ¹/₄ cup chopped black olives
> 1 clove garlic, crushed
> 2-pound boneless sirloin steak, 1-inch thick
> 1 tablespoon Worcestershire sauce
> liquid smoke, optional

Preheat the broiler.

Drain the sun-dried tomatoes and combine with the canned tomatoes, wine, basil, olives, and garlic in a large skillet. Bring to a boil, reduce heat to a simmer, and allow to cook while the steak is prepared and broiled.

To prepare the steak, combine the Worcestershire sauce and a few drops liquid smoke to taste, if desired; brush on the steak. Broil 3 to 4 inches from the heating element for a total of about 12 (for medium-rare) or 15 minutes (for medium). Place on a serving platter and slice; pour half the sauce over the steak and serve the rest on the side.

Steak Français

Servings: 4 to 6

> 2-pound boneless round steak, cut 1¹/₂
>   inches thick
> 1 tablespoon olive oil

Marinade:
> ¹/₂ cup white wine
> ¹/₄ cup olive oil
> ¹/₂ teaspoon tarragon
> 1 clove garlic, crushed

Topping:
> ¹/₂ cup soft bread crumbs
> 1 tablespoon chopped fresh parsley
> 2 tablespoons Dijon mustard
> ¹/₄ teaspoon pepper
> ¹/₄ teaspoon tarragon
> dash thyme

In a small bowl, combine the marinade ingredients. Place the steak and marinade in a sealed plastic food bag or covered glass dish, and turn to coat. Marinate in the refrigerator 8 hours or overnight, turning occasionally.

When ready to cook steak, preheat the oven to 350°F. In a small bowl, combine bread crumbs and parsley. In another bowl, combine mustard, pepper, tarragon, and thyme. Remove meat from the marinade and pat dry. In a skillet, heat the oil over medium-high heat and brown the steak well on both sides. Place on a flat rack in a

(continued)

shallow roasting pan and brush with the mustard mixture, then spread the crumb mixture on top and pat down evenly.

Bake about 40 minutes, or until a meat thermometer registers 155°F (medium). Remove from oven and allow to stand 5 minutes. Slice to serve.

Chuck Steak and Vegetables

Servings: 4 to 6

2-pound beef chuck steak, ³/₄- to
*   1-inch thick*
1 can artichoke hearts
1 small red bell pepper
1 small yellow bell pepper
1 small green bell pepper
4 ounces whole mushrooms
1 onion, quartered
4 10-inch bamboo skewers

Marinade:
³/₄ cup bottled Italian dressing
¹/₂ teaspoon crushed red pepper

Combine marinade ingredients, reserving ¹/₄ cup. Place the steak and marinade in a sealed plastic food bag or glass dish, turning to coat. Marinate in the refrigerator at least 6 hours or overnight, turning occasionally.

Drain and halve the artichokes. Seed the peppers and cut into chunks. Toss the artichokes, peppers, mushrooms, and onion in the reserved marinade to coat. Marinate up to 2 hours in the refrigerator (do not exceed this time).

When ready to cook the meat, preheat the broiler. Meanwhile, soak the bamboo skewers in water 10 minutes, then drain. Remove the meat from the marinade and pat dry. Remove the vegetables from the marinade and place them on the skewers. Place the steak and the vegetable skewers on the broiler pan and broil 4 inches from the heat until done, a total of 16 to 20 minutes. Turn the steak once and the vegetables several times; the vegetables will probably need to be removed before the steak is done. Serve the steak and vegetables together.

Mom's Meatloaf

Servings: 6

1½ pounds lean ground beef or
meatloaf mix
1 cup soft bread crumbs
½ cup chopped celery
⅓ cup chopped onion
½ teaspoon dry mustard
1 tablespoon dried parsley, optional
salt and pepper to taste
1 egg
¼ cup milk
1 tablespoon Worcestershire sauce
¼ cup ketchup

Preheat the oven to 350°F.

Combine the meat, bread crumbs, celery, onion, mustard, parsley, salt, and pepper. Beat the egg lightly and add the milk and Worcestershire sauce; add the liquid ingredients to the meat mixture. Combine well. Turn into a lightly greased 8 x 11-inch baking dish, patting into a loaf shape.

Bake 45 minutes, then top with ketchup, spreading to cover. Return to the oven for an additional 15 minutes.

Lucia's Meatloaf

Servings: 8

Meatloaf:
2 pounds lean ground beef
10-ounce box frozen chopped spinach,
thawed and well drained
16 ounces shredded mozzarella cheese
2 cloves garlic, crushed
1 teaspoon basil
1 cup Italian seasoned bread crumbs
salt and pepper to taste
1 egg

Marinara Sauce:
2 tablespoons olive oil
2 cloves garlic, crushed
1 teaspoon basil
dash thyme
28-ounce can crushed tomatoes
salt and pepper to taste
dash red pepper

Preheat oven to 350°F.

Mix all meatloaf ingredients except the egg together. Beat the egg lightly and add it to the meat mixture, stirring to combine thoroughly. Form into one large loaf or two smaller ones. Bake in a lightly greased 8 x 11-inch baking dish for about 1½ to 2 hours.

Meanwhile, in a medium skillet, heat the oil and sauté the garlic. Add basil and thyme, and stir for about 1 minute. Add the tomatoes, salt, and peppers, and simmer for about an hour.

When the meatloaf is done, remove from the oven and allow to stand for about 10 minutes before cutting. Serve with sauce.

Meat Safety

In cooking:

* Thaw meat in the refrigerator. Do not refreeze.
* Marinate meat in the refrigerator.
* Wash cutting boards thoroughly after handling meat on them.
* Use separate utensils and plates for cooked and uncooked meats.

In storing:

* Never leave cooked meat at room temperature more than 2 hours before refrigerating.
* Reheat leftovers until very hot.
* Use leftovers within 3 days

Oven Barbecued Hamburgers

Servings: 8

Burgers:

³/₄ cup rolled oats
³/₄ cup milk
1¹/₂ pounds lean ground beef
¹/₂ cup chopped onion
salt and pepper to taste

Sauce:

1 cup ketchup
¹/₂ cup water
2 tablespoons vinegar
3 tablespoons sugar
3 tablespoons chopped onion
2 tablespoons Worcestershire sauce

Preheat oven to 325°F.

Mix together the oats and milk and allow to stand for 5 minutes, then combine with the beef and onion. Add salt and pepper to taste. Shape into 8 patties and place in a 9 x 13-inch baking dish. Mix all sauce ingredients together and pour over the beef patties. Cover the pan with foil and bake about 1¹/₂ hours.

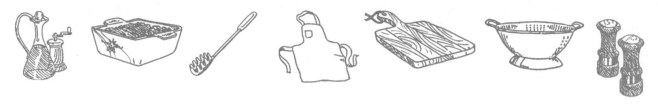

Veal Parmigiana

Servings: 4

> 1 pound veal scaloppine or cutlets or veal
>   steak, ⅛- to ¼-inch thick
> 1 egg
> ¾ cup dry bread crumbs
> ¼ cup grated Parmesan cheese
> 1 tablespoon dried parsley
> ⅛ teaspoon pepper
> olive or vegetable oil
> ⅔ cup grated mozzarella cheese

Sauce:*

> ¼ cup chopped onion
> 1 clove garlic, crushed
> 16-ounce can plum or Italian tomatoes
> 1 teaspoon Italian seasoning
> 1 teaspoon sugar
> ¼ teaspoon salt

Cut the veal into serving-size pieces. If it's more than ⅛-inch thick, pound with a meat mallet to ⅛-inch thickness. In a small shallow dish, beat the egg lightly. In another small shallow dish, combine the bread crumbs, Parmesan cheese, parsley, and pepper. Bread the cutlets on both sides by dipping first in the egg, then in the crumb mixture. (It is not necessary to use all of the breading mixture.) Set aside on a plate as they are completed. In a large skillet, heat 1 tablespoon or more oil over medium heat. When it is hot, cook the veal until done, about 4 to 5 minutes, turning once. Remove from skillet.

In the same skillet, cook the onion and garlic until tender. Chop the tomatoes and add, along with the juice, to the skillet. Add the Italian seasonings, sugar, and salt. Bring to a boil, then reduce the heat and allow to simmer for 5 minutes. Return the veal to the skillet, spooning the sauce over the top, and cook until thoroughly reheated. Turn off the heat, sprinkle the mozzarella cheese evenly over the cutlets, and cover the skillet until the cheese melts, no more than 5 minutes.

*For a quick dinner, substitute a 16-ounce jar of spaghetti or Italian cooking sauce.

Quick Tangy Cubed Veal Steaks

Servings: 4

> 2 tablespoons butter
> 1 pound cubed veal steaks
> juice of 1 lemon
> ¼ cup yogurt, lemon or plain, or
>   sour cream

In a large skillet, heat the butter over medium heat. Sauté the cube steaks until done, turning once (about 5 to 7 minutes). Remove to a serving platter. Reduce the heat to low and deglaze the skillet with the lemon juice. Add the yogurt or sour cream and stir in thoroughly, warming through. Pour over cubed steaks and serve.

Elegant Veal Loaf

Servings: 4 to 5

1 pound ground veal
$\frac{1}{4}$ cup soft bread crumbs
$\frac{1}{8}$ teaspoon white pepper
$\frac{1}{4}$ cup fresh chopped parsley
1 egg
1 tablespoon butter
4 ounces Gorgonzola or blue cheese, crumbled
2 tablespoons chopped toasted walnuts
1 tablespoon snipped fresh chives

Preheat oven to 350°F.

Mix together the veal, bread crumbs, pepper, and parsley. Lightly beat the egg and combine with the veal mixture. Shape into a loaf in a lightly greased 8 x 11-inch baking dish, then press a well the entire length of the loaf, about two thirds of the way to the bottom of the loaf.

Soften the butter and combine with the cheese, walnuts, and chives. Spoon the mixture into the well in the loaf, ending within $\frac{1}{2}$ inch of each end. Reshape the veal over the cheese filling. Bake 50 minutes, or until juices run clear.

Veal Chops with Mushroom Sauce

Servings: 4

4 veal loin chops, $\frac{3}{4}$- to 1-inch thick
2 teaspoons vegetable oil
$\frac{1}{4}$ cup chopped shallots
1 clove garlic, minced
2 cups diced fresh mushroom caps*
$\frac{1}{8}$ teaspoon white pepper
2 tablespoons chopped fresh parsley
$\frac{1}{4}$ teaspoon thyme
$\frac{1}{4}$ cup dry white wine, or 1 tablespoon water plus 2 teaspoons white wine or Worcestershire sauce
$\frac{2}{3}$ cup beef broth
1 teaspoon cornstarch

Preheat the broiler, adjusting the rack so that the chops will be 4 inches from the heating element.

Broil the chops until done, turning once (up to 17 minutes).

Meanwhile, heat the oil in a skillet over medium heat. Add the shallots and garlic and cook for about 2 minutes. Add the mushrooms along with the pepper, parsley, and thyme, and cook for about 3 minutes. Add the wine and broth, reserving 1 tablespoon of the broth, and cook for an additional 5 minutes. Dissolve the cornstarch in the reserved broth and add to the skillet, stirring until thickened. Serve sauce over the chops.

*If desired, a mixture of several varietal mushrooms, such as shiitake or Portobello, can be used.

Easy Honey-Herb Chops

Servings: 4

> 2 tablespoons honey
> 1/4 cup Dijon mustard
> 1/2 teaspoon rosemary
> 1/4 teaspoon thyme
> 1/4 teaspoon pepper
> 4 boneless pork chops, about 1-inch thick

Preheat the broiler.

Combine honey, mustard, rosemary, thyme, and pepper, whisking to combine well. Brush over the chops and place on a broiler pan that has been lightly greased or sprayed with cooking spray. Broil the chops 4 inches from the heating element, turning once and basting two additional times on each side with the honey mixture. Total cooking time will be about 12 minutes.

Stuffed Pork Chops

Servings: 6

> 6 pork chops, 1 1/2-to-2 inches thick, with
>   pockets cut for stuffing*

Stuffing Mix:
> 1/4 cup chopped dried apricots

> 1 1/4 cups water
> 1 tablespoon sugar
> 1/2 cup uncooked long-grain rice
> 1/4 cup chopped onion
> 1 tablespoon chopped parsley
> 2 tablespoons butter
> 1 teaspoon grated orange zest
> 1/2 teaspoon salt
> 1 tablespoon slivered almonds, toasted

(continued)

Does Pork Have to be Well Done?

Today's leaner pork should still be cooked to 160°F (medium to medium well). Juices should run clear. Grilled pork and pork cooked with tomatoes and some other ingredients will remain pink even if it is well done.

Preheat the oven to 350°F.

In a saucepan, bring to a boil the apricots, water, and sugar. Stir in the rice, onion, parsley, butter, orange zest, and salt. Reduce heat and simmer 20 minutes or more until water is absorbed and rice is cooked. Allow mixture to cool about 15 minutes.

Stir in almonds. Stuff about ¼ cup mixture into each pork chop pocket, packing firmly. Press the edges of the chops together and seal with toothpicks or metal skewers (sold inexpensively at grocery and variety stores as turkey trussing kits).

Lay the chops in a 9 x 13-inch baking dish and bake for about 1½ hours, or until chops are tender.

*Pork chops with pockets cut for stuffing are available at most groceries. You can also cut the pockets yourself. Purchase thick cut, bone-in chops. With a small, sharp knife, make a horizontal cut through the fat side of the chop, 2 to 3 inches wide. While keeping the opening slit no more than 3 inches wide, work the knife back and forth to make the inside of the pocket larger. Cut the pocket almost through to the bone.

Pork Loin Hawaiian

Servings: 6

1 pork loin roast, about 2 pounds

Marinade:
1½ cups unsweetened pineapple juice
¼ cup plus 2 tablespoons soy sauce
3 tablespoons molasses
1½ teaspoons ground ginger
1½ teaspoons dry mustard
2 cloves garlic, crushed

Mix marinade ingredients together well, reserving about ½ cup. Cover and refrigerate the reserved marinade. Place the roast and the remaining marinade in a glass dish or sealing plastic food bag, turning several times to coat thoroughly. Cover and refrigerate 12 to 24 hours, turning often. Discard marinade after removing roast.

When ready to cook the roast, preheat the oven to 325°F. Place on the rack of a shallow roasting pan and roast about 1¼ hours, or until a meat thermometer reads 160°F. Baste occasionally with the reserved marinade. Remove from the oven, cover with foil, and allow to stand for 15 minutes before slicing.

Country-style pork ribs are the meatiest of the rib varieties and are usually eaten with a fork and knife. *Back ribs* have less meat. *Spareribs* have the least meat of all per pound, but they are the traditional rib of choice for barbecuing.

Stuffed Pork Tenderloin

Servings: 4

1¼ pound pork tenderloin
2 tablespoons butter
1 cup packaged dry herb-flavored or
  sage-and-onion-flavored stuffing mix,
  or 1 cup small dry bread cubes plus
  ¼ teaspoon poultry seasoning
½ cup chopped apple
2 tablespoons raisins
2 tablespoons apple juice
salt and pepper to taste

Preheat oven to 350°F.

Slice the tenderloin lengthwise, but do not cut completely through. Spread the halves open. Place plastic wrap over them and use a meat mallet to flatten to an even thickness.

Melt the butter and combine with the bread stuffing, apple, raisins, and apple juice. Salt and pepper to taste. Spread the stuffing over the pork to within ½ inch of all edges. Beginning from the short end, roll the tenderloin like a jelly roll. Tie securely in three places with white kitchen string. Bake in an appropriately-sized baking pan for 45 to 50 minutes, or until a meat thermometer reads 160°F.

After removing from the oven, allow to stand (covered with foil) for about 15 minutes before slicing.

Oven-Barbecued Spareribs

Servings: 6 to 8

4 pounds spareribs, back ribs, or
  country-style ribs

Marinade:
2 cups chopped onion
2 cups ketchup
⅔ cup brown sugar
⅔ cup red wine or other vinegar
2 tablespoons Worcestershire sauce

Combine the marinade ingredients well. Place the ribs and 2 cups of the marinade in a glass dish or sealing plastic food bag, turning several times to coat. Marinate in the refrigerator 8 hours or overnight, turning occasionally. Reserve the remaining marinade in a covered container in the refrigerator.

When ready to cook, remove the ribs from the marinade and discard it. Preheat oven to 450°F. Bring the reserved marinade to a boil, then reduce heat and simmer about 10 minutes until thickened slightly. Wipe ribs with the marinade. Place on a flat rack in a shallow roasting pan and bake at 450°F for ½ hour. Reduce heat to 325°F and continue baking for 1 to 1½ hours or until very tender, basting frequently with the sauce.

Baked Glazed Ham

Servings: varies with size of ham

1 fully cooked ham
whole cloves
1 recipe glaze (see below)

Preheat oven to 325°F.

Place the ham fat side up on the rack of a shallow roasting pan and score the top in a diamond-shaped pattern. Cuts should be between $\frac{1}{8}$- and $\frac{1}{4}$-inch deep and about 2 inches apart. Insert whole cloves into the ham where the cuts intersect (that is, at the corners of the diamonds).

Follow the general instructions for roasting a ham on page 135. One hour before the ham will be done, begin basting with one of the following glazes and baste every 15 minutes until done.

Tangy Glaze: In a saucepan, combine $\frac{1}{2}$ cup brown sugar, $1\frac{1}{2}$ cups of water, and 2 teaspoons cornstarch. Bring to a boil and stir until clear and thickened. Remove from heat and stir in 1 teaspoon dry mustard, 2 teaspoons grated orange zest, and $\frac{1}{2}$ cup raisins.

Cranberry Glaze: In a saucepan, combine half of a 16-ounce can of jellied cranberry sauce, $\frac{1}{2}$ cup brown sugar, 2 tablespoons apple juice or water, $\frac{1}{4}$ teaspoon cinnamon, and $\frac{1}{4}$ teaspoon allspice.

Ham Facts

Fully-cooked hams are ready to eat when purchased. Often, they are heated or "baked" and served hot. They can be smoked or unsmoked. Fully-cooked hams are the most common variety today, but hams that are not fully cooked are sometimes available. They *must* be roasted or baked before eating.

A canned ham is ham meat with the bone and much of the fat removed. The meat is then re-formed into a hamlike shape.

Marinated Lamb Kebobs

Servings: 4

> 1 pound boneless leg of lamb chops, cut
>   into 1¼-inch cubes
> 4 14-inch skewers
> 16 green onions, cut into 2-inch pieces
>   (whites and greens)

Marinade:
¼ cup lemon juice
¼ cup olive oil
3 tablespoons dry sherry
3 tablespoons water
1 tablespoon chopped shallots
½ teaspoon oregano
½ teaspoon rosemary

Combine marinade ingredients in a small bowl; reserve about ¼ cup in a covered container in the refrigerator. Place remaining marinade and lamb cubes in a glass dish or sealing plastic food bag; turn several times to coat. Marinate in the refrigerator 6 to 8 hours, turning occasionally.

When ready to cook, preheat the broiler. Assemble kebobs by threading lamb cubes on the skewers with several green onion pieces between each (the equivalent of 4 whole green onions per skewer). Broil 3 to 4 inches from the heat for 10 to 15 minutes, brushing twice with reserved marinade.

Garlic-Glazed Leg of Lamb

Servings: 8

> 1 boneless leg of lamb, about 3½ to 4
>   pounds, rolled and tied

Glaze:
⅓ cup dry sherry
1 tablespoon paprika
2 tablespoons soy sauce
2 tablespoons olive oil
4 cloves garlic, minced
⅓ cup water

Combine the glaze ingredients in a small bowl. Place the lamb on a rack in a shallow roasting pan, brush with the glaze. Roast 2¾ to 3 hours, brushing about every 20 minutes with the glaze.

Greek-Style Lamb Patties

Servings: 6

> 1 pound ground lamb
> ½ cup dry bread crumbs
> ½ cup crumbled feta cheese
> 2 tablespoons finely chopped onion
> 2 tablespoons chopped fresh parsley
> 1 clove garlic, crushed
> 1 teaspoon dried mint

Preheat the broiler and adjust the rack so the patties will be 5½ to 6 inches from the heating element.

Combine all ingredients, mixing well. Divide the mixture into 6 portions and shape into 4-inch patties. Place on the rack of a broiler pan that has been lightly greased or sprayed with cooking oil. Broil 4 to 5 minutes per side, turning once, or to desired doneness.

When you grill or broil meat (cook it over or under a source of high heat), use a basting brush to prevent the meat from drying out. Extra-long handled brushes are available for use on the grill.

When you braise meat, or cook it covered in a pan with added liquid, you are actually alllowing the meat to self-baste, since the steam from the liquid condenses on the lid, then falls back on to the meat. No added basting is needed.

Steak and Potato Potpie

Servings: 6

> 1 pound boneless sirloin steak, ¾-inch thick
> 1 tablespoon vegetable oil
> 8 ounces mushrooms, sliced
> 1 clove garlic, crushed
> 1 medium onion, thinly sliced
> 1 cup baby carrots
> 1 cup sugar snap peas, trimmed (fresh or frozen)
> 3 tablespoons butter
> ¼ cup flour
> 2½ cups beef broth, divided
> ¼ teaspoon thyme
> ¼ teaspoon pepper
> 3 cups mashed potatoes or garlic mashed potatoes

Preheat the oven to 450°F.

Trim any fat from the steak and cut into strips about ¼-inch thick and 2 inches long. In a large skillet, heat the oil over medium-high heat; add the beef, and stir-fry until no longer pink. Place in an 8 x 11-inch baking dish. Add mushrooms, garlic, and onion to the skillet; cook until onion is tender, about 3 minutes. Remove the vegetables from the skillet and sprinkle on top of the meat.

Steam or boil the carrots and snap peas until just crisp-tender, and add to dish. Melt the butter in the skillet; stir in the flour, then add the broth all at once. Bring to a boil, stirring constantly. Reduce heat, add the

(continued)

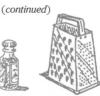

How to Read a Meat Label

A standard meat label tells you what part of the animal the meat comes from (the primal, or wholesale, cut) and what the retail name of the cut is. (Retail names for certain cuts can vary slightly from region to region in the United States.) It will also tell you the weight, price per pound, and total price. Some supermarkets also provide sell-by dates and cooking instructions on labels.

The label sometimes states the grade of the meat as well. Usually, the more fat marbled in the meat, the higher its grade, because fat adds flavor, juiciness, and tenderness (as well as those pesky calories and health risks!). Prime meats have the most marbling and are the most expensive, choice has less marbling, and select has even less, making it leaner but not as flavorful. Meat grading is done by USDA inspectors if the meat processor chooses to have it done and to pay for it. Meat *safety inspection*, on the other hand, is required by law and is supported by your tax dollars.

thyme and pepper, and allow to cook for 1 minute. Pour over the meat. Divide the potatoes into six ½ cup portions, and place on top of the meat mixture, using an ice cream scoop if available or a large spoon.

Bake for 15 to 20 minutes, or until the potatoes are browned.

Chili Mac

Servings: 4

½ pound ground beef
¼ cup chopped onion
¼ cup chopped green pepper
29-ounce can whole tomatoes
1½ teaspoons chili powder
1 teaspoon salt
dash pepper
4 ounces elbow macaroni

Spray a large skillet with cooking spray, or add about 1 teaspoon vegetable oil, and heat over medium-high heat. Brown the meat along with the onion and pepper. Add the tomatoes, chili powder, salt, and pepper, mixing well, and breaking up the tomatoes slightly. Bring to a boil and stir in the macaroni. Cover, reduce heat, and simmer about 20 minutes, or until macaroni is done.

Cowboy Beef and Beans

Servings: 12

1 pound dry pinto beans
1 tablespoon butter
1 3 to 4 pound beef rump roast
1 cup green pepper strips
2 medium onions, sliced
2 cups tomato juice
8-ounce can tomato sauce
½ cup water
2 teaspoons cider vinegar
2 tablespoons brown sugar
2 teaspoons salt
1 teaspoon dry mustard
1 teaspoon thyme

Rinse the beans. Place in a large oven-proof stockpot, cover with cold water, and soak overnight. Or bring the beans to a boil, boil 1 minute, and allow to stand for 1 hour.

When ready to begin preparing the dish, bring the beans to a boil, then reduce the heat and cook 1 hour. Drain, discarding the water.

In a large Dutch oven, heat the butter over medium heat; brown the roast evenly in the butter for about 10 to 15 minutes.

Preheat oven to 350°F. Add peppers and onions to the pot, and cook until tender. Add the beans and all remaining ingredients. Cover and bake for 2½ to 3 hours or until beans are tender and meat is done.

Beef Stroganoff

Servings: 4

 4 tablespoons flour, divided
 1 teaspoon paprika
 1 teaspoon salt
 ¹/₂ teaspoon pepper
 1 pound beef sirloin, cut into ¹/₄-inch-thick
   strips
 4 tablespoons butter, divided
 1 clove garlic, minced
 ¹/₂ cup chopped onion
 4-ounce can mushrooms
 14¹/₂-ounce can beef broth
 1 tablespoon tomato paste
 1 cup sour cream
 2 tablespoons dry white wine (optional)

In a plastic food bag, combine 2 table-spoons flour and the paprika, salt, and pepper. Add the beef slices and shake to coat. In a large skillet, heat 2 tablespoons butter over medium-high heat, and cook the garlic and onion 2 minutes. Shake the excess flour from the beef, then add it to the skillet and brown it quickly.

Drain the mushrooms and reserve the juice. Add the mushrooms to the skillet and cook for about 1 minute, or until heated through. Push the meat and vegetables to one side of the skillet. Add the two remaining tablespoons butter and allow to melt, then blend the remaining 2 table-spoons flour into it. Add the beef broth and reserved mushroom juice to the skillet and stir, gradually incorporating the meat, until the broth becomes thickened and bubbly. Stir in the tomato paste. Stir in the sour cream and the wine, and continue cooking and stirring until heated through. Serve over hot noodles or over rice.

Stuffed Peppers

Servings: 6

 6 large, squat green peppers
 ¹/₂ cup converted (parboiled) long-grain rice
 ¹/₂ cup water
 ¹/₂ pound ground beef
 ¹/₄ cup diced celery
 ¹/₄ cup chopped onion
 16-ounce can diced tomatoes
 salt and pepper
 8-ounce can tomato sauce

Slice off the tops of the peppers and clean and seed the insides. Bring a large kettle of water to a boil and blanch the peppers about 5 minutes. Remove and invert to drain. In a small saucepan, bring the rice and ¹/₂ cup water to a boil; cover and simmer for 5 to 10 minutes, or until water is absorbed.

In a large bowl, mix the beef, celery, onion, and rice. Stir in the tomatoes, and salt and pepper to taste. Fill the peppers, mounding the filling on top if there is

(continued)

enough. Place upright in a deep-sided baking dish; peppers may be touching. Pour tomato sauce over the peppers.

Cover and bake 1 hour; uncover and bake an additional 15 minutes. Filling may remain somewhat pink even when well done.

Variation: If desired, make a tomato gravy to serve with mashed potatoes. Substitute a 16-ounce can of tomato sauce for the 8-ounce can; pour about half over the peppers and the remainder around them. When peppers are done, remove them from the dish. Combine 1 tablespoon instant or all-purpose flour and $1/4$ cup water in a small bowl; stir into the tomato juices and cook and stir until bubbly and thickened.

Cabbage Rolls

Servings: 8

>*1 cup converted (parboiled) long-grain rice*
>*1 cup water*
>*1 pound ground beef*
>*$1/2$ cup chopped onion*
>*16-ounce can diced tomatoes*
>*salt and pepper to taste*
>*2 large heads cabbage*
>*1 large can tomato juice (46 ounces)*

In a small saucepan, bring the rice and water to a boil; cover and simmer for about 10 minutes, or until water is absorbed. In a large bowl, mix the beef, onion, and rice. Stir in the tomatoes, and salt and pepper to taste.

Place about 4 inches of water in a large kettle and bring to a boil. Core the cabbages and remove any bruised outer leaves. Place the whole cabbages in the boiling water and partially cover. When top leaves have softened, remove them from the cabbage, using long-tined forks to avoid being burned with the steam. Continue repeating this process until you've gathered enough leaves for all the filling.

Turn the cabbage leaves ribs side up and with a sharp paring knife, pare away the raised rib so the leaf is easier to roll. Turn the leaf over, rib side down. Place about two heaping tablespoons of the filling on the leaf, centered crosswise and about 2 inches from the bottom lengthwise edge of the leaf. Roll the bottom lengthwise edge over the meat filling, then fold in the side edges over it. Continue to roll lengthwise, then place on a platter seam side down.

When all the filling has been used, slice the remaining cabbage thickly and place in a large Dutch oven. Carefully place the rolls on top of the cabbage in layers, seam sides down. Pour the tomato juice over all. Cover and simmer 3 hours or longer. Serve with mashed potatoes, if desired.

Simple Beef Goulash

Servings: 4

2 tablespoons butter
2 medium onions, finely chopped
1 clove garlic, minced
1 pound cubed beef
1 tablespoon paprika
$\frac{1}{2}$ teaspoon caraway (optional)
$\frac{1}{2}$ teaspoon salt
$\frac{1}{4}$ teaspoon pepper
1 tablespoon flour
$\frac{1}{4}$ cup water

In a Dutch oven, melt the butter. Brown the onions and garlic in the butter. Add the beef, and brown until the meat is no longer pink, stirring constantly. Add water to cover and add paprika, caraway, salt, and pepper. Simmer until tender, about 1 hour.

Mix the flour with $\frac{1}{4}$ cup water and stir into the broth, cooking until thickened and bubbly. Adjust salt and pepper to taste.

Beef Goulash a la Vasiloff

Servings: 8

3 tablespoons butter
2 large onions, chopped
1 clove garlic, minced
2 pounds cubed beef
$\frac{1}{2}$ pound cubed pork
1 teaspoon sugar
$\frac{1}{4}$ cup ketchup

2 tablespoons paprika
1 teaspoon caraway
dash of cayenne
1 bay leaf
2 tablespoons flour
$\frac{1}{4}$ cup water
salt and pepper

In a large skillet, melt the butter. Sauté the onion and garlic in the butter. Add the meat and sprinkle with sugar; brown the meat slightly. Add water to cover, ketchup, paprika, caraway, cayenne, and the bay leaf, and simmer until tender, at least $1\frac{1}{2}$ hours.

To make gravy, add the flour to the water in a small bowl; stir into the broth. Cook and stir until thickened and bubbly. Add salt and pepper to taste.

Swedish Meatballs

Servings: 6

$\frac{1}{4}$ cup milk
$1\frac{1}{2}$ cups soft bread cubes, about
     $\frac{1}{4}$-inch square
$\frac{1}{4}$ cup finely chopped onion
$\frac{1}{4}$ cup + 1 tablespoon butter, divided
$1\frac{1}{2}$ pounds meatloaf mix (a combination
     of ground beef, pork, and veal)
$\frac{1}{2}$ teaspoon paprika
$\frac{1}{8}$ teaspoon nutmeg
$\frac{1}{2}$ teaspoon dry mustard
$\frac{1}{2}$ teaspoon salt
$\frac{1}{8}$ teaspoon pepper

(continued)

2 eggs
2 tablespoons flour
$\frac{1}{2}$ cup beef broth
2 teaspoons tomato paste
$\frac{1}{2}$ cup sour cream

Combine milk and the bread cubes. Allow to stand for 5 minutes, then using your fingers, squeeze or press the excess liquid from the bread cubes. In a small skillet, sauté the onion in 1 tablespoon of butter. In a large bowl, mix together well the meats, bread, onion, paprika, nutmeg, mustard, salt, and pepper. Beat the eggs lightly and add to the meat mixture. Shape the meat into 18 small meatballs.

In a large skillet, melt $\frac{1}{4}$ cup butter over medium heat, brown the meatballs in batches, about 5 minutes on each side. Remove meatballs from the skillet as they are done and set aside. Reduce the heat and stir the flour into the pan drippings. Add the beef broth and tomato paste, and cook over medium heat until thick. Add the meatballs to the skillet, cover, and simmer 15 minutes. Stir in the sour cream and serve.

Steak Salad

Servings: 4 main-dish servings

$1\frac{1}{4}$ pounds beef sirloin steak, at least 1-inch thick
salt to taste
1 large head romaine lettuce

$\frac{1}{2}$ cup crumbled blue or Gorgonzola cheese
$\frac{1}{4}$ cup toasted chopped hazelnuts or walnuts
16 cherry tomatoes
1 cup prepared Italian dressing with balsamic vinegar, or to taste

Rub Ingredients:

1 teaspoon oregano
1 clove garlic, crushed
$\frac{1}{4}$ teaspoon pepper

Preheat the broiler.

Combine the rub ingredients and press into both sides of the meat, distributing it evenly. Broil steak to desired degree of doneness. When done, season with salt and slice across the grain into strips $\frac{1}{8}$- to $\frac{1}{4}$-inch thick.

Slice the lettuce across the rib into 1-inch-thick slices (do not prepare ahead of time; lettuce that is cut with a knife quickly browns around the edges). Place a quarter of the lettuce on each serving plate and top with a quarter of the meat. Sprinkle with cheese and nuts and garnish each plate with 4 tomatoes. Drizzle with dressing.

Wella's Veal Potpie

Servings: 6

1 pound cubed veal
1 medium onion, chopped

¹/₂ teaspoon salt
¹/₈ teaspoon pepper
4 stalks celery, sliced
2 medium carrots, sliced
3 medium potatoes, peeled and diced
1 tablespoon flour
¹/₄ cup cold water

Biscuits:

²/₃ cup milk
2¹/₄ cups all-purpose baking mix,
*   such as Bisquick*

Put the veal and onion in a Dutch oven. Cover with water (approximately 2 quarts), add the salt and pepper, and simmer until tender, about 1 hour.

Add the celery and carrots, and simmer about 20 minutes. Add the potatoes, and simmer for an additional 20 to 30 minutes, or until potatoes are tender.

Preheat oven to 400°F. To make the biscuits, stir the milk into the baking mix until a soft dough forms. Turn onto a floured surface and knead about 10 times. Roll to a ¹/₂-inch thickness and cut with a 2¹/₂-inch biscuit cutter into 9 biscuits.

When biscuits are ready, combine the flour with the cold water, then stir into the broth and cook until it is thickened and bubbly. Turn the veal mixture into a square baking dish and arrange the biscuits on top, in three rows of three. Bake 10 to 15 minutes, or until the biscuits are golden brown.

Skillet Pork Chops and Sauerkraut

Servings: 4

2 tablespoons or more butter
3 medium potatoes, peeled and thinly
*   sliced*
1 small onion, thinly sliced
salt and pepper to taste
4 pork chops
¹/₄ teaspoon paprika
¹/₄ teaspoon garlic powder
16-ounce jar sauerkraut
1 cup water

In a large skillet, melt the butter over medium-high heat. Add the potatoes and onion, season with salt and pepper, and brown lightly. Remove the potatoes from the skillet and add the pork chops. Season with salt, pepper, paprika, and garlic powder. Brown the pork chops.

When the chops are browned, place the potatoes and onions on top of them, then top with the sauerkraut. Pour water over all. Reduce heat, cover, and simmer for 1 hour, or until pork chops are done.

Pork Chops and Rice

Servings: 4

4 pork chops
salt and pepper to taste
4 slices onion

(continued)

169

½ cup long-grain rice
28-ounce can whole tomatoes

Preheat oven to 350°F.

Spray a medium skillet with cooking spray, or heat 1 teaspoon vegetable oil over medium heat. Brown the pork chops well, seasoning with salt and pepper, about 5 minutes on each side.

Place chops in a baking dish (chops should not overlap). Top each chop with an onion slice, then sprinkle rice over all. Place the tomatoes on top of the dish, with 1 nice sized tomato centered on top of each of the chops. Pour the juice from the tomatoes over all. Cover and bake about 1 ¼ hours, or until chops are tender.

Scalloped Apples and Pork Chops

Servings: 4

2½ cups sliced apples
4 small sweet potatoes, pared and sliced
⅓ cup raisins
⅓ cup brown sugar
dash nutmeg
3 tablespoons currant jelly
3 tablespoons prepared mustard
4 pork chops, cut ¾-inch thick
salt and pepper

Preheat oven to 350°F.

Place half the apples at either end of a greased 8 x 11-inch baking dish. In the center, place the sweet potato slices. Scatter the raisins over all and sprinkle with brown sugar and nutmeg. Combine the jelly and mustard, mixing until smooth.

Trim fat from chops and coat both sides of each with the jelly mixture. Place chops on the sweet potatoes and sprinkle with salt and pepper. Cover and bake 1 hour and 40 minutes, or until the chops are tender.

Ham 'n' Cornbread Potpie

Servings: 4

1 potato, peeled and cubed
1 carrot, thinly cut
½ cup broccoli cut into small pieces
¼ cup chopped onion
1 cup cubed ham
4-ounce can mushrooms, drained
3 tablespoons butter
¼ cup flour
2½ cups chicken broth
¼ teaspoon thyme
⅛ teaspoon pepper

Topping:
8-ounce package cornbread mix
1 cup grated Cheddar cheese
⅓ cup milk
1 egg

In a medium saucepan, combine the potato, carrot, broccoli, and onion in enough water to cover, and cook until crisp-tender. Drain and reserve. Place the ham in a 9 x 9-inch baking dish; place the cooked vegetables and the mushrooms on the ham. In a medium saucepan over medium heat, melt the butter. Stir in the flour, then gradually whisk in the broth. Stir in the thyme, and allow the sauce to heat to a simmer, stirring constantly. Add pepper and simmer for 1 minute. Pour over the vegetables and set aside while making the topping.

Preheat oven to 400°F.

In a medium bowl, combine the cornbread mix and the cheese. In a separate bowl, whisk together the milk and egg, then stir into the cornbread mixture. Spoon the cornbread batter over the meat mixture as evenly as possible and smooth lightly with a spatula. Bake 25 to 30 minutes, or until the cornbread is lightly browned and pulling away from the sides of the pan.

Moussaka

Servings: 8 to 10

5 large eggplants, about 1½ pounds each
1 teaspoon salt, divided, + salt for sprinkling
10 tablespoons butter, divided
3 pounds ground lamb or beef
1½ cups chopped onion
2 tablespoons tomato paste

¼ cup chopped parsley
½ cup red wine
⅛ teaspoon pepper
½ cup water
⅛ teaspoon ground cinnamon
¾ cup grated Parmesan cheese, divided
½ cup bread crumbs, divided
½ cup all-purpose flour
4 cups hot milk
pepper to taste
⅛ teaspoon grated nutmeg
3 eggs, slightly beaten
hot sauce, optional
vegetable oil

Remove ½-inch-wide strips of peel lengthwise from eggplants, leaving ½ inch of peel between strips. Cut eggplants into ½-inch rounds, sprinkle with salt, and let stand in a colander under a heavy or weighted plate for 30 minutes. Rinse and dry eggplant rounds.

Melt 4 tablespoons butter in a saucepan; sauté meat and onion in the saucepan until brown. Add tomato paste, parsley, wine, ½ teaspoon salt, pepper, and water. Simmer until liquid has been absorbed. Cool. Stir in cinnamon, ½ cup cheese, and half of the bread crumbs.

To prepare the sauce, melt 6 tablespoons butter in a saucepan over low heat. Add flour and stir until well blended. Remove from heat, and gradually stir in milk. Return to heat and cook, stirring, until sauce is thick and smooth. Add ½ teaspoon salt, pepper, and nutmeg. Combine

(continued)

eggs with a little of the hot sauce, then stir egg mixture into the sauce and cook over low heat for 2 minutes, stirring constantly.

Preheat the broiler. Lightly brush the eggplant slices with oil on both sides. Place on an ungreased cookie sheet and broil until lightly browned. Set aside to cool. Preheat oven to 350°F.

Sprinkle a 10 x 16-inch pan with the remaining ¼ cup bread crumbs. Place a layer of eggplant slices on the bread crumbs, then spread the meat mixture over the eggplant slices. Cover the meat with the remaining eggplant. Spoon the sauce over the eggplant; sprinkle with the remaining ¼ cup grated cheese. Bake for 40 minutes, or until golden brown. Cool for 10 minutes before cutting. Serve warm.

Lamb and Eggplant Balls

Servings: 4

> 1 pound ground lamb
> 1 small eggplant, peeled and diced
> ½ cup chopped onion
> 1 clove garlic, pressed or minced
> ½ cup soft bread crumbs
> 1 egg, lightly beaten
> 3 tablespoons chopped fresh parsley
> 1 teaspoon salt
> ¼ teaspoon pepper
> 2 tablespoons olive or other cooking oil
> 16-ounce can tomato sauce
> 1 teaspoon dry mustard

> 2 cups fresh green beans, trimmed and cut
> into pieces, or frozen cut green beans

In a large bowl, mix together well the ground lamb, eggplant, onion, garlic, bread crumbs, egg, parsley, salt, and pepper. Shape into 10 to 12 balls. In a large, deep skillet with a lid, heat the oil over medium heat; brown the meatballs well on all sides in the oil. Drain any excess oil.

Combine the tomato sauce and mustard, and pour over the meatballs. Cover and simmer for 30 minutes. Uncover the pan and add the beans. Simmer, uncovered, for 15 more minutes, or until beans are tender. Serve with Basic Rice Pilaf, page 275.

Quick Fajitas with Pico de Gallo

Servings: 4

> 1 pound well-trimmed boneless beef
> top round or top sirloin steak cut
> ¾-inch thick
> 8 small flour tortillas
> lime wedges
> cilantro sprigs

Marinade:
> 2 tablespoons fresh lime juice
> 2 tablespoons olive oil
> 2 large cloves garlic, crushed

Pico de Gallo:

1 cup seeded and chopped tomato
½ cup diced zucchini
¼ cup chopped fresh cilantro
¼ cup picante sauce or salsa
1 tablespoon fresh lime juice

Place beef in a plastic bag. Add marinade ingredients, turning to coat. Close securely and marinate in refrigerator 20 to 30 minutes, turning once. Wrap tortillas in heavy aluminum foil. Combine pico de gallo ingredients, mixing well.

Remove steak from the marinade. Discard marinade. Place steak on the grill over medium heat and cook 8 to 9 minutes (10 to 12 minutes for top sirloin), turning occasionally. During the last 5 minutes, place the tortilla packet on the edge of the grill to heat through. Trim the fat from the steak and carve crosswise into very thin slices. Serve beef in tortillas with pico de gallo garnished with lime wedges and cilantro sprigs.

Szechuan Beef

Servings: 4

1 pound beef top round steak
5 carrots, cut into thin "sticks"
2 tablespoons dry sherry
1 tablespoon Chinese soy sauce
1 tablespoon hot bean sauce*
1 teaspoon chili oil**
1 tablespoon sesame oil

2 cups fresh pea pods or 6-ounce package
  frozen pea pods, thawed
15-ounce can straw mushrooms, drained
½ cup chopped peanuts
chopped green onions, for garnish

Partially freeze the beef, and cut on the bias into thin strips. Cook carrots, covered, in a small amount of boiling salted water, about 3 minutes. Drain. Stir together the sherry, soy sauce, and hot bean sauce. Set sauce aside.

Preheat wok over high heat and add chili oil and sesame oil. Add more oil if necessary. Stir-fry carrots in hot oil for 30 seconds. Add pea pods and stir-fry for 1 minute. Add straw mushrooms and stir-fry 1 minute. Remove the vegetables from the wok. Add half of the beef to the hot wok. Stir-fry for 2 to 3 minutes, or until done. Remove the beef. Stir-fry the remaining beef for 2 to 3 minutes. Return all the beef to the wok. Push beef from the center of the wok.

Add the sauce to the center of the wok and cook and stir about 30 seconds or until heated through. Return the vegetables to the wok, and stir all ingredients to coat with sauce. Cook and stir for 1 minute. Stir in peanuts. Garnish with green onions. Serve immediately.

*Hot bean sauce (4-ounce glass jars) can be found in the Asian section of most well-stocked supermarkets or in Asian food stores.

**Spiced chili oil is found in Asian food stores (5-ounce bottles).

Chapter 7

Poultry Dishes

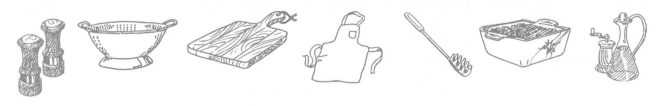

Everyone likes chicken and turkey. No doubt that's because they're tasty and easy to fix. Poultry is low in fat and cholesterol, if you are conscientious about removing the skin and trimming away any visible fat.

But most importantly, poultry is versatile. You can spread a grilled chicken breast with a bit of pesto, place it between two slices of bread with some lettuce and tomato, and you have a quick lunch. Or, you can go all out and create a dish that will fit right in with a gourmet dinner.

Broiling Chicken and Turkey

Chicken and Cornish hen halves, chicken and turkey pieces, ground poultry patties, and poultry kebobs can all be prepared by the quick, lower-fat method of broiling.

- Poultry can be broiled with the skin on or the skin removed. It can be marinated or rubbed with a seasoning mix before broiling.
- To prepare the poultry: Rinse with water and dry with paper towels. (Poultry should be rinsed and dried before marinating or applying a rub.) If desired, brush with a little vegetable oil and season.
- To prepare the broiler: If desired, line the broiler pan with foil to make cleanup easier. Adjust the rack so that the poultry will be 5 inches from the heating element if broiling poultry pieces, patties, or kebobs; 7 or 8 inches if broiling chicken halves; and 6 inches

if broiling Cornish hens. Preheat the broiler about 10 minutes.
- To broil: Place the poultry skin side down, if applicable. Turn once about halfway through the recommended broiling time unless otherwise noted. After turning, brush again with oil if desired. Poultry may also be basted with sauces while broiling. Turn with tongs, not a fork.
- To test doneness: the meat should no longer be pink and the juices should run clear when the poultry is cut to the center of the thickest part.

Roasting Poultry

- Chicken and turkey can be roasted stuffed or unstuffed. If stuffing the bird, do it just before roasting, for safety purposes; do not stuff and store ahead of time.
- To prepare the poultry: Remove the giblets, which are packed inside the

176

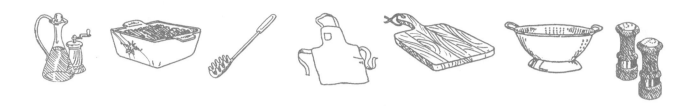

Poultry Safety

Poultry is highly perishable. To avoid the possibility of bacterial growth and contamination . . .

When purchasing and storing:

Always check the sell-by date.

Do not allow poultry to sit in a hot car. Make grocery shopping your last stop.

Refrigerate raw chicken promptly! Do not allow it to sit out on the countertop.

Poultry can be refrigerated in its store wrapping. To freeze chicken and turkey parts, unwrap, rinse, dry, and repackage in freezer-safe bags or freezer paper.

Freeze uncooked chicken if you will not be using it within two days.

Never freeze stuffed poultry.

When preparing:

Always wash your hands, countertops, cutting boards, dishes, and utensils well in hot soapy water after they have been in contact with raw chicken.

Rinse poultry and pat dry with paper towels (then discard them) before cooking

Do not place cooked chicken onto the same (unwashed) plate that held raw chicken.

Always marinate in the refrigerator.

Discard marinades after removing the poultry. It is best not to use them for basting or as sauces—if a recipe calls for them to be reused, bring them to a full boil for 1 minute first.

When serving and storing leftovers:

Remove all stuffing from poultry when you carve it to serve.

Serve immediately after cooking. Do not allow poultry to stand at room temperature for more than 1 hour to prevent the formation of bacteria.

Remove all meat from the bone to store. Use shallow containers to help it cool quickly and thoroughly.

Refrigerate leftover stuffing separately from leftover poultry.

Bring leftover gravy to a full boil before reusing.

body or neck cavity of some birds. If legs are locked in a plastic or metal lock, release them. Rinse the bird thoroughly, inside and out, and pat dry with paper towels. If the bird will not be stuffed, rub the inside cavity with salt.

- If stuffing the bird, see instructions on page 180.
- Tuck or twist the wing tips under the bottom of the turkey (to prevent their burning) and skewer in place. Tuck the drumsticks under the skin flap, if present, or tie in place together with the tail using white kitchen twine, or return to the metal lock.
- Place the bird breast side up on a rack in a shallow roasting pan and brush with cooking oil or melted butter. Herb rubs may be used if desired. Place a meat thermometer in the thickest part of the thigh muscle (whole bird) or into the thickest part of the breast if roasting only the whole breast. Do not allow the thermometer to touch bone.
- Preheat the oven to 325°F unless instructions state otherwise. Do not add water to the pan. Do not cover chicken. Do not cover turkey until it begins to turn golden brown, then make a loose tent of heavy-duty aluminum foil. If using a bird with a pop-up timer, check to see if its instructions differ.
- Baste the bird at least once an hour (unless it is a self-basting variety).

- Roast until the thermometer registers 180° to 185°F for whole birds. The bird is done when drumsticks rotate freely in their sockets and juices run clear when a long-tined fork is inserted in the bird near the leg joint. Roast until the thermometer reads 170°F for whole breasts only.
- After removing the bird from the oven, allow to stand about 10 minutes before carving if small, and 15 to 20 minutes if large. Cover loosely while standing.

Foil-Wrapped Turkey: A whole turkey can also be roasted wrapped entirely in foil, in a shorter time at a higher temperature. Place a large sheet of heavy-duty foil under the turkey, bring it over the breast, seal the edges, and tuck around the ends of the turkey. Place in a roasting pan, but it is not necessary to use a rack. Open the foil the last half hour to allow browning. This method will not produce as many drippings for gravy. Roast at 450°F according to the following time chart. Using a meat thermometer, check for doneness. The thermometer should read 180°F in the thighs; 160°F in the breast for a whole turkey.

WEIGHT IN POUNDS	ROASTING TIME IN HOURS
8 to 12	$2^{1}/_{4}$ to $2^{3}/_{4}$
13 to 20	3 to $3^{1}/_{2}$
20 to 24	$3^{1}/_{2}$ to $3^{3}/_{4}$

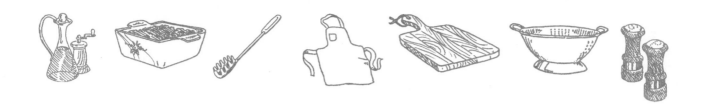

Thawing Poultry

Uncooked frozen poultry should be thawed in the refrigerator or in cold water. It *should not* be thawed simply by leaving out at room temperature, because there is a danger that bacteria will grow in it. Poultry can also be thawed in a microwave oven; check the manufacturer's directions for your oven.

To thaw in the refrigerator: Place the poultry in a dish or pan so that it will not drip on other food as it thaws. A whole chicken will thaw in about 24 hours; cut up pieces will thaw in 2 to 8 hours, depending on how it is packaged. Thaw in the original wrapping.

A turkey under 12 pounds will take 1 or 2 days; a 12- to 16-pound turkey will take 2 or 3 days; a 16- to 20-pound turkey will take 3 or 4 days; and a turkey over 20 pounds will take 4 to 5 days.

To thaw on the countertop in cold water: Place the chicken or turkey, in its original wrap or in a sealed plastic bag, in a large pan or bowl of cold water. Change the water every 30 minutes. It will take about 30 minutes per pound of poultry. Allow up to 2 hours to thaw a whole chicken. For turkey, allow up to 6 hours for under 12 pounds; up to 8 hours for 12 to 16 pounds; up to 10 hours for 16 to 20 pounds; and up to 12 hours for over 20 pounds.

Cooked frozen poultry should be thawed in the refrigerator. Allow up to 8 hours for cubed chicken or turkey, and up to 24 hours for whole pieces.

Stuffing a Turkey or Chicken

For purposes of food safety, poultry should not be stuffed until immediately before it is to be cooked. To save time, you can combine the dry ingredients in one pan and the wet ingredients in another ahead of time, and store separately.

- Use day old or dry bread to make stuffing, cutting it into ½-inch cubes. If you do not have dry bread, dry some fresh bread in a single layer on a cookie sheet or jellyroll pan in a 300°F oven for about 15 minutes. Allow to cool before cutting. (You can also cut the bread first and then dry the cubes; if using this method, stir once or twice.) Allow about 2 slices of bread per cup of dried cubes desired.
- Allow ½ to ¾ cup stuffing per pound of poultry.
- Spoon stuffing into the neck cavity, then pull the skin over the opening and secure with a metal skewer. Spoon stuffing into the body cavity, and tie the legs together in front of the opening or return to the metal lock. Fill both cavities lightly, and do not pack stuffing down. If it is too tightly packed, the stuffing might not reach a safe temperature, which should be at least 165°F at its center. You can measure stuffing temperature with an instant-read ther-

mometer or by inserting a regular meat thermometer into the center of the cavity and waiting about 5 minutes for an accurate reading.

- Additional stuffing, or an entire recipe of stuffing, can be baked in a lightly greased, covered casserole at 325°F for about 45 minutes.
- Always remove **all** the stuffing from the cooked turkey when the bird is carved to be served. For food safety, do not leave, store, or refrigerate leftover stuffing inside the cavity of the bird.

Basic Bread Stuffing

Yield: stuffs a 10-pound turkey

8 cups dry bread cubes
3 or 4 stalks celery (with leaves attached)
1 large onion, chopped
1 teaspoon salt
¼ teaspoon pepper
1 teaspoon poultry seasoning, or ¾
teaspoon sage and ¼ teaspoon thyme
½ cup butter
chicken broth or water (up to 1 cup)

Place the bread cubes in a very large bowl. Chop the celery, including the leaves, and toss it and the onion with the bread. Sprinkle with the seasonings and toss again. Melt the butter and drizzle over the bread mixture, tossing lightly. Add broth until the bread mixture is evenly moist but

(continued)

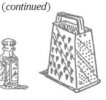

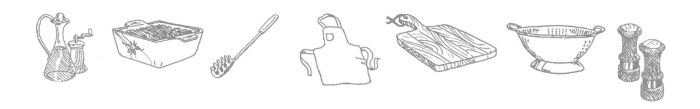

Cooking Poultry

Poultry should always be cooked to "well done."

For **chicken**, a meat thermometer should read 180°F for a whole chicken, 170°F for bone-in parts, and 160°F for boneless parts.

To check visually for doneness, pierce chicken with a long-tined fork in its thickest part. Juices should run clear. An alternative method is to make a small cut with a thin, sharp knife into the thickest part of the chicken. Meat should no longer be pink.

For **turkey**, a meat thermometer should read 180°F in the thighs and 170°F in the breast for a whole turkey. Stuffing should read 165°F. Turkey breasts should read 170°F when cooked alone.

Many turkeys have pop-up thermometers inserted in them when purchased, which pop up when the correct temperature is reached. Industry representatives say that these are accurate to within 2°F if they were placed correctly. We still recommend double checking with your own meat thermometer.

not wet; the amount will depend on how dry the cubes are.

To bake separately, place in a lightly greased 3-quart baking dish and bake uncovered at 325°F for about 45 minutes.

Variation: To make giblet stuffing, place the neck and giblets of a turkey or chicken in a small saucepan, along with 1 quartered onion and 1 stalk celery, cut into pieces. Cover with water. Salt lightly, bring to a boil, then reduce heat to a simmer for about 1 to 1½ hours, or until tender. Discard the neck and vegetables, chop the other organs finely, and strain the broth. Add up to ½ cup of the chopped giblets to the stuffing mix; use the broth instead of chicken broth or water to moisten.

Fruit Stuffing

Yield: stuffs a 10-pound turkey

6 cups dry bread cubes
1 cup chopped celery
½ cup chopped onion
2 cups chopped dried apples, apricots, cranberries, or mixed fruits; up to ½ cup can be raisins
1 teaspoon poultry seasoning, or ½ teaspoon sage and ½ teaspoon thyme
½ teaspoon salt
1 cup whole cranberry sauce or cranberry-orange relish
chicken broth or water (up to 1 cup)

Place the bread cubes in a very large bowl and add the celery, onion, fruit, and seasonings. Toss to combine. Add the cranberry sauce and stir to combine, then add broth until the mixture is evenly moist but not wet; the amount will depend on how dry the cubes are.

To bake separately, place in a lightly greased 3-quart baking dish and bake uncovered at 325°F for about 45 minutes.

Cornbread Sausage Stuffing

Yield: stuffs a 10-pound turkey

1 pound pork or turkey sausage
1 cup chopped onion
½ cup chopped celery
½ cup chopped green pepper
3 cups coarsely crumbled cornbread
3 cups dried bread cubes
1 teaspoon poultry seasoning, or ½ teaspoon sage and ½ teaspoon thyme
¼ teaspoon pepper
⅓ cup butter
chicken broth or water (up to 1 cup)

Brown together the sausage, onion, celery, and green pepper; drain well. Combine with the cornbread and bread cubes and sprinkle with seasonings. Melt the butter and drizzle over the stuffing, then add broth until the mixture is evenly moist but not wet.

(continued)

How to Carve a
Whole Turkey or Chicken

Allow the cooked bird to stand, covered with foil, for 15 minutes before carving. This allows the flesh to firm up.

1 Place the bird on a clean cutting board and remove any stuffing. Begin carving by pulling the drumsticks to the side of the body. Cut through the thigh meat on the side of the body and through the leg joint.

2 Cut the drumsticks and thighs apart at the joint.

3 If you wish to cut the meat from the drumsticks, hold them by the tip and slice parallel to the bone.

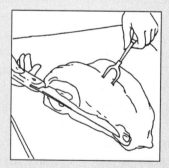

4 Pull the wings away from the body and cut through the wing joints.

5 Just above the wing joints, cut *horizontally* through to the ribs. This cut will be the bottom of the breast meat slices.

6 Beginning at the outer top of each breast side, slice down vertically to the horizontal cut, making slices of breast meat.

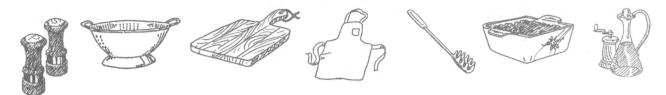

To bake separately, place in a lightly greased 3-quart baking dish and bake covered at 325°F for about 45 minutes.

Basic Poultry Gravy

pan drippings from roasted poultry
chicken broth (can be canned or bouillion)
flour
salt

For *each cup of gravy* you wish to make, you will need: 2 tablespoons poultry fat, 2 tablespoons instant or all-purpose flour, and 1 cup of drippings/broth mixture.*

To prepare the drippings: remove the poultry from the roasting pan and pour the drippings into a large glass measuring cup, using a large-holed strainer to remove large bits. Add 1/2 to 1 cup of chicken broth to the roasting pan and deglaze, scraping well to remove all bits. Add the deglazing broth to the measuring cup, straining if necessary to remove large bits. Let stand for a few minutes to allow the fat to rise to the top. Spoon or pour off as much fat as possible, reserving in another cup. Check to see that you have enough drippings/broth mixture to make the desired amount of gravy; if you do not, add more broth.

To make the gravy: *for each cup of gravy,* place 2 tablespoons fat in a saucepan and whisk in 2 tablespoons flour. Add 1 cup of drippings/broth to the flour mixture all at once. Cook and stir over medium heat until the mixture begins to boil and thickens, then cook for one minute more, stirring constantly. Add salt to taste.

Giblet Gravy: Place the neck and giblets of a turkey or chicken in a small saucepan, along with one quartered onion and one stalk celery, cut into pieces. Cover with water. Salt lightly, bring to a boil, then reduce heat to a simmer for about 1 to 1 1/2 hours, or until tender. Discard the neck and vegetables; chop the other organs finely, and strain the broth. Use the broth to make the gravy; if desired, chopped organs can be added to the gravy.

The ratio of drippings will affect the flavor of the gravy, but you will still have gravy of some sort even if you use mostly broth. Since the amount of drippings can vary, as can the amount of gravy people like to make, most instructions I've checked seem to be written somewhat like these.

Glazed Turkey Breast

Yield: 8 to 10 servings

4 to 6 pound turkey breast
glaze (see below)

Preheat the oven to 325°F. Place the turkey breast on a rack in a shallow roasting pan. Roast uncovered about 2 to 2½ hours, or until a meat thermometer reads 175°F. During the last 30 minutes of roasting, brush with one of the following glazes:

Honey Mustard Glaze: Combine ¼ cup honey and 2 tablespoons sweet or Dijon mustard.

Citrus Glaze: Combine ⅓ cup orange marmalade, 1 tablespoon lime juice, and ½ teaspoon dried mint leaves.

Herb-Roasted Turkey Breast

Yield: 8 to 10 servings

4 to 6 pound turkey breast
1 tablespoon chopped fresh sage
½ tablespoon chopped fresh thyme
½ tablespoon chopped fresh marjoram
vegetable oil
salt and pepper

Preheat the oven to 325°F.
Gently loosen the skin of the turkey breast on both sides, but do not detach it from the breast bone. Mix the chopped herbs together and gently spread them under the skin. Place the turkey breast skin side up on a rack in a shallow roasting pan. Rub the turkey skin generously with oil, then sprinkle with salt and pepper.

Roast the turkey uncovered about 2 to 2½ hours, or until a meat thermometer reads 175°F. Baste with pan drippings or additional oil during the last half hour of roasting.

Turkey Types

Turkey hens are female turkeys and usually weigh up to 15 pounds.

Turkey toms are male and usually weigh from 15 pounds and up.

The two are very similar in tenderness and ratio of white to dark meat. Choose on the basis of size.

For holiday turkeys, allow about 1 pound per person if you want leftovers.

Turkey Breast Southwestern Style

Yield: 8 to 10 servings

4 to 6 pound turkey breast
2 cloves garlic, finely minced
1 tablespoon fresh minced cilantro
$\frac{1}{2}$ teaspoon sage
$\frac{1}{2}$ teaspoon oregano
vegetable oil
salt and pepper

Dressing:

1 pound pork sausage
1 cup chopped onion
$\frac{1}{2}$ cup chopped celery
3 cups coarsely crumbled cornbread
3 cups dried bread cubes
1 tablespoon fresh chopped cilantro
1 tablespoon fresh chopped parsley
1 teaspoon poultry seasoning, or $\frac{1}{2}$
    teaspoon sage and $\frac{1}{2}$ teaspoon thyme
$\frac{1}{2}$ teaspoon salt
$\frac{1}{4}$ teaspoon pepper
2 eggs, lightly beaten
1 cup chicken broth or water
$\frac{1}{4}$ cup seeded and chopped jalapeño
    peppers

Preheat the oven to 325°F.

Gently loosen the skin of the turkey breast on both sides, but do not detach it from the breast bone. Mix the garlic, cilantro, sage, and oregano together and gently spread them under the skin. Place the turkey breast skin side up on a rack in a shallow roasting pan. Rub the turkey skin generously with oil, then sprinkle with salt and pepper. Roast uncovered about 2 to $2\frac{1}{2}$ hours, or until a meat thermometer reads 175°F. Baste with pan drippings or additional oil during the last half hour of roasting.

To prepare the dressing: Brown together the sausage, onion, and celery; drain well. Combine with the cornbread and bread cubes and sprinkle with the herbs and seasonings. Mix in the eggs, broth, and jalapeño peppers. Place in a lightly greased 3 quart baking dish and bake covered at 325°F for the last hour the turkey roasts; dressing will take 50 to 60 minutes.

Oven-Fried Turkey Tenderloins

Servings: 4

2 tablespoons honey
1 tablespoon Dijon mustard
$\frac{1}{4}$ teaspoon paprika
$\frac{1}{8}$ teaspoon onion powder
$\frac{2}{3}$ cup fine corn flake crumbs
$\frac{1}{3}$ cup finely chopped pecans
4 small turkey tenderloins
    (about 6 ounces each)

Preheat oven to 400°F.

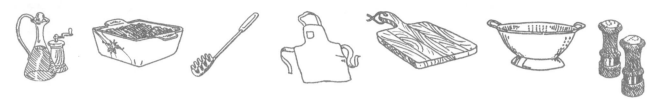

Combine honey, mustard, paprika, and onion powder in a shallow bowl, mixing well. Combine corn flake crumbs and pecans in another shallow bowl. With a basting brush, brush the tenderloins all over with the honey-mustard mixture, then roll in the corn flake mixture. Place the tenderloins on a cookie sheet that has been sprayed with cooking oil. Allow to stand for about 10 minutes.

When ready to bake, spray the pieces lightly with cooking oil spray and bake for 30 minutes, or until the turkey is no longer pink.

Turkey Tuscan

Servings: 4

> 1 medium onion
> 6 or more cloves garlic, to taste
> 2 16-ounce cans whole Italian tomatoes
> 1 tablespoon olive oil
> 1 to 1¼ pounds turkey tenderloins
> ½ cup sliced black olives
> ¼ cup sun-dried tomatoes, soaked in ½
>   cup very hot water
> 1 tablespoon balsamic vinegar
> 2 teaspoons Italian seasoning
> ⅛ teaspoon red pepper flakes
> salt and pepper to taste

Peel and slice the onion thinly; peel the garlic cloves and halve. Halve the tomatoes, reserving the liquid. In a large skillet with a tight-fitting lid, heat olive oil over medium heat. Add the turkey and brown on all sides. Remove and set aside. Add the onions and garlic to the skillet and cook until the onion is softened, about 3 minutes.

Add the tomatoes and their liquid to the skillet along with olives, *drained* sun-dried tomatoes, vinegar, and seasonings. Return the turkey to the skillet. Bring to a boil, then cover and reduce the heat. Simmer about 40 minutes, or until the tenderloins are fully cooked. Serve with pasta, if desired.

Salsa Turkey

Servings: 4

> 1 red bell pepper
> 1 green bell pepper
> 1 to 1¼ pounds turkey cutlets
> vegetable oil
> salt and pepper to taste
> 1 clove garlic, minced
> ⅛ teaspoon cumin
> ⅛ teaspoon oregano
> 1 tablespoon chopped fresh parsley
> 1 cup chunky salsa
> ½ cup shredded Cheddar cheese
> 1 tablespoon chopped fresh cilantro

Preheat the oven to 350°F.

Seed the peppers and slice them in about ¼-inch slices. Slice the cutlets into ¼-inch thick slices. In a medium skillet, heat about 1 tablespoon of oil and brown the

(continued)

cutlets quickly on both sides, a few at a time, and remove. Add more oil if necessary to complete. Transfer the cutlets to a round or oval shallow baking dish.

Place the pepper rings on the turkey, and season with salt and pepper. Stir the garlic and herbs into the salsa, then spread over the turkey and peppers. Cover and bake for 30 to 40 minutes, or until the turkey is cooked.

Remove from the oven and sprinkle with the cheese, then return to the oven uncovered and allow the cheese to melt. Before serving, sprinkle with cilantro. Serve with rice, if desired.

Turkey Schnitzel

Servings: 4

> 1 egg
> ²⁄₃ cup dry bread crumbs
> ¼ cup flour
> ¼ teaspoon pepper
> 1 pound turkey cutlets, cut ⅛- to
>   ¼-inch thick
> ¼ cup butter
> 2 tablespoons vegetable oil
> 1 lemon, cut in wedges

In a small shallow dish, beat the egg lightly. In another small shallow dish, combine the bread crumbs, flour, and pepper. Bread the cutlets on both sides by dipping first in the egg, then in the crumb

mixture. (It is not necessary to use all of the breading mixture.) Set cutlets aside on a plate as they are completed.

In a large skillet, heat half the butter and half the oil over medium heat. When it is hot, cook half the cutlets, turning after 2 minutes, then turning again and continuing to cook until done, about an additional 5 minutes. Remove and repeat with the remaining butter and cutlets. Before serving, squeeze the lemon over the cutlets.

Jerky Turkey Kebobs

Servings: 4

> about 2 pounds turkey thighs, skinned,
>   boned, and cut into 1-inch cubes
>   (or 1 pound boneless, skinless turkey
>   dark meat)

Jamaican Marinade:
¼ cup lime juice
1 tablespoon soy sauce
4 chopped green onions
1 jalapeño pepper, seeded
2 cloves garlic, peeled
1 teaspoon each ginger, allspice, thyme,
   cumin, ground black pepper
½ cup water

Combine the marinade ingredients in a blender and purée until smooth. Pour into a glass bowl, add the turkey cubes, and stir to coat well. Cover and refrigerate 4 to 5 hours, stirring occasionally.

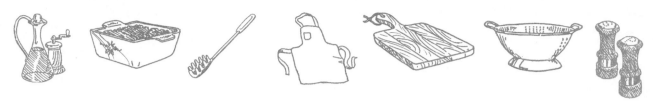

When ready to cook, preheat the broiler. Remove the turkey from the marinade and reserve the marinade. Thread the turkey onto 4 metal skewers. Spray the broiler pan with cooking oil spray, place the skewers on it, and broil 5 inches from the heat a total of 10 to 12 minutes, turning once. Meanwhile, bring the reserved marinade to a full boil and allow to boil for 1 minute. Keep warm and serve on the side as a sauce.

Thanksgiving in a Loaf

Servings: 6

²/₃ cup packaged herbed bread stuffing
1¹/₂ pounds lean ground turkey
1 small potato, grated
¹/₂ cup chopped onion
¹/₂ cup chopped celery
1 egg
¹/₄ teaspoon poultry seasoning
¹/₂ teaspoon salt
¹/₄ teaspoon pepper

Preheat oven to 350°F.

If the packaged stuffing mix is cubed rather than crumbed, crush it slightly. Combine it with the meat, grated potatoes, onion, and celery in a bowl. Beat the egg lightly and add to the meat mixture with the seasonings, mixing well. Shape into a loaf and turn into an appropriately sized lightly greased baking dish. Bake 50 to 60 minutes, or until the juices run clear. Serve with gravy, if desired.

Citrus-Glazed Roasted Chicken

Servings: 6

1 lemon
1 lime
2 tablespoons dry white wine
2 tablespoons packed brown sugar
3 to 3¹/₂ pound whole broiler-fryer chicken
vegetable oil
¹/₄ teaspoon rosemary
¹/₈ teaspoon tarragon
¹/₈ teaspoon thyme
¹/₂ teaspoon salt
¹/₄ teaspoon pepper

Preheat the oven to 375°F.

Prepare the Glaze: Cut the lemon and lime in half. Squeeze *one half of each* to obtain up to 2 tablespoons of juice; discard any extra juice, but reserve the unsqueezed citrus halves. Combine the juice, wine, and brown sugar; set aside.

Prepare the chicken for roasting as directed on page 176. Place the reserved citrus halves in the body cavity. Rub the skin lightly with oil, then rub with the herbs, salt, and pepper. Place on the rack of a shallow roasting pan. Roast for 1¹/₄ to 1³/₄ hours, or until meat thermometer reads 185°F. During the last 30 minutes of roasting, brush at least twice with the glaze.

Herb-Roasted Chicken with Wine Gravy

Servings: 6

1/4 cup butter
2 cloves garlic, finely minced
1 tablespoon dry mustard
1/2 teaspoon thyme
1/2 teaspoon tarragon
1/2 teaspoon salt
1/4 teaspoon pepper
3 to 3 1/2 pound whole broiler-fryer chicken
1 onion, quartered
1 bay leaf
dry white wine and/or chicken broth
2 tablespoons flour

Preheat the oven to 350°F.

Soften the butter and combine it in a small bowl with the garlic, mustard, thyme, tarragon, salt, and pepper. Prepare the chicken for roasting using the instructions on page 176. Place the chicken breast side up on the rack of a shallow roasting pan. Put the onion and bay leaf in the body cavity (discard after cooking). Gently separate the skin from the breast and sides of the chicken. Spread half the butter-herb mixture under the skin. Tuck the wings under the chicken and tie the legs. Rub about half of the remaining butter mixture on the skin of the chicken. Cover the chicken with a loose foil tent and place in the oven.

After 45 minutes, brush the chicken with the remaining butter-herb mixture. Total roasting time will be about 1 1/2 hours, or until the meat thermometer reads 180°F. After removing the chicken from the oven, allow it to stand, covered, for 15 minutes before carving.

Make the gravy: Pour the juices from the pan into a glass measuring cup and skim the fat from the top. Add dry white wine or chicken broth (or a combination) to make 1 3/4 cups. Pour about a third of the liquid into a small saucepan. Stir in the flour and cook for 1 minute over medium-low heat. Slowly whisk in the additional liquid, raise the heat to medium and cook, stirring constantly, until the gravy boils and thickens. Season to taste.

Oven-Braised Chicken

Servings: 4 to 6

3-pound broiler-fryer, cut up
1/3 cup flour
1/2 teaspoon paprika
1 teaspoon salt
1/2 teaspoon pepper
2 tablespoons vegetable oil or butter
water

Preheat oven to 350°F.

Rinse the chicken pieces and pat dry. Place the flour and seasonings in a plastic

(continued)

How to Bone a Chicken Breast

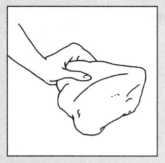

1 Place the breast skin side down on a clean cutting board.

The wider end should be nearest you.

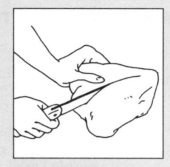

2 Cut through the white cartilage, starting from the V at the neck end.

3 Pick the breast up in both hands and bend the sides back to pop out the keel bone.

4 Loosen the meat from the bone. Run your thumbs around both sides and pull out the bone and cartilage.

5 Cut or pull the breast meat from the bone by inserting the tip of the knife close to the long rib bone. Work one side at a time

6 Cut and scrape all meat from the bone. Work from the ends of the wishbone.

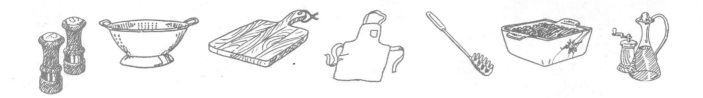

food bag and dredge the chicken pieces in the mixture, two pieces at a time. As they are completed, place on a platter. In a large skillet, heat about 2 tablespoons of oil or butter over medium heat. Brown the chicken pieces on all sides, about 15 minutes.

Remove the chicken to a large baking dish or a roaster. Deglaze the skillet with about ½ cup water and add to the baking dish. Cover and bake for about 1 hour, or until the juices run clear. Check during baking and add more water if necessary.

Southern Baked Chicken

Servings: 4 to 6

3 to 3½ pound broiler-fryer, cut up
½ teaspoon salt
¼ teaspoon pepper
2 tablespoons molasses
2 tablespoons brown mustard
2 tablespoons vinegar
¼ teaspoon celery salt
¼ teaspoon onion powder

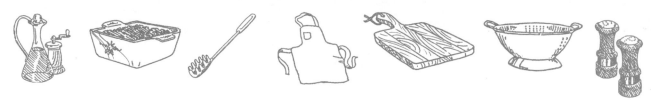

Preheat oven to 400°F.

Rinse the chicken pieces and pat dry. With your hands, rub the salt and pepper over the chicken. In a small bowl, combine the molasses, brown mustard, vinegar, celery salt, and onion powder. Coat the chicken thoroughly with the molasses mixture, using your hands to rub it over the pieces. Place the chicken in a large lightly greased roasting pan (do not crowd) and bake 40 to 45 minutes, or until the juices run clear. Turn with tongs halfway through baking time.

Southern Fried Chicken

Servings: 4 to 6

3 to 3½ pound broiler-fryer, cut into pieces
1 cup buttermilk
1 cup flour
⅓ cup yellow cornmeal
½ teaspoon celery salt
½ teaspoon onion powder
1 teaspoon paprika
1 teaspoon salt
½ teaspoon pepper
vegetable oil for frying

Rinse the chicken pieces and pat dry. Place them in a bowl and pour the buttermilk over the chicken; allow to sit in the refrigerator for 30 minutes. In a large plastic food bag, combine the flour, cornmeal, spices, and seasonings. Remove the chicken pieces from the milk (shake, but don't pat dry), and dredge in the flour two at a time. As they are done, place on a rack and allow

(continued)

Kinds of Chicken

Broiler-fryers usually weigh from 3 to 3½ pounds. They are an all-purpose, tender chicken and can be broiled, fried, or roasted.

Roasting chickens are older and larger than broiler-fryers, usually weighing from 4 to 6 pounds. They are not as tender as broiler-fryers and should not be broiled or fried. But when cooked by a slow method like roasting, they become tender and flavorful.

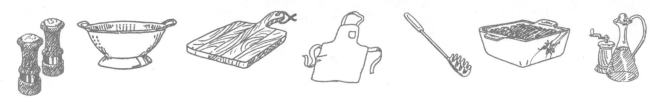

Kinds of Chicken

Stewing chickens are also usually between 4 and 6 pounds. They are more mature and less tender birds, and should be cooked by simmering or stewing, as in soups or stews, or to make cut up chicken for recipes.

Cornish hens, also called Rock Cornish game hens, weigh only 1 to 1½ pounds and are all white meat.

to sit until the flour is pastelike, about 30 minutes.

In a large, heavy skillet (preferably cast iron), add oil to a depth of about ¾ inch. Heat the oil over medium-high heat. (The oil is ready when it's 350°F, or when a cube of white bread dropped in the oil browns in about 1 minute.) Place chicken in the oil *carefully,* skin side down. Do not crowd; fry in two batches if necessary. Cook for about 15 minutes, turning once to brown on both sides. Reduce heat to medium and cover; allow to cook for an additional 20 minutes. Uncover (to crisp the chicken) and cook for 10 minutes more or until the juices of the largest pieces run clear, or their temperature measured with a meat thermometer is about 185°F. Drain on paper towels before serving.

Oven-Fried Chicken

Servings: 4 to 6

> 6 boneless, skinless chicken breasts, or a
>   3 to 3½ pound broiler-fryer, cut into
>   pieces and skin removed
> ⅓ cup flour
> ½ teaspoon salt
> ¼ teaspoon pepper
> 1 egg
> 1 tablespoon water
> 1 cup fine corn flake crumbs or crisp
>   rice cereal crumbs
> 3 tablespoons melted butter

How to Quarter a Whole Chicken

Place the chicken breast side up on a clean cutting board.

  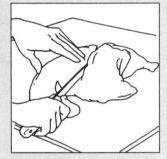

1 Cut in half along the breastbone with a sharp knife.

2 Pull the two halves apart. Break the ribs away from the backbone and finish cutting through the skin and meat with a knife to separate the halves.

3 Separate the thigh quarter from the breast quarter. Bend to locate the joint. Cut through the body above the joint and on through the joint to separate.

Preheat oven to 375°F.

Rinse the chicken pieces and pat dry. Place the flour, salt, and pepper in a sealable plastic food bag and add the chicken pieces; coat evenly. Remove the chicken from the bag and shake off any excess flour. In a shallow bowl, beat the egg lightly with the water. In another shallow bowl, place the crumbs. Coat the chicken by dipping in the egg then rolling in the crumbs.

Place the pieces on a cookie sheet that has been well sprayed with cooking oil spray.

Drizzle with the butter. Bake for about 30 minutes for the boneless breasts or 50 minutes for the chicken pieces, or until the meat of the thickest pieces is no longer pink. Do not turn while baking.

Chicken Fingers

Servings: 4 to 6

> 1 to 1¼ pounds chicken breast tenders, or
>   boneless, skinless chicken breasts
> 1 cup flour
> 1 teaspoon salt
> 1 cup fine corn flake crumbs, or fine
>   saltine cracker crumbs
> 2 eggs
> 2 tablespoons water
> vegetable oil

Preheat the oven to 450°F.

If using chicken breasts, cut the chicken into strips about ½ x 3 inches. In a plastic food bag, combine the flour and salt. In a shallow dish place the corn flake crumbs; in a similar dish beat the eggs well with the water. Dredge the chicken strips first in the flour, coating well on all sides. Then one at a time, dip in the egg and roll in the crumb mixture. Place on a rack as they are completed.

In a large skillet, heat about ⅛ inch vegetable oil over medium-high heat. Brown half the fingers until golden on all sides, about 5 minutes, then transfer them to a cookie sheet. Add more oil to the skillet if necessary, allow to heat, and repeat with the second half of the fingers. When all fingers have been browned, place in the hot oven for 5 to 8 minutes, or until crispy.

Serve with dipping sauces, such as bottled barbecue sauce or honey mustard sauce. (Honey mustard sauce can be made easily by combining 2 parts honey to 1 part sweet mustard.)

Curry-Glazed Chicken Breasts

Servings: 6

> 6 half chicken breasts, bone in, with skins
> ¼ cup orange marmalade
> 1 teaspoon curry powder
> ⅛ teaspoon ginger
> ⅛ teaspoon cumin
> ⅛ teaspoon cayenne pepper

Preheat the oven to 350°F.

Rinse the chicken breasts and pat dry. Place on the rack of a shallow roasting pan and roast for about 40 minutes, or until the juices run clear. Whisk together all the remaining ingredients. Brush the chicken with the glaze after the chicken has roasted for 10 minutes, and again after 20 minutes.

Broiled Chicken Leg Quarters

Servings: 4

> ¼ cup butter
> 1 tablespoon finely minced shallots
> 1 clove garlic, minced
> ¾ teaspoon parsley flakes

(continued)

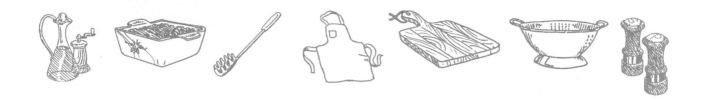

Cubed, Cooked Chicken

1 whole chicken breast, bone in (about 1½ pounds) will yield about 2 cups of cubed cooked white meat chicken.

1 pound of boneless, skinless breasts will yield about 2¾ cups of cubed cooked white meat chicken.

1 whole broiler-fryer (about 3 to 3½ pounds) will make about 2½ to 3 cups of cubed cooked white and dark meat chicken.

Cooked chicken in cubes, strips, and other shapes is available prepackaged in the meat departments of most grocery stores. Of course, the cost per pound is much higher than the cost of making your own cooked chicken cubes or strips at home.

To make your own quickly, place boneless, skinless chicken breasts in a large saucepan or skillet. Cover the chicken with water, bring to a boil, and simmer about 15 minutes, or until chicken is no longer pink. Drain, cool, and cut up.

¹/₄ teaspoon salt
¹/₈ teaspoon pepper
4 chicken leg quarters with thighs

Preheat the broiler and adjust the rack so the chicken will be about 8 inches from the heating element.

Soften the butter and combine with the herbs and seasonings. Gently loosen the skin on the thigh end of each chicken piece and spread each with a quarter of the butter-herb mixture. Spread the mixture under the skin by pressing gently on the top of the skin. Place the prepared chicken on the broiler *skin side up.* Total broiling time will be 35 to 45 minutes; turn the quarters after 20 minutes.

Chicken Breasts in Fruit Sauce

Servings: 4

1 medium onion, sliced
1 stalk celery with leaves, cut in 4 pieces
¹/₄ teaspoon salt
2 peppercorns or ¹/₈ teaspoon cracked pepper
4 boneless, skinless chicken breasts
1 cooking apple, pared and diced
²/₃ cup orange juice
¹/₄ cup dried cranberries or raisins
1 tablespoon orange marmalade or apple jelly
¹/₈ teaspoon ground ginger

In a large skillet with a lid, place the onion slices, celery salt, and pepper, and enough water to cover the chicken breasts. Bring to a boil, carefully add the breasts, then cover loosely and reduce the heat to a simmer. Simmer about 15 minutes, or until the chicken is no longer pink in the middle.

Meanwhile, combine the apple, orange juice, cranberries, marmalade, and ginger in a small saucepan and cook until apples are tender but not mushy. When the chicken is done, remove it from the liquid, place on a serving plate and spoon the sauce over the chicken.

Brie-Stuffed Chicken Breasts

Servings: 4

olive oil
1¹/₂ cups thinly sliced onion
2 cloves garlic, peeled and thinly sliced
²/₃ cup dry white wine
2 ounces Brie cheese
¹/₂ teaspoon salt
¹/₄ teaspoon pepper
4 half chicken breasts, bone in and skin on
1 tablespoon butter, melted

In a large skillet, heat about 1 teaspoon olive oil over medium heat. Add the onions and sauté about 3 minutes until golden

(continued)

How to Cut Up a Whole Chicken

1 Place the chicken breast side up on a clean cutting board. Cut through the skin and meat between the thighs and tail end of the body.

2 Grasp the legs in your hands and bend them back, while lifting the chicken, until the hip joints pop out.

3 Cut the thigh from the body by cutting through the joint and remaining skin. The tip of the knife should point toward the tail end of the bird while making this cut.

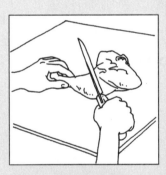   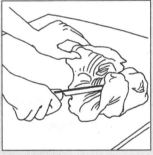

4 Separate the legs and thighs. Bend the joint to locate it, then cut through it.

5 Cut the wings from the body. Pull the wings out slightly from the body and cut down through the body near the wing and through the joint, following its shape with the knife. Cut from the top down.

6 Separate the breast from the back. Hold the chicken up with its neck end on the board and cut through the joints along each side of the rib cage. Cut from the top toward the board.

7 Place the breast skin side down and cut through the white cartilage at the V of the neck. Grasp in both hands and bend the sides back to pop out the keel bone. Remove it. Cut the breast in half through the wishbone using the knife or a kitchen scissors.

brown. Add the sliced garlic and sauté an additional 5 minutes. Stir in the wine and cook about 5 minutes or until the wine is almost evaporated. Remove the onion mixture to a bowl. Cut the Brie into small pieces (rind should be removed) and stir into the onion mixture along with the salt and pepper; allow to cool slightly.

Preheat the oven to 375°F. Remove the bones (but not the skins) from the chicken breasts. Loosen the skin from the breasts by working your fingers between the skin and the meat and gently separating them; leave the skin attached around 3 edges. Stuff a quarter of the onion-Brie mixture under the skin of each breast.

Place the chicken in a greased square baking pan, skin side up, and drizzle with the butter. Bake uncovered about 50 minutes, or until the chicken is no longer pink when cut.

Pan-Grilled Chicken Ancho

Servings: 4

4 boneless, skinless chicken breasts

Marinade:
2 teaspoons minced shallots
1 teaspoon minced garlic
2 tablespoons ground ancho chili peppers*
juice of 1 lime
½ cup olive oil
2 teaspoons salt

Place the chicken breasts between two pieces of plastic wrap and pound lightly with the flat side of a meat mallet to flatten slightly. Combine all other ingredients in a glass dish and place the chicken breasts in it, turning to coat thoroughly. Allow to marinate 2 to 3 hours in refrigerator, covered.

When ready to cook, spray a heavy skillet or stovetop grill pan with cooking oil spray and heat to medium-high. Remove the chicken from the marinade and pat dry; discard the marinade. Cook the chicken breasts for a total of 10 to 12 minutes, turning once, or until juices run clear.

*The ancho chili pepper, the dried form of the Mexican poblano chili pepper, can be purchased in a well-stocked supermarket or specialty food shop.

Chicken Piccata

Servings: 4

4 boneless, skinless chicken breasts
3 tablespoons flour
2 teaspoons lemon pepper
1 teaspoon salt
butter
¼ cup dry sherry, white wine, or chicken broth
¼ cup lemon juice
1 tablespoon capers
1 lemon, cut into wedges

Slice the chicken breasts crosswise into pieces about ¼-inch thick. Place them between pieces of plastic wrap, and with a meat mallet gently flatten to scallops about ⅛-inch thick. Dredge the chicken lightly in a mixture of the flour, pepper, and salt. In a large skillet, heat about 1 tablespoon of butter and quickly sauté the scallops several at a time, until golden brown on both sides, about 4 or 5 minutes. Continue until all are done, adding more butter to the skillet as necessary. As scallops are cooked, transfer to a plate and keep warm.

When all are done, add the wine and lemon juice to the skillet. Stir gently and cook about 2 minutes, until the sauce thickens a little. Stir in the capers and spoon the sauce over the scallops. Serve with lemon wedges.

Chicken Paprikash à la Vasiloff

Servings: about 6

butter, up to ½ cup
1 cup finely chopped onion
3 to 3½ pound broiler-fryer
  chicken, cut up
1¼ teaspoons salt, divided
2 teaspoons paprika, divided
1 cup water

¼ teaspoon pepper
dash of cayenne
chicken broth
2 tablespoons flour
½ cup sour cream

In a large skillet with a lid, melt about 2 tablespoons of butter over medium-high heat, sauté the onions until lightly browned. Remove from the pan and reserve. Add more butter to the skillet, about 2 tablespoons at a time as needed, and brown the chicken pieces on all sides. Return the onions to the skillet, and sprinkle with 1 teaspoon of salt and 1 teaspoon of paprika; cover, and cook over low heat for about 30 minutes.

Add the water, ¼ teaspoon salt, pepper, cayenne, and 1 teaspoon paprika to the skillet. Bring to a boil, then reduce the heat, cover, and simmer about 30 minutes more, or until the chicken is done.

Remove the chicken and keep warm. Add enough chicken broth to the skillet to make about 1¾ cups liquid. Blend the flour with ¼ cup water, then add to the skillet. Cook and stir until thickened, then stir in the sour cream. Serve the sauce over the chicken.

Coq au Vin

Servings: 4 to 6

3 to 3½ pound broiler-fryer, cut into pieces
¼ cup flour
½ teaspoon salt
¼ teaspoon pepper
2 tablespoons butter
¼ cup brandy
2 cloves garlic, crushed
12 pearl onions, peeled
1 cup dry red wine
8 ounces small fresh whole mushrooms
2 teaspoons fresh chopped thyme
1 bay leaf

Rinse the chicken pieces and pat dry. Combine the flour, salt, and pepper in a plastic food bag and shake the chicken pieces 2 at a time until coated, shaking off excess flour as you remove them from the bag. In a large skillet, melt the butter over medium-high heat and brown the chicken on both sides. Turn off the heat, add the brandy, and *carefully* ignite; allow the alcohol to burn off. Remove the chicken and set aside.

Reheat the skillet and add the garlic and peeled onions. Cook for about 2 minutes but do not allow to brown. Add the wine to the skillet and stir in the mushrooms, thyme, and bay leaf.

At this point you can: Return the chicken to the skillet, cover, and simmer for 45 minutes to 1 hour, or until the chicken is tender; or you can preheat the oven to 350°F, place the chicken pieces in a large baking dish, and pour the mushroom mixture over top. Cover tightly and bake for 45 minutes to 1 hour, or until the chicken is tender. Serve with egg noodles, if desired.

Chicken Cacciatore

Servings: 6

3 to 3½ pound broiler-fryer, cut into pieces
½ cup flour
2 tablespoons olive oil
2 cloves garlic, crushed
2 16-ounce cans diced tomatoes
½ cup dry red wine, optional
2 onions, thinly sliced
8 ounces fresh sliced mushrooms*
1 teaspoon oregano
½ teaspoon basil
½ teaspoon celery seed
½ teaspoon salt

Rinse the chicken pieces and pat dry. Dredge in flour. Heat the oil in a large skillet over medium-high heat and brown the chicken well on both sides, about 15 to 20 minutes.

Drain excess oil. Add the garlic to the skillet and cook about 2 minutes, but do not brown. Stir in the tomatoes, wine, onions, mushrooms, herbs, celery seed, and salt. Heat to boiling, then reduce heat and cover. Simmer for 30 to 40 minutes, or until

the largest pieces of chicken are no longer pink in the center. Serve with spaghetti noodles, if desired.

*One 8-ounce can of mushrooms, undrained, may be substituted.

Busy Day Chicken 'n' Gravy

Servings: 4

2 tablespoons flour
¹/₂ teaspoon paprika
¹/₂ teaspoon pepper
4 chicken breast halves, bone in, or any 4 chicken pieces of your choice
1 tablespoon vegetable oil
4 ounces frozen pearl onions
1 can cream of chicken soup
1 can cream of onion soup
¹/₂ teaspoon poultry seasoning

Preheat the oven to 350°F.

Mix together the flour, paprika, and pepper in a plastic food bag. Rinse the chicken pieces and pat dry, then shake in the flour mixture. Heat vegetable oil in a medium skillet over medium-high heat. Brown the chicken on both sides, about 10 minutes total.

Place the chicken pieces in a deep-sided baking dish; they should fit snugly but without stacking. Sprinkle with the onions. Combine the soups and poultry seasoning

and add to the skillet, scraping to remove all bits. Pour over the chicken. Cover and bake for about 1 to 1¹/₄ hours, or until the largest pieces are no longer pink in the center. The chicken makes a gravy-type sauce as it bakes. Serve with mashed potatoes if desired.

Elegant Skewered Chicken

Servings: 4

Marinade:
¹/₂ cup chopped green onions
¹/₃ cup olive oil
¹/₄ cup balsamic vinegar
1 tablespoon Worcestershire sauce
2 cloves garlic, minced
1 teaspoon basil

Kebobs:
4 boneless, skinless chicken breasts, cut into 1 to 1¹/₂ inch cubes
4 whole Portobello mushrooms, quartered
8 medium button mushroom caps
8 pearl onions, peeled
8 cherry tomatoes

Combine the marinade ingredients. Place the chicken cubes, mushrooms, and onions in a glass bowl or sealing plastic food bag and pour the marinade over, turning to coat well. Refrigerate for 2 to 4 hours.

(continued)

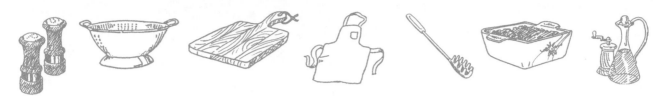

When ready to cook, preheat the broiler. Remove the ingredients from the marinade, shake off any excess, and thread them, along with the cherry tomatoes, onto four metal skewers. Discard the marinade. Spray the broiler pan with cooking oil and place the skewers on it. Broil 5 inches from the heat for a total of about 12 minutes, turning once.

Thai Wings

Servings: 4

> 3 pounds chicken wings
> 1 recipe marinade (see below)

Prepare the wings by cutting off the tips with a sharp knife and discarding, then dividing the wing into two sections at the joint. Prepare the marinade according to instructions, then place the marinade and wings in a sealable plastic food bag or a covered glass dish and marinate in the refrigerator, turning often.

When ready to cook, remove wings from the marinade and discard the marinade; if you want additional marinade for basting, double the recipe, and reserve half of it in a separate dish. Spray the broiler pan with cooking oil spray and place the wings on it; do not crowd. Broil 5 inches from the heating element, 10 to 15 minutes, turning once.

Thai Marinade: Combine 3 tablespoons creamy peanut butter, 3 tablespoons water, 1 tablespoon soy sauce, 1 tablespoon lemon juice, 2 teaspoons brown sugar, 1 finely chopped green onion, and 1 or 2 drops hot pepper sauce. Add wings and marinate in the refrigerator 2 to 12 hours.

Barbecue in a Loaf

Servings: 6

> 1½ pounds lean ground chicken
> 1 cup dry bread crumbs
> ½ cup chopped onion
> ⅓ cup shredded carrot
> ⅓ cup finely chopped celery
> 1 egg
> 2 teaspoons Worcestershire sauce
> ¾ cup bottled barbecue sauce, divided
> 1 tablespoon brown sugar
> ½ teaspoon salt
> ½ teaspoon pepper

Preheat oven to 350°F.

In a bowl, combine the chicken, bread crumbs, and vegetables. Beat the egg lightly and combine with the Worcestershire sauce, ½ cup barbecue sauce, and brown sugar. Add to the meat mixture along with the salt and pepper and combine well. Shape into a loaf and place in a lightly greased baking dish. Spread about ¼ cup of barbecue sauce on top. Bake for 50 minutes to an hour, or until juices run clear.

Oven Barbecued Cornish Hens

Servings: 4

2 Cornish hens, about 24 ounces each
salt and pepper
2 tablespoons frozen orange juice
    concentrate
1/4 cup white wine vinegar
2 tablespoons tomato paste
1 tablespoon grated orange zest
2 tablespoons vegetable oil

Preheat the oven to 350°F.

Cut the hens in half, using a kitchen scissors, starting at the tail and cutting along the backbone and breastbone. Sprinkle the halves with salt and pepper and place on the rack of a roasting pan. Combine the orange juice, vinegar, tomato paste, zest, and oil, and brush over both sides of the hens. Bake for 1 to 1 1/4 hours brushing the poultry with the sauce and turning occasionally as it bakes. Hens are done when meat is no longer pink at the center of the thigh.

Variation: Use a honey apple glaze: Combine 1/4 cup plus 2 tablespoons honey, 3 tablespoons apple juice, 1 1/2 tablespoons fresh lemon juice, 1 1/2 teaspoons soy sauce, and 1 teaspoon grated lemon zest. Prepare and bake as directed.

Where's the Fat?

Even though it's a pain to remove the skin from chicken, and you feel like you're missing out by not eating that crunchy, satisfying skin, consider these figures:

- A 1/2- pound chicken breast—one serving— without the skin contains 9 grams of fat.
- A 1/2- pound serving from a whole chicken with the skin removed contains 13 grams of fat.
- A 1/2- pound serving from a whole chicken with the skin left on contains 38 grams of fat.

Souper Chicken

Servings: 4 to 6

1 can cream of mushroom soup
1 can cream of chicken soup
1 can cream of celery soup
⅔ cup chopped celery
1 cup long-grain rice
3–3½ pound chicken, cut up, or 6 pieces chicken
¼ cup butter, melted

Preheat oven to 350°F.

In a large bowl, combine the three soups, celery, and rice. Turn into a 9 x 13-inch baking dish. Arrange the chicken pieces on the soup, and rice mixture and drizzle the melted butter over the chicken pieces. Cover and bake about 1½ hours, or until the largest chicken pieces are no longer pink in the center.

Easy Chicken–Wild Rice Casserole

Servings: 4

6-ounce package long-grain and wild rice mix, such as Uncle Ben's
¼ cup butter
4 large chicken breast halves, skin on
1 can cream of chicken soup
8-ounce jar button mushrooms
½ cup dry white wine or chicken broth
½ cup diced celery

In a large saucepan, cook rice mix following package directions; set aside. In a large skillet, heat butter over medium heat; brown the chicken breasts well in the butter, about 25 to 30 minutes total.

Preheat oven to 350°F. Remove chicken from skillet and stir in the soup and *undrained* mushrooms. Add the wine and bring to a boil. Pour half of the sauce into the rice mix; add the celery, and stir to combine.

Turn the rice into an 8 x 11-inch baking dish and arrange the chicken breasts on top. Pour the remaining sauce over all. Cover and bake 30 minutes; uncover and bake 15 minutes more, or until the chicken is no longer pink in the center.

Easy Chicken Ratatouille

Servings: 4

4 boneless, skinless chicken breasts
1 medium zucchini, cut into ½–inch thick slices
1 small eggplant, peeled and cut into chunks
16-ounce can stewed tomatoes
8-ounce can tomato sauce
½ cup chopped onion
1 clove garlic, pressed or minced
1 tablespoon chopped fresh parsley
½ teaspoon dried oregano, or 2 teaspoons chopped fresh oregano

Preheat oven to 350°F.

Place the chicken breasts in an 8- or 9-inch-square baking dish that has been sprayed with cooking spray. Cover and bake for 15 minutes.

In a bowl, combine the vegetables with all remaining ingredients. Spoon over the chicken. Cover the dish, and bake for 45 minutes or more, until vegetables are tender and chicken is done. Baste chicken twice with the juice during baking.

Elegant Chicken Potpie

Servings: 4

1 teaspoon oil
1 cup pearl onions, peeled if fresh or thawed if frozen
¹/₂ cup water
8 ounces cremini or other mushrooms, quartered
¹/₄ cup dry white wine
1¹/₂ cups asparagus cut into 1-inch pieces
1 cup chicken broth
¹/₄ cup sour cream
3 tablespoons flour
1 tablespoon chopped fresh parsley
¹/₂ teaspoon tarragon
1 teaspoon Dijon mustard
salt and pepper
2 cups cubed cooked chicken

Biscuits:

1³/₄ cups flour
1 tablespoon baking powder
1 teaspoon salt
¹/₄ cup + 2 tablespoons grated Parmesan cheese
¹/₂ teaspoon rosemary
5 tablespoons butter, cut into pieces
¹/₂ cup milk

In a large skillet, heat the oil over medium-high heat; sauté the onions in the oil until well browned, about 5 minutes. Add water to the skillet and continue cooking until it evaporates. Add the mushrooms, and sauté for about 3 minutes, then add the wine and asparagus and cook for about 1 minute. Reduce heat to low.

In a small bowl, combine the chicken broth, sour cream, flour, parsley, tarragon, and mustard, whisking until smooth. Stir into the mushroom mixture and bring to a simmer. Stir and cook until thickened, about 3 minutes. Salt and pepper to taste. Remove from the heat and stir in the chicken. Place mixture in an 8 x 8-inch baking dish.

Preheat the oven to 450°F. To make the biscuits: In a medium bowl, combine the flour, baking powder, salt, ¹/₄ cup of the cheese, and rosemary. With a pastry cutter cut the butter into the mixture until it resembles small peas. Stir in the milk to form a dough, then turn onto a floured surface. Knead until smooth, about 8 times.

(continued)

Pat the dough to a thickness of about $\frac{1}{2}$-inch, and cut into 9 squares. Place the biscuits in a well-buttered 8 x 8-inch baking pan and sprinkle with the remaining Parmesan cheese.

Bake both the biscuits and the chicken mixture for about 12 minutes, or until the biscuits are just beginning to brown. Using a spatula, carefully transfer the biscuits to the top of the chicken mixture. Bake for an additional 5 minutes or more, or until the biscuits are golden brown.

Chicken Caesar Salad

Servings: 4 main-dish servings

4 slices French bread, about $\frac{1}{2}$–inch thick
4 boneless, skinless chicken breasts
$\frac{1}{3}$ cup grated Parmesan cheese + more
    for sprinkling
8 cups romaine lettuce torn into
    bite-sized pieces

Marinade:

1 tablespoon olive oil
1 clove garlic, crushed
1 teaspoon parsley
1 teaspoon grated lemon zest
$\frac{1}{4}$ teaspoon white pepper
$\frac{1}{2}$ teaspoon salt

Caesar Dressing:

3 tablespoons mayonnaise
2 teaspoons Dijon mustard
1 teaspoon Worcestershire sauce
2 cloves garlic
3 tablespoons lemon juice
4 anchovies, rinsed and dried
2 tablespoons olive oil

Preheat the broiler and adjust the rack so the chicken will be 5 inches from the heat. Spray the broiler pan lightly with cooking spray.

Whisk together all marinade ingredients. Coat both sides of the bread slices with the marinade, then coat the chicken breasts with the remaining marinade. Place the bread on the broiler pan. Sprinkle the bread lightly with Parmesan cheese and broil until golden brown; turn, sprinkle the second side with cheese, and broil. Remove bread and broil the chicken until done, a total of about 12 to 15 minutes, turning once.

Meanwhile, cut the bread into cubes for croutons. To make the Caesar dressing, in a blender or food processor, combine all the dressing ingredients except the olive oil. Blend until smooth. With the blender or food processor still running, slowly add the olive oil.

Toss the lettuce with the Caesar dressing. Sprinkle with $\frac{1}{3}$ cup Parmesan cheese, add the croutons, and toss again. Divide onto 4 serving plates. When the chicken is done, slice into pieces about $\frac{1}{4}$-inch thick and place on top of the lettuce to serve.

Turkey Spinach Toss

Servings: 4

> 1 cup long-grain rice
> 1 cup chicken broth
> 1 cup water
> 2 tablespoons butter
> 1 medium onion, chopped
> 1 cup sliced mushrooms
> 2 cloves garlic, minced
> 1½ cups cut-up cooked turkey
> 1 tablespoon lemon juice
> ½ teaspoon oregano
> 3–4 ounces fresh spinach leaves, trimmed
>   and torn into bite-sized pieces
> ½ cup crumbled feta cheese
> salt and pepper to taste

In a medium saucepan, bring the rice, chicken broth, and water to a boil; reduce heat, cover, and simmer for 20 minutes, or until water is absorbed.

Meanwhile, in a large skillet heat the butter over medium heat; sauté the onion, mushrooms, and garlic until mushrooms are reduced. Add the turkey and sauté quickly to heat. Stir in the lemon juice and oregano. Add the spinach and cheese, and toss continuously until spinach is wilted. Gently toss with the rice to combine. Add salt and pepper to taste.

Turkey Divan

Servings: 4

> 2 heads broccoli or 1 large bunch
>   asparagus, about 1¼ pounds
> 4 tablespoons butter
> ¼ cup flour
> ⅛ teaspoon nutmeg
> ⅛ teaspoon salt
> ½ teaspoon white pepper
> 1 cup milk
> ½ cup turkey or chicken broth
> ¼ cup dry white wine
> 4 large slices turkey white meat, or
>   enough sliced turkey for 4 servings
> ¼ cup grated Parmesan cheese +
>   additional for sprinkling

Preheat the oven to 350°F. Cut the broccoli into spears (or clean the asparagus and break off the woody part of the stalk.) Blanch in boiling salted water until just tender. Arrange in an 8 x 11-inch baking dish.

In a saucepan, melt the butter; add the flour, nutmeg, salt, and pepper. Stir in the milk and broth, and simmer until thick and bubbly. Stir in the wine. Pour half the sauce over the broccoli, then top with the turkey slices. Add ¼ cup Parmesan cheese to the remaining sauce and pour over the turkey.

Bake for about 20 minutes, or until heated through, then sprinkle the top with Parmesan cheese and cook under the broiler for about 5 minutes, or until the top is golden.

Easy Turkey Potpie

Servings: 6

1 potato, cut into cubes
1 teaspoon butter
¼ cup diced onion
½ cup sliced celery
10-ounce jar turkey or chicken gravy
¼ cup water
10-ounce package frozen mixed vegetables
*2 cups cut-up turkey, white or dark meat
    or a combination*
salt and pepper to taste
1 can refrigerated biscuits

Preheat oven to 400°F.

Boil or steam the potato until just tender. In a medium ovenproof skillet, heat butter over medium heat and sauté the onion and celery in the butter about 3 minutes. Stir in the gravy, water, vegetables, turkey, and seasonings. Bring to a boil then remove from the heat.

Arrange the biscuits on top of the mixture. Bake 12 to 14 minutes, or until the biscuits are golden brown.

Turkey-Chutney Salad

Servings: 4 main-dish servings

2 cups diced turkey
8-ounce can pineapple tidbits
1 cup thinly sliced celery
⅓ cup sliced green onions

1 unpeeled apple, cored and cubed
¼ cup cashews

Dressing:
1 cup mayonnaise
3 tablespoons chutney
2 tablespoons lime juice
½ teaspoon grated lime zest
2 teaspoons ginger
½ teaspoon curry powder
½ teaspoon salt

Combine the mayonnaise with other dressing ingredients, mixing well. Toss the salad ingredients together, then stir in the dressing until well combined. Serve on lettuce leaves, if desired.

Fajita-Style Burritos

Servings: 8

Sauce:
*2 tablespoons canned mild green chili
    peppers, chopped and well drained*
2 tablespoons sour cream
*3½ tablespoons mild or medium
    picante sauce*
½ teaspoon chili powder
¼ teaspoon paprika

Filling:
½ tablespoon olive oil
1 cup chopped sweet red peppers
1 cup chopped white onions
3 cups sliced mushrooms

1¼ pounds boneless, skinless chicken
    breast, cubed
¼ cup mild or medium picante sauce
2 tablespoons mild green chili peppers,
    chopped and drained
1 teaspoon chili powder
1 cup coarsely diced tomatoes
⅓ cup coarsely sliced scallions
¼ teaspoon salt, optional
pinch of black pepper
2 tablespoons sour cream

Fajitas:

8 large flour tortillas (8 inch)
1 ounce Cheddar cheese, shredded
1 cup coarsely cubed tomatoes
¼ cup fresh cilantro, chopped
chopped scallions, sliced jalapeño peppers,
    or shredded lettuce for garnish

To prepare the sauce: In a small bowl, stir together the peppers, sour cream, picante sauce, chili powder, and paprika. Set aside.

Preheat the oven to 375°F. To prepare the filling: In a 12-inch nonstick skillet over medium heat, warm the oil. Add the red peppers and onions. Cook, stirring frequently, for 3 minutes, or until slightly soft. Add the mushrooms. Cook, stirring often, for 4 minutes or until the mushrooms release their juices. Raise the heat to high. Stir in the chicken, picante sauce, chili peppers, and chili powder. Cook, stirring frequently, for 4 to 5 minutes, or until

the liquid has almost completely evaporated from the skillet. Be careful not to scorch the ingredients. Stir in the tomatoes, scallions, salt, and black pepper. Cook for 1 minute. Remove from heat and stir in the sour cream.

To prepare the fajitas: Coat a 3-quart baking dish with nonstick spray. Divide the filling evenly among the tortillas and roll them up to enclose the filling. Arrange the fajitas, seam side down, in the dish. Cover with foil and bake for 10 minutes. Spoon the sauce over the fajitas. Sprinkle with the cheese. Cover and bake for 10 minutes longer. Serve garnished with tomatoes, cilantro, and scallions, peppers, or lettuce.

Tamale Pie

Servings: 4 to 6

1 pound ground chicken
1 onion, chopped
1 jalapeño pepper, finely chopped
1 package taco seasoning mix
¾ cup water
14-ounce can crushed tomatoes
¼ cup water
1 cup frozen corn
3 flour tortillas (10 inch)
1 cup grated Cheddar cheese

(continued)

In a skillet over medium heat, stir and cook ground chicken until no pink remains. Stir in onion, jalapeño pepper, taco seasoning, and $3/4$ cup water. Stir and cook until no liquid remains. Add crushed tomatoes, $1/4$ cup water, and corn, and simmer for 10 minutes.

Preheat oven to 350°F. Line a 9-inch pie plate with tortillas, overlapping them to cover the edges of the pie plate. Sprinkle half of the cheese over the tortillas. Spread the meat mixture evenly in the pie plate and top with the remaining cheese. Bake until heated through, about 30 minutes.

When preparing hot peppers, wear rubber gloves for protection against oils that cause a burning sensation on the skin.

Spicy Chicken with Cashew Nuts

Servings: 4 to 6

3 whole skinless, boneless chicken breasts, cut crosswise into $1/2$-inch-wide strips
2 tablespoons cornstarch
1 egg white
3 tablespoons peanut oil
1 cup raw cashews
1-inch piece fresh gingerroot, grated
2 green onions
$1/2$ teaspoon hot pepper paste
(recipe follows)
2 teaspoons hot bean sauce*

1 tablespoon dry sherry
$1/2$ teaspoon salt
1 teaspoon sesame oil
1 teaspoon sugar

Place the chicken strips in the cornstarch and coat well. Beat the egg white in a bowl; add the chicken pieces to the egg white; stir. Refrigerate for 30 minutes.

Heat the oil in a wok over medium heat; when it develops a slight haze over the oil (do not let it smoke), fry the cashews until they are light golden brown. Drain them and set them aside on a paper plate. When the chicken has finished chilling, reheat the oil, if necessary, over a medium-high setting, and stir-fry the chicken pieces until firm and light golden. Drain them over a wok with a slotted spoon and set aside on paper plates. In the same oil, fry the ginger and green onions for 1 minute, stirring constantly. Stir in all the remaining ingredients except the sesame oil and the sugar. Add the chicken pieces to the wok again and stir-fry for 1 minute. Stir in the sesame oil, sugar, and cashew nuts. Immediately transfer to a serving platter and serve hot with steamed rice.

*Hot bean sauce can be found in the Asian food section of most well-stocked supermarkets, usually in 4-ounce sized glass jars.

Korean Style Chicken

Servings: 6

1½ pounds skinless and boneless chicken
   breasts
2 tablespoons lemon juice
2 tablespoons sesame seeds
2 cloves garlic, finely chopped
6 green onions, sliced thinly
¼ cup dry vermouth
½ cup light soy sauce
2 tablespoons sugar
1½ tablespoons Asian sesame oil
2 teaspoons fresh minced ginger
½ teaspoon ground black pepper

Place chicken between 2 pieces of plastic wrap and, using a meat pounder, gently pound the chicken to ¼-inch thickness. Place in a bowl and rub gently with lemon juice.

In a small frying pan over low heat, toast the sesame seeds, stirring frequently, until light brown, about 3 to 5 minutes. Set aside 1 tablespoon of the seeds. Transfer the remaining tablespoon of seeds to a spice grinder or mortar and pestle, and grind to a powder. In a small bowl, stir together the ground sesame seeds with all the remaining ingredients. Pour over the chicken, turning to coat, refrigerate for at least 3 hours.

Prepare the grill. When coals are hot, place chicken directly on the rack. Grill until slightly charred, about 5 minutes. Turn and char slightly on the other side, about 3 to 4 minutes longer. Transfer to a serving platter

and sprinkle with reserved sesame seeds. Serve with steamed rice and leafy greens.

Chicken Satay

Servings: 4

¼ cup chopped shallots, divided
5 cloves garlic, halved, divided
3 red serrano chili peppers, halved, divided
2 tablespoons peeled and finely chopped
   fresh lemongrass, divided
2 tablespoons ground coriander, divided
2 teaspoons sugar
1½ teaspoons salt, divided
4 tablespoons water, divided
2 tablespoons unsweetened coconut cream*
1 pound skinless, boneless chicken breast,
   cut into 1-inch pieces
2 tablespoons peanut oil
¼ cup chunky peanut butter
1 teaspoon brown sugar
1 teaspoon fish sauce, or to taste
¼ cup unsweetened coconut milk
¼ cup lime juice
1 small cucumber, peeled and thinly sliced
   for garnish

In a blender, combine half the shallots, 2 cloves garlic, 1 chili pepper, and 2 tablespoons of the lemongrass. Process until finely chopped. Add 1 tablespoon of the coriander, along with the sugar, 1 teaspoon salt, and 2 tablespoons water. Process until smooth a paste forms. Pour

(continued)

into a bowl and add the coconut cream, mixing well. Add the chicken, turning it to coat evenly. Refrigerate for several hours or overnight.

Prepare a grill and place the cooking rack about 2 inches from the fire. Use metal or wood skewers for grilling the chicken. If using wood, soak for 20 minutes in water before grilling. In a blender, combine the remaining shallots, garlic, chilies, lemongrass, coriander and 2 table-spoons of water. Process until smooth.

In a saucepan, warm the oil. Add the spice paste and cook, stirring occasionally, about 3 minutes. Add the peanut butter and cook 2 minutes longer. Stir in the brown sugar, fish sauce, 1/2 teaspoon salt, and coconut milk. Cook about 5 minutes, stirring occasionally. Stir in the lime juice. Add more coconut milk if necessary to make a creamy sauce. Pour into a shallow bowl.

Remove the chicken from the marinade and discard the marinade. Thread chicken pieces onto the skewers. Place directly on the grill rack, and cook, turning once, about 8 to 10 minutes per side. Serve on a platter garnished with cucumber slices and the peanut sauce.

*The rich layer of fat that rises to the top of a can of coconut milk should be spooned off and used when coconut cream is called for. The remaining coconut milk can be used in a variety of Asian dishes.

Japanese Teriyaki Chicken

Servings: 4

- 1/2 cucumber
- 2 tablespoons rice vinegar (or 1 tablespoon regular white vinegar)
- 1 tablespoon Japanese soy sauce*
- 1/2 teaspoon sugar
- 4 chicken breasts, halved
- 2 tablespoons peanut oil

Teriyaki Sauce:
- 1/4 cup mirin* or 3 tablespoons sweet sherry
- 1/2 cup basic fish sauce
- 1/2 cup Japanese soy sauce
- 1 tablespoon sugar

Cut the ends of the cucumber off and discard. Score the cucumber lengthwise with a fork. Cut the 1/2 cucumber in half length-wise, and scoop out the seeds. Cut the halves crosswise into thin slices. Combine the vinegar, soy sauce, and sugar in a nonmetal bowl and marinate for 20 minutes.

Warm the mirin in a small saucepan. Stir in the fish sauce, soy sauce, and sugar; bring to a boil, then cool. Marinate the chicken in all the teriyaki sauce for 10 minutes. Remove the chicken and pat dry with a paper towel. Reserve the sauce. Heat the oil in a wok and stir-fry the chicken breasts for 5 minutes, turning frequently. Remove to drain on paper towels. Pour the oil from the wok (discard the oil), and return the chicken breasts to

the wok. Pour the reserved marinade (teriyaki sauce) over the chicken and cook for 2 minutes, turning 2 or 3 times. Remove the wok from the heat. Remove the cucumber slices from the marinade and arrange on a serving plate. Lift the chicken breasts from the sauce and place them on the serving plate. Serve accompanied with cooked short-grained rice.

*Mirin is Japanese sweet rice wine, which can be found in most liquor stores and well-stocked supermarkets. Japanese soy sauce can also be found in most supermarkets.

Tandoori Chicken Kebobs

Servings: 4

1 pound boneless, skinless chicken
8–12 wooden skewers

Marinade:
1 cup low-fat plain yogurt
1 tablespoon lemon juice
1 clove garlic, minced
1 small onion, finely chopped
1½ teaspoons curry powder
1 teaspoon ground cumin
1 teaspoon ground coriander
1 teaspoon ground ginger
½ teaspoon salt

Tandoori Sauce:
1 cup whipping cream
½ cup dry white wine

3 tablespoons tomato paste
1 teaspoon curry powder
½ teaspoon ground coriander
½ teaspoon cumin
½ teaspoon garam masala*
½ cup chopped fresh cilantro

Cut chicken into bite-sized pieces and thread on skewers. Place skewers into large plastic bag. Combine marinade ingredients and pour over chicken. Make sure each piece is well coated. Close bag and refrigerate for at least 4 hours.

Combine all tandoori sauce ingredients and refrigerate in an airtight container until ready to use. Preheat the grill to medium heat. Remove chicken from the marinade and place on the grill. Throw out the marinade bag. Grill the chicken, with the barbecue lid down, for about 10 minutes (or until the chicken is no longer pink), turning at least 3 times. While the chicken is grilling, transfer the Tandoori Sauce to a medium-sized saucepan. Bring to a slow boil, stirring continuously, being careful not to burn the sauce. Reduce the heat to low. Simmer the sauce until slightly thickened, stirring occasionally. Cover and keep warm until chicken is cooked.

Transfer the chicken kebobs to a serving platter and drizzle Tandoori sauce over the kebobs. Sprinkle with fresh cilantro and serve.

*Garam masala is an Indian spice which can be found in specialty food stores.

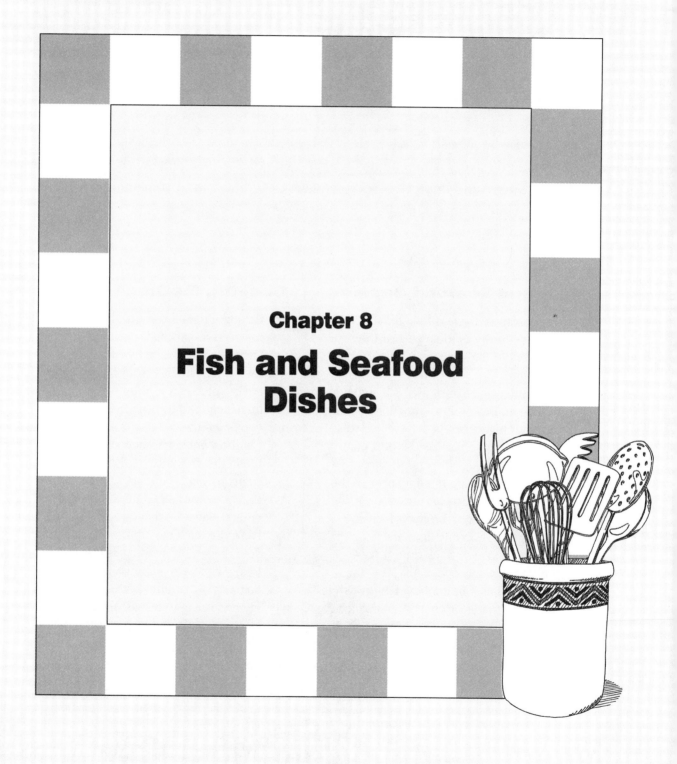

Chapter 8

Fish and Seafood Dishes

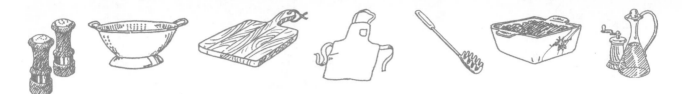

Fish is the ultimate convenience food, as it cooks to perfection easily and quickly. It can be baked, sautéed, steamed, or broiled in minutes, and when combined with a fresh salad or steamed vegetable, makes a nutritious and sophisticated meal. Fish contains high amounts of omega-3 fatty acids, which lower blood pressure and improve blood circulation. Adding fish to your menus will save meal preparation time and satisfy a wide variety of appetites.

Fish and Seafood Basics

- Fresh fish or thawed frozen fish should be kept in the coldest part of the refrigerator and cooked within one or two days.
- When thawing frozen fish, place fish in a dish and allow it to thaw for 24 hours in the refrigerator.
- The "10-minute rule" is the best guide to cooking seafood by conventional methods. Measure the thickness of the fish at its thickest part and cook it 10 minutes per inch, turning it halfway through the cooking time. Pieces of fish less than ½-inch thick do not have to be turned when cooking.
- Add 5 minutes in cooking time if fish is wrapped in foil or cooked in a sauce.
- Double cooking time for frozen fish that has not been defrosted.

Cooking Methods

- Baking: Preheat oven to 450°F and bake uncovered, basting if desired.
- Oven-broiling: Place fish 1-inch thick or less, 2 to 4 inches from heat. Place thicker pieces 5 to 6 inches away. Baste frequently and turn halfway through the cooking time.
- Charcoal grilling: Heat coals. Lightly brush the grill and the fish with oil. See oven-broiling for directions regarding distance from heat. Use a hinged fish grill or place the fish directly on the grill.
- Pan-frying or sautéing: Dip the fish in flour, batter, or breading just before frying. Heat a small amount of oil or butter in a pan until hot but not smoking. Fry according to the 10-minute rule.
- Deep-frying: Bread or batter the fish. Heat oil to 350°F. Completely submerge the fish in hot oil without crowding,

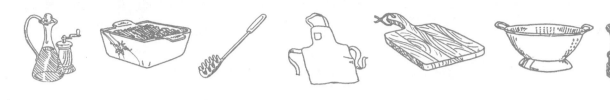

and cook until the fish is golden brown. Drain on absorbent paper towels.

- Poaching: Boil sufficient water or other liquid to cover the fish. Place the fish in the liquid and return to a boil. Reduce the heat to simmer, cover, and begin timing the fish according to the 10-minute rule. Remove the fish from the liquid when the fish just begins to flake but is still firm and moist.
- Microwaving: The 10-minute rule does not apply. Place the fish in a shallow dish, and cover with plastic wrap, keeping one corner open for venting. Cook on high for 3 minutes per pound of boneless fish. Rotate during cooking. Remove from the microwave when the edges of the fish are firm and opaque and the center is slightly translucent. Let the fish stand, covered, for 5 minutes.

Barbara's Scallops

Servings: 2

2 cloves garlic, crushed
6 tablespoons butter
½ cup pale dry sherry
½ pound chopped mushrooms
3 scallions, chopped
½ cup chopped fresh parsley
½ pound baby scallops
2 tablespoons flour
½ cup half-and-half

Combine the garlic, butter, sherry, mushrooms, scallions, and parsley in a saucepan and sauté 2 minutes over medium heat. Add the scallops; stir and simmer for 1 minute. Add the flour and stir until scallops are lightly browned. Slowly add the half-and-half. Stir and cook until thickened and scallops are just done.

 When purchasing fresh fish, check for clear and bright eyes, firm skin that bounces back when touched, and a fresh, clean smell. Try not to keep fresh fish more than a day in your refrigerator before cooking.

Herbed Scallops with Tomatoes

Servings: 4

1 tablespoon extra-virgin olive oil
1 clove garlic, minced
1 pound bay scallops, patted dry
1 tablespoon chopped fresh parsley
¼ teaspoon salt or to taste
freshly ground pepper
1 tablespoon fresh lemon juice
3 tablespoons half-and-half
8 cherry tomatoes, quartered
2 teaspoons fresh tarragon, minced

Heat oil in large skillet over low heat. Add garlic and cook until garlic begins to soften, but does not brown, about 2 minutes. Increase heat to high and add

(continued)

scallops, parsley, salt, and pepper. Cook, stirring constantly, until scallops are cooked through, 1 to 2 minutes. Sprinkle with lemon juice and cook briefly. Remove scallops with a slotted spoon.

Add half-and-half and tomatoes to the liquid in the pan. Boil until tomatoes are warmed through and liquid has thickened slightly, about 1 minute. Return scallops to pan and add tarragon. Cook 10 seconds. Adjust seasoning.

The creamy and translucent scallop has the most complex flavor and enjoyable texture of any mollusk. Scallops are sold with their tendon, a white strip that attaches the muscle to the shell. To refine cleaning and preparation, strip this off before cooking.

Spiced Scallops

Servings: 4

1½ pounds sea scallops
½ teaspoon salt
¼ teaspoon black pepper
1 tablespoon olive oil
⅓ cup sweet red wine
2 tablespoons fresh lemon juice
¼ cup chopped fresh parsley
5 cloves garlic, minced
2 cups cooked long-grain rice

Sprinkle scallops with salt and pepper. Heat 1½ teaspoons of the oil in a 10-inch

cast-iron skillet or other heavy skillet until very hot—about 3 minutes. Add half of scallops; cook 2 minutes on each side or until browned. Remove scallops from pan and keep warm. Repeat procedure with 1½ teaspoons oil and the remaining scallops. Remove scallops from pan.

Stir in wine and lemon juice, scraping pan to loosen bits. Add scallops, 3 tablespoons of the parsley, and garlic. Sauté 30 seconds over high heat. Serve the scallops over rice. Sprinkle with the remaining tablespoon of parsley.

Scallop and Pepper Stir-Fry

Servings: 4

1 tablespoon olive oil
1 pound bay scallops
1 green bell pepper, chopped
1 red bell pepper, chopped
1 red onion, chopped
1 teaspoon red pepper flakes
2 cups cold cooked white rice
salt and pepper to taste

In a large skillet or wok, heat the oil over medium-high heat. Add the scallops, bell peppers, onion, and red pepper flakes. Stir-fry until scallops are cooked and tender, about 5 minutes. Add the rice and cook, stirring until heated through. Season with salt and pepper to taste. Serve immediately.

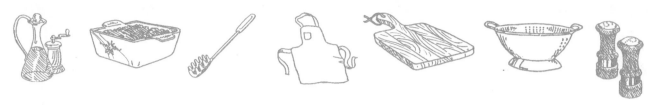

Steamed Salmon Steaks with Ginger

Servings: 4

4 fresh salmon steaks, each about
   1-inch thick
1 teaspoon salt
4 green onions
thin 2 tablespoons shredded fresh ginger
2 tablespoons hoisin sauce
2 tablespoons soy sauce
2 cloves garlic, coarsely chopped
½ teaspoon sugar
1 teaspoon minced peeled ginger
pepper to taste
¼ cup peanut oil
cilantro for garnish

Blot salmon dry and sprinkle with salt. Using a large knife blade, flatten the green onions and cut them in 2-inch-long sections. Place half the onions and half the shredded ginger on a shallow, heatproof plate. Arrange the salmon steaks on top of the onions and ginger and scatter the remaining green onion sections and ginger over the steaks.

Combine the hoisin sauce, soy sauce, garlic, sugar and the teaspoon of minced ginger. Spread over the salmon. Fill the bottom of a steamer with water to 1 inch from the bottom of the steamer rack. Bring the water to a boil. Place the plate of salmon in the steamer and cover. Steam over medium to high heat until done, about 10 minutes.

Uncover the steamer, tilting the lid away from you. Allow the steam to escape before reaching in to tip the plate slightly to drain off excess moisture. Sprinkle pepper and chopped green onions over fish. Heat peanut oil in a small saucepan until just hot. Drizzle the oil over the fish just before serving. Garnish with cilantro.

 Steaming preserves the delicacy of ocean or freshwater fish better than any other method of cooking. Use a lidded container (a wok or deep pot) and a rack large enough to hold the fish in a single layer above the water. For large quantities, a Chinese steamer with trays can be used.

Grilled Glazed Salmon

Servings: 4

½ cup orange marmalade
2 teaspoons sesame oil
2 teaspoons tamari sauce
½ teaspoon grated gingerroot
1 clove garlic, crushed
3 tablespoons white rice wine vinegar
1 pound boneless, skinless salmon fillet,
   cut into 4 pieces
6 scallions, thinly sliced
¼ cup toasted sesame seeds

Combine the marmalade, oil, tamari sauce, ginger, garlic, and vinegar. Heat the grill. Brush orange glaze on each side of

(continued)

salmon and grill about 5 minutes on each side. Top with scallions and sesame seeds before serving.

 The way fish is cooked depends more on its texture than its size. Dense and sturdy fish like salmon can be prepared almost any way. Steaks and fresh fillets of Atlantic or pacific salmon are readily available. Salmon's high fat content (except for Coho) makes it suitable for grilling, roasting, or sautéing.

Roast Salmon with Citrus-Chili Marinade

Servings: 2

1 jalapeño pepper, cored, seeded, and minced
2 tablespoons fresh lime juice
3 tablespoons fresh lemon juice
1 tablespoon chopped fresh parsley
4 teaspoons honey
1 tablespoon olive oil
$1/4$ teaspoon salt
freshly ground pepper
10-ounce salmon fillet
2 lime slices

Preheat the oven to 500°F. Stir together jalapeño pepper, lime and lemon juices, parsley, honey, olive oil, salt and pepper to taste. Set aside.

Place salmon on a greased rack over a baking sheet. Roast until cooked through, 8 to 10 minutes. Remove from oven and garnish with lime slices. Divide salmon in half and spoon the citrus-chili marinade on the fillets.

Poached Salmon with Béarnaise Sauce

Servings: 4

$1/2$ cup water
$1/4$ cup white wine
2 salmon steaks

Béarnaise Sauce:

$1/4$ cup mayonnaise
2 tablespoons lemon juice
1 tablespoon Dijon mustard
1 teaspoon sugar
1 teaspoon tarragon
salt and fresh ground pepper to taste

In skillet, bring water and wine to a gentle simmer. Add salmon and cook without boiling for 8 to 10 minutes or until fish flakes easily when tested with a fork. Divide steaks in half and arrange on warmed plates.

In small saucepan, whisk together mayonnaise, lemon juice, mustard, sugar, and tarragon. Cook over medium-low heat, whisking, for about 3 minutes or until warmed through but not boiling. Season with salt and pepper to taste. Spoon over salmon.

One-Pot Salmon Dinner

Servings: 4

> 2 cups fusilli (pasta)
> 1 cup milk
> 1 cup ricotta cheese
> 1 cup frozen green peas
> 1/4 cup green onion, chopped
> 2 tablespoons Dijon mustard
> 2 tablespoons lemon juice
> 1 tablespoon chopped fresh dill
> 3/4 teaspoon salt
> 1/4 teaspoon freshly ground pepper
> dash hot pepper sauce
> 7 1/2-ounce can red salmon

Cook fusilli in a pot of boiling salted water until firm. Drain well and set aside. Reserve 1/4 cup of the pasta cooking water. In a blender, blend the milk with the ricotta until smooth, pour into a saucepan. Add reserved cooking water, peas, green onion, mustard, lemon juice, dill, salt, pepper, and hot pepper sauce. Heat through over medium heat, stirring often.

Drain salmon, keeping it in chunks. Stir the salmon into the saucepan along with the fusilli. Remove from heat, cover, and let stand for 3 to 4 minutes until sauce has thickened slightly.

The following recipes for fish fillets are grouped together, as any fish fillets available at your market can be used. Fish such as sea trout, pollack, and ocean perch are often underused and make delicious main dishes. Many are sold frozen and should be thawed slowly in the refrigerator.

Baked Fish Fillets

Servings: 4

> 1 1/2 pounds leeks, trimmed, washed, and chopped
> 1/2 cup fish stock or water
> salt and freshly ground pepper to taste
> 1 tablespoon Dijon mustard
> 1 1/2 pounds cod, halibut, or salmon fillets

Preheat oven to 400°F. Combine leeks in an ovenproof casserole with fish stock, salt, pepper, and mustard. Spread the leeks out in the casserole. Place fish on top of the leek mixture and sprinkle with salt and pepper. Cover casserole and bake 10 to 15 minutes or until a knife inserted meets no resistance when inserted into the thickest part of the fillet. Serve with leek mixture spooned over the fish.

Baking fish in a sealed baking dish allows the fish to steam in its own juices. Fresh herbs like thyme and curry powder can be used to spice fish fillets.

Fillets of Sole

Servings: 2

1/3 cup flour
1 1/4 teaspoons salt
1/4 teaspoon freshly ground pepper
1 1/2 pounds sole fillets
6 tablespoons butter
1 tablespoon olive oil
2 tablespoons lemon juice
1 1/2 teaspoons fresh parsley, minced

Preheat the oven to 225°F. Put an oven-proof platter in the oven. Combine the flour, salt, and pepper in a shallow dish. Coat each fish fillet with the flour mixture and shake off extra. In a large skillet, heat 3 tablespoons of the butter with the oil. Without crowding the fillets, pan-fry each over medium heat until golden—about 1 to 2 minutes.

As each fillet is done, put it on the platter in the oven. When all the fish fillets are cooked, turn the heat to high, stir in the lemon juice, and cook for a few seconds. Add the parsley, and drizzle over the fish fillets just before serving.

Skillet Fillet Dinner

Servings: 4

5 tablespoons butter or olive oil
1 cup chopped red onion
1 1/2 cups diced small red potatoes
*   with skins*
1 cup corn
1 pound fish fillets (cod, bass, snapper, or
*   halibut), cut into 1-inch chunks*
salt and freshly ground pepper
1/3 cup chopped parsley

Heat 4 tablespoons of the butter or olive oil in a large skillet over medium-high heat, then add the onion and potatoes and cook slowly until tender. Stir in the corn and the remaining tablespoon of butter. Add the fish chunks and salt and pepper to taste. Continue cooking, stirring occasionally, until fish is cooked through—about 5 minutes. Do not break up fish chunks. Sprinkle with parsley and serve.

Oven-Fried Snapper

Servings: 4

2 pounds red snapper fillets
1/2 cup olive oil
1 teaspoon salt
3 cloves garlic, pressed
1 cup Parmesan cheese
1 cup dry bread crumbs

Rinse fish with cold water and pat dry with paper towel. Cut fish into 4 equal portions. Combine oil, salt, and garlic in a 9 x 12-inch baking dish. Place fish in the mixture and marinate for 10 minutes. Turn and marinate for an additional 10 minutes.

Preheat the oven to 450°F. Remove the fish from the marinade. Roll in Parmesan cheese and then the bread crumbs. Place on a well-greased cookie sheet and bake for 12 to 15 minutes or until fish flakes when tested with a fork.

A soft and delicate fish like red snapper should be baked or sautéed, as it can easily fall apart during cooking.

Cajun Rainbow Trout

Servings: 4

1½ teaspoons paprika
¾ teaspoon freshly ground pepper
1 teaspoon salt
½ teaspoon each dried oregano, chili powder, and dry mustard
pinch cayenne pepper
1 pound rainbow trout fillets (½-inch thick)
2 teaspoons olive oil
2 teaspoons fresh parsley, chopped
1 green onion, chopped
lemon wedges

Preheat the broiler. In a small bowl, combine paprika, pepper, salt, oregano, chili powder, mustard, and cayenne pepper; set aside. Pat fillets dry and place skin side down on a broiler rack. Lightly brush both sides of fillets with oil. Sprinkle both sides evenly with paprika mixture. Broil 4 to 6 inches from heat for 4 to 5 minutes or until fish flakes easily when tested with a fork.

Arrange fish on a warmed serving platter and sprinkle with parsley and chopped green onion. Squeeze one of the lemon wedges over the fish. Serve with remaining wedges.

Until recently most farm-raised trout was almost tasteless compared to salmon. Now, several farm-raised fish like steelheads and orange-fleshed rainbow trout look and taste like salmon. These are best cooked like salmon and can be used in any salmon recipe.

Fillets of Fish with Lime and Cumin

Servings: 4

12 fish fillets
2 tablespoons lime juice
1 teaspoon cumin
¼ cup plain low-fat yogurt
salt and freshly ground pepper to taste

(continued)

Preheat the oven to 350°F. Arrange fish in a single layer in a baking dish. Combine lime juice and cumin, and pour over fish, turning to coat. Bake uncovered for 10 to 15 minutes or until fish flakes easily when tested with a fork.

In a bowl, combine the yogurt with 1 tablespoon of the juice from the baking dish. Season with salt and pepper to taste and serve over the fish.

Any fresh fish fillet baked with a little lime juice and cumin makes a quick and tasty main dish. Serve with whole-grain rice.

Fish Fillets Almandine

Servings: 4

¹/₃ cup slivered almonds
4 tablespoons butter
¹/₂ teaspoon seasoned salt
freshly ground pepper to taste
1¹/₂ pounds fresh fish fillets
1¹/₂ tablespoons lemon juice
2 tablespoons fresh chopped parsley
6 lemon wedges

Toast slivered almonds by heating over medium heat in a cast iron or other heavy skillet until browned (about 5 minutes). Set aside. Melt the butter and blend with seasoned salt and pepper. Coat fish fillets

with the butter, salt, and pepper mixture and sauté 2 minutes per side.

Remove to serving platter and sprinkle fillets with lemon juice. Top with toasted almonds, fresh chopped parsley and serve with lemon wedges.

Grilled Fish Fillets with Herbed Mustard Sauce

Servings: 4

4 fillets grey sole, Pacific tuna, or gulf
  snapper
1¹/₂ tablespoons olive oil
salt and freshly ground pepper to taste
2 tablespoons unsalted butter
1 clove garlic, minced
¹/₃ cup whipping cream
1 teaspoon Dijon mustard
1 tablespoon seasoned rice vinegar
¹/₄ cup fresh minced dill
1 tablespoon fresh minced mint

Heat gas or charcoal grill until hot. Brush fillets with olive oil and season with salt and pepper. Grill fillets, 2 to 4 minutes per side. Grill until fish flakes when tested with a fork at its thickest part. Remove to serving platter and keep warm.

Melt butter over medium heat in a skillet, add the garlic, and cook for 30

226

seconds. Add cream and mustard. Heat to a boil and cook until thickened slightly, about 1 minute. Remove from heat and stir in the vinegar, dill, mint, and salt and pepper to taste. Spoon sauce over fish just before serving.

When grilling fish, place fish steaks or fillets on a hot, well-oiled grill. Grill for about 10 minutes per inch of thickness of the fillet, measured at its thickest part. Turn once while on the grill. Thoroughly brush fish with vegetable oil or basting sauce several times during grilling. Grill until fish flakes when tested with a fork at its thickest part.

Fish Patties

Servings: 5

*2 cups cooked salmon
   (or 6 ounces canned)
6 soda crackers, crushed
1 egg, slightly beaten
1/3 cup milk
1 small onion, grated
1 tablespoon chopped fresh parsley
1 tablespoon flour
salt to taste
1–2 tablespoons light oil
flour*

If using canned salmon, drain fish well; place the fish in a bowl and flake with a fork. Add the crushed crackers. Combine the egg, milk, onion, parsley, and flour. Mix into fish and cracker crumbs, then salt to taste. Gently form into 5 patties.

Heat oil in a large skillet over medium heat. Lightly dust patties with flour, then fry on both sides until browned, about 5 minutes per side. Serve with lettuce, tomatoes, and onions on whole-wheat buns.

Fish You Can Grill

- Mahi-mahi
- Marlin fillets
- Whole baby coho salmon
- Chunk Norway salmon
- Shark fillets
- Whole gulf snapper
- Whole grey sole
- Swordfish fillets
- Pacific tuna

227

Smoked Fish Salad with Cilantro Dressing

Servings: 4

Dressing:

2 tablespoons plain yogurt
1 tablespoon each fresh lemon juice, white wine vinegar, and minced cilantro
1/4 teaspoon salt
1/8 teaspoon freshly ground pepper
dash ground red pepper
1/2 cup olive oil

Salad:

1 head romaine lettuce
1/3 to 1/2 pound smoked fish (salmon or whitefish) flaked into bite-sized pieces
1 cup small black olives
15-ounce can chickpeas, drained
1/2 medium-sized red onion, thinly sliced

Mix yogurt, lemon juice, vinegar, cilantro, salt, black pepper, and red pepper. Set aside. Trim romaine and discard stem ends. Slice remaining inner leaves into 1½-inch pieces. Wash and dry. Place in a large bowl with the smoked fish, olives, chickpeas, and onion. Whisk olive oil into vinegar mixture; adjust seasoning. Pour over salad and toss.

Seafood on English Muffins

Servings: 6

2 tablespoons butter
2 tablespoons all-purpose flour
1/8 teaspoon white pepper
1 cup 2% milk
1 egg, beaten
2 teaspoons lemon juice
2 cups seafood (crab, lobster, or firm whitefish), flaked into large pieces
8 English muffins, toasted
fresh parsley, chopped

In a heavy 1-quart saucepan, melt the butter over low heat. Blend in the flour and the pepper. Cook over low heat, stirring, until the mixture is smooth and bubbly. Remove from heat and gradually stir in the milk.

Over medium heat, bring the white sauce to a boil, stirring constantly. Simmer for 1 minute, stirring constantly. Stir in the beaten egg. Heat for 1 to 2 minutes. Stir in the lemon juice and the seafood. Heat for 2 minutes. Serve over toasted English muffins and garnish with parsley.

Elegant Pike

Servings: 6

> 3 quarts water
> 1 medium onion, quartered
> 3 stalks celery, cut up
> 1/2 cup lemon juice
> 3 tablespoons salt
> 3 pounds pike fillets, skinned
> 1/4 cup melted butter
> paprika
> lemon wedges and melted butter

Preheat broiler, setting rack 6 inches below the element. Fill a large saucepan with 3 quarts of water. Add onion, celery, lemon juice, and salt. Bring to a boil. Cut the pike fillets into 2-inch pieces. Drop the fish into the boiling water, and cook 3 minutes and no longer. Drain immediately, discarding the onion and celery.

Place fish pieces on a foil-lined baking sheet. Brush with 1/4 cup melted butter and sprinkle with paprika. Broil 2 minutes, or just until fish starts to turn golden. Serve with lemon wedges and melted butter in small bowls for dipping.

Batter-Fried Shrimp

Servings: 6

> oil for deep-frying
> 1/2 cup oil
> 1 egg, beaten
> 1 cup all-purpose flour
> 1/2 cup milk
> 3/4 teaspoon seasoned salt
> 1/4 teaspoon salt
> 1 1/2 pounds shrimp, peeled and deveined

Preheat oil for deep-frying to 350°F. Combine 1/2 cup oil and egg and beat well. Add remaining ingredients except shrimp and stir until well blended.

Dip shrimp into batter to coat. Drop shrimp into hot oil and fry for 30 to 60 seconds or until golden brown. Remove with a slotted spoon and drain on a paper towel.

Avoid prepeeled and deveined shrimp, as cleaning before freezing may remove some of the flavor and texture from the shrimp. Shrimp should have no black spots on their shell; the spots indicate a breakdown of the meat has begun. Shrimp, like most fish, should smell of saltwater and nothing else.

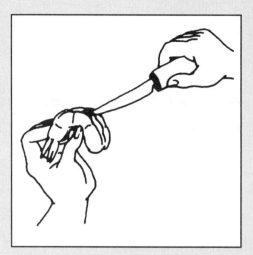

To devein a shrimp: Use the tip of a knife to make a cut along the back of a peeled shrimp. Use the knife tip to pull out the vein.

To butterfly a shrimp: Laying the peeled shrimp on its side, make a deep cut along the curl of the shrimp. Using your fingers, open the shrimp.

Shrimp Linguine

Servings: 6

- ½ cup butter
- ¼ cup olive oil
- 1 clove garlic, minced
- 1 cup sliced mushrooms
- ½ cup chopped green onion
- 1 pound cooked shrimp, peeled and deveined
- 2 tablespoons chopped parsley
- 8 ounces linguine, cooked according to package directions and drained
- Parmesan cheese

Melt butter with olive oil in a large skillet. Add garlic, mushrooms, and green onion. Sauté until tender. Add shrimp and heat through. Stir in parsley. Serve over hot cooked linguine and sprinkle with Parmesan cheese.

Citrus Shrimp and Scallops

Servings: 4

- ½ pound sea scallops
- 12 large shrimp, peeled, and deveined (about ½ pound total)
- 1 teaspoon finely shredded orange zest
- ½ cup orange juice
- 1 teaspoon peeled and grated fresh ginger
- ¼ teaspoon cayenne pepper
- 2 tablespoons soy sauce
- 1 clove garlic, minced
- 12 fresh or frozen snow peas
- 1 orange, cut into 8 wedges

Halve any large scallops. Place the scallops and shrimp in a plastic bag set in a deep bowl. In a small bowl, stir together the orange zest, orange juice, ginger, cayenne pepper, soy sauce, and garlic. Pour

over the seafood. Seal the bag. Marinate in the refrigerator for 30 minutes. Prepare the fire in a gas or charcoal grill.

Drain the seafood. If using fresh snow peas, cook in boiling water for about 2 minutes, then drain. If using frozen snow peas, thaw and drain well. Wrap 1 snow pea around each shrimp. Thread the shrimp onto four 10- to 12-inch long skewers alternately with the scallops and orange wedges.

Place the skewers on the grill rack and grill over medium-hot coals for 5 minutes. Turn and grill until the shrimp turn pink and the scallops are opaque, 5 to 7 minutes longer. Brush the kebobs occasionally as they cook.

If preferred, kebobs can also be broiled about 4 inches from the heat source. Broil 4 minutes on the first side and 4 to 6 minutes on the second.

Crab-Stuffed Avocados

Servings: 6

2 cups fresh crabmeat, drained and flaked
11-ounce can mandarin oranges, drained
1/4 cup plus 1 tablespoon olive oil
1/2 cup sliced green onions with tops
2 tablespoons white wine vinegar
1/2 teaspoon garlic salt
3 small avocados, peeled
2 tablespoons lemon juice
lettuce leaves

Combine crabmeat, oranges, oil, green onions, vinegar, and garlic salt, mix well. Cut avocados in half lengthwise and remove seeds. Brush avocado halves with lemon juice and fill with crabmeat mixture. Arrange avocado halves on lettuce leaves and serve.

East Coast Crab Cakes

Servings: 6

2 pounds fresh crabmeat, drained
1 cup soft whole-wheat bread crumbs
2/3 cup minced onion
2/3 cup minced celery
1/4 cup mayonnaise
1 egg white, lightly beaten
2 teaspoons Old Bay seasoning or other
   seafood seasoning mix
2 teaspoons Dijon mustard
2 teaspoons Worcestershire sauce
1/4 teaspoon ground red pepper
2 teaspoons olive oil
3/4 cup lemon sauce (recipe follows)

Combine first 10 ingredients. Shape mixture into 12, 1/2-inch-thick patties. Cover and chill 1 hour. Heat the olive oil on a griddle over medium-hot heat. Add crabmeat cakes in batches and cook 4 to 5 minutes on each side or until golden brown. Serve crab cakes with tangy lemon sauce.

(continued)

Lemon Sauce:

1 tablespoon cornstarch
1/2 teaspoon sugar
dash ground white pepper
1 cup chicken broth
2 tablespoons water
1/2 teaspoon grated lemon rind
1/3 cup fresh lemon juice
2 teaspoons chopped fresh parsley

Combine first 3 ingredients in a small saucepan and stir well. Gradually stir in chicken broth and water. Cook over medium heat, stirring constantly, until mixture comes to a boil. Reduce heat and simmer 1 minute or until mixture is thickened, stirring constantly. Remove from heat and stir in lemon rind, lemon juice, and parsley. Serve warm over fish or steamed vegetables.

Crab Louis

Servings: 4

2 6-ounce packages frozen crabmeat, thawed
2 tablespoons sliced green onions
1 stalk celery, thinly sliced
1/2 cup mayonnaise
2 tablespoons chili sauce
1/4 teaspoon salt
freshly ground pepper to taste
1/2 cup whipping cream, whipped
2 avocados, halved and skinned
lettuce leaves

Drain crabmeat thoroughly on paper towels. Set aside. Combine green onions, celery, mayonnaise, chili sauce, salt, and pepper and blend well. Stir in crabmeat. Fold in whipped cream. Spoon into avocado halves and arrange on lettuce leaves.

Steamed Clams

There are three varieties of clams: soft shelled, hard shelled, and razor clams from the Pacific. Soft-shelled clams are oval; hard-shelled clams are round and are known as littlenecks, medium cherrystones, or large chowder clams. Small clams are eaten raw or steamed or on the half shell. When buying clams, be sure the shells are clamped tightly together, as this indicates the clam is alive. Discard broken or cracked shells. Scrub each under running water and soak in salt brine for about 1/2 hour.

1 quart clams per serving
1/4 cup melted butter per serving
lemon juice or vinegar

Scrub shells well with a brush until no sand is visible. Put clams in a large saucepan with 2 tablespoons of water for each quart of clams. Cover tightly and cook over low heat until the clams open, about 15 minutes. Do not overcook. Remove the clams with a slotted spoon to soup bowls.

Strain the broth and serve in small bowls on the side. Also serve with small bowls of

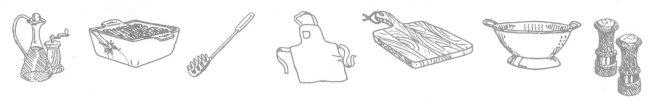

melted butter to which a little lemon juice or vinegar has been added. Add a small amount of boiling water so the butter will float to the top and stay hot. To eat, lift the clam from the shell by the neck and dip in clam broth, then butter.

Tomato Seafood Stew

Servings: 6

  1 tablespoon olive oil
  1 cup chopped onion
  2 cloves garlic, minced
  16-ounce can tomatoes, chopped
  8-ounce can tomato sauce
  1 potato, peeled and diced
  1 green bell pepper, chopped
  1 celery stalk, chopped
  1 carrot, shredded
  1 teaspoon crumbled dried thyme
  1/4 teaspoon pepper
  4 dashes Tabasco sauce
  1/2 pound shrimp, peeled, deveined, and
      halved lengthwise
  20-ounce can whole baby clams, drained
  2 tablespoons snipped fresh parsley

In a large saucepan, heat the oil over medium heat. Add the onion and garlic and sauté until soft, about 10 minutes. Stir in the tomatoes and their juice, tomato sauce, potato, bell pepper, celery, carrot, thyme, pepper, and Tabasco sauce. Bring to a boil. Cover, reduce the heat to low, and simmer until the vegetables are tender, 20 to 25 minutes.

Stir in the shrimp, clams, and parsley. Bring to a boil. Cover, reduce the heat to low, and simmer until the shrimp turn pink, about 2 minutes. Spoon into serving bowls and serve immediately.

Steamed Lobster

Lobsters range from 1 to about 30 pounds in weight. When buying a lobster, select one that is lively and active. Killed lobsters should be cooked as soon as possible after purchase. The meat of the claws, body, and tail are eaten.

  salt
  lobsters
  butter

Fill a large kettle with water to cover the lobsters. Add 2 teaspoons of salt for each quart of water. Bring to a boil and put lobsters in the pot. Allow 10 minutes cooking time for small lobsters, 15 minutes for medium lobsters, and up to 25 minutes for large lobsters.

Lift lobsters from the pot with tongs, and cool a few minutes before handling. To prepare, twist off the claws and break with a hammer or nutcracker, so meat can be removed. Gently pull the tail from the body, and holding with the hard shell

(continued)

down, cut the length with a scissors. Bend it apart, so meat loosens. Insert a knife down the center and remove the long intestine. Serve the lobster meat with melted butter for dipping.

Tuna Casserole

Servings: 4

4 medium potatoes, cubed
2 6-ounce cans tuna, well drained
1 cup peas, fresh or frozen
1 can cream of mushroom soup
$\frac{1}{4}$ cup milk
salt and pepper to taste
1 cup chow mein noodles

Preheat oven to 400°F.

Boil or steam the cubed potatoes until just tender. In a large bowl, toss the potatoes together with the tuna and peas. Stir the soup and milk together thoroughly, and stir into the potato mixture. Season to taste with salt and pepper. Turn into a 2-quart baking dish and sprinkle the noodles on top. Bake 20 to 30 minutes, or until the center is bubbly.

Salad Nicoise

Servings: 4 main-dish servings

3 medium potatoes (1 pound)
8 ounces fresh green beans, trimmed, or 9-ounce package frozen cut green beans, thawed
$\frac{1}{2}$ cup pared, diced cucumber
$\frac{1}{4}$ cup sliced black olives
7-ounce can white tuna, drained and flaked
$\frac{2}{3}$ cup Simple Vinaigrette Dressing, page 119, or oil-and-vinegar-style "French" dressing
lettuce leaves, optional
2 ripe tomatoes, cut in wedges
2 hard-boiled eggs, sliced

Pare and dice the potatoes, and boil or steam until tender. Meanwhile, cook or steam green beans until barely tender. In a bowl, layer the green beans, cucumbers, olives, tuna, and potatoes. Drizzle the dressing over the top. Cover and refrigerate until well chilled.

When ready to serve, toss the salad. Arrange on lettuce leaves, if desired, and top each serving with tomato wedges and hard-boiled egg slices.

Northwest Salmon Vegetable Pie

Servings: 4

   2 tablespoons butter
   1 cup broccoli florets
   1 medium carrot, thinly sliced
   1 small onion, cut into wedges
   1 clove garlic, minced
   $\frac{1}{3}$ teaspoon crushed dried oregano
     or savory
   $12\frac{1}{2}$-ounce can skinless, boneless salmon,
     drained and flaked
   1 prepared pie crust
   2 eggs
   $\frac{1}{3}$ cup light cream
   salt and pepper to taste

Preheat the oven to 350°F.

In a large skillet, melt the butter; stir-fry the broccoli, carrot, onion, and garlic until they are crisp-tender. Stir in the oregano. Gently stir the salmon into the vegetable mixture. Turn into the prepared pie crust. Beat the eggs and cream together well. Pour evenly over the salmon mixture.

Season with salt and pepper to taste. Cover with aluminum foil and bake for 15 minutes.

Remove foil, and bake for 5 to 10 minutes more or until set. Let stand 5 minutes before serving.

Shrimp Creole

Servings: 4

   2 tablespoons butter
   2 onions, chopped
   2 cloves garlic, crushed
   $\frac{1}{2}$ cup finely chopped celery
   1 medium green pepper, finely chopped
   8-ounce can tomato sauce
   $\frac{1}{4}$ cup tomato paste
   $\frac{3}{4}$ cup water
   1 tablespoon minced fresh parsley
   1 bay leaf
   $\frac{1}{8}$ teaspoon cayenne pepper
   1 pound medium shrimp, peeled and
     deveined
   salt
   3 cups cooked rice

In a medium skillet, melt the butter over medium heat; sauté the onions, garlic, celery, and green pepper in the butter about 5 minutes. Add the tomato sauce and paste, water, parsley, bay leaf, and cayenne pepper to the skillet. Slowly bring to a boil; add shrimp, and reduce heat to medium. Simmer for about 15 minutes, or until shrimp are done. Remove bay leaf, salt to taste, and serve over hot rice.

Paella

Serves: 4

> *about 3 tablespoons olive oil, divided*
> *4 large or 8 small shrimp, peeled and*
> *   deveined*
> *1 pound boneless, skinless chicken thighs*
> *   or breasts*
> *8 ounces chorizo*
> *1 cup rice*
> *1 clove garlic, halved*
> *2 cups chicken broth*
> *½ red bell pepper, sliced*
> *½ yellow or orange bell pepper, sliced*
> *1 medium tomato, seeded and chopped*
> *¼ teaspoon saffron, or more to taste*
> *1 cup fresh or frozen peas*
> *4 canned or frozen artichoke hearts, or*
> *   1 cup fresh or frozen corn*

If you do not have a paellero, or paella pan, use a large, covered casserole dish that can be used on the stovetop. Paella is served in the pan in which it is cooked.

In a separate skillet (not the paella pan), heat 1 tablespoon olive oil; sauté the shrimp in the oil 3 to 4 minutes; remove and set aside. Cut the chicken into strips that are approximately ½ inch wide and 3 inches long. Add another 1 to 2 tablespoons olive oil to the skillet and sauté the chicken in the oil until no longer pink; remove and set aside.

Slice the sausage into 1-inch chunks. Brown the sausage in the paella pan; set aside. Drain the drippings from the pan but do not clean or wipe it. Over medium-low heat, brown the rice lightly along with the garlic. Remove the garlic and discard. Add the chicken broth. Stir in the sliced peppers, tomato, sausage, and saffron. Bring to a boil, then reduce heat to a simmer. Cover and cook for about 15 minutes.

Uncover and stir in the peas and artichokes. Place the chicken on top. Cover and cook for an additional 10 minutes. Arrange the shrimp on top of the dish, cover, and cook for an additional 5 minutes, or until the rice is tender, the broth is absorbed, and the shrimp is heated through.

Paella Salad

Servings: 4 main-dish servings

Salad:

> *1 cup uncooked long-grain rice*
> *2 cups chicken broth or water*
> *¼ teaspoon saffron or turmeric*
> *8 ounces small shrimp, peeled and*
> *   deveined*
> *1½ cups cubed cooked chicken breast*
> *1 tomato, seeded and chopped*
> *½ cup frozen peas, thawed*

4 artichoke hearts, canned or
    frozen, quartered
¼ cup sliced green onions
salt to taste

Dressing:
3 tablespoons white wine vinegar
3 tablespoons olive oil
1 clove garlic, minced
⅛ teaspoon curry powder
⅛ teaspoon dry mustard
⅛ teaspoon white pepper

Combine the rice, chicken broth, and saffron in a medium saucepan. Bring to a boil; reduce heat, and cover. Simmer about 20 minutes, or until rice is tender and broth is absorbed.

Meanwhile, place the shrimp in a medium skillet, cover with water, bring to a boil, and simmer for about 3 minutes. Drain and reserve.

In a small bowl, whisk together the dressing ingredients. In a large bowl, combine all salad ingredients, and pour the dressing on top. Toss until well combined; cover and refrigerate at least 4 hours before serving. Serve on lettuce leaves, if desired.

Hoisin Sesame Salmon

Servings: 4

1 piece (½ inch) gingerroot, minced
¼ cup hoisin sauce*
7 skinless salmon fillets
¼ cup sesame seeds
1 tablespoon olive oil
1 package udon noodles, cooked according
    to package directions*
3 green onions, minced
2 teaspoons sesame oil
¼ teaspoon salt, or to taste
freshly ground black pepper

Stir together the ginger and hoisin sauce in a small bowl. Reserve 1 tablespoon of the mixture in another small bowl. Brush the sauce over the salmon fillets. Coat each fillet with sesame seeds. Heat the olive oil in a large skillet over medium heat. Add the fillets and cook, turning once, until seeds are browned and fish is cooked through, about 6 minutes per side.

Toss the noodles, reserved hoisin sauce, green onions, sesame oil, salt, and pepper to taste in a large bowl. Divide noodles among plates and top each serving with a fillet.

*Look for hoisin sauce and udon noodles in the Asian section of most supermarkets.

Chapter 9

Vegetable Entrees and Side Dishes

Vegetable side dishes can be renamed vegetable center dishes, as they often play a pivotal role in meal planning. Busy nutrition-conscious cooks who want to add color, flavor, texture, and variety to meals turn to preparing easy and yet sensational vegetable dishes for family and friends.

Glazed Onions

Servings: 6–8

> 18 medium white or yellow onions
> 4 teaspoons sugar
> 1 teaspoon dry mustard
> 1/2 teaspoon salt
> 6 tablespoons butter, melted
> 1/4 teaspoon paprika

Peel onions and simmer whole in water for 15 minutes.

Preheat the oven to 325°F. Drain the onions and arrange in a shallow baking dish. Combine sugar, mustard, salt, and butter, pour over the onions. Sprinkle with paprika and bake for 20 minutes or until tender when pierced with a sharp knife.

Baked Corn Soufflé

Servings: 4

> 2 eggs, well beaten
> 1 tablespoon butter, melted
> 2 teaspoons flour
> 2 tablespoons milk
> 2 tablespoons cream or half-and-half

> 1 teaspoon salt
> 16-ounce can cream-style corn

Preheat oven to 350°F. Beat eggs with an electric mixer until golden and fluffy. Add butter, flour, milk, cream, salt, and canned corn. Bake in a 2-quart casserole or 9-inch-square glass baking dish for 45 minutes or until edge pulls away from baking dish. Serve immediately.

Belgian Carrots

Servings: 4

> 2 pounds fresh carrots, sliced thinly
> 1/2 cup butter, melted
> 1 teaspoon salt
> 1/3 cup fresh chopped parsley
> 2 bunches fresh green onions, chopped

Preheat oven to 350°F. Place sliced carrots in a 2-quart baking dish. Set aside.

Sauté butter, salt, parsley, and green onions in a saucepan over medium heat for 5 minutes or until onions become slightly translucent. Pour over carrots, stirring slightly. Bake for 50 minutes or until carrots are tender. Serve immediately.

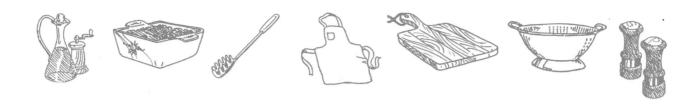

Wash Those Veggies!

- Vegetables should be washed carefully to remove dust and dirt.

- To retain the peel of root vegetables, wash with a stiff brush. Do not use a woven plastic or metal pad to wash vegetables as bits of each can loosen and fall unseen into the food.

- Leave the peel/skin on vegetables whenever possible unless you know or suspect the vegetable has been sprayed or waxed.

- The easiest and most efficient tool for peeling vegetables is a carbon-steel swivel bladed peeler which can be purchased at most supermarkets.

Vegetable Brush

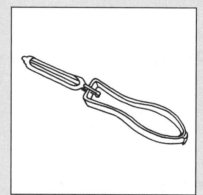

Peeler

Puréed Parsnips

Servings: 4

6 parsnips
½ cup 2% milk
3 tablespoons butter
1 teaspoon ground cumin
¼ teaspoon paprika
½ teaspoon salt
¼ teaspoon freshly ground pepper

Peel parsnips and cut into ½-inch cubes. Cook parsnips in gently boiling water for 10 to 12 minutes or until tender. Drain well. In food processor or with hand masher, purée parsnips with all remaining ingredients until smooth.

For a special presentation, use a pastry bag to decoratively pipe parsnip purée onto plates surrounding roasted meat

Honey-Orange Beets

Servings: 4

6 medium-sized fresh beets
1 teaspoon grated orange zest
2 tablespoons orange juice
2 teaspoons butter
1 teaspoon honey
¼ teaspoon ground ginger
salt and freshly ground pepper to taste

In a pot of boiling water, cook beets for 40 minutes or until tender.

Drain beets and let cool slightly. Slip off skins and slice. In a saucepan, heat the orange zest, orange juice, butter, honey, and ginger over low heat until the butter melts. Add the beets, and toss to coat. Season with salt and pepper.

Rutabaga Casserole

Servings: 8

1 orange
3 cups water
6 medium-sized carrots, chopped
5 cups peeled and cubed rutabaga
2 tablespoons maple syrup or honey
2 tablespoons butter
salt and pepper
½ cup sour cream
pinch cinnamon
pinch nutmeg

Grate 2 tablespoons of zest off the orange. Remove and discard the remaining peel and white pith from the rest of the orange. Slice and then chop the orange.

In a large saucepan, combine water, orange zest, orange, carrots, rutabaga, maple syrup, butter, and salt and pepper to taste. Bring to a boil and then reduce heat and simmer for 30 to 40 minutes or until water evaporates and vegetables are tender.

In food processor, purée mixture in batches, adding sour cream, cinnamon, and nutmeg to the last batch. Transfer to

warmed vegetable bowls and serve immediately, stirring to distribute the sour cream.

 Rutabagas and turnips contribute fiber and are good sources of vitamin C and potassium. The rutabaga is a dense vegetable that keeps well either in the refrigerator for up to 3 weeks or in a cool, dry storage place for up to 2 months. Turnips soften quickly when cooking and can be stored in a plastic bag in the refrigerator for up to 1 week.

Glazed Turnips or Rutabagas

Servings: 4

2 pounds rutabagas or turnips
2 tablespoons butter
$^1/_4$ cup honey
$^1/_4$ teaspoon ground ginger
salt and freshly ground pepper to taste

Peel rutabagas or turnips and cut into $^1/_2$-inch thick, quarter-sized slices. In a pot of boiling water, cook rutabagas for 15 minutes, or turnips for 8 minutes or just until tender.

Drain. Stir in butter and cook over high heat, shaking pan often, until vegetables are coated with butter. Stir in honey, ginger, and salt and pepper to taste. Cook, stirring often, for 1 minute or until glazed. Serve immediately.

Cheese Asparagus Bake

Servings: 4

$^3/_4$ to 1 pound asparagus, sliced in 1-inch
    pieces, tough ends removed
4 tablespoons butter, divided
2 tablespoons chopped yellow onion
$^1/_2$ teaspoon sugar
1 teaspoon salt, divided
2 tablespoons water
6 eggs
$^1/_3$ cup heavy cream
freshly ground pepper
2 tablespoons butter
$1^1/_2$ cups grated Muenster cheese
2 tablespoons grated Parmesan cheese

Peel and cut the asparagus into 1-inch pieces. Melt 2 tablespoons butter in a saucepan and sauté onion until soft and golden. Add the asparagus; sprinkle with the sugar and $^1/_2$ teaspoon salt, and toss for 1 minute. Add water, cover, and shaking the pan, steam-cook for 1–2 minutes. Remove cover, and cook until liquid is evaporated. Cool for 2 minutes.

Preheat the oven to 350°F. Beat together the eggs, cream, $^1/_2$ teaspoon salt, and pepper to taste. Melt 2 tablespoons butter in an ovenproof 10 x 10-inch baking dish. Pour in the egg mixture and cook over medium heat until the bottom is set—about 3 minutes. Arrange asparagus and onions in a single layer on top of the eggs. Bake for 5 minutes.

(continued)

Remove from the oven and cover the asparagus with the grated cheeses, then bake for an additional 10 minutes. When eggs have puffed and cheese has lightly browned it is done.

Fresh asparagus in spring is best cooked simply. Simmer in boiling water until the asparagus is tender and still crisp (about 5 minutes). Top with a pat of sweet butter.

Oven-Roasted Asparagus

Servings: 4

1 pound asparagus
2 cloves garlic, slivered
1 teaspoon chopped fresh parsley
2 tablespoons water
2 tablespoons dry white wine or
   nonalcoholic white wine
2 teaspoons lemon juice
1 teaspoon olive oil
$1/4$ teaspoon salt
$1/8$ teaspoon freshly ground pepper

Preheat the oven to 400°F. Break off tough ends of asparagus spears. With a vegetable peeler, peel the bottom half of the asparagus stalks. Scatter the garlic and parsley in a 13 x 9-inch baking dish. Arrange the asparagus spears in a single layer.

In a small bowl, combine the water, wine, lemon juice, oil, salt, and pepper.

Pour over the asparagus. Bake for 10 minutes. Turn the asparagus over and bake for 8 to 10 minutes more, or until the asparagus are tender but slightly crisp and the liquid is almost gone.

Green Beans and Tomatoes

Servings: 4 to 6

1 pound fresh green beans
2 tablespoons butter
1 tablespoon olive oil
$3/4$ cup chopped green onions
1 clove garlic, minced
2 cups peeled, seeded, and chopped
   tomatoes
$1/2$ teaspoon oregano
1 teaspoon salt
freshly ground pepper to taste
grated Parmesan cheese

Blanch or steam the beans and cut into $1 1/2$-inch pieces. Heat the butter and olive oil in a saucepan and sauté the onions until just soft, about 5 minutes. Add the garlic and cook for 1 minute. Add tomatoes, oregano, salt, and pepper, and simmer 5 minutes. Mix in the beans and cook 2 minutes longer to heat through. Serve with Parmesan cheese.

French Beans

Servings: 10

2¹/₂ pounds French-cut green beans
2 tablespoons peanut oil
2 tablespoons walnut oil
1 tablespoon honey
2 teaspoons freshly ground black pepper
1 tablespoon fresh lemon juice
1 teaspoon lemon zest
³/₄ cup walnuts, chopped

In a sauté pan, toss green beans in hot peanut and walnut oils until tender, about 3–5 minutes. Add honey, pepper, lemon juice, and lemon zest. Continue to cook for 2 more minutes. Add walnuts and serve.

Cauliflower Curry

Servings: 4 to 6

1¹/₂ pounds cauliflower florets
2 teaspoons ground ginger
2 teaspoons ground cumin
1 teaspoon ground cinnamon
1 teaspoon ground turmeric
¹/₄ teaspoon cayenne pepper
2 teaspoons salt
dash of sugar
2 tablespoons olive oil
4 tablespoons butter, divided

1 cup chopped onions
¹/₂ teaspoon mustard seeds
1¹/₂ cups puréed tomatoes
2 tablespoons chopped green chilies
2 tablespoons chopped parsley

Trim and cut florets into equal-sized pieces. Combine spices, salt, and sugar. Heat the olive oil and 2 tablespoons of the butter in a large sauté pan. Lightly brown the cauliflowers. Remove and set aside.

Add the remaining butter and the onions and cook until the onions are wilted, 5 to 10 minutes. Add mustard seeds and tomatoes. Simmer for 4 to 5 minutes until the sauce is slightly thickened.

Add the cauliflower, stirring until coated with sauce. Add the chilies. Simmer, covered, for approximately 20 minutes or until the cauliflower is tender. Sprinkle with parsley and serve with basmati rice.

Cauliflower, raw or cooked, stores poorly, as it quickly acquires a strong and unpleasant odor. Store for 2 to 3 days in a perforated plastic bag in the refrigerator when raw. Do not store in a sealed container, as cauliflower needs oxygen.

Cauliflower Gratin

Servings: 8

juice of 1 lemon
salt to taste
1 large cauliflower head, cut into small
* florets, core sliced thinly*
2 tablespoons unsalted butter
2 medium yellow onions, diced
2 cloves garlic, minced
crushed red pepper flakes
1½ cups whipping cream
1 cup grated sharp Cheddar cheese
½ cup grated mozzarella cheese
½ cup grated farmer cheese
salt and freshly ground black pepper
1 cup grated Parmesan cheese
1 cup chopped chives

Heat a large pot of water to boiling over high heat. Add lemon juice and season with salt. Add cauliflower florets (but not the core); cook until firm to the bite, about 3 minutes. Transfer florets to a colander and drain, saving water. Add sliced cauliflower core to same water and cook until firm to the bite, about 2 minutes. Transfer to another colander to drain.

Heat butter in a large skillet over medium heat and add onions and garlic; cook until onions are tender, about 10 minutes. Season with salt and crushed red pepper flakes. Add cream, and heat mixture to simmer. Reduce heat and add

Cheddar, mozzarella, and farmer cheeses, stirring until melted but not boiling. Add cauliflower slices and stir to coat with mixture. Remove skillet from heat and add salt and pepper to taste.

Preheat oven to 350°F. Spoon ¼ of the cauliflower slices mixture across the bottom of a baking dish, pour with ¼ of the florets. Season with ¼ of the Parmesan cheese and chives. Cover florets with another ¼ of the cauliflower slices, followed by florets, Parmesan cheese, and chives. Repeat layers with remaining ingredients. Bake until golden brown, about 30 minutes. Cool slightly before serving.

Garden Vegetable Platter

Servings: 6

Dressing:
⅔ cup olive oil
¼ cup red wine vinegar
3 tablespoons chopped fresh oregano
2 tablespoons chopped fresh basil
1 tablespoon Dijon mustard
3 cloves garlic, minced
½ teaspoon each salt and pepper

1 small eggplant
1 each green and golden zucchini,
* thinly sliced*
8 ounces Italian green beans, trimmed

8 ounces asparagus, trimmed
1 each red and yellow tomato, sliced
1 sweet green pepper, sliced
fresh basil and oregano for garnish
fresh peas for garnish (removed
*   from pods)*

In a small bowl, whisk together all dressing ingredients. Cut eggplant into ¼-inch-thick slices. Lightly brush eggplant and zucchini with some of the dressing; place on a greased grill over medium-high heat. Grill zucchini for 5 to 6 minutes and eggplant for 10 to 15 minutes, basting with dressing and turning occasionally until vegetables are tender.

In a large pot of boiling salted water, cook beans for 4 to 5 minutes or until tender-crisp. Remove with slotted spoon to a colander. Pour cold water over the beans and drain.

Add asparagus to the pot and cook for 3 minutes until tender-crisp. Drain and pour cold water over asparagus. Drain again. Brush tomatoes with 2 tablespoons of dressing; toss beans, asparagus, and green pepper with remaining dressing.

Decoratively arrange beans, asparagus, and green pepper on a large platter along with the grilled eggplant and zucchini. Garnish with basil, oregano, and peas.

Stir-Fried Spinach

Servings: 4

2 pounds fresh spinach
1 small yellow onion
3 tablespoons peanut oil
1 clove garlic
2 slices ginger, ⅛-inch thick
salt
1 tablespoon dry sherry
1½ tablespoons tamari sauce
1 teaspoon sugar

Wash and trim spinach and cut leaves into wide strips or tear into 2-inch squares. Chop onion and stir-fry in a large pan with the oil, garlic, and ginger over high heat for 1 minute. Add the spinach, sprinkle with salt, and stir for 3 minutes. Add the sherry, tamari sauce, and sugar. Turn the heat down to medium, cover, and cook for 3 minutes longer.

Remove ginger and garlic, and serve immediately. The Chinese flavors of this dish go well with roast pork or chops.

Creamed Spinach

Servings: 6

10-ounce package fresh spinach
1 small onion, finely chopped
1 teaspoon olive oil
3 tablespoons all-purpose flour
1¼ cups 1% milk
1 teaspoon salt
½ teaspoon pepper

(continued)

Wash the spinach. Place the spinach in a heavy skillet over medium heat, cover, and steam, stirring occasionally, until wilted, about 5 minutes. (There is no need to add water other than what clings to the leaves while washing.) Place the spinach in a sieve and press with the back of a spoon to remove as much moisture as possible.

In a nonstick saucepan, sauté the onion in the olive oil over medium heat until translucent, about 7 to 10 minutes. Stir in the flour until a smooth paste forms. Gradually add milk, stirring constantly. Bring just to a boil; reduce the heat to low, and simmer, stirring often, until thickened, about 10 minutes. Add the salt and pepper.

Process the spinach in a blender or food processor until it's fine, then add to the cream sauce. Serve hot.

Baked Mashed Squash

Servings: 4

2¹/₂–3 pound winter squash
5 tablespoons butter, divided
salt and freshly ground pepper to taste
brown sugar
¹/₄–¹/₃ cup chopped pecans
sour cream for garnish

Peel squash and steam or bake until tender. Mash.

Preheat the oven to 350°F. Add 4 tablespoons butter to squash and season to taste with salt and pepper. Place squash in a buttered 1-quart baking dish, dot with remaining butter, and cover with a sprinkling of brown sugar and pecans. Bake for 30 minutes. Garnish with sour cream.

Winter squash such as acorn and buttercup store well and there is no need to can or freeze them. Cooked squash freezes easily and is convenient to have on hand for a quick and easy side dish.

Steamed Cabbage

Servings: 4

1 tablespoon olive oil
3 cups shredded green cabbage
1 cup thinly sliced celery
1 green pepper, chopped
¹/₂ cup chopped yellow onion
salt and pepper to taste

In a large deep skillet with a lid, heat the oil over medium heat. Add the vegetables, stirring and cooking for 1 minute. Cover the pan tightly, and allow to steam for approximately 5 minutes, stirring occasionally. Remove from the heat, season with salt and pepper, and serve immediately.

Brussels Sprouts with Mustard Cream

Servings: 6

1½ pounds Brussels sprouts, trimmed
2 tablespoons unsalted butter
1 large shallot, minced
½ cup whipping cream
1 teaspoon fresh minced tarragon or
    ½ teaspoon dried tarragon
¾ teaspoon Dijon mustard
¼ teaspoon salt
¼ teaspoon freshly ground pepper

Cook Brussels sprouts in boiling water until tender, 5 to 6 minutes. Drain well. Sprouts can be cooked several hours in advance and kept at room temperature. Melt the butter in the same pan and add the shallot. Cook over medium-high heat until shallot soften, about 2 minutes. Add Brussels sprouts and toss gently. Add all the remaining ingredients. Cook just until the cream thickens slightly, about 1 minute.

Crosshatch the bottom of Brussels sprouts for more even cooking. Add Brussels sprouts sliced lengthwise to mixed vegetable soups and clear consommés. Add steamed leaves to clear soups for garnish.

Sautéed Broccoli and Sweet Peppers

Servings: 4

1 pound broccoli
1 tablespoon olive oil
2 teaspoons unsalted butter
½ each red bell pepper and yellow bell
    pepper, julienned
2 cloves garlic, minced
salt and pepper

Cut broccoli into bite-sized florets and blanch in boiling water until tender, about 2 to 3 minutes. Shock in ice water to preserve color, and drain. Set aside.

Heat oil and butter in a sauté pan or skillet over medium-high heat. Sauté peppers for 3 minutes. Add broccoli and garlic. Sauté until thoroughly heated and lightly browned, 3 to 4 minutes. Season with salt and pepper to taste.

Add the peeled stalks of broccoli, thinly sliced diagonally, to stir-fries. Use raw, peeled stems cut in quarter-sized pieces in Chinese recipes as a substitute for water chestnuts. Use julienned blanched broccoli stalks as a clear soup garnish.

Leeks with Tomatoes

Servings: 4

¼ cup olive oil
2 cups chopped fresh tomatoes
2 cloves garlic, minced
1 teaspoon fresh chopped thyme
6 cups cleaned and sliced leeks
1 tablespoon lemon juice
½ teaspoon freshly ground pepper
salt to taste

Heat oil in a large skillet over medium heat. Add the tomatoes, garlic, and thyme, stirring to coat; sauté 10 minutes, stirring frequently.

Add the leeks and cook 10 minutes, stirring occasionally. Add lemon juice and pepper. Remove from heat, cover, and let stand 30 minutes. Season to taste with salt.

Grilled Portobello Mushrooms

Servings: 4

4 large Portobello mushrooms
olive oil
salt and pepper to taste
10 fresh sage leaves
1 teaspoon fresh chopped parsley
¼ cup unsalted butter
lemon wedges

Preheat the grill. Brush mushrooms with olive oil and sprinkle with salt and pepper. Put the sage leaves, parsley, and butter into a small pan and set over low heat (or on the grill); cook for 5 minutes or until the butter is aromatic. Grill the mushrooms about 2 minutes on each side or until tender.

Put the mushrooms on individual plates and spoon the seasoned butter (including the sage leaves) over each mushroom. Squeeze fresh lemon juice over the mushrooms just before serving.

Wilted Asian Greens with Sesame Seeds

Servings: 6

¼ cup water
¼ cup tamari sauce*
2 tablespoons rice wine vinegar
1 tablespoon sesame oil
1 teaspoon peanut oil
1 clove garlic, minced
6 cups mixed Asian greens
1 mango, pitted, peeled, and julienned
¼ medium red onion, thinly sliced
toasted sesame seeds**

Whisk together water, tamari sauce, vinegar, and sesame oil in a small bowl. Set aside.

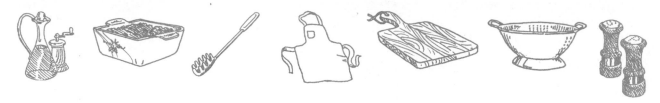

Heat the peanut oil in a medium saucepan over medium heat. Cook garlic in the oil for 1 minute. Add the vinaigrette mixture and heat 2 minutes.

Toss the greens, mango, and onion in a large serving bowl. Pour the warm dressing over the salad; sprinkle with toasted sesame seeds to taste.

*Tamari sauce can be found in the Asian section of grocery stores or at Asian markets.

**To toast sesame seeds, heat seeds in a small dry pan, stirring often, until lightly browned. Immediately remove from the pan to stop cooking.

Sugar Snap Peas and Carrots

Servings: 4 to 6

1 pound sugar snap peas
1 pound carrots
salt
2–3 teaspoons sugar, divided
6 tablespoons butter, divided
freshly ground pepper to taste

Shell the peas. Set aside. Peel the carrots and cut into logs approximately 3 inches long by ½ inch thick. Bring 3 quarts of water to a rolling boil. Add 2 teaspoons salt and 2 teaspoons sugar, and drop in the carrot logs. Cook at a medium boil until barely tender, about 4 to 8 minutes. Drain.

Melt 3 tablespoons butter in a large sauté pan, add carrots; roll the carrots in butter until coated. Sprinkle with sugar if a light glaze is desired. Heat through and season with salt and pepper. Stack the carrot logs down the center of a warm platter and keep warm.

Meanwhile, melt 3 tablespoons butter in a large sauté pan. Stir in the peas, cover, and cook over medium heat for 2 to 3 minutes to barely cook the peas, shaking the pan occasionally. Do not let them brown. Serve peas arranged on each side of the carrot logs.

Baked Peppers and Onions

Servings: 4

1–1½ pounds green and red peppers
(4–5 medium sized)
1 pound small red new potatoes
1 large yellow onion
*¼ cup olive oil**
salt and freshly ground pepper

Preheat the oven to 425°F. Wash the peppers and cut into 1½-to 2-inch pieces. Scrub the potatoes and cut into 1-inch slices or chunks. Peel the onion and cut into chunks.

(continued)

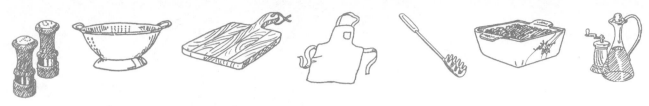

Place everything in a shallow ovenproof dish; pour the oil over the vegetables. Rub the vegetables with the oil. Sprinkle with salt and lots of pepper. Bake for approximately 30 minutes or until the potatoes are tender.

*A heavy green olive oil is preferable and blends well with the peppers and onions.

Sautéed Swiss Chard

Servings: 4

2 bunches young Swiss chard
2 tablespoons olive oil
2 tablespoons butter
1 clove garlic, chopped
salt and pepper to taste

Leave the chard whole or slice it. In a sauté pan, heat the oil and butter over medium heat until butter is just melted. Stir in the chopped garlic and the raw chard. Toss until coated with butter and oil.

Cover the pan, reduce the heat, and cook for 3 to 4 minutes, stirring occasionally. Uncover the pan and raise the heat to evaporate the moisture. Shake the pan so chard does not stick. Add more butter if necessary and season to taste.

Substitute Swiss chard in most spinach recipes to get a heartier texture and taste. Refrigerated, unwashed chard in a perforated plastic bag will hold for 3 to 5 days.

Fresh Vegetable Pot

Servings: 4

3–4 small young carrots cut in thirds
1 rutabaga cut in large cubes*
1/2 small head cauliflower, cut into florets
1/4 small head of cabbage, cut in wedges
6 small white onions (not pearl),
    cut in half
1 cup new green beans, ends trimmed
    (young, small green beans)
3 cloves garlic, split
1 cup green peas*
salt and freshly ground pepper

In a large, heavy saucepan, layer vegetables (except peas, if they are frozen) in order given, seasoning each layer with salt and freshly ground pepper. Add 1 inch of water, cover tightly, bring to a boil, and simmer over medium to medium-low heat steaming vegetables until just tender, about 15 minutes.

If using frozen peas, thaw and sprinkle over the vegetables a minute or so before cooking is finished, just to heat through.

*New red-skinned potatoes and broccoli florets can be substituted for the rutabagas and peas if desired.

Zucchini Bake

Servings: 4 to 6

> 6 tablespoons butter
> 1 clove garlic, split
> 2 pounds zucchini (4 medium)
> 2 eggs
> 1/3 cup half-and-half
> salt and freshly ground pepper to taste
> 2 tablespoons grated Parmesan cheese

Preheat oven to 375°F. In a small skillet, slowly melt the butter, and add the split garlic. Let stand while preparing zucchini. Cube unpeeled zucchini. Cook until tender in just enough lightly salted water to cover. Drain well in a colander. Mash the zucchini.

Beat the eggs and add to the zucchini. Remove the garlic halves from the butter, discarding them. Mix the butter and the half-and-half into the zucchini along with salt and pepper to taste. Pour into a buttered 1 1/2-quart, deep casserole. Sprinkle with cheese. Bake 45 minutes.

Baked Garlic

Servings: 4

> 4 heads garlic
> 4 tablespoons butter
> salt and freshly ground pepper
> olive oil
> crusty French bread
> goat cheese

Preheat the oven to 250°F. Make a slight cut around the circumference of each garlic head about 1/2 inch up from the base. The upper skin then peels off easily, leaving the whole head intact with each clove covered by skin. Set the garlic heads in a baking dish, and top each with 1 tablespoon butter. Sprinkle with salt and pepper and drizzle with olive oil. Bake uncovered for 30 minutes, then add just enough water to film the bottom of the pan.

Cover and bake another 1 1/2 hours or until the cloves are tender. Serve with fresh crusty bread and a French goat cheese. Each person squeezes the garlic out of its skin and spreads it on the bread.

Garlic can also be squeezed out and puréed with a bit of soft butter.

Corn and Chive Soufflé

Servings: 4

> 2 cups corn, scraped fresh from cobs
> 1/2 cup shredded Cheddar cheese, packed
> 6 egg yolks
> 1/2 cup minced chives
> salt and freshly ground pepper
> 8 egg whites
> 1/4 teaspoon cream of tartar

Preheat the oven to 425°F. Butter a 2-quart soufflé dish.

(continued)

Blend together the corn, cheese, and egg yolks. Add chives and season to taste with salt and pepper.

Beat the egg whites to soft peaks, adding the cream of tartar when they become foamy. Stir a quarter of the whites into the corn mixture to lighten it, then fold in the remaining whites. Pour into the soufflé dish and bake for 10 minutes, then reduce the temperature to 375°F and bake for 30 minutes longer.

Kernels *cut* from 6 plump ears equal approximately 4 cups whole kernels. Kernels *scraped* from 6 ears equal approximately 3½–4 cups flesh and liquid.

Don't Forget the Herbs

When preparing vegetable dishes, don't forget fresh herbs and spices. Use fresh herbs whenever possible. Use a mortar and pestle to grind them for the freshest and fullest flavor. Add dried herbs such as ginger, thyme, rosemary, and marjoram to dishes for a more pungent flavor, but use them sparingly.

Meatless Burritos

Servings: 4

16-ounce can kidney beans, drained
10-ounce can enchilada sauce, mild or hot
1 cup water
16-ounce can whole tomatoes, diced, liquid reserved
1 cup corn (fresh or frozen)
½ cup peas (frozen or fresh)
1 cup shredded carrot
1½ cups cooked brown rice
10–12 flour tortillas
1½ cups shredded Monterey Jack or Cheddar cheese
sour cream

In a large, deep skillet with a lid, combine the beans, enchilada sauce, water, tomatoes, and vegetables. Mix well and bring to a boil over medium heat. Stir in the cooked rice. Cover and reduce heat. Simmer until the liquid is absorbed, about 20 minutes, stirring occasionally.

Warm the tortillas in the microwave or conventional oven. Place ½ cup of the mixture in the middle of the tortilla and top with cheese. Fold and serve with sour cream.

Meatless Tacos

Servings: 4

1 tablespoon olive oil
1 small yellow onion, chopped

1 stalk celery, chopped
1/3 cup chopped sweet red or green pepper
1 teaspoon finely chopped jalapeño pepper
1 clove garlic, minced
19-ounce can chickpeas, drained
2 tablespoons picante sauce or salsa
1/2 teaspoon ground cumin
salt and pepper
8 taco shells, warmed

Toppings:
1 1/2 cups shredded Cheddar cheese
1 cup shredded iceberg lettuce
1 cup salsa
1 teaspoon chopped fresh cilantro

In a large, heavy skillet, heat oil over medium-high heat; cook onion, celery, red pepper, jalapeño pepper, and garlic in the oil, stirring often, for 3 minutes or until softened. Add chickpeas, picante sauce, and cumin. Cook, stirring, for 2 minutes or until heated through. Season with salt and pepper to taste. Spoon into taco shells. Top each taco with cheese, lettuce, salsa, and cilantro.

To put the crunch back into iceberg lettuce (the only kind to serve in tacos), plunge leaves into cold water and let stand for 5 minutes. Drain, dry well and store, wrapped in cotton towels, in crisper of refrigerator.

Szechuan Stir-Fried Cabbage with Hot Peppers

Servings: 4 to 6
1/4 cup + 2 tablespoons vegetable oil
8 dried red chili peppers, seeded and cut into quarters
1-inch piece fresh gingerroot, peeled and minced
1 medium head cabbage (any variety), washed, drained, and chopped into 2-inch pieces
1/2 teaspoon cornstarch
1 tablespoon soy sauce
1 teaspoon pale, dry sherry
1 teaspoon sugar
1 teaspoon rice wine vinegar
1 teaspoon sesame oil

Heat 1/4 cup of oil in a wok over high heat. Stir in the peppers and fry, stirring, for 1 minute, or until peppers turn a dark red-brown. Immediately empty the oil and peppers into a small bowl and set aside.

Pour remaining 2 tablespoons of oil into the wok and, still over high heat, fry the ginger for a few seconds. Immediately add the cabbage and stir well. Fry, stirring, for 1 minute. Stir the cornstarch, soy sauce, and sherry together in a small bowl; add to the wok. Stir the mixture until the cornstarch cooks and begins to glisten and thicken, then add sugar and vinegar. Sprinkle with sesame oil and pour in the red peppers and their oil. Stir again and transfer to a serving bowl.

Chapter 10

Potato, Rice, and Bean Entrees and Side Dishes

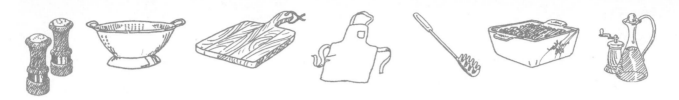

For vegetarians, potatoes, rice, and beans are an essential staple in a healthy diet. For meat-eaters, they serve as healthy and delicious alternatives in entrees and the perfect accompaniment as side dishes. All three contain tons of important vitamins, and are a necessary part of any balanced diet. In this chapter you'll find sides and main courses made with potatoes, rice, and beans that will satisfy any palate.

Kinds of Potatoes

The most commonly sold kinds of potatoes are:

Russets—The all-purpose variety, available year-round. They are widely grown in the Northwest, and are sometimes called Idaho or Burbank potatoes. Russets are longish and slightly rounded, and have rough brown skin with "eyes." They have a high starch content and become fluffy when cooked. Russets make the best baked potatoes and French fries.

Round Whites—Widely grown in the East, they are available year-round and are also called boiling potatoes. They have a smoother, light tan skin and less starch than other varieties. Round whites hold their shape after cooking and are the best variety for mashed or roasted potatoes and potato salads.

Long Whites—Grown in California and Arizona, they are available in the spring and summer. They are oval shaped with a thin tan skin and have a medium starch content. They are best used for baking and boiling, and they're great in soups, stews, and scalloped potatoes.

Round Reds—Primarily available in the late summer and fall, they are often called "new potatoes." They have a red skin and white flesh and are best used for boiling, roasting and frying; they're also great in salads.

Yellow Flesh Potatoes—Traditionally very popular in Europe, they have recently gained in popularity in the United States. Common varieties are Yukon Gold and Yellow Finn. They are available in the late summer and early fall. They have a buttery flavor and are best used for baking, mashing, or roasting.

Other Varieties—Purple- or blue-fleshed potatoes, which originated in South America, are sometimes available in the fall. They have a nutty flavor and are best prepared in the microwave to preserve the color.

New Potatoes—Round red potatoes are most often called new potatoes, but actually the term refers to any small potato that has been harvested when it is very young. It will have a thin skin and a higher sugar content because it has not matured long enough to convert the sugar to starch. New potatoes are best used in salads and for roasting or boiling.

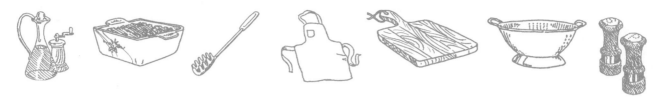

Basic Ways to Cook Potatoes

Wash or scrub potatoes. If possible, leave peels on to help preserve nutrients. (Be aware that you will have to allow potatoes to cool first if they must be pared to be used in mashed potatoes or another recipe.) Otherwise, peel potatoes and remove any eyes. Leave whole or cut into large pieces, equivalent to the size of a quartered medium potato.

Boiling—Place potatoes in a heavy saucepan with a tight-fitting lid. Add enough salted water to cover and boil for 35 to 40 minutes if whole, 20 to 25 minutes if cut up, or until fork tender.

Steaming—Place a wire rack in the bottom of a large kettle, or use a saucepan with a steamer insert. Add water to just below the level of the rack or steamer insert. Bring the water to a boil, then add the potatoes. Cook, tightly covered, until fork-tender, about 30 to 40 minutes if whole, 20 to 30 minutes if cut up.

Boiling and Steaming New Potatoes—Follow instructions in the two preceding paragraphs, but do not cut up potatoes. Allow about 20 minutes to boil or steam.

Boiling and Steaming Sweet Potatoes and Yams—Follow the instructions for potatoes.

Baked Potatoes

Wash or scrub the potatoes. Pierce the top with a fork in several places; this allows steam to escape and prevents the potato from exploding in the oven. Place the potatoes directly on the rack of the

Potato Equivalents

One medium potato equals:

- 1 cup peeled, sliced potatoes
- a little more than $\frac{2}{3}$ cup peeled, diced potatoes
- $\frac{2}{3}$ cup mashed potatoes
- 1 serving of potato salad

One pound of potatoes equals about *3 medium* potatoes, or:

- 3 cups peeled, sliced potatoes
- $2\frac{1}{2}$ cups peeled, diced potatoes
- 2 cups mashed or French-fried potatoes
- 3 servings of potato salad

oven. If a soft skin is desired, rub the potato with a little vegetable oil before baking. Potatoes can also be wrapped in foil, but most chefs do not recommend this method because it causes the potato to cook by steaming (moist heat) rather than baking (dry heat).

Baking temperatures and times for potatoes can be adjusted (between 325°F and 450°F) to match those of other foods being cooked at the same time. **Medium-sized** potatoes will take:

- about 40 minutes at 425°F
- 45 to 50 minutes at 400°F
- 50 to 60 minutes at 375°F
- 1 to 11/4 hours at 350°F
- 11/4 to 11/2 hours at 325°F

If baking **large potatoes**, increase the cooking time. Baking several potatoes at once, however, does not lengthen the baking time. Baked potatoes are done if they feel soft when squeezed (wear an oven mitt!) or when they can be *easily* pierced with a fork.

Baking Sweet Potatoes and Yams— Follow the instructions and time chart for baking potatoes.

Baking Potatoes in the Microwave— Scrub and pierce potatoes as for conventional oven preparation. For 1 potato, placke on a paper towel and microwave on high 3¹/₂ to 4¹/₂ minutes, turning over once. Allow to stand for 5 minutes. For 4 potatoes, arrange them in a circle on a paper towel at least 1 inch apart. Cook 9 to 11 minutes, turning once. Allow to stand for 5 minutes.

Twice-Baked Potatoes—are prepared by scooping the flesh from halved baked potatoes, leaving a shell of potato flesh about ¼-inch thick in the skin. The scooped out flesh is mixed with other ingredients and returned to the shell to bake again until thoroughly warmed.

Pan-Roasted Potatoes

Roasted Alone—Boil or steam small whole peeled potatoes or halved medium potatoes for 10 minutes. Arrange in a shallow baking pan and brush with butter. Bake uncovered at 400°F for about 45 minutes, turning occasionally to baste with the butter.

Roasted with Meat—Arrange small whole or halved medium peeled potatoes around the meat in a roasting pan, adding them about 1¹/₂ hours before the meat will be done. Do not precook the potatoes. Baste with the pan drippings when they are added to the roasting pan, and turn and baste frequently while they cook.

Basic Mashed Potatoes

Servings: 4

> 4 medium potatoes (1¹/₃ pounds)
> ¹/₂ cup milk
> 2 tablespoons butter
> at least ¹/₄ teaspoon salt, or to taste
> ¹/₈ teaspoon pepper

Wash and peel the potatoes and boil or steam until they're tender. Turn off the burner and drain the potatoes, then return the potatoes in the pan to the burner. Shake the pan for about 1 minute to allow the potatoes to dry.

Warm the milk and butter in a small saucepan or in a glass measuring cup in the microwave, to prevent it from cooling the potatoes. Add the seasonings to the hot potatoes and mash them slightly with a hand masher or large fork. Then add the milk gradually while beating vigorously with a hand masher or using an electric mixer at medium-low speed. Beat until fluffy. The total amount of milk needed will vary with the kind of potato and will also determine their texture: the more milk, the creamier or thinner the potatoes will be.

Whipped Potatoes: After adding the milk, beat 1 minute at low speed then 1 minute at high speed, or until the potatoes are very smooth.

Garlic Mashed Potatoes

Servings: 4

> 4 medium potatoes (1¹/₃ pounds)
> 2 tablespoons butter
> 3 cloves garlic, minced*
> ¹/₂ cup milk
> at least ¹/₄ teaspoon salt, or to taste
> ¹/₈ teaspoon pepper

Wash and peel the potatoes and prepare them by boiling or steaming. Turn off the burner and drain the potatoes, then return the potatoes in the pan to the burner. Shake the pan for about 1 minute to allow the potatoes to dry.

Meanwhile, melt the butter in a small skillet and cook the garlic in the butter for about 3 minutes to soften, but do not allow to brown. Add the milk and warm over medium-low heat until heated through. Mash the hot potatoes slightly with a hand masher or large fork. Then add the milk-garlic mixture gradually, while beating vigorously with a hand masher or using an electric mixer. Beat until fluffy and season to taste with salt and pepper.

*Or use 3 cloves mashed roasted garlic, and omit cooking the garlic as directed in the recipe. Amount of garlic can be increased (or decreased) to taste.

Pepper Potatoes

Servings: 6

1 pound Yukon Gold or other yellow flesh
    potatoes
1 tablespoon olive oil
$^1/_2$ cup diced yellow bell pepper
$^1/_2$ cup diced red bell pepper
$^1/_2$ cup diced green bell pepper
$^1/_4$ cup milk
2 tablespoons butter
salt and pepper to taste
2 tablespoons mashed roasted garlic

Wash and peel the potatoes and prepare by boiling or steaming. Turn off the burner and drain the potatoes, then return the potatoes in the pan to the burner. Shake the pan for about 1 minute to allow the potatoes to dry.

Meanwhile, heat the olive oil in a medium skillet over medium heat and saute the peppers until crisp-tender. Warm the milk and butter in a small saucepan or in a glass measuring cup in the microwave. Add the seasonings and garlic to the hot potatoes and mash them slightly with a hand masher or large fork. Whip until smooth. Stir the peppers into the potatoes, mixing well.

Roasting Garlic for Garlic Mashed Potatoes

Slice about $^1/_2$ inch off the top of a garlic bulb. Place the root or bottom side down in a small baking dish and drizzle with about 2 teaspoons of olive oil. Bake at 350°F for about 45 minutes, or until fork-tender. Squeeze the garlic out of each clove and mash.

Elegant Mashed Potatoes

Servings: 4

4 medium potatoes
$^1/_3$ cup milk
3 tablespoons butter
$^1/_4$ teaspoon rosemary
$^1/_4$ teaspoon thyme
salt and pepper to taste
3 tablespoons crumbled Gorgonzola cheese

Wash and peel the potatoes and prepare by boiling or steaming. Turn off

the burner and drain the potatoes, then return the potatoes in the pan to the burner. Shake the pan for about 1 minute to allow the potatoes to dry. Warm the milk, butter, and seasonings in a small saucepan or in a glass measuring cup in the microwave. Mash the hot potatoes slightly with a hand masher or large fork. Sprinkle with the cheese, then add the milk and butter mixture gradually while beating vigorously with a hand masher or using an electric mixer at medium-low speed. Beat until smooth.

Spicy Low-Fat Mashed Potatoes

Servings: 4

4 medium potatoes (1$^1\!/_2$ pounds)
1$^1\!/_4$ cups water
$^1\!/_2$ teaspoon salt
$^1\!/_4$ cup chopped fresh parsley
1 teaspoon yellow mustard
2 teaspoons grainy brown mustard
2 teaspoons prepared horseradish
$^1\!/_4$ cup low-fat sour cream

Scrub the potatoes and cut into cubes of $^1\!/_2$ to 1 inch, leaving skins on. Place potatoes, water, salt, and parsley in a heavy saucepan and bring to a boil. Reduce heat and simmer about 25 minutes total. During the last 10 minutes of cooking, break the

potatoes up and mash them as they soften, adding a little more hot water if they become too dry. When done, potatoes will be soft but lumpy. Remove from the heat. Stir in the mustards, horseradish, and sour cream, and serve.

Basic Twice Baked Potatoes

Servings: 4 to 6

4 potatoes
1 tablespoon butter
2 tablespoons chopped onion
$^1\!/_3$ cup sour cream
up to $^1\!/_4$ cup milk
2 strips bacon, cooked hard and crumbled (optional)
$^1\!/_3$ cup shredded Cheddar cheese
salt and pepper to taste

Bake the potatoes and allow to cool until they can be handled. Meanwhile, melt the butter in a small skillet and cook the onion until softened, about 3 minutes. Cut the potatoes in half lengthwise and scoop out the flesh, being careful to leave a shell of $^1\!/_4$ to $^1\!/_2$ inch.

In a medium bowl, combine the potato, sour cream, onion, and butter. Mash them together thoroughly, then beat by hand or with an electric mixer, adding as much milk as necessary for a smooth

(continued)

consistency. Potato mixture will be slightly firmer than mashed potatoes. Stir in the bacon and the cheese, and season to taste.

Mound the mixture in the potato shells and place them on an ungreased baking sheet. Bake at 350°F for about 30 minutes, or microwave on high for about 10 minutes, until well heated.

Twice Baked Potatoes 'n' Chives

Servings: 4 to 6

4 potatoes
1/4 cup milk
3-ounce package cream cheese, softened
1/4 cup thinly sliced green onions
1/4 cup butter, softened
salt and pepper to taste
1/4 cup chopped fresh chives

Bake the potatoes and allow to cool until they can be handled. Combine the milk and the cream cheese. Cut the potatoes in half lengthwise and scoop out the flesh, being careful to leave a shell of 1/4 to 1/2 inch.

In a medium bowl, combine the potato, cream cheese, and butter. Mash them together thoroughly, then beat by hand or with an electric mixer. Stir in the chives and onions and season to taste. Mound the mixture in the potato shells and place

them on an ungreased baking sheet. Bake at 350°F for about 30 minutes, or microwave on high for about 10 minutes, until well heated.

Twice-Baked Veggie Potatoes

Servings: 4 to 6

4 potatoes
8 medium broccoli florets
1/4 cup skim milk
2/3 cup shredded sharp white Cheddar or Swiss cheese, divided
salt and pepper to taste

Bake the potatoes and allow to cool until they can be handled.

Meanwhile, steam the broccoli until just tender, then chop finely. Cut the potatoes in half lengthwise and scoop out the flesh, being careful to leave a shell of 1/4 to 1/2 inch. In a medium bowl, mash the potato and milk together. Add the broccoli and 1/3 cup cheese, and continue mashing. The potato mixture will become pale green. Season to taste with salt and pepper.

Mound the mixture in the potato shells and sprinkle with reserved cheese. Place on an ungreased baking sheet and bake at 350°F for about 30 minutes, or until well heated.

Basic Scalloped Potatoes

Servings: 6 to 8

6 medium potatoes
1 small onion
$\frac{1}{4}$ cup flour
1 teaspoon salt
$\frac{1}{4}$ teaspoon pepper
2 cups milk
1 tablespoon butter

Preheat oven to 350°F. Peel the potatoes and slice them thinly.

Peel and slice the onion thinly. In a well-greased 2 to 2½-quart baking dish, layer about a third of the potato slices. Top with about half the onion, and sprinkle half the flour and seasonings on top. Repeat, ending with a potato layer. Heat the milk (do not scald) and pour over the potatoes. Dot the top with butter. Cover and bake for 1 hour; uncover and bake for $\frac{1}{2}$ hour longer, or until potatoes are tender.

Scalloped Potatoes and Mushrooms

Servings: 6

3 tablespoons butter
8 ounces fresh mushrooms, chopped
1 tablespoon chopped onion
3 tablespoons flour
1 teaspoon salt
$\frac{1}{4}$ teaspoon pepper

2 cups milk
6 medium potatoes
1 tablespoon chopped fresh parsley
1 tablespoon butter

Preheat oven to 350°F.

Melt $\frac{1}{4}$ cup butter in a medium skillet over medium-high heat, sauté the mushrooms and onions in the butter until tender. Stir in the flour, salt, and pepper. Cook until smooth, then add the milk; heat to boiling, stirring constantly.

Peel the potatoes and slice them thinly. In a well-greased 2 to 2 ½-quart baking dish, layer about a third of the potato slices, sprinkle with parsley and top with about a third of the mushroom sauce. Repeat twice, ending with sauce. Dot the top with 1 tablespoon butter. Cover and bake for 1 hour; uncover and bake for $\frac{1}{2}$ hour longer, or until potatoes are tender.

Potatoes au Gratin
Servings: 6

2 tablespoons butter, divided
1 tablespoon flour
$\frac{1}{2}$ teaspoon salt
$\frac{1}{4}$ teaspoon pepper
1 cup milk
1 teaspoon paprika
6 medium potatoes
1 cup grated sharp Cheddar cheese, divided
$\frac{1}{4}$ cup soft bread crumbs

(continued)

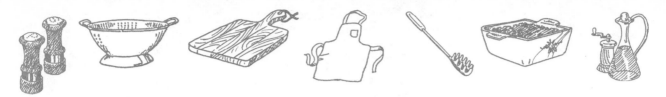

Preheat oven to 375°F. Make a white sauce: Melt 1 tablespoon of the butter and stir in the flour, salt, and pepper. Add the milk and cook over medium heat until the sauce is bubbly and thickened, stirring constantly. Stir in the paprika.

Peel the potatoes, halve them lengthwise, then slice thinly. In a well-greased 2 to 2½-quart deep-sided casserole dish, make three layers of potatoes, topping the first

and second layers with ¼ cup of the cheese, and topping the third layer with the remaining ½ cup. Carefully pour the white sauce over all.

In a small skillet, melt the remaining tablespoon of butter; add the bread crumbs, and stir to absorb. Sprinkle the crumbs on the potatoes. Bake uncovered about 1 hour and 15 minutes.

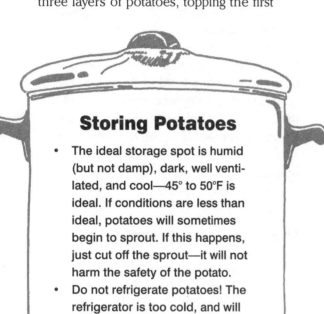

Storing Potatoes

- The ideal storage spot is humid (but not damp), dark, well ventilated, and cool—45° to 50°F is ideal. If conditions are less than ideal, potatoes will sometimes begin to sprout. If this happens, just cut off the sprout—it will not harm the safety of the potato.
- Do not refrigerate potatoes! The refrigerator is too cold, and will cause the starch in the potato to turn to sugar. The taste will be different, and the potato flesh will turn dark when cooked.

Potato Fans

Servings: 4

4 large potatoes
¼ cup butter
1 tablespoon finely grated lemon zest
¼ teaspoon garlic powder
salt
1 tablespoon chopped fresh parsley

Preheat oven to 350°F.

Scrub the potatoes. With a sharp knife, make crosswise cuts in each potato about ¼ inch apart; cut to within ½ inch of the bottom, but do cut through to the bottom. Immerse the potatoes in ice water for 10 minutes to crisp them. Drain, dry well with paper towels, and place cut side up in a 9 x 13-inch baking dish; do not crowd. Gently spread or "fan" the potatoes by gently pressing down at the ends, then spreading the slices.

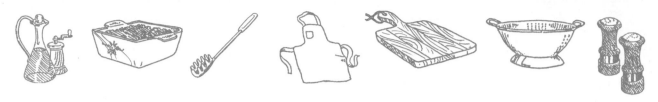

Combine the butter, lemon zest, and garlic powder; heat in the microwave or in a small saucepan until the butter is melted. Brush the tops and sides of the potatoes with the butter mixture. Cover and bake 45 minutes, brushing once during that time with more butter.

Uncover and drizzle the remaining butter over the potatoes. Bake an additional 15 to 20 minutes, or until tender. Remove from the oven and sprinkle with salt and parsley before serving.

Parsleyed New Potatoes

Servings: 4

> 1¼ pounds very small new potatoes,
>   red- or tan-skinned
> ¼ cup butter
> ¼ cup chopped onion
> 1 cup vegetable or chicken broth, or water
> ½ cup chopped fresh parsley
> salt and pepper to taste

Wash the potatoes well. The traditional method for preparing new potatoes is to peel a thin strip around the middle of the potato; potatoes can also be completely peeled or completely unpeeled, according to preference.

In a medium skillet, melt the butter and cook the onion until tender, about 3 minutes. Add the broth, parsley, salt, and pepper, then place the potatoes in the skillet in a single layer. Bring to a boil, then cover

and reduce heat. Simmer about 20 minutes or until the potatoes are tender. Remove the potatoes to a serving bowl, then pour the remaining sauce over them to serve.

Roasted Reds

Servings: 4

> 1 pound small new red potatoes
> 2 leeks, thickly sliced
> 2 cloves garlic, chopped
> 3 tablespoons olive oil
> 1 teaspoon each chopped fresh rosemary
>   and thyme
> 1 tablespoon chopped fresh parsley
> salt and pepper to taste

Preheat oven to 375°F.

If the potatoes are larger than 1½ inches diameter, halve or quarter into chunks of 1 to 1½ inches. Place potatoes, leeks, and garlic, rosemary and thyme in a bowl, drizzle the oil over all, and toss to combine. Turn into a 9 x 13-inch baking pan and roast until potatoes are cooked and browned, about 1 hour. Stir every 15 minutes. When done, toss with the parsley, salt, and pepper before serving.

Oven-Baked Red Potatoes

Servings: 2

1 pound small red potatoes, halved
¼ cup fresh lemon juice
1 teaspoon olive oil
1 teaspoon salt
¼ teaspoon pepper

Preheat oven to 350°F.

Arrange potatoes in a 13 x 9-inch oven-proof casserole dish. Combine lemon juice, olive oil, salt, and pepper, and pour over potatoes. Bake for 30 to 40 minutes or until potatoes are tender, turning 3 to 4 times to baste.

Basic French Fries

Servings: 4

6 medium potatoes (2 pounds)
vegetable oil
salt

Peel potatoes and cut into ¼-inch lengthwise strips. As the strips are cut, place them in a bowl of ice water to crisp and prevent browning. When ready to fry, drain and dry well, using paper towels. (If potatoes are not dry they will not brown properly, and the hot oil will spatter.)

In a large, deep skillet, heat 2 inches of oil to 375°F (if you do not have a deep enough skillet, use a Dutch oven). For best results, measure the temperature with a meat thermometer. As an alternative, test by dropping a 1-inch cube of bread into the oil; it should brown evenly in about 45 seconds. Cook the potatoes in batches; do not crowd. Fry for about 5 to 6 minutes, or until golden brown. Remove with a slotted spoon or spatula, drain well on paper towels and salt immediately.

Selecting Potatoes

Look for potatoes that:

- *Are not* soft to the touch and do not have excessive cut, cracked, wrinkled, decayed, or bruised areas.
- *Are not* green. A greenish tint indicates improper storage and over-exposure to light. It causes a bitter taste, so green areas should be cut out before cooking.
- *Are* clean, firm, smooth, and reasonably regular in shape. Extremely irregular shapes can cause more waste when the potato is peeled.

Between batches, add more oil if necessary, and allow oil to return to the proper temperature. Cooked fries can be kept warm in a 300°F oven.

Note: For successful fries, cut accurately (do not make them too thick) and have the oil at the correct temperature.

Oven French Fries

Servings: 4

6 medium potatoes (2 pounds)
cooking oil spray
salt

Preheat oven to 500°F.

Peel potatoes and halve lengthwise. Place the halves cut side down on the cutting board and cut into ¼-inch lengthwise strips. As the strips are cut, place them in a bowl of ice water to crisp. When ready to cook, drain and dry well, using paper towels. (If potatoes are not dry they will not brown properly.)

Spray two cookie sheets or jellyroll pans with cooking spray. Arrange the potatoes on the sheets and spray the potatoes with cooking oil spray. Sprinkle with salt and bake about 10 minutes, then remove from the oven, turn potatoes over, and spray and salt the second side. Return to the oven for another 10 to 15 minutes. Fries are done when they are fork tender and golden brown.

Spicy fries: Before placing on the baking sheet, toss the potatoes with a mixture of ¼ teaspoon garlic powder, ¼ teaspoon onion powder, ⅛ teaspoon cayenne, and ½ teaspoon salt. Sprinkle this mixture again on the fries halfway through the cooking process.

Oven Wedges

Servings: 4

4 large potatoes (about 2 pounds)
2 tablespoons butter, melted
seasoned salt

Preheat oven to 400°F.

Do not peel potatoes; scrub well. Cut them into quarters, then cut each quarter into two or more wedges about 1-inch wide on the skin side.

Coat a jellyroll pan well with cooking oil spray. Place the potato wedges in the pan, standing upright with the skin side down. Drizzle with the butter and sprinkle with seasoned salt. Bake 12 to 15 minutes, or until fork tender and nicely browned.

Potatoes Lyonnaise

Servings: 6

4 medium potatoes
1 medium onion
2 tablespoons butter
2 tablespoons vegetable oil
1 clove garlic, minced
1/2 teaspoon salt
1/8 teaspoon pepper
paprika

Boil the potatoes in their skins until almost but not quite tender, about 20 minutes.

When cool enough to handle, peel and slice the potatoes thinly. Peel and slice the onion thinly. In a large skillet, melt half the butter and all the vegetable oil. Add the potatoes and cook until golden brown.

In a small skillet, melt the remaining 1 tablespoon butter and cook the onion and garlic until tender. To serve, combine the potatoes and onions, season with salt and pepper, and sprinkle with paprika.

Black Forest Potato Salad

Servings: 4 to 6

4 medium red potatoes
4 slices bacon, chopped
2 tablespoons chopped onions
vegetable oil if necessary
2 tablespoons cider vinegar

1 tablespoon sugar
1/2 teaspoon dry mustard
1/2 teaspoon salt
1/8 teaspoon pepper

Scrub the potatoes well and boil or steam, whole and unpeeled. When done, drain well and slice thinly.

Meanwhile, sauté the bacon and onion until the bacon is done; remove and reserve the drippings, adding enough vegetable oil to make 2 tablespoons. Return the bacon and onion to the skillet and add the vinegar, sugar, mustard, salt, and pepper. Mix well and bring to a boil.

Add the potatoes and toss gently. Serve warm.

Pie Fry

Servings: 4 to 6

1 small onion
2 medium tomatoes
4 medium potatoes
1/4 cup butter, divided
1/2 teaspoon rosemary
1/2 teaspoon salt
1/4 teaspoon freshly ground pepper

Peel the onion and slice very thinly. Slice the tomatoes thinly. Peel the potatoes and slice very thinly. In a medium oven-proof skillet or 10-inch round casserole dish that can be used on the stovetop and in the

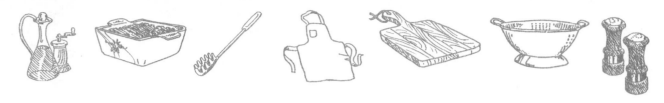

oven, melt about 2 tablespoons of the butter. Arrange the potatoes in the dish, cover with the tomato slices, sprinkle with rosemary, and top with the rings of onion. Sprinkle with salt and pepper. Cover and cook over medium heat for 20 minutes.

Preheat the broiler and adjust the rack so that the top of the potato pan will be 5 inches from the heat. Remove the cover from the pan and dot with the remaining butter. Broil for about 6 minutes, checking doneness by inserting a long-tined fork into the potatoes. To serve, cut in wedges like a pie.

Hash-Brown Casserole

Servings: 8 to 10

> 2 pounds shredded hash-brown potatoes, partially thawed if frozen
> $\frac{1}{4}$ cup chopped onion
> $\frac{1}{4}$ cup chopped green pepper
> 8 ounces (2 cups) shredded Colby and Jack cheese, mixed
> 4 ounces (1 cup) shredded Cheddar cheese, divided
> 1 teaspoon salt
> $\frac{1}{2}$ teaspoon pepper
> 1 tablespoon chicken bouillon granules
> 8 ounces sour cream

Preheat oven to 350°F.

In a large bowl, toss the potatoes, onion, pepper, Colby-Jack cheese, half the Cheddar cheese, salt, and pepper. Stir the bouillon into the sour cream; add to the potatoes, mixing well to combine.

Turn into a 9 x 13-inch baking dish, spread out evenly, and smooth the top. Sprinkle with the remaining Cheddar cheese. Bake for about 1 hour, or until the edges are brown and the center is cooked.

Preventing Boil-Over

A lump of butter or a few teaspoons of cooking oil added to water when boiling potatoes will prevent the liquid from boiling over.

Gingered Mashed Sweet Potatoes

Servings: 5 or 6

> 4 medium sweet potatoes or yams
>   (about 1¹/₂ pounds)
> ¹/₄ cup milk
> 2 tablespoons butter
> 1 tablespoon mashed candied ginger or
>   1 tablespoon brown sugar plus ¹/₂
>   teaspoon ground ginger

Peel and quarter the sweet potatoes and cook in boiling salted water until tender, about 20 minutes. Drain and return to the pan. In a small saucepan or in the microwave, heat the milk and butter. Add along with the candied ginger to the potatoes and mash by hand or with an electric mixer. Texture will be thicker than mashed white potatoes.

Baked Candied Sweet Potatoes

Servings: 6

> 6 medium sweet potatoes (about 2
>   pounds)
> ¹/₄ cup butter
> ¹/₂ cup brown sugar
> 1 teaspoon salt
> ¹/₂ cup toasted pecans

Scrub the sweet potatoes and boil or steam them whole until tender. When cool enough to handle, peel and cut into ¹/₂-inch slices. Preheat the oven to 375°F. Melt the butter in the microwave or a small saucepan and stir in the brown sugar and salt. Butter an 8 x 11-inch baking dish well and layer about a third of the potatoes in the dish. Drizzle with about a fourth of the butter-sugar mixture, and sprinkle with about a third of the pecans. Repeat layers twice, ending with the remaining butter-sugar on top. Bake uncovered for about 30 minutes.

Rice Cooking Tips

For 1 cup of:	Liquid	Cooking Time
Regular long grain	2 cups	15 minutes
Medium or short grain	$1^3/_4$ cups	15 minutes
Converted	$2^1/_2$ cups	20 or more minutes
Brown	$2^1/_2$ cups	45 or more minutes
Basmati	$1^1/_2$ cups	15 or more minutes
Jasmine	$1^3/_4$ cups	15 or more minutes
Wild	4 cups	45 to 60 minutes

Kinds of Rice

There are more than 40,000 varieties of rice in the world, but most rice used in the United States falls into the following categories:

White Rice—The most common form of rice, it is also called milled or polished rice. The hull, bran, and germ layers have been removed from the rice kernel. Often white rice is enriched. White rice comes in long-, medium-, and short-grain varieties. The primary difference is their cooking characteristics. The shorter the grain, the more the grains will stick together when cooked; shorter-grained rices have more starch than longer-grained rices. If the cooking characteristic is not crucial, however, white rices can be substituted for each other.

- *Long-grained rice* is light and fluffy when cooked, and the grains remain separate. It is the best choice for pilafs and similar dishes.

- *Medium-grained rice* is more moist and tender than long grain, and is often used in risottos and desserts when a creamier texture is desired.
- *Short-grained rice* is soft when cooked and clumps together. It is a good choice for sushi or Asian-style cooking.

Brown Rice—Brown rice differs from white rice in the way it is processed, not in the variety of the grain. Brown rice has only the hull removed from the rice kernel; the bran is left intact. It takes longer to cook than white rice, and when cooked has a slightly chewy and nutty flavor.

Arborio Rice—Arborio rice is classified as a medium-grained rice; it has a characteristic white dot at the center of each grain. When cooked it absorbs flavors well and develops a creamy texture with a firmer center.

Aromatic Rice—Often used in Indian and Middle Eastern cooking, aromatic rices

273

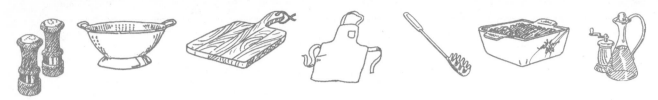

have an aroma and flavor similar to nuts or popcorn. Common varieties are jasmine, which sticks together when cooked; and basmati, which develops long, thin, separate grains when cooked.

Wild Rice—Wild rice is not a true rice, but an aquatic grass. Native to North America, this dark brown grain has a chewy texture and nutty flavor. It takes longer to prepare and cook than white rice.

Common Forms of Rice

Precooked Rice—has been cooked and dehydrated before packaging. It is usually called *instant* or *quick-cooking rice* because it can be prepared in a very short time. *Boil-*

in-the-bag rice is precooked rice that has been measured into perforated cooking bags before packaging. Both white and brown rice are available in quick-cooking form.

Converted Rice—also called *parboiled rice*—is white rice that has undergone a steam-pressure process before milling. This processing preserves some of the original nutrients and keeps the grains separate when they cook.

Basic Ways to Cook Rice

Always check package directions and follow them when available.

On the stove top—Combine rice, liquid, 1 teaspoon of salt, and 1 tablespoon of butter. Bring to a boil, stir, cover, and reduce heat to a simmer. If rice has not absorbed all the liquid at the end of the cooking time, re-cover and allow to cook for 2 or more minutes. Fluff with a fork before serving.

In the oven—In a casserole dish with a tight-fitting lid, combine 1 cup rice with *boiling* liquid (refer to the chart above for amount), 1 teaspoon of salt, and 1 table-spoon of butter, or desired seasonings. Bake at 350°F for about 30 minutes for regular white rice; about 40 minutes for converted rice; or about 1 hour for brown rice. Fluff with a fork before serving.

Rice in a Hurry

Unlike most foods, rice does not cook faster in a microwave oven. It *can* be prepared in the microwave, however, if desired. If speed is important, use instant rice.

In the microwave—In a microwave-safe dish that is 2½ quarts or larger, combine 1 cup rice with 1 teaspoon of salt and 1 tablespoon of butter, or desired seasonings, and liquid (refer to the chart for the amount). Cover and cook on high for 5 minutes or until boiling. Cook on medium an additional 15 minutes for regular white rice, 20 for converted rice, or 30 for brown rice. Fluff with a fork before serving.

To Cook Wild Rice—Place 1 cup rice in a colander and rinse thoroughly under running water. Drain. Combine the rice, 4 cups water, and 1 teaspoon salt in a large saucepan. Bring to a boil, cover, and reduce heat. Simmer 45 minutes to an hour, or until rice kernels are partially open and tender, but not mushy. All water is not usually absorbed; drain the excess liquid.

Basic Rice Pilaf

Servings: 4

> 2 tablespoons butter
> ¼ cup chopped onion
> 1 cup uncooked regular long-grain rice
> 2 tablespoons pine nuts
> 2 cups vegetable or chicken broth,
>   or water
> 1 tablespoon parsley flakes
> salt to taste

(continued)

Rice Yields

- Most regular (not instant or converted) white, Arborio, and aromatic rices triple in volume when cooked.

- Converted white rice, brown rice, and wild rice will more than triple; 1 cup uncooked will yield between 3 and 4 cups cooked.

- Most instant rices double in volume when prepared.

Melt the butter in a large saucepan to medium heat; cook the onion in the butter about 3 minutes or until tender but not brown. Add the rice and pine nuts. Cook and stir in the butter for about 5 minutes. Add the broth, parsley, and salt; bring to a boil. Stir, cover, and reduce the heat to a simmer. Cook for 15 or more minutes, or until water is absorbed. Allow to stand covered at least 5 minutes before fluffing with a fork and serving.

Oven Preparation: Preheat the oven to 350°F. In a medium skillet (do not add fat), toast the rice and pine nuts slowly over medium heat until golden brown, stirring frequently. Place the rice, onion, and parsley in a 2¹/₂ to 3-quart casserole. Heat just 1¹/₂ cups broth to boiling, and pour over the rice. Cover and bake about 30 minutes or until water is absorbed. Fluff with a fork before serving.

Rice Dishes

- A pilaf (say "pill-OFF" or "PEA-lof") includes onions and bits of various vegetables, nuts, or raisins. It is usually cooked in a broth and seasoned with spices. The rice is often sautéed before cooking.

- A *risotto* (say "rih-ZOT-oh") is prepared by first browning the rice, then cooking it very slowly in broth, which it absorbs to produce a creamy texture.

Veggie Rice

Servings: 8

¹/₂ cup wild rice
3 cups chicken broth or water
¹/₄ cup chopped onion
1 teaspoon salt
¹/₄ teaspoon pepper
1 cup long-grain white rice
10-ounce package frozen French-cut
    green beans
¹/₄ teaspoon tarragon
2 tablespoons butter
¹/₂ cup toasted slivered almonds

Rinse the wild rice thoroughly. Drain and set aside. In a large saucepan, bring the broth, onions, salt, and pepper to a boil. Add the wild rice; cover, reduce heat, and simmer about 20 minutes.

Add the white rice, and simmer an additional 10 minutes.

Add the beans, tarragon, and butter, cover, and continue cooking an additional 10 to 15 minutes, until all liquid is absorbed

and rice is tender. Before serving, stir in the almonds.

Fruited Brown Rice Pilaf

Servings: 4

> 2 tablespoons butter
> 1 tablespoon minced onion
> 2¼ cups water or chicken broth
> 1 cup uncooked brown rice
> ⅓ cup chopped dried apricots or apples
> ¼ cup raisins
> ⅛ teaspoon pepper
> salt to taste
> ¼ cup toasted almonds

Melt the butter in a large saucepan over medium heat; cook the onion in the butter about 2 minutes or until the onion is tender but not brown.

Carefully pour in the water, then stir in the rice, fruit, pepper, and salt. Bring to a boil. Stir, cover, and reduce the heat to a simmer. Cook for 45 or more minutes, or until water is absorbed. Fluff with a fork and stir in almonds before serving.

Curried Rice

Servings: 4

> 1 cup uncooked long-grain rice
> 2 cups water

> 1 teaspoon salt
> ⅓ cup raisins
> 2 tablespoons butter
> 2 tablespoons chopped onion
> 2 tablespoons chopped celery
> ½ teaspoon curry powder
> ⅛ teaspoon allspice
> ¼ teaspoon pepper

In a large saucepan, bring the rice, water, and salt to a boil. Cover, reduce heat, and cook for 10 minutes; add the raisins and cook an additional 5 minutes, or until water is absorbed.

Meanwhile, in a small skillet, melt the butter. Cook the onion and celery in the butter about 3 minutes, or until softened. Stir in the curry powder, allspice, and pepper, and combine the mixture with the rice.

Basic Risotto

Servings: 4

> 2 tablespoons butter
> ¼ cup chopped shallots or
>   green onions
> 1 cup Arborio rice or medium-grain white
>   rice
> ½ cup dry white wine or
>   chicken broth
> 2 cups chicken broth
> 1 cup water
> ¼ cup grated Parmesan cheese
> ⅛ teaspoon pepper
> salt to taste

(continued)

Melt the butter in a large skillet and cook the shallots in the butter over medium-high heat until tender. Add the rice and cook, stirring frequently, until it just begins to brown. Add the wine and stir until absorbed.

Meanwhile, in a small saucepan warm the broth. Stir 1 cup broth into the rice and cook until it is absorbed, stirring constantly. Add the remaining broth and water $\frac{1}{2}$ cup at a time, *stirring frequently,* until each cup is absorbed. Cook until rice is tender and creamy, a total of about 25 to 30 minutes. Stir in the cheese and seasonings.

Lemon Asparagus Risotto

Servings: 4

2 tablespoons butter, divided
$\frac{1}{4}$ cup chopped green onions
1 cup Arborio rice or medium-grain
  white rice
3 cups vegetable or chicken broth
1 cup fresh asparagus pieces, about
  1-inch long
1 tablespoon lemon juice
1 teaspoon grated lemon zest
$\frac{1}{4}$ cup chopped fresh parsley
$\frac{1}{8}$ teaspoon pepper
salt to taste

Melt the butter in a large skillet and cook the onions in the butter until tender over medium-high heat. Add the rice and cook, stirring frequently, until it just begins to brown. Stir in 1 cup broth and cook until it is absorbed, stirring constantly. Add an additional $\frac{1}{2}$ cup broth and the asparagus, cooking until liquid is absorbed. Add the remaining broth $\frac{1}{2}$ cup at a time, *stirring frequently,* until each cup is absorbed. With the last $\frac{1}{2}$ cup, add the lemon juice.

Cook until rice is tender and creamy, a total of about 25 to 30 minutes. Stir in the lemon zest, parsley, and seasonings.

Storing Rice

White or milled rice of all kinds can be stored almost indefinitely in a tightly closed container, although it's best to use it within two years.

Brown rice cannot be stored as long as white rice because the fat in the bran layer will spoil. Store in a tightly closed container, on the shelf or in the refrigerator, for up to 6 months.

Wild Rice with Mushrooms

Servings: 6 to 8

> 1/4 cup butter
> 1/4 cup chopped onion
> 8 ounces sliced fresh mushrooms
> 2 tablespoons dry sherry or broth
> 3 1/2 cups vegetable, beef, or chicken broth
> 1 teaspoon salt
> 1/4 teaspoon pepper
> 1 cup wild rice
> 1 cup sliced celery

In a large saucepan, melt the butter. Cook the onion and mushrooms in the butter until onion is tender, 3 to 4 minutes. Carefully add the liquids and salt and pepper, then stir in the rice and celery. Bring to a boil; cover, reduce heat, and simmer for 45 to 55 minutes, or until rice kernels are open and tender but not mushy.

Hoppin' John

Servings: about 8

> 1 cup dried black-eyed peas
> 3 slices bacon, chopped
> 1 medium onion, chopped
> 1/8 teaspoon crushed red pepper
> 3/4 cup uncooked long-grain white rice
> salt and pepper to taste
> 1 3/4 cups water

(continued)

Rice Tips

- Do not rinse rice before or after cooking, unless it is imported or the package instructs otherwise.
- For firmer rice, reduce the cooking liquid by 1/4 cup and reduce the cooking time by 5 or more minutes.
- For softer rice, allow rice to sit in the covered pan for up to 10 minutes afer cooking.
- Use a pan with a tight-fitting lid and keep it tightly covered during cooking to prevent steam from escaping.
- Do not stir rice during cooking.
- Fluff cooked rice with a fork before serving to separate the grains.

Wash the black-eyed peas and bring to a boil in about 6 cups of water. Boil 2 minutes, then remove from heat, cover, and let stand for 1 hour. Meanwhile, sauté the chopped bacon and onion in a medium skillet over medium-high heat until onion is tender, about 3 minutes. (Bacon will not be crisp.) Drain any excess accumulated fat from the skillet. Drain the black-eyed peas and transfer to a large saucepan. Add the bacon-onion mixture, crushed pepper, rice, and 1³/₄ cups of water. Bring to a boil, cover, and reduce heat. Simmer about 20 minutes, or until peas and rice are tender and liquid is absorbed.

Bean Maurine

Servings: 10 to 12

> 8 ounces bacon
> 2 medium onions, chopped
> ¹/₂ cup brown sugar
> ¹/₂ cup white sugar
> ¹/₂ cup cider vinegar
> ¹/₂ teaspoon garlic powder
> 1 teaspoon dry mustard
> 1 teaspoon salt
> 16-ounce can chickpeas, drained
> 16-ounce can red kidney bean, drained
> 16-ounce can great northern beans, drained
> 16-ounce can cut green beans, drained
> 16-ounce can baked beans, undrained

Preheat oven to 350°F.

Chop the bacon into small pieces and sauté in a medium-large skillet together with the onion until the onion is tender but not brown. Add the sugars, vinegar, spices, and salt to the skillet and simmer for 20 minutes.

Combine the chickpeas and beans and place in a large 4-quart casserole or baking dish. Pour the bacon-onion mixture over the top and bake for 1 hour.

Old-Fashioned All-Day Beans

Servings: 10 to 12

> 2 pounds dry navy beans
> 1 pound salt pork or bacon
> 1 medium onion

Legumes

Legumes—dried beans, peas, and lentils—are a delicious way to add fiber and nutrients to your diet. Legumes are high in protein, as well as being rich in iron and calcium.

My favorite quick meal is to cook some spaghetti and top it with some spaghetti sauce, garbanzo beans, scallions, and Parmesan cheese.

¹/₂ cup sugar
²/₃ cup molasses
¹/₄ cup ketchup
2 teaspoons dry mustard
4 teaspoons salt
¹/₂ teaspoon pepper

Cover the navy beans with 2–3 inches of water and allow to soak overnight; or bring to a boil, boil 2 minutes, remove from heat, cover, and let stand 1 hour.

Drain the beans well in a colander. Cut the salt pork or bacon into small pieces (do not cook). Peel the onion and cut it in half. Place one half of the onion in the bottom of a 2-quart bean pot or a 2 to 3-quart casserole dish. Combine the beans with all remaining ingredients and place into the dish. Place the remaining half onion on top. Cover and bake at 300°F for 6 hours.

Beans can also be cooked in a slow cooking Crock-Pot: Cook on high for 1 hour, then reduce heat to low and cook for an additional 7 to 9 hours.

Plain Boiled Rice

Servings 4 to 6

2 cups raw short-grained rice
2¹/₂ cups cold water

Wash the rice well in a colander with several changes of water. After water runs clear, let the rice drain in a sieve or colander for 10 minutes. Place rice in a saucepan and add the water. Cover, and bring to a boil over high heat (standing by to watch that it does not boil over); reduce the heat to low and let the rice simmer for 15 minutes.

Remove the saucepan from the heat and let it stand, still covered, for 10 minutes to allow the rice to cook in the residual steam. Uncover and fluff the rice with a fork or chopsticks. If you're not ready to serve, place a towel over the saucepan to absorb any extra moisture, and then replace the lid.

Glutinous or "Sweet Sticky" Rice

Servings: 4

2 cups (15¹/₂ ounces) raw glutinous rice
4 cups cold water

Place the rice in a saucepan and pour in enough water to cover; soak for 30 minutes.

Pour off the soaking water and wash the rice, agitating the grains in several changes of water until the water runs clear. Pour away the water, using the lid to help it drain, and pour 4 cups of fresh water into the rice. Let stand for 10 more minutes.

Cover the pan and place it over high heat. Bring to a boil and immediately reduce the heat to low. Simmer the rice for

(continued)

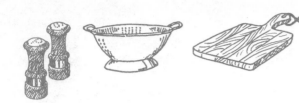

30 minutes, or until all the water is absorbed. Do not lift the lid while the rice is cooking, but remove it at the end of the cooking time to check if the water is absorbed. If it is not, cover again and let it simmer for a few minutes longer. The rice is now ready to use.

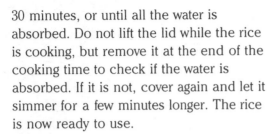 Although most varieties of rice do not need preliminary soaking, glutinous rice must be soaked at least 30 minutes before cooking. Some cooking experts recommend longer, but half an hour will do.

Fried Rice with Eggs

Servings: 4

½ cup sliced carrots (¼-inch slices)
8–12 spears asparagus, trimmed and cut into ½-inch diagonal slices
4 large eggs
1½ teaspoons salt, divided
3 tablespoons peanut oil, divided
1 tablespoon minced fresh ginger
1 tablespoon minced fresh garlic
3 cups cooked long-grain rice, cold or at room temperature
1 cup cooked baby shrimp
1 cup tiny red radishes, trimmed and washed
1 cup frozen baby peas, thawed
2 cups baby spinach leaves, rinsed and drained

3 tablespoons soy sauce
2 teaspoons toasted sesame oil or to taste
freshly ground black pepper
½ cup sliced green onions, white and green parts
fresh cilantro, chopped

Steam carrots for 2 minutes in a vegetable steamer. Add asparagus. Cover and steam 2 minutes more. Transfer vegetables to a plate and set aside.

Whisk eggs and ½ teaspoon salt in bowl. Heat a 12-inch nonstick skillet or wok over medium heat until hot enough to evaporate a drop of water upon contact. Add 1 tablespoon of peanut oil and tilt skillet to coat evenly. When the oil is hot, add the eggs all at once. Push them to the center with a spatula as the edges set, about 3 minutes. Transfer to a plate and break the eggs up into ½-inch pieces. Reserve.

Wipe out the wok or skillet and reheat. Add remaining 2 tablespoons peanut oil, ginger, and garlic, and stir-fry until sizzling, about 5 seconds. Add rice and stir-fry until rice is heated through, about 3 minutes. Add asparagus, carrots, shrimp, radishes, and peas. Stir-fry about 3 minutes. Add cooked eggs and spinach, and stir-fry until spinach is wilted and ingredients are blended. Add soy sauce, sesame oil, the remaining 1 teaspoon salt, and pepper to taste. Garnish with green onions and fresh cilantro.

Dhal

Servings: 4

1 cup dried lentils
2 cups water
1 teaspoon salt
½ teaspoon ground turmeric
¼ teaspoon cayenne pepper
2 tablespoons Asian sesame oil
1 medium onion, thinly sliced
1 teaspoon ground cumin
1 teaspoon ground coriander

In a saucepan, combine the lentils, water, salt, turmeric, and cayenne pepper. Bring to a boil. Meanwhile, in a large saucepan, heat the sesame oil over medium heat. Add the onion and sauté until soft, about 5 minutes. Add the cumin and coriander, and cook for 5 minutes longer.

Add the onion mixture to the lentils; cover and cook over medium heat until the lentils are tender, about 30 minutes.

Indian dhal recipes have a souplike consistency and are offered in many Indian restaurants as a soup course. This spiced vegetarian side dish is made from lentils or split peas.

Curried Potatoes and Cauliflower

Servings: 6

1½ pounds new red potatoes, peeled and cubed

2 teaspoons brown mustard seeds*
2 tablespoons vegetable oil
1 yellow onion, sliced
2 cloves garlic, minced
2 teaspoons minced fresh ginger
1 teaspoon ground cumin
½ teaspoon ground turmeric
¼ teaspoon cayenne pepper
2 cups cauliflower florets
1 cup water
salt and black pepper to taste
1 cup fresh peas
2 tablespoons fresh cilantro, chopped

Peel the potatoes and cut into 1-inch cubes. Place in a bowl of water and set aside. In a large saucepan over medium heat, cook the mustard seeds until they begin to pop, about 1 to 2 minutes. Add the vegetable oil, onion, garlic, and ginger; cook, stirring occasionally, until the onion begins to soften, about 1 minute. Sprinkle in the cumin, turmeric, and cayenne, and cook, stirring constantly, until fragrant, about 30 seconds.

Drain the potatoes. Add the potatoes and cauliflower to the pan, and stir to coat with spices. Add the water, cover, and cook until the potatoes are almost tender, about 15 minutes. Season with salt and pepper. Add the peas and cook until tender and the liquid is absorbed, about 3 minutes longer. Garnish with cilantro and serve hot.

*Brown Mustard seeds can be found in the spice section of most well-stocked supermarkets or in specialty food stores.

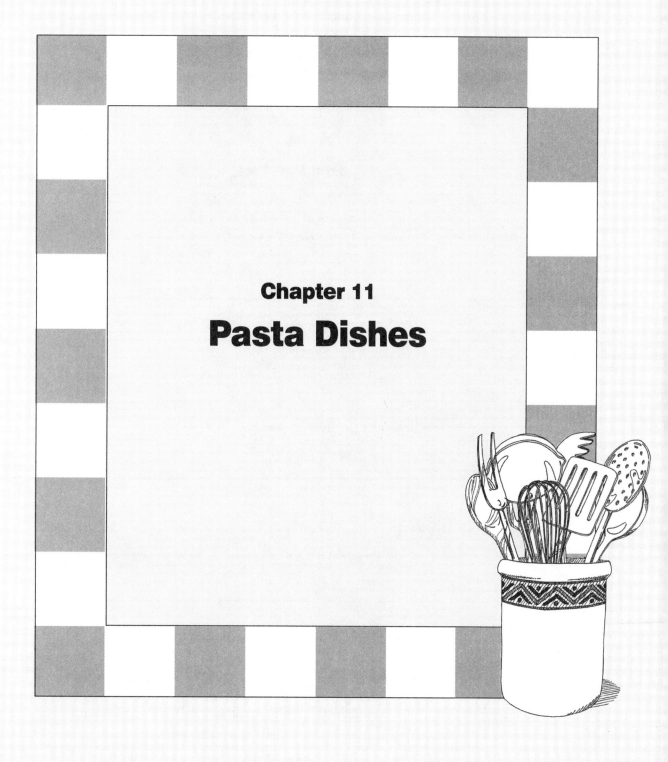

Chapter 11

Pasta Dishes

Wherever there was flour, people created pasta: German *spaetzle*, Polish *pierogi*, Japanese *udon*, Chinese *mein*, Indian *sevika*, and French *nouilles* name merely a few incarnations. Here you'll find not only different types of pasta, but also cooking tips, tempting fillings, and delicious meat and vegetable sauces and garnishes. So get some water boiling, and enjoy!

Long Pastas

The strand that started it all was spaghetti. This "little string" is the simple tune on which a great symphony was composed. In time, the strands became narrower and wider, and then narrower and wider still, and then flatter and fatter and curled and twisted. The same and yet different, the small, appealing variations are emblematic of what makes pasta so endlessly alluring.

Italian Name	English	Description	Comments
spaghetti	little strings	long, slim solid pasta	The most common form used for a variety of sauces
spagellini		short, thin pieces of *spaghetti*	
spaghettini	fine strings	slim *spaghetti*	Used with garlic and oil sauce, fish and clam sauces
spaghetti all chitarra	guitar string	thin cut strand	
fedelini	little faithfuls	very thin strands	
capellini or *capelli d'angelo*	fine hairs or angel hair	thinner than *fedelini*	Used for very delicate sauces Sometimes sold as a ring for soups
vermicelli	little worms	thinner than *spaghettini*	Thicker than angel hair. Used for tomato, butter and cheese sauces
linguine	small tongues	flat or oval strands	Often used with seafood sauces
liniguine fini	little tongues	narrower than *linguine*	Also used with thin oil-based sauces like clam sauce
bavettine		very narrow *linguine*	
fusilli lunghi	long springs	curly strand	Excellent for chunky sauces that cling

Ribbons

Smooth, slippery ribbons run along the tongue with a silky feel. Most are made with eggs in addition to the basics, flour and water. They taste best either homemade or bought fresh. Their porous nature makes them fabulous partners for cream- and butter-based sauces, the most famous being fettuccine Alfredo. While herbs permeate these shapes, bits of medium-fine sauces adhere to them, creating a complexity of taste and texture.

Italian Name	English	Description	Comments
tagliatelle	from the verb "to cut"	$1/3$ inch wide, fresh egg pasta	Classically paired with meat
fettuccine	ribbons	$1/5$ inch wide, medium width	Best for cream sauces; available available in many flavors, especially spinach
fettucce	ribbons	wider than *fettuccine*	
fettucelle	little ribbons	narrower than *fettuccine*	
tagliolini or *taglierini*		extremely narrow fresh egg pasta	Mostly used in broth
tonnarelli		$1/16$ inch square ribbons	
pappardelle		$3/4$ inch wide, ripple or plain edged	
pizzoccheri		earthy, brown color, medium wide, 3" or 4" lengths	Buckwheat flour added to eggs and white flour
malfade		wide ribbon with frilly edges	
paglia e fieno	straw and hay	green and white *linguine* or *fettuccine* mixed together	

Tubes

Tubes are muscular pastas that can stand deliciously alone with a little butter and cheese. But tubes are also welcoming receptacles for every nuance a sauce has to offer.

Italian Name	English	Description	Comments
maccheroni	"macaroni" general term for tubed pasta	slightly curved tubes	
penne	pens or quills	1" long, $\frac{1}{4}$" wide, slanted	Available in smooth (*lisce*) or ridged (*rigate*)
perciatelli	small pierced	hollow tube like a straw	Good for thicker sauces
bucatini	from bucato "with a hole."	heavier tube than *perciatelli*	
penne piccoline	little quills		All forms of *penne* are good for meat, vegetable and cheese sauces
mostaccioli	mustache	same as *penne*	
ziti	bridegrooms	wider than *penne*, straight edged	Often used in backed dishes Good for thick sauces
zitoni	husky bridegrooms	thicker than *ziti*	Excellent for heavy ragu sauces
rigatoni	big ridges	large slightly curved tubes with ridges	Excellent for meat sauces or delicious barely adorned with butter and cheese
gnocchetti rigati	thin *rigatoni*		Fine for hearty tomato sauces
millerighe	thousand lines	straight-sided large tube with many ridges	Good for meat sauces
gigantoni	super giants	very large tubes	Suited only for baking
elicoidali	helixes	straight-edged tubes with wrap-around ridges	Excellent for cheese and ricotta sauces

(*continued*)

Tubes

Italian Name	English	Description	Comments
sedani	celery stalks	long, ridged like celery than *penne*	Longer and thinner
chifferi or gomiti	short, bent tubes		Good for light cheese sauces
cavatappi	corkscrews	snake-shaped tubes	Holds sauce very well. Good for vegetable sauces
manicotti	little muffs	large tube	Similar to *cannelloni* Used filled or baked
candele	candles	pipes of $1/2$" to $3/4$" diameters	
canneroncini	narrow pipes	$1/2$" long tubes	
canneroni	pipes	longer than *canneroncini*	
garganelii		squares rolled diagonally	The only tube made by hand from egg pasta

Soup Shapes

The general term for a small pasta used in soup is pastina. Many are variations on the same theme, and others are individual diminutive works of art.

Italian Name	English	Description	Comments
acini di pepe	peppercorns	tiny beads	
anelli	little rings	small circles	
anelli rigati	little ridged rings	small circles with ridges	

(continued)

289

Soup Shapes

Italian Name	English	Description	Comments
funghetti	little mushrooms	mushroom shaped	
conchigliette	little shells	small snail shells with ridges	
farfalline	little butterflies	small bow ties	
semi di melone	melon seeds		
orzo	barley	rice-shaped	Also known as *pasta a riso*
orzi piccoli		thinner than *orzo*	
alfabetini	little alphabet	pasta to spell with	
tubetti	little tubes	short and stubby pipes	
perline	little pearls	small beads	
stelline	little stars	small stars	
ditalini	little thimbles	tiny tubes, smaller than *ditali*	
quadretti	small squares		
salamini	tiny sausages		

Stuffed Shapes

Ever since the awareness of stuffed pastas has broadened beyond meat-filled ravioli in a can, their popularity has soared. And no wonder. Filled with vegetables and cheese, meat and seafood, and any combination thereof, stuffed pastas are interesting and endlessly variable. The very best balance pasta, stuffing, and sauce so that the integrity of each is not compromised.

Italian Name	English	Description	Comments
cannelloni	from *canna*, "hollow cane"	4" tube made by rolling a rectangle of pasta	
agnollotti or angolotti		crescent shaped	Also called *raviolini*
agnolini		smaller than *ravioli*	
tortellini		circles stuffed, then folded in half and pinched into a ring	Usually stuffed with meat or cheese
cappelletti	little hats	similar to *tortellini*, but made from a square so that a "peak" forms into a hat shape	
tortelloni		similar to *cappeletti*, but smaller	Also a square usually stuffed with riccota. Also called *tortelli*.
ravioli	stuffed squares		Shapes may differ according to regions
pansotti	little bellies	stuffed triangles	
lasagna		wide strips of pasta	Layers of *lasagna* with filling created the dish that bears their name

Special Shapes

These fancy shapes were most likely regional specialties or simply the result of singular imagi-nations—with a sense of humor. No one could name a pasta "radiators" without a smile. And who can explain the impetus for an Italian wagon wheel, more a symbol of the American Wild West than its Sicilian home territory? Each appeals to the eye as well as to the taste buds, an important element in any culinary effort.

Italian Name	English	Description	Comments
ruote	cartwheels	wheels complete with spokes	*Ruote* can be ridged or smooth
rotelle	wagon wheels	another name for *ruote*	*Rotelle* can also refer to spirals
conchiglie	shells	snail shell design	Middle-sized *conchiglie* are for sauces
conchiglioni	large shells		Used for stuffing
radiatori	radiators	shaped like small heaters	
gnocchi		pasta shaped like the "real" potato version	
gnocchetti		smaller than gnocchi	
gemelli	twins	one ½" length, folded and curled to look like two pieces	
casareccia	twists	curved ½" lengths of "S" shaped pasta	
fusilli	springs	short, telephone cord pieces	Sometimes called *fusilli corti*, meaning "short springs"
fusilli bucati		fusilli made from a tube	

Special Shapes

Italian Name		English	Description	Comments
orecchiette		little ears	circles pressed between fingers	less than 1 inch
cavatelli		cylinder bent into a "C"	less than 1 inch
farfalle		butterflies or bow ties	ridged squares pinched in the center	Also made with egg pasta
campanelle		bells	small cones with frilled edges	
lumache		snails	snail-like shape	*Lumanchine* is the smallest size
lumachone		fat snail		
cappelli de pagliaccio		clown's hats		
capelvenere		maidenhair fern	fine noodles for soup	

Colored and Flavored Pastas

Italians are apt to think of colored and flavored pastas as a gimmick that has crashed somewhere off the culinary track. Spinach and tomato are the traditional classics and you can serve them knowing that a noble history is behind them. But it seems very stodgy to reject innovation without experimenting, so here is a list of some pastas, new and old, that, at first, seem strange, but may be wonderful. Except for the squid, which would seem to have a natural affinity for seafood, most of these would best be served with simply butter, oil, or light cream sauces.

Estelle's Meatballs and Spaghetti

Servings: 8

Sauce:

28-ounce can tomato purée
12-ounce can tomato paste
28-ounce can tomato sauce
$\frac{1}{4}$ cup grated Parmesan cheese
1 teaspoon garlic powder
1 tablespoon Italian seasoning or oregano
2 tablespoons parsley flakes
salt and pepper to taste

Meatballs:

2 pounds meatloaf mix (ground beef,
    pork, and veal)
2 eggs, lightly beaten
2 slices soft bread, crumbed
1 small onion, finely chopped
1 medium potato, peeled and grated
$\frac{1}{4}$ cup grated Parmesan cheese

Combine the sauce ingredients in a large pot and bring to a boil; reduce heat to simmer. In a large bowl, combine the meatball ingredients, mixing well. Shape into 2-inch meatballs. Drop the *raw* meatballs into the hot spaghetti sauce. Simmer at least 2 hours, gently stirring occasionally. Serve with spaghetti noodles.

Fettuccine Alfredo

Servings: 4

9-ounce package refrigerated fettuccine,
    or 8 ounces dry pasta
$\frac{1}{2}$ cup butter
2 cloves garlic, minced
1 tablespoon flour
$1\frac{1}{2}$ cups milk
2 tablespoons cream cheese
1 cup grated Parmesan cheese
salt and freshly ground black pepper
    to taste
Parmesan cheese for garnish

Prepare the pasta according to package directions, cutting or breaking into thirds before cooking. Drain and keep warm.

In a large saucepan, melt the butter, sauté the garlic in the butter for about 2 minutes. Stir in the flour, then add the milk all at once, cooking and stirring over a medium heat until thick and bubbly. Add the cream cheese, stirring until blended. Add the Parmesan cheese, and continue cooking and stirring until all the cheese has melted. Toss with the fettuccine and add salt and pepper; serve with additional Parmesan cheese.

Basic Lasagna

Servings: 12

> 2 tablespoons olive oil, divided
> 3 cloves garlic, crushed
> ½ cup chopped onion
> 1 pound ground beef
> 1 tablespoon Italian seasoning
> salt and pepper to taste
> 2 26- to 28-ounce jars spaghetti sauce
> 16-ounce box lasagna noodles
> 3 eggs
> 16-ounce container ricotta cheese
> 3 tablespoons dried parsley flakes, or
>   ½ cup chopped fresh parsley
> 4 cups shredded, or 16 ounces sliced,
>   mozzarella cheese
> ½ cup grated Parmesan cheese

In a large skillet, heat 1 tablespoon of the olive oil; cook the garlic and onion in the oil about 3 minutes. Add the beef and sprinkle with Italian seasoning and salt and pepper. Brown the beef. Add the spaghetti sauce, reserving about ½ cup. Allow to simmer about 15 minutes. Cook the lasagna noodles as directed on the package, adding 1 tablespoon olive oil to the cooking water. In the blender or food processor, combine the eggs and ricotta cheese, then stir the parsley into the mixture.

Preheat the oven to 350°F. To assemble the lasagna, place a small amount of plain sauce (without the meat) on the bottom of a well-greased lasagna pan. Make a layer of noodles, topped with the ricotta cheese mixture, sauce, and mozzarella cheese. Repeat layers, ending with noodles. Spread the remaining plain sauce (without the meat) on top, and sprinkle with Parmesan cheese. Bake for 1¼ to 1½ hours, or until the center is bubbly. Allow to stand for 10 minutes before cutting to serve.

Vegetable Lasagna

Servings: 12

> 2 tablespoons olive oil, divided
> 4 cloves garlic, crushed
> ½ cup chopped onion
> 26- to 28-ounce jar spaghetti sauce, or 3½
>   cups Quick Tomato Sauce (page 117)
> 16-ounce can diced tomatoes
> 1 medium zucchini, peeled and diced
> 8 ounces sliced mushrooms
> 1 tablespoon Italian seasoning
> 16-ounce box lasagna noodles
> 3 eggs
> 16-ounce container ricotta cheese
> 3 tablespoons dried parsley flakes, or ½
>   cup chopped fresh parsley
> 1 red bell pepper, sliced
> 1 yellow bell pepper, sliced
> 1 green bell pepper, sliced
> 4 Roma tomatoes, sliced lengthwise
> 4 cups shredded, or 16 ounces sliced,
>   mozzarella cheese
> ½ cup Parmesan cheese

(continued)

In a small skillet, heat about 1 tablespoon of the olive oil; cook the garlic and onion in the oil about 3 minutes. In a large pot, combine the spaghetti sauce and diced tomatoes. Reserve about ½ cup of this mixture, then add the zucchini, mushrooms, Italian seasoning, and onion and garlic; bring to a boil. Allow to simmer about 15 minutes. Cook the lasagna noodles as directed on the package, adding 1 tablespoon olive oil to the cooking water. In the blender or food processor, combine the eggs and ricotta cheese, then stir the parsley into the mixture.

Preheat the oven to 350°F. To assemble the lasagna, place a small amount of the reserved sauce on the bottom of a well-greased lasagna pan. Make a layer of noodles, topped with the ricotta cheese mixture, sauce, sliced peppers, sliced tomatoes, and mozzarella cheese. Repeat layers, ending with noodles. Spread the remaining reserved sauce on top, and sprinkle with Parmesan cheese. Bake for 1¼ to 1½ hours, or until the center is bubbly. Allow to stand for 10 minutes before cutting to serve.

Note: This lasagna will be somewhat less "saucy" than a meat lasagna, because the tomatoes will add some moisture in baking.

Seafood Lasagna

Servings: 12

8 lasagna noodles
1 tablespoon olive oil
5 tablespoons butter, divided
1 cup chopped onion
8-ounce package cream cheese
1 egg
1½ cups ricotta cheese
1 teaspoon salt, divided
¼ teaspoon white pepper, divided
¼ cup flour
2 cups light cream or milk
½ cup dry white wine
1 teaspoon tarragon
*1 pound small or medium shrimp, peeled
   and deveined*
8 ounces crabmeat, flaked
½ cup shredded Swiss cheese
¼ cup Parmesan cheese

Cook the lasagna noodles according to package directions, adding the olive oil to the cooking water. In a large saucepan, melt 1 tablespoon of the butter; cook the onion in the butter until tender, then blend in the cream cheese. Beat the egg well. Add the egg, ricotta cheese, and half the salt and pepper, mixing well.

In a separate saucepan, melt 4 tablespoons butter; blend in the flour and remaining salt and pepper. Add the cream and cook until thick and bubbly, then stir in the wine and allow to cook for 1

minute, stirring constantly. Stir in the tarragon and seafood.

Preheat the oven to 350°F. Grease well a small lasagna pan or a 9 x 13-inch baking dish. Place 4 noodles in the pan; top with half the ricotta cheese mixture and half the seafood sauce; repeat layers. Sprinkle with the Swiss cheese, then top with Parmesan. Bake for 50 to 60 minutes, or until the center is bubbly. Allow to stand 10 minutes before cutting to serve.

Spinach Manicotti

Servings: 4 to 5

> 8–10 manicotti shells
> 5–6 ounces fresh spinach leaves
> 16-ounce container ricotta cheese
> ½ cup grated Parmesan cheese
> 1 egg, well beaten
> ½ teaspoon salt
> ¼ teaspoon pepper
> 16-ounce jar spaghetti sauce, or 2 cups
>   Quick Tomato Sauce (page 117)
> ½ cup shredded mozzarella cheese

Cook the manicotti shells according to package instructions. Tear the spinach into smaller pieces and steam in a vegetable steamer, in batches, until just wilted. In a large bowl, combine the ricotta cheese, Parmesan cheese, egg, salt and pepper; then stir in the spinach.

How to Cook Pasta

1. Fill a large pot with water— at least 4 quarts of water for 1 pound of pasta, 6 quarts if a large enough pot is available.
2. Bring the water to a boil and add 1 teaspoon of salt.
3. Add 1 tablespoon olive or vegetable oil if desired, which will help prevent the water from boiling over. It will also help prevent the pasta from sticking together.
4. Add the pasta when the water is at a roiling boil— not before.
5. Stir occasionally to prevent the pasta from sticking to the bottom of the pot.

(continued)

Preheat the oven to 350°F. Stuff the shells lightly and place in an 8 x 11-inch or similar baking dish. Pour the sauce over all and sprinkle with mozzarella cheese. Bake uncovered for 30 to 40 minutes, or until bubbly in the middle.

Chicken-Stuffed Shells

Servings: 6 to 8

1 stalk celery with leaves, cut into chunks
1 pound boneless, skinless chicken breasts
12-ounce package jumbo shells
2 tablespoons olive oil
2 cloves garlic, minced
8 ounces fresh mushrooms, finely chopped
8 sun-dried tomatoes packed in oil, drained and finely chopped
1/4 cup snipped fresh parsley
1 teaspoon basil
1 egg
2 tablespoons butter
2 tablespoons flour
1/4 teaspoon salt
1/4 teaspoon pepper
1 1/2 cups chicken broth
1/2 cup shredded Swiss or mozzarella cheese
1/2 cup shredded sharp Cheddar cheese

Fill a large saucepan with salted water, add the celery, and bring to a boil. Add the chicken breasts and poach until no longer pink in the middle, about 15 minutes.

Discard the water and celery; allow the chicken to cool, then chop finely. Cook the shells according to the package directions.

In a large skillet, heat the olive oil over medium heat; cook the garlic and the chopped mushrooms in the oil for about 3 minutes; add the tomatoes, parsley, and basil, and allow to thicken. Remove from heat and allow to cool for about 10 minutes. Beat the egg lightly and stir the egg and chicken into the mushroom mixture. Stuff the cooked shells and reserve on a platter.

In a medium saucepan, melt the butter and stir in the flour, salt, and pepper. Add the chicken broth, and cook and stir until thick and bubbly. Add the cheeses a little at a time and stir until melted. Spread about 1 cup of sauce in a large baking dish, and arrange the shells on the sauce. Spoon the remaining sauce over the shells. Cover and bake about 30 minutes, or until hot and bubbly.

Baked Penne

This recipe can easily be halved

Servings: 10 to 12

16 ounces penne pasta
1 pound ground beef
2 cloves garlic, crushed
1/4 cup chopped onion
1 teaspoon Italian seasoning

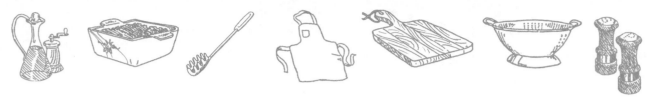

salt and pepper to taste
2 26- to 28-ounce jars basil-flavored
    spaghetti sauce
4 cups shredded mozzarella cheese, divided

Cook the penne as directed on the package, but undercook slightly.

Preheat oven to 350°F. In a large skillet, brown the ground beef, garlic, and onion, sprinkling with the Italian seasoning and salt and pepper to taste as it cooks. In a large bowl, combine the cooked meat mixture, penne, spaghetti sauce, and 3 cups of cheese. Turn into a greased 9 x 13-inch baking dish, and sprinkle with the remaining cup of cheese. Bake 45 to 55 minutes, or until hot and bubbly in the center.

Turkey Tetrazzini

The world's best leftover turkey casserole

Servings: 5 to 6

8–10 ounces spaghetti or linguine
4-ounce can mushrooms (reserve the liquid)
2 or more cups cubed cooked turkey
4 tablespoons butter
¼ cup flour
salt and pepper to taste
16-ounce can chicken broth, or 1¾ cups
    turkey broth
1 cup half-and-half
½ cup grated Parmesan cheese

Break the spaghetti into pieces, and cook according to package directions, but undercook slightly. Drain. In a large bowl, toss the noodles with the drained mushrooms and turkey.

Preheat the oven to 350°F. Melt the butter over low heat. Stir in the flour, salt, and pepper, and cook until the mixture is bubbly. Remove the pan from the heat, and

(continued)

Pasta for Sauced Dishes

When cooking pasta to be used in sauced pastas rather than baked dishes:

- Follow the timing directions on the package. Fresh pasta cooks in a much shorter time than dried pasta.
- Test the pasta when the end of the cooking time nears to determine when it is done "al dente" (say "all dantay") or "to the tooth." Al dente describes pasta that is firm to the bite. It will be chewy rather than soft or mushy. Al dente is the preferred level of doneness for most pasta recipes.

stir in the broth, half-and-half, and reserved mushroom liquid. Stirring constantly, heat the sauce until it boils; boil 1 minute.

Pour the sauce over the noodle mixture and mix thoroughly. Place mixture in an 8 x 11-inch baking dish. Sprinkle the Parmesan cheese on top. Bake about 45 minutes, or until hot and bubbly in the center.

Chicken Noodle Bake

Servings: 8

8 ounces wide egg noodles
2¹/₂ cups milk
3 tablespoons flour
1 tablespoon chicken bouillon granules
2 cups cubed cooked chicken
2 cups broccoli pieces, thawed
¹/₂ cup plain yogurt
¹/₂ cup shredded Swiss cheese

Cook the noodles according to package directions, undercooking slightly. Preheat the oven to 375°F. In a medium saucepan, combine the milk, flour, and bouillon, and cook over medium heat until it thickens slightly. Combine all the other ingredients except the cheese in a large bowl. Pour the milk mixture over, and toss to combine well. Turn into a lightly greased 2-quart baking dish and sprinkle the cheese on top. Cover and bake 25 to 30 minutes, or until the center is hot and bubbly.

Variation: Cubed cooked turkey or ham may be substituted for the chicken.

Noodle Casserole

Servings: 12 side-dish servings

16-ounce package medium-width
    egg noodles
16 ounces creamy cottage cheese
3 eggs
8 ounces sour cream
2 tablespoons sugar
1 tablespoon parsley flakes, optional
1 teaspoon salt
1 teaspoon paprika
2 tablespoons butter, melted

Cook the noodles according to package directions. Preheat oven to 350°F. In a blender or food processor, blend the cottage cheese, eggs, sour cream, sugar, parsley, and seasonings until smooth. Pour over the noodles and toss well to combine. Place in a lightly greased 9 x 13-inch baking dish and drizzle the melted butter on top. Bake about 40 minutes, or until the center is hot.

Corny Macaroni

Servings: 6 to 8 side-dish servings

¹/₄ cup butter
¹/₄ cup finely chopped onion
¹/₄ cup finely chopped pepper
1 cup uncooked elbow macaroni
*1 cup shredded Colby or Colby-Jack
    cheese, seasoned for tacos*
16-ounce can whole kernel corn, drained
16-ounce can cream-style corn
salt and pepper to taste

In a small skillet, melt the butter over medium heat; cook the onion and pepper in the butter about 3 minutes, or until soft. Combine the butter-onion mixture with all other ingredients. Turn into a lightly greased, high-sided 2-quart casserole dish. Bake for 1 hour, stirring every 15 minutes.

Patti's Pasta

Servings: 6 to 8

2 teaspoons olive oil
1 green pepper, sliced in julienne strips
10 scallions, sliced in julienne strips
4 tablespoons butter, divided
2 cups halved and sliced mushrooms
16 ounces spiral pasta
dried pepper flakes (optional)
shredded Parmesan cheese

Sauce:

1 tablespoon butter
1 tablespoon flour
2 cups heavy cream
¹/₄ cup grated Swiss cheese
*¹/₂ pound deli sliced smoked ham,
    sliced in julienne strips*
freshly ground pepper to taste

(continued)

Pasta for Baking

***When cooking pasta to be used
in baked dishes:***

Undercook by 1 or 2 minutes. Cook 1 or 2 minutes less than the shortest cooking time given in the package directions. The pasta will be a better consistency when the dish has been baked.

In a small skillet, sauté the green pepper and scallions briefly in the olive oil. In another small skillet, melt 2 tablespoons butter and sauté the mushrooms until just soft. Set both aside.

To make the sauce, melt the butter over low heat in heavy 2-quart saucepan. Add the flour and stir for 30 seconds. Remove from heat until the bubbling stops, then add the cream all at once. Return to the heat, and bring to a simmer, stirring constantly. Add Swiss cheese and stir until melted. Add ham to sauce and pepper to taste and heat through over low heat.

Cook pasta according to package directions. Drain, return to the pan, and toss with 2 tablespoons butter. Place pasta in a serving bowl. Add the green peppers and scallions to the sauce, along with the pepper flakes if desired. Pour sauce over the pasta, and top generously with shredded Parmesan cheese.

Quick Pasta with Basil and Tomatoes

Servings: 4

> 8- to 10-ounce package refrigerated angel
>   hair pasta, or 8 ounces dried pasta
> 4 tablespoons olive oil, divided
> 12 medium Roma tomatoes (use fewer if
>   tomatoes are large)
> 2 or more cloves garlic, to taste, crushed
> ¹/₄ cup chopped fresh basil

¹/₂ cup fresh shredded Parmesan cheese

Break or cut the pasta into smaller pieces, and cook according to package directions, adding 1 tablespoon olive oil to the cooking water. Seed and coarsely chop the tomatoes (do not peel). In a large skillet, heat 3 tablespoons olive oil. Cook the garlic in the oil about 1 minute, then add the tomatoes and basil; cook just until warmed—do not allow the tomatoes to become mushy. In a large bowl, toss together the hot pasta, tomato mixture, and Parmesan cheese.

Raw Veggie Pasta Toss

Servings: 4

> 1 small yellow squash
> 1 small zucchini
> ¹/₄ cup extra-virgin olive oil
> 3 ripe Roma tomatoes, seeded
>   and chopped
> 1 cup shredded broccoli (available at
>   groceries as "broccoli slaw")
> 3 green onions, sliced
> 1 clove garlic, finely minced
> ¹/₄ cup chopped fresh basil
> salt and pepper to taste
> 8 ounces ziti or penne pasta
> ³/₄ cup shredded Italian cheese blend, or
>   use ¹/₂ cup shredded mozzarella cheese
>   and ¹/₄ cup shredded Parmesan cheese

Partially peel the squash and zucchini by removing ¼-inch-wide strips of skin, ¼ inch apart, with a vegetable peeler; dice the squash and zucchini. In a large bowl combine the olive oil, vegetables, garlic, basil, and salt and pepper. Allow to stand while the pasta is prepared.

Cook the pasta according to package directions. Immediately after draining, toss with the cheese until the cheese melts, then toss with the vegetable-olive oil mixture. Serve immediately.

Pasta Creole

Servings: 4

> 8- to 10-ounce package refrigerated
>   linguine, or 8 ounces dried pasta
> ¼ cup + 1 tablespoon olive oil, divided
> ⅓ cup diced purple or red onion
> 2 cloves garlic
> ⅓ cup diced green pepper
> ⅓ cup diced red pepper
> 1½ pounds medium shrimp, peeled
>   and deveined
> 1 tablespoon Cajun seasoning
> 1 teaspoon red pepper flakes
> salt to taste
> ¾ cup dry white wine
> ¾ cup seeded, diced tomatoes
> ¼ cup shredded Parmesan cheese

How to Peel Tomatoes

Many pasta recipes call for the use of egg-shaped plum or Roma tomatoes, which have more meat and fewer seeds than slicing tomatoes. To peel them easily:

1. Bring a large pan of water to a boil.
2. Drop the tomatoes, a few at a time, into the water for about 1 minute or until the skin begins to split.

Remove from the water with a long-tined fork or slotted spoon. Allow to cool slightly. Place them on the end of a long-tined fork and peel; the skin will slip off easily. Start the peel with a sharp paring knife, if necessary.

(continued)

Break or cut the linguine into small pieces, then cook according to package directions, adding 1 tablespoon olive oil to the cooking water. Drain and keep warm.

In a large skillet, heat $1/4$ cup olive oil over medium heat and sauté the onion, garlic, and peppers about 2 minutes. Add the shrimp and cook until they turn color, stirring frequently. Add the seasonings and simmer 1 minute, then add the wine and bring to a boil. Add the tomatoes and cooked linguine to the skillet and toss gently until heated through. Top with Parmesan cheese. Serve immediately.

Mushroom Linguine

Servings: 4

> 4 tablespoons butter
> 2 cloves garlic, finely minced
> $1/2$ cup finely chopped onion
> 2 cups grated carrots
> 16 ounces mushrooms, sliced
> 1 tablespoon flour
> 8 ounces linguine
> 1 tablespoon olive oil
> $1/3$ cup grated Parmesan cheese
> $1/4$ cup snipped fresh parsley
> salt and pepper to taste

Melt the butter in a large skillet over medium-high heat. Sauté the garlic, onion, and carrots in the butter for about 2 minutes, then add the mushrooms and sauté

for 3 minutes more, or until liquid begins to form. Sprinkle the flour over the mushrooms, and continue to cook and stir until mushrooms are coated with a thin sauce.

Meanwhile, break the linguine into small pieces and cook according to package directions, adding olive oil to the cooking water. Drain and add to the skillet, sprinkle with the Parmesan cheese, parsley and salt and pepper. Toss gently until well mixed. Serve immediately.

White Mushroom Pasta

Servings: 3 to 4

> 8 ounces bow tie pasta
> 1 tablespoon olive oil
> 8 ounces assorted fresh mushrooms, chopped (shiitake, Portobello, chanterelle)
> 2 teaspoons freshly ground black pepper
> 1 cup cottage cheese
> 1 cup crumbled blue cheese (Gorgonzola or other)
> $1/4$ cup grated Parmesan cheese

Cook pasta according to package directions. While pasta is boiling, heat oil in a deep skillet over high heat. Reduce heat slightly and add mushrooms and pepper; stir occasionally until mushrooms are tender, about 4 to 5 minutes. Reduce heat to medium-low. If any excess liquid remains, lightly drain.

Drain pasta, and add noodles to mushrooms in skillet. Add cottage cheese and blue cheese. Stir well until all cheese is melted and pasta is coated. Remove from heat and sprinkle with Parmesan. Serve immediately.

Penne with Chicken, Asparagus, and Pine Nuts

Servings: 4

> 8 ounces penne pasta
> ½ cup pine nuts
> 3 boneless, skinless chicken breasts
> 2 tablespoons olive oil, divided
> 4 cloves garlic, sliced thinly
> 16-ounce can chicken broth
> 1 pound asparagus, stems trimmed and broken into 2-inch pieces
> ½ cup grated Parmesan cheese

Cook the pasta according to package directions. While the water is boiling, toast the pine nuts in a dry skillet, stirring frequently, until golden brown. Set aside. Slice the chicken into thin 1-inch-long pieces. In a large skillet, heat 1 tablespoon olive oil over medium-high heat; stir-fry the chicken for 5 to 7 minutes or until cooked through and no longer pink.

In a large pot, heat 1 tablespoon olive oil over high heat; cook the garlic in the oil for 2 to 3 minutes. Add the broth and bring to a boil. Add the asparagus to the broth; reduce heat to a simmer and cook until just tender. Drain the pasta. Toss together the pasta, pine nuts, chicken, Parmesan, and broth mixture. Serve immediately.

Chicken Fettuccine

Servings: 4

> olive oil
> 3 boneless, skinless chicken breasts, diced
> 2 cups diced fresh mushrooms
> ¾ cup sun-dried tomatoes packed in oil, drained and chopped
> 4 cloves garlic, crushed
> 2 tablespoons chopped shallots
> ¾ cup white wine
> 1½ cups chicken broth
> 3 tablespoons chopped fresh basil
> 1 teaspoon salt
> ⅛ teaspoon pepper
> 3 tablespoons butter
> 12 ounces fettuccine
> ¾ cup shredded Parmesan cheese

Heat about 2 tablespoons olive oil over medium-high heat; sauté the diced chicken until partially browned. Add the mushrooms and tomatoes, and cook until mushrooms are reduced and fully cooked. Add the garlic and shallots, and sauté about a minute longer, then add the wine, chicken broth, basil, salt, and pepper. Simmer until reduced, then add the butter.

(continued)

Cook the fettuccine according to package directions (break into thirds before cooking). Toss with sauce and sprinkle with Parmesan cheese.

Pesto

Yield: about ³⁄₄ cup

¹⁄₃ cup pine nuts
1 clove garlic, peeled and chopped
1¹⁄₂ cups fresh basil leaves, firmly packed*
2 tablespoons + ¹⁄₃ cup olive oil, divided
2 tablespoons grated Parmesan cheese
¹⁄₂ teaspoon salt

Toast the pine nuts. In a blender or food processor, combine the pine nuts, garlic, basil, and 2 tablespoons olive oil. Blend just until evenly puréed. Place in a bowl and stir in the cheese and salt, then slowly stir in ¹⁄₃ cup olive oil. (Pesto is not cooked or heated.)

*To prepare the basil, wash the leaves and trim off the stems before packing in the measuring cup.

Pesto Pasta

Servings: 4 side-dish servings

¹⁄₃ cup pine nuts
9-ounce package refrigerated fettuccine or linguine, or 8 ounces dried pasta
1 recipe pesto
shredded Parmesan cheese

Toast the pine nuts. Cook the pasta (cut or break into thirds before cooking) according to the directions on the package, and drain. Toss the pasta with the pesto and pine nuts. Serve with shredded Parmesan cheese.

Pepper Pesto Pasta

Servings: 4

9-ounce package refrigerated angel hair pasta, or 8 ounces dry pasta
1 red bell pepper
1 pound sirloin steak
¹⁄₄ cup olive oil
2 cloves garlic, minced
1¹⁄₂ teaspoons seeded and crushed red chili peppers
¹⁄₂ cup pesto
salt to taste

Cook the pasta according to package directions, cutting or breaking into thirds before cooking, and drain. Seed the red pepper and cut into lengthwise strips. Slice the beef into pieces ¹⁄₈- to ¹⁄₄-inch thick and 2 to 3 inches long.

In a large skillet, heat the oil over medium-high heat; sauté the garlic and chili peppers for 1 minute, then add the beef and brown until no longer pink. Add the pepper strips and sauté for about 2 minutes more, or until peppers are crisp-tender. Stir in the pesto and salt to taste. Toss with the pasta and serve.

Pasta Fagioli

Servings: 6 to 8

16 ounces ziti pasta
2 tablespoons olive oil
2 cloves garlic, minced
1½ cups fresh or frozen sugar snap pea pods, thawed and drained
1½ cups diced cooked ham
16-ounce can cannellini beans, drained
¼ cup sun-dried tomatoes in oil, drained and chopped
1½ cups chicken broth
½ teaspoon salt
¼ teaspoon pepper
¼ cup grated Parmesan cheese

Cook the pasta as directed on the package. Meanwhile, in a large skillet, heat the oil over medium heat; sauté the garlic in the oil for about 2 minutes. Add the pea pods and stir-fry for about 3 minutes. Stir in the ham, beans, tomatoes, broth, salt and pepper, and simmer for 5 minutes. Toss the pasta, Parmesan cheese, and bean mixture together.

Fettuccini a la Brie

Servings: 3 or 4

4 Roma tomatoes
½ pound Brie cheese
2 cloves garlic, minced
½ teaspoon salt
¼ teaspoon pepper
¼ cup olive oil
¼ cup chopped fresh basil
9-ounce package refrigerated fresh fettuccini, or 8 ounces dry pasta

(continued)

Pasta for Salads

When cooking pasta to be used in marinated salads:

Undercook by 1 or 2 minutes. Cook 1 or 2 minutes less than the shortest cooking time given in the package directions. The pasta will absorb the flavors of the other ingredients in the dish more easily.

Peel, seed, and chop the tomatoes. Remove the rind from the cheese. Grate enough to make $1/4$ cup; set aside. (Cheese will grate more easily if it is placed in the freezer for $1/2$ hour.) Cut the remaining cheese into half-inch cubes. Combine the tomatoes, cheese, garlic, salt, and olive oil in a bowl; cover and allow to stand at room temperature for 2 hours. When ready to serve, cut or break the pasta into smaller pieces and prepare according to package directions. Drain and immediately toss with the tomato-cheese mixture and the basil. Sprinkle with the grated brie and serve immediately.

Easy Beef and Ramen Noodles

Servings: 4

1 pound top round or sirloin steak
2 teaspoons soy sauce
1 tablespoon vegetable oil
2 3-ounce packages Asian (or Oriental) flavor instant ramen noodles
2 cups frozen Asian (or Oriental) vegetable mix
2 cups water
$1/8$ teaspoon ginger
2 tablespoons sliced green onion (whites and part of the green)
1 tablespoon sesame seeds

Slice the beef into pieces $1/8$ to $1/4$ inch thick and 2 to 3 inches long, and toss with the soy sauce. In a large skillet, heat the oil over medium-high heat. Brown the beef in the oil until no longer pink. Remove beef from the skillet to a bowl; toss it with the seasoning packet from one package of the noodles.

To the skillet, add the noodles, broken up, Asian vegetables, water, ginger, and the remaining seasoning packet. Bring to a boil. Cover, reduce the heat, and simmer for about 3 minutes or until noodles are tender. Stir in the beef, green onion, and sesame seeds, and heat through.

Basic Pasta Salad

Servings: 8 side-dish servings

8 ounces tricolored corkscrew pasta
1 cup or more Italian salad dressing
$1/4$ cup sliced green onions
1 cup chopped broccoli
1 cup chopped cauliflower
1 cup shredded or chopped carrot
$1/4$ cup sliced black olives
$1/3$ cup shredded Jack or mozzarella cheese
$1/3$ cup cubed Cheddar cheese
$1/3$ cup shredded Parmesan cheese
1 cup julienned summer sausage (optional)
salt and pepper

Cook the pasta according to package directions, undercooking slightly. While it is still warm, toss in a deep bowl with about ¼ cup salad dressing. Allow to cool at room temperature 30 minutes, stirring occasionally.

Meanwhile, combine all the vegetables in a deep narrow bowl or container. Add about ½ cup dressing and stir to coat; add up to ¼ cup more if necessary. Allow to marinate about 30 minutes at room temperature, stirring occasionally. Cover both bowls and refrigerate. Allow the pasta and the vegetables to marinate separately, at least 6 hours or overnight.

When ready to serve, add the vegetables and their dressing to the pasta, and toss with the cheeses and sausage. If the salad seems too dry, add dressing to taste. Season with salt and pepper to taste.

Pesto Pasta Salad

Servings: 6 side-dish or 3 main-dish servings

9-ounce package refrigerated pesto-filled tortellini
about 1 cup prepared vinaigrette salad dressing, or Simple Vinaigrette Dressing (page 119)
1 medium cucumber or zucchini
¾ cup grated or shredded carrot

¼ cup chopped red onion
½ cup shredded packaged Italian cheese mix, or ¼ cup shredded mozzarella and ¼ cup Parmesan cheese
1 tablespoon snipped fresh parsley
salt and pepper

Cook the pasta according to package directions, undercooking slightly. While it is still warm, toss in a deep bowl with about ¼ cup salad dressing. Allow to cool at room temperature 30 minutes, stirring occasionally.

Meanwhile, partially peel the cucumber by removing ¼-inch strips of skin ¼-inch apart. Quarter the cucumber lengthwise, and slice. Combine the cucumber with the carrot and onion in a deep narrow bowl or container. Add about ½ cup dressing and stir to coat. Allow to marinate about 30 minutes at room temperature, stirring occasionally. Cover both bowls and refrigerate. Allow the pasta and the vegetables to marinate separately for at least 4 hours or overnight.

When ready to serve, add the vegetables and their dressing to the pasta and toss with the cheese and parsley. Season with salt and pepper to taste.

Bacon and Tomato Pasta Salad

Servings: 6 side-dish or 3 main-dish servings

> half of a 9-ounce refrigerated package
>   white (plain) cheese-filled tortellini
> half of a 9-ounce refrigerated package
>   green (spinach) cheese-filled tortellini
> ½ cup vinaigrette or Italian salad dressing
> 1 cup cut green beans, fresh or frozen
> 1 tablespoon chopped red onion
> 6 slices bacon, cooked and crumbled
> 4 medium Roma tomatoes, seeded
>   and chopped
> ¼ cup or more ranch-style salad dressing
> 1 tablespoon snipped fresh parsley
> salt and pepper

Cook the pasta according to package directions, undercooking slightly. While it is still warm, toss in a deep bowl with about ¼ cup of the vinaigrette. Allow to cool at room temperature 30 minutes, stirring occasionally.

Meanwhile, blanch the beans, then place in a bowl with the onion and ¼ cup vinaigrette dressing; stir to coat. Allow to marinate about 30 minutes at room temperature, stirring occasionally. Cover both bowls and refrigerate. Allow the pasta and the vegetables to marinate separately at least 4 hours or overnight.

Fresh or Dried Pasta?

Most of us eat dried pasta that has been stored in a box. If you've ever eaten fresh pasta, it may actually seem mushy to you.

Fresh pasta can be heavenly in taste and texture, but since it is fresh, it needs only a minute or two of cooking, just to heat through. Nowadays, you can buy freshly made pasta (usually refrigerated) in the supermarket, and although it's more expensive than the boxed variety, you can look at it as a special treat.

When ready to serve, add the beans and their dressing to the pasta, along with the tomato and bacon. Add the ranch dressing and parsley, and toss. Season with salt and pepper to taste.

Braised Noodles with Vegetables

Servings: 4

3 quarts water
1½ teaspoons salt, divided
1 pound Shanghai-style noodles (or Chinese-style egg noodles)
¼ pound fresh shiitake mushrooms
3 tablespoons peanut oil, divided
2 cloves garlic, chopped
1 carrot, peeled and julienned
4 cups finely shredded Chinese cabbage
8 green onions, cut into 2-inch pieces
¾ cup chicken broth
3 tablespoons dark soy sauce
2 tablespoons rice wine vinegar
2 teaspoons sesame oil
¼ teaspoon sugar
freshly ground black pepper to taste

In a large pot, bring the water and 1 teaspoon salt to a boil. Add the noodles; stir well and cook until just tender, 3 to 4 minutes. Drain and rinse well under cold water. Set aside.

Remove shiitake stems and discard. Cut mushrooms into ¼-inch pieces. Heat the wok over medium-high heat. Add 2 tablespoons of the oil and the remaining ½ teaspoon salt. Add the garlic and mushrooms, stirring until wilted, about 3 minutes. Set aside. Raise heat to high and add the remaining 1 tablespoon oil to the wok. Add the carrot and cabbage, and toss and stir for 2 minutes. Add the green onions and stir for 10 seconds. Remove from heat for a moment.

Place wok over medium-high heat and add the broth, soy sauce, vinegar, sesame oil, sugar, and pepper. Bring to a boil and cook until the liquid is slightly reduced, about 1 minute. Add the noodles and toss to coat evenly. Cook until the liquid is completely reduced, about 3 minutes. Divide among individual plates and serve immediately.

Stir-frying is the technique of sautéing small pieces of meat, fish, and/or vegetables in a little oil over very hot heat while stirring and tossing the ingredients continuously to cook them evenly on all sides. The average stir-fry dish takes between 3 to 5 minutes to cook.

Pad Thai

Servings: 4

> $\frac{1}{2}$ pound dried rice ribbon noodles*
> 2 tablespoons vegetable oil, divided
> 3 cloves garlic, minced
> $\frac{1}{4}$ cup minced shallots
> 3 tablespoons tomato paste
> 2 tablespoons fish sauce*
> 2 tablespoons fresh lime juice
> 1 tablespoon sugar
> 1 egg
> pinch of red pepper flakes
> chicken broth
> $\frac{1}{3}$ pound mung bean sprouts
> 8 green onions, chopped
> $\frac{1}{2}$ cup chopped roasted peanuts, divided
> cilantro for garnish

Place the noodles in a bowl, add warm water to cover, and soak until soft, about 15 minutes. Heat a wok over medium-high heat, and add 1 tablespoon of the oil. Add the garlic and shallots and stir until golden, about 1 minute. Raise the heat to high and add the tomato paste, fish sauce, lime juice, and sugar. Stir until thickened, about 30 seconds. Break the egg into the middle of the wok, lightly beat, then cook without stirring, until set, about 20 seconds. Gently fold the egg into the sauce. Add the noodles and red pepper flakes, tossing to coat with sauce. Add the chicken broth slowly to moisten the noodles and cook until the noodles begin to cling together, about 3 minutes. Add the bean sprouts, green onions, and half the peanuts. Toss to combine and cook until the bean sprouts begin to wilt. Serve on individual plates and garnish with cilantro and remaining peanuts.

*Look for fish sauce in the Asian section of most supermarkets. Rice ribbon noodles are usually only found in Asian food stores.

Peanut Sesame Noodles

Servings: 4–5

> 1 pound dry spaghetti or spaghettini
> 1 cup snow peas, sliced diagonally
> $\frac{1}{2}$ cup chunky peanut butter
> $\frac{1}{3}$ cup rice wine vinegar
> $\frac{1}{3}$ cup sugar
> 3 tablespoons Japanese soy sauce
> 2 tablespoons water
> 1 tablespoon toasted sesame oil*
> $\frac{1}{4}$ cup Thai chili sauce**
> $1\frac{1}{2}$ teaspoons minced garlic
> 1 teaspoon minced fresh gingerroot
> 1 tablespoon sesame seeds, lightly toasted in a frying pan
> $\frac{1}{4}$ cup chopped fresh cilantro
> 1 large carrot, sliced into tiny matchstick pieces
> 9 green onions, thinly sliced
> $\frac{1}{2}$ cup chopped roasted peanuts

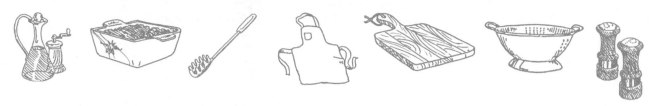

Break spaghetti in half and cook in boiling water according to package directions. Drain and rinse in cold water. Set aside. Bring a small pan of water to a boil. Add snow peas and count to 5. Drain immediately and rinse in cold water.

In a large bowl, whisk together peanut butter, vinegar, sugar, soy sauce, water, sesame oil, chili sauce, garlic, and ginger until very smooth. Add cooked pasta, snow peas, sesame seeds, cilantro, carrot, green onions and peanuts to the dressing. Toss together, coating the pasta and vegetables well with the dressing.

*Toasted sesame oil can be found in the Asian section of well-stocked supermarkets or in Asian food stores.

**Thai chili sauce is available at most well-stocked supermarkets. It is not the same as spicy Chinese chili paste.

Japanese Teriyaki Chicken (page 214) can be sliced very thin and served on top of Peanut Sesame Noodles.

Toasting Nuts

Toasting nuts brings out their flavor. When a recipe calls for toasted nuts, you can toast them:

- In the oven, by placing on a jellyroll pan and baking at 300°F, turning often, until golden brown, or

- On the stovetop, by placing them in a nonstick skillet over low heat. Do not add any fat and stir frequently until browned.

Chapter 12

Meatless Main Dishes

Polenta

Servings: 4

¹/₄ cup olive oil

3 teaspoons kosher salt

2 cups coarse cornmeal

4 tablespoons (¹/₂ stick) unsalted butter at room temperature

¹/₂ cup grated Parmesan cheese

Bring 8¹/₂ cups of water to a boil in a large, heavy pot. Add the olive oil and salt. Slowly add the cornmeal in a steady stream and stir continuously. After all the cornmeal has been added, cook and stir over low heat until the polenta pulls away from the sides of the pot. When using coarse cornmeal, this may take up to 20 minutes. The polenta should be thick, smooth, and creamy.

Stir in the butter and the cheese. Either serve immediately or allow to cool in a 9 x 11-inch pan.

Other cheeses can be used, depending on the dish you are preparing. Good choices are provolone, Cheddar, and smoked cheeses of all kinds.

Note: A nonstick saucepan is best for making polenta as it takes the pressure off the "continuous stirring" direction, although it still cannot be left unattended for more than a minute or two.

Polenta is cooked cornmeal—the cornmeal can be either fine or coarsely ground. When using finely ground cornmeal, water is absorbed quickly and it is done almost immediately. When making polenta, a good rule of thumb is to use 1 cup of water per serving. Each cup of boiling water absorbs about ¹/₃ cup of cornmeal, which makes a proper serving. Polenta is a wonderful basic dish that easily absorbs the flavors of vegetables and seasonings and allows endless creative main-dish ideas.

Polenta with Red Sauce and Smoked Cheese

Servings: 4–6

polenta made with
*   2 ounces smoked grated cheese*
*   instead of Parmesan*

Basic Tomato Sauce (page 117) made with
*   1 tablespoon of chipotle puree**
*   (added when sautéing the onions)*

³/₄ pound shiitake mushrooms, sliced, about 4 cups

³/₄ teaspoon salt, divided

4 tablespoons olive oil, divided

4 cloves garlic, finely chopped, divided

1 medium-sized zucchini, diced

¹/₂ medium red bell pepper, diced

1 teaspoon cumin seed, toasted and ground**

pinch of cayenne pepper

1 tablespoon chopped cilantro, divided

1 tablespoon chopped fresh marjoram or oregano, divided

¹/₄ pound grated smoked mozzarella cheese, about 1¹/₂ cups

Make the polenta and while it cools, make the tomato sauce. When the polenta is cool, cut into squares and then triangles.

Sauté the mushrooms until golden brown over medium-high heat with ½ teaspoon of the salt and 2 tablespoons olive oil. Add half the garlic, and sauté for 1 minute more. Set aside in a bowl.

Sauté the zucchini, pepper, cumin, the remaining ¼ teaspoon salt, cayenne pepper and remaining olive oil for 7 to 8 minutes. Add the remaining garlic and sauté for an additional 2 minutes. Remove from heat and toss with the mushrooms and half the fresh herbs.

Preheat the oven to 375°F. Pour the tomato sauce into a 9 x 13-inch baking pan. Arrange the polenta triangles in rows, overlapping where necessary to fill the baking dish. Sprinkle the vegetables in and around the polenta triangles. Sprinkle the cheese over the polenta and vegetables. Bake for 30 to 40 minutes. When ready to serve, sprinkle remaining fresh herbs over each serving.

*Chipotle peppers can be found canned in the Mexican section of most well-stocked food stores. Purée them in the blender and refrigerate the remainder in a well-sealed container for later use.

**Cumin seeds can be toasted by heating 3–4 minutes in a dry-fry pan.

The mix of flavors in this dish is delightful. Serve this dish with a green garden salad, and you'll have a complete meal.

Penne with Asparagus

Servings: 4

8 ounces uncooked penne or ziti pasta
1 tablespoon olive oil
2 medium shallots, finely chopped
2 cups tomato sauce
⅔ cup 1% milk
2 pounds pencil-thin asparagus, trimmed and cut into 1-inch pieces
½ teaspoon dried tarragon
½ teaspoon salt
½ teaspoon freshly ground pepper
freshly grated Parmesan cheese

Bring a large pot of water to boiling and add a little salt. Add the pasta and cook until just tender, about 10 minutes. Drain well in a colander.

In a large skillet, heat the olive oil over medium heat. Add the shallots and sauté until soft, about 6 to 7 minutes.

Stir in the tomato sauce and milk; increase the heat and bring to a boil. Add the asparagus and tarragon, and reduce the heat to low. Partially cover and cook until asparagus is tender and sauce is slightly thickened, about 10 to 12 minutes.

Add the pasta to the asparagus mixture along with the salt and pepper. Toss until well coated. Sprinkle with Parmesan cheese (optional) and serve hot.

Capellini with Pesto

Servings: 4

> 2–3 cups vegetable broth
> ³/₄ pound capellini
> 5 cups tightly packed fresh basil leaves,
>   preferably small leaves
> ¹/₄ cup extra-virgin olive oil
> 2 tablespoons coarsely chopped
>   flat-leafed parsley
> 2 tablespoons chopped garlic
> ¹/₂ cup pine nuts or walnuts or pecans
> 1 teaspoon salt
> ¹/₂ cup freshly grated Parmesan cheese

Bring 2 cups of the broth to a boil in a medium soup pot; add the pasta and cook until done, stirring constantly. All of the broth should be absorbed by the pasta. If the broth is absorbed and the pasta is not done, add enough broth to finalize cooking. Pasta can also be made with lightly salted water if broth is not available.

Put the basil, olive oil, parsley, garlic, nuts, and salt in a food processor and blend just until puréed; be careful not to overprocess. Add enough broth to the pesto to make it creamy, not thick. (Pesto can be made before the pasta is cooked.) Add the pesto to the pasta and gently toss; serve immediately with a dusting of Parmesan cheese.

 Pesto is an uncooked or lightly cooked sauce that has been blended to a paste.

It can be made very easily with a food processor in a matter of minutes. In America, the classic pesto is made with basil, garlic, pine nuts, and olive oil. Walnuts or pecans can be substituted for pine nuts, however, it is important to use extra-virgin olive oil and fresh garlic.

Leek and Cheese Bake

Servings: 4 to 6

> 9-inch pastry shell
> 2 leeks, cleaned and sliced into rounds
> 2 tablespoons butter
> pinch of cayenne pepper
> pinch of ground nutmeg
> 3 eggs
> ¹/₃ cup milk
> ¹/₃ cup sour cream
> ¹/₄ teaspoon salt
> ³/₄ cup grated Cheddar cheese

Preheat the oven to 375°F. Prebake the pastry shell for 5 minutes. Set aside. Turn the oven temperature up to 400°F. In a saucepan, sauté the leeks in butter just until tender. Season with cayenne pepper and nutmeg. Let cool.

Whisk eggs, milk, sour cream, and salt together. Sprinkle half the cheese on the bottom of the pastry shell. Spread the leeks on top and cover with the remaining cheese. Pour the egg custard over the cheese. Bake for 30 minutes or until golden. Serve warm or cold.

Summer Squash Casserole

Servings: 6

> 2 pounds yellow summer squash or
>   zucchini
> salt to taste
> 4 eggs
> 1/2 cup milk
> 1/2 cup chopped parsley
> 3 tablespoons flour
> 2 teaspoons baking powder
> 1 teaspoon salt
> 4-ounce can diced green chilies
> 8 ounces ricotta cheese
> 8 ounces sharp Cheddar cheese, grated
> 3 cups small, fresh bread cubes
> 3–4 tablespoons butter
> 1/2 cup sesame seeds

Preheat oven to 325°F. Cube or slice the squash and place in a medium saucepan or skillet with 1/2 cup water and salt to taste. Cover and cook until barely tender, about 3 to 5 minutes. Drain water and set aside to cool.

Beat the eggs in a medium bowl. Mix in the milk, parsley, flour, baking powder, salt, chilies, ricotta cheese, and Cheddar cheese, in that order. Add the cooked squash.

Butter an 8 x 11-inch shallow baking dish. Pour in the squash mixture and top with the bread cubes. Dot the top with butter and sprinkle with sesame seeds. Bake uncovered for 30 minutes.

Vegetarian Chili

Servings: 8

> 3 tablespoons vegetable oil
> 2 medium-large yellow onions
>   (about 1 pound), chopped
> 1/4 cup flour
> 2–4 cloves garlic, finely chopped
> 1/2 of a 6-ounce can tomato paste
> 3 cups crushed tomatoes, or 3 cups roughly
>   chopped whole tomatoes
> 5 cups water or vegetable broth
> 1 teaspoon powdered red chilies
>   (or to taste)
> 2 teaspoons whole or ground cumin
> 1 teaspoon oregano
> 1/2 teaspoon black pepper
> 2 teaspoons salt
> 3 tablespoons cider vinegar
> 1/2 cup wild rice, cooked and drained
> 1/2 cup vegetable protein
> 1 or 2 chopped chipotle chilies (optional)*
> 1 bell pepper, chopped
> 4 cups red kidney beans, home cooked
>   or canned

Heat the oil in a large skillet and add the chopped onions. Cover the pan to "sweat" them over low heat for about 5 minutes. Remove the lid, raise the heat to medium, and stir the onions until they are uniformly light brown, but not at all charred. Sprinkle the flour over the onions and stir. Add all the remaining ingredients except the bell pepper and beans, and place

(continued)

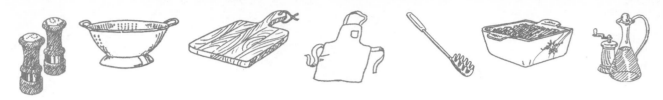

over medium heat. Bring to a simmer and cook gently, covered, for 1 hour, stirring occasionally.

At the end of the simmering time, add the chopped bell pepper and the beans. Include some of the bean liquid if the stew needs further thinning. Simmer 10 minutes longer.

Serve immediately or chill and serve, heated, the next day. Chile aficionados prefer a second day stew. Bring to room temperature before reheating and serve with sourdough bread, cornbread, or flour tortillas. Toppings such as grated cheddar cheese, black olives, sour cream, squirts of lime juice or chopped cilantro can also be added for additional excitement.

*These are dried jalapeños with a distinct smoky flavor that can be purchased ready-made.

Vegetarian chile can be a hearty dish when wild rice and/or vegetable protein is added to enhance both flavor, texture, and balanced protein content.

Four-Cheese Quiche with Red Pepper

Servings: 6 to 8

4 ounces blue cheese, crumbled
3 ounces Swiss cheese, grated
4 ounces Brie, broken into small pieces
1½ cups half-and-half
3 eggs
⅛ teaspoon nutmeg
salt and freshly ground pepper to taste
¼ cup grated Parmesan cheese
1 large or 2 small red bell peppers
2 tablespoons butter, melted
9- or 10-inch pie crust, prebaked 5 minutes
    at 375°F

Preheat oven to 400°F. Mix together the blue cheese, Swiss cheese, and Brie. Set aside. In a blender or food processor, blend the half-and-half, eggs, nutmeg, salt, pepper, and Parmesan cheese on medium-high for 1 minute. Slice the peppers in rounds, removing seeds and membrane. Sauté the peppers in the butter until soft.

Sprinkle the cheese on the pie crust. Top with sautéed pepper rings. Pour the egg mixture over peppers. Bake 10 minutes. Reduce heat to 350°F and continue cooking 20 to 25 minutes until a knife stuck into the quiche comes out clean.

Roasted Vegetable Calzone

Servings: 4

2 teaspoons olive oil
1 sweet red pepper, thinly sliced
1 zucchini, thinly sliced
1 yellow summer squash, thinly sliced
1 small onion, thinly sliced

2 cloves garlic, minced
salt and freshly ground pepper
cornmeal
1 loaf frozen French bread dough, thawed
2 tablespoons crumbled Gorgonzola cheese
2 tablespoons shredded mozzarella cheese
1 cup tomato sauce

Preheat the oven to 500°F.

In a large ovenproof frying pan over medium heat, heat the oil, sauté the red pepper, zucchini, squash, onion, and garlic in the oil for 2 minutes, or until tender. Put the pan in the oven and bake for 10 minutes, stirring vegetables occasionally. Remove from the oven and add salt and pepper to taste. Allow to cool while shaping the dough. Turn the oven down to 350°F.

Dust a baking sheet with cornmeal and set aside. Divide the dough into 4 pieces; form each into a 7-inch round. Place the rounds on the cornmeal-dusted baking sheet. Spoon the vegetable mixture evenly over half of each round. Sprinkle the cheeses evenly over the vegetable mixture. Brush the outside edges of the rounds with water and fold the dough over the vegetables. Seal the edges and bake each for 15 to 20 minutes, or until golden brown. Serve with tomato sauce drizzled over each calzone.

Spinach and Feta Pie

Servings: 8

10-inch deep-dish pie crust, prebaked 5
*   minutes at 375°F*
1 bunch fresh spinach (about 4 cups)
3 tablespoons olive oil
1 yellow onion, chopped
1 cup grated Swiss cheese
2 eggs
1¼ cups light cream
½ teaspoon salt
¼ teaspoon freshly ground pepper
⅛ teaspoon nutmeg
¼ cup grated Parmesan cheese
6 ounces Feta cheese, grated or crumbled
2 medium tomatoes, sliced

Preheat oven to 350°F. Wash and stem the spinach; steam the spinach until wilted. Squeeze out excess water, and chop. Heat the olive oil and sauté the onion in the oil until golden. Toss with the spinach. Mix the Swiss cheese with the onion and spinach.

Mix the eggs, cream, salt, pepper, nutmeg, and Parmesan cheese in a blender on medium-high for 1 minute. Spread the spinach-cheese mixture on the crust. Top with Feta cheese and decorate with tomatoes. Pour on the egg mixture over the tomatoes, making sure it soaks through to the crust. Use your fingers or a spoon to spread. Bake 40 to 50 minutes or until a

(continued)

knife inserted in the pie comes out clean. Serve hot or at room temperature.

Cabbage Rolls

Servings: 6

1 head green cabbage, trimmed and cored
3 tablespoons butter, divided
1 tablespoon olive oil
1 leek, thinly sliced
2 cloves garlic, minced
1 cup finely diced carrots
1 cup finely diced rutabaga
2½ cups cooked short-grained rice
¼ cup chopped fresh parsley
¼ cup chopped fresh dill
½ teaspoon dried thyme
½ teaspoon salt
¼ teaspoon freshly ground pepper
8-ounce can tomato sauce
1 tablespoon brown sugar
1 tablespoon cider vinegar

Trim and core the cabbage. In a large pot, cover the cabbage with boiling water and let stand for 8 to 10 minutes or until outer leaves can easily be removed. Carefully remove 12 leaves, dip each leaf into boiling water for 3 minutes until softened.

In a large skillet, melt 2 tablespoons of the butter with the olive oil over medium heat. Cook the leek and the garlic in the oil, stirring occasionally, for 3 minutes or until softened. Add the carrots and rutabaga. Cover and cook over medium-low heat for 3 minutes. Remove from heat and stir in the rice, parsley, dill, thyme, salt, and pepper.

Preheat the oven to 350°F. Spoon the rice mixture onto the cabbage leaves, using about ½ cup for large leaves and ⅓ cup for small ones. Roll up the leaves, tucking in the sides. Arrange the rolls in a greased 13 x 9-inch baking dish. Brush the rolls with the remaining butter. Combine the tomato sauce, brown sugar, and vinegar, and spoon over the rolls. Cover and bake for 1½ hours.

Potato Mushroom Strudel

Servings: 4

1 tablespoon butter
1 medium yellow onion, sliced
1 clove garlic, minced
1 cup sliced mushrooms
4–6 medium red potatoes, scrubbed and chopped coarsely
1 cup chopped fresh marjoram, divided
2 tablespoons water
¼ cup grated Parmesan cheese
2–3 green onions, chopped
salt and freshly ground pepper to taste
4 sheets fresh phyllo pastry
¼ cup butter, melted

In a large skillet, melt 1 tablespoon butter over medium heat; cook onion, garlic, and mushrooms in the butter, stirring often, for 5 minutes or until liquid has evaporated. Stir in potatoes and 2 teaspoons of the marjoram. Add water and cover and cook for 8 to 10 minutes or until potatoes are tender. Remove from heat. Stir in the Parmesan cheese, green onion, salt, and pepper to taste. Let cool.

Preheat the oven to 400°F. Place one sheet of phyllo dough on a work surface, keeping the remaining dough covered with a damp towel. Brush the sheet of dough lightly with butter. Layer the remaining phyllo on top of the first sheet, brushing each sheet with butter. Spoon the potato mixture over the phyllo, leaving a 2-inch border along one long side and a 1-inch border at each short end. Starting at the other long side, carefully roll up jellyroll-style, folding in the edges while rolling. Place, seam side down, on a greased baking sheet. Brush with butter. Bake for 18 to 20 minutes or until golden.

Let stand for 5 minutes. Sprinkle with remaining marjoram. Slice diagonally with a serrated knife.

Vegetable Casserole with Mozzarella Cheese

Servings: 6

2 cups sliced carrots
1 onion, sliced
1 package chopped frozen spinach
*   thawed slightly*
1½ cups water, divided
1 tablespoon butter
3 tablespoons all-purpose flour
1½ cups skim milk
1 cup shredded mozzarella cheese
¼ teaspoon salt
pepper to taste

Place carrots, onion, and spinach on a rack in a pressure cooker. Add ½ cup of the water. Secure the lid in place. Place over high heat. As soon as the pressure regulator begins to rock (about 5 minutes), reduce the pressure with the quick release method.

Remove vegetables from pressure cooker and set aside in a bowl.

In a small saucepan, melt the butter over low heat. Add the flour and cook and stir until well blended, 1 to 2 minutes. Gradually add the milk, stirring constantly. Continue to cook, stirring, until the sauce thickens, about 4 minutes. Remove from the heat and stir in the cheese, salt, and pepper. Stir until the cheese is melted.

Place half of the spinach in a 6-cup metal bowl that will fit loosely in the pressure

(continued)

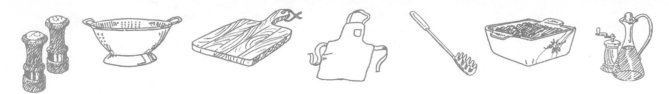

cooker. Top with half of the carrots and the onions. Cover with half of the cheese sauce. Repeat the layers, ending with the sauce. Cover the bowl tightly with foil. Pour in remaining 1 cup water into the cooker, place the cooking rack in place, and place the bowl on the rack. Secure the lid. Bring to high pressure over high heat. Adjust the heat to maintain high pressure and cook for 7 minutes. Allow the pressure to reduce naturally, which takes about 10 minutes. Remove the lid, tilting it away from you to allow excess steam to escape. Serve directly from the bowl.

German Potato Pancakes

Servings: 6

> 1 egg
> ¹/₂ cup half-and-half
> 5 medium-sized white potatoes, peeled
>   and cubed
> 1 medium white onion, chopped
> salt and freshly ground pepper to taste
> ¹/₂ tablespoon canola oil

Place the egg and half-and-half in the blender and blend on medium-high for 1 minute. Add the cubed potatoes, ¹/₂ cup at a time, and purée. Add the onion and blend the entire mixture one more minute on medium-high. Pour into a medium-sized bowl and season to taste with salt and pepper.

Heat a griddle or large cast-iron frying pan over medium heat, add the oil. (Griddle should be thinly coated with oil to avoid a greasy pancake.) Spoon batter onto the griddle in thin (¹/₄-inch) cakes. Fry 2 to 3 minutes before turning (edges should be crispy). Brown the second side. Top with butter and/or sour cream and serve with applesauce and a field green salad.

Baked Macaroni and Cheese

Servings: 8

> 1 pound uncooked macaroni elbow
>   or shells
> 2 cups milk
> 4 tablespoons butter (¹/₂ stick)
> salt and freshly ground pepper to taste
> 1¹/₂ pounds Velveeta cheese, diced
> ¹/₂ pound Colby cheese, diced
> 1 whole egg, slightly beaten
> ¹/₂ pound sharp Cheddar cheese, grated

Cook macaroni according to package directions. Rinse, drain, and set aside.

Preheat the oven to 350°F. Bring milk to a boil and add butter, salt, and pepper. Add Velveeta and Colby cheeses to the milk. Stir until creamy and the sauce thickens. Add the egg to the cooled macaroni, then add the cheese sauce; combine well.

Lightly grease a 9 x 13-inch pan or spray with cooking spray. Layer the macaroni with Cheddar cheese. Bake for 30 to 45 minutes, or until cheese is bubbly and melted to a golden brown.

Classic Swiss Fondue

Servings: 6

1 clove garlic, halved
2½ tablespoons flour
1 cup fat-free vegetable broth
⅔ cup evaporated skim milk
½ teaspoon brandy extract
2 ounces reduced-fat Swiss cheese, shredded
2 tablespoons grated reduced-fat Parmesan cheese
3 ounces reduced-fat cream cheese, cubed
⅛ teaspoon freshly ground pepper
⅛ teaspoon ground nutmeg
1 loaf crusty French bread, cubed

Rub the inside of a fondue pot or saucepan with cut sides of the garlic. Discard the garlic. Whisk flour and ¼ cup of the broth in a measuring cup until blended. Add the remaining broth and milk to the pot, and heat over low heat until very hot but not boiling. Whisk in the extract and the flour mixture. Cook, stirring constantly, 2 to 6 minutes. Stir in Swiss, Parmesan, and cream cheeses, pepper, and nutmeg. Cook, stirring constantly, until the cheeses melt and the mixture is very smooth.

If you don't have a fondue pot, transfer to a Crock-Pot or casserole with a warming unit. Serve with bread cubes.

Vegetable Potpie

Servings: 6

¾ cup all-purpose flour
pinch of salt
3 tablespoons canola oil
⅓ cup dry sherry or apple juice
1 onion, sliced thinly
2 cups cubed red potatoes
½ cup chopped carrots
2 leeks, cleaned and sliced into rounds
2 tomatoes, chopped coarsely
1 cup chopped greens (spinach, collard, kale, or turnip)
3 teaspoons chopped fresh parsley
1 teaspoon arrowroot powder
1 cup cold vegetable stock
1 tablespoon tamari sauce
2 tablespoons grated Parmesan cheese
1 egg, slightly beaten

In a large bowl or food processor, mix together the flour and salt; add the oil. Mix until a pliable dough is formed, adding a small amount of water if needed. Lightly flour a dry surface and roll dough into a 9-inch round. Wrap carefully in plastic wrap and refrigerate.

(continued)

Lightly oil a 9-inch round baking dish. In a 10-inch nonstick skillet over medium-high heat, heat the sherry or juice; add the onion. Cook, stirring occasionally, until very soft, but not browned. Add the potatoes and carrots, and reduce the heat to medium. Cook 5 minutes. Add the leeks, tomatoes, greens, and parsley. Cover and cook 5 minutes.

Preheat the oven to 350°F. In a small bowl, dissolve the arrowroot in the cold vegetable stock; add to the skillet. Cook for 8 to 10 minutes, or until thick. Pour into the prepared casserole dish; add the tamari sauce and Parmesan cheese. Lay the pastry dough over the vegetable mixture; seal the top around the lip of the dish. Cut two small steam holes. Brush with the beaten egg. Bake 30 minutes, or until pastry is lightly browned.

Quiche Lorraine

Servings: 6

1 teaspoon olive oil
1½ cups thinly sliced yellow onion
½ cup + 1 tablespoon imitation bacon bits
4 eggs, beaten
1 cup light cream
1 cup milk
1 tablespoon all-purpose flour
½ teaspoon salt
dash nutmeg

1½ cups shredded Swiss cheese
9-inch pastry shell, prebaked 5 minutes at 375°F

Preheat the oven to 450°F.

Sauté the onion in the olive oil until translucent. Add the imitation bacon bits, and cook an additional minute. Stir together the eggs, cream, milk, flour, salt, and nutmeg. Stir in the onion, bacon bits, and Swiss cheese. Mix well and set aside.

Bake pastry shell for 5–7 minutes. Remove from the oven and reduce the oven temperature to 325°F. Pour the cheese mixture into the hot pastry shell. Cover the edge of the crust with aluminum foil. Bake for 45 to 50 minutes or until a knife inserted in the center comes out clean. Let stand 10 minutes before serving.

Cheese Soufflé

Servings: 6

6 tablespoons butter
⅓ cup all-purpose flour
½ teaspoon salt
dash cayenne pepper
1½ cups 2% milk
2 cups shredded cheddar cheese
1 cup grated fontina cheese
6 egg yolks
6 egg whites

Measure enough foil to go around a 2-quart soufflé dish plus a 2- to 3-inch overlap. Fold foil into thirds lengthwise. Lightly butter one side. With the buttered side in, position the foil around the dish, letting the collar extend 2 inches above the top of the dish; fasten with tape. Set aside.

Melt the butter in a saucepan; stir in the flour, salt, and cayenne. Add milk all at once. Cook and stir till thickened and bubbly. Cook and stir 1 to 2 minutes more. Remove from heat. Add the cheeses, stirring until cheese is melted. Beat egg yolks until thick. Slowly add cheese mixture to the egg yolks, stirring constantly. Cool slightly.

Preheat the oven to 300°F. Using clean beaters, beat egg whites until stiff peaks form. Gradually pour the cheese-yolk mixture over the beaten whites, folding to combine. Pour into the ungreased soufflé dish. Bake about 1½ hours or until a knife inserted in the soufflé comes out clean. Gently peel off the collar. Serve immediately.

Soufflés should be served immediately after they are taken out of the oven, as they will fall within minutes. To cut the soufflé into servings, insert two forks, back to back, into the soufflé, and gently pull the soufflé apart. Use a large spoon to transfer the soufflé to individual plates.

Zucchini Egg Skillet

Servings: 4

¼ cup butter or olive oil, divided
potatoes, peeled and diced
½ cup zucchini, coarsely grated
¼ cup fresh chives or green onions
4 eggs
salt and pepper to taste

In a 10-inch heavy skillet, melt half the butter over medium heat. Cook potatoes, stirring often, for about 5 minutes, or until tender. Add zucchini and chives and cook, stirring, for 1 minute. In large bowl, beat eggs slightly. Stir in vegetables and season with salt and pepper. Clean the skillet and melt remaining butter/oil. Pour in egg mixture. Reduce heat to medium-low and cook, shaking pan occasionally, for about 5 minutes or until bottom is slightly browned. Cover and cook for 5 to 6 minutes longer or until top is firm. Serve in wedges.

Asparagus Frittata

Servings: 4

2 small red potatoes, diced
10–12 asparagus spears cut into
*   2-inch pieces*
3 teaspoons olive oil
1 small yellow onion, thinly sliced
1 clove garlic, chopped

(continued)

1 teaspoon fresh rosemary, chopped
1 tomato, cored, seeded, and chopped
½ teaspoon salt
½ teaspoon freshly ground pepper
4 large eggs
4 large egg whites
¼ cup Romano cheese
fresh chives

Place potatoes in a steamer basket over boiling water and cook for 4 minutes. Add asparagus and cook until the vegetables are tender, 2–3 minutes more. Transfer to bowl to cool. Preheat the broiler. Heat 2 teaspoons olive oil in a large, ovenproof, nonstick skillet over medium heat. Add onion, garlic, rosemary and half the chopped tomato. Cook, stirring, until the onions are limp, about 8 minutes. Add the mixture to the reserved potatoes and asparagus. Season with salt and pepper and set aside.

Brush skillet with remaining olive oil. Return to low-heat. In a medium-sized bowl, lightly whisk together whole eggs, egg whites and Romano cheese. Add the vegetables to the egg mixture and pour into skillet, gently stirring to distribute the vegetables. Cook over low heat until the underside is light golden, 5–8 minutes. Place the skillet under the oven broiler and broil the frittata until the top is golden brown, 1–2 minutes. Slide on to a platter, garnish with chives and remaining chopped tomato.

Chickpeas and Red Onions

Servings: 4

½ cup slivered red onion
19-ounce can chickpeas, drained and rinsed
½ cup fresh parsley, chopped
2 tablespoons lemon juice
1 tablespoon olive oil
1 tablespoon capers, drained, rinsed, and coarsely chopped
½ cup Feta cheese, crumbled
salt and pepper
red lettuce leaves

In a medium-sized bowl, cover onions with cold water and let soak for 10 minutes. Drain well and place in a bowl. Add chickpeas, parsley, lemon juice, oil, capers and Feta cheese. Stir to combine. Season with salt and pepper. Serve on lettuce leaves.

Eggplant-Couscous Rolls

Servings: 4

1 pound eggplants
4 teaspoons olive oil, divided
1 cup couscous, preferably whole wheat
½ teaspoon dried thyme
½ teaspoon salt
¾ cup + 2 tablespoons crumbled feta cheese
3 tablespoons fresh mint, chopped
freshly ground pepper to taste
1 cup tomato sauce

Preheat oven to 425°F. Lightly oil two baking sheets or coat them with nonstick cooking spray. Trim both ends of the eggplant. Stand one eggplant on end and remove a thin slice of skin from two opposite sides and discard. Repeat with second eggplant. Cut each eggplant lengthwise into 6 or more ³/₈-inch slices. Using 2 teaspoons of the oil, brush both sides of the slices and arrange in a single layer on the baking sheets. Bake for 10–15 minutes or until lightly brown and tender. In a medium-sized saucepan, bring 1¹/₂ cups water to a boil. Stir in couscous, thyme, salt and remaining 2 teaspoons olive oil. Remove from the heat, cover and let stand for 5 minutes, or until the water is absorbed. Uncover and let cool for 15 minutes. With a fork, stir in ³/₄ cup of the feta, 2 tablespoons of the mint and pepper. Lightly oil a 9 x 13-inch baking dish or coat it with nonstick cooking spray. Place some of the couscous mixture in the center of each eggplant slice. Roll up the eggplant firmly around the filling and place, seam-side down, in the prepared dish. Cover with foil and bake for 15 minutes. Uncover, spoon tomato sauce on top and bake for 5 minutes more. Sprinkle with the remaining 2 tablespoons feta cheese and 1 tablespoon mint.

Italian Vegetable Bake

Servings: 8

28-ounce can tomatoes, coarsely chopped,
   juices reserved
1 yellow onion, sliced
¹/₂ pound green beans, cut into pieces
¹/₂ pound okra, cut into ¹/₂-inch lengths
³/₄ cup finely chopped green bell peppers
2 tablespoons lemon juice
1 tablespoon fresh basil, chopped
1 tablespoon oregano
medium zucchini, cut into 1-inch cubes
1 eggplant, peeled and cut into
   1-inch chunks
2 tablespoons Parmesan cheese, grated

Preheat oven to 325°F. In a baking dish, combine the tomatoes and their liquid, onion, green beans, okra, bell peppers, lemon juice, basil, and oregano. Cover with foil or a lid. Bake for 15 minutes. Mix in the zucchini and eggplant, cover, and continue to bake, stirring occasionally, until the vegetables are tender, about 1 hour. Sprinkle the top with Parmesan cheese just before serving.

Chapter 13

Soups, Stews, and Chilies

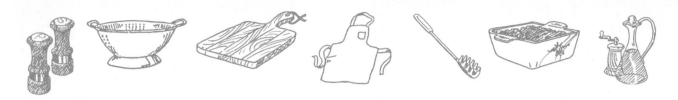

What could be better on a blustery winter day than a bowl of hot soup? To make a fabulous homemade soup that will warm you right up, start with a meat, chicken, or vegetable stock. Prefer something heavier? Pick your favorite vegetable and make a rich cream soup or chowder, or cook up a hearty beef stew. These dishes freeze well, so make them in large quantities and freeze half for a rainy day.

Chicken Stock

Yield: 24 cups

> *6 pounds chicken, whole or in parts*
> *8 quarts water*
> *2 teaspoons salt*
> *1¹/₂ pounds onions, coarsely chopped*
> *³/₄ pound carrots, coarsely chopped*
> *³/₄ pound celery, coarsely chopped*
> *2 whole cloves*
> *3 cloves garlic, mashed*
> *3 bay leaves, crumbled*
> *¹/₂ teaspoon black peppercorns*
> *¹/₂ teaspoon thyme*
> *5-6 stalks parsley, tied in a bundle*

Wash the chicken under cold running water. Place in a stockpot and cover with water, about 8 quarts. Bring the stock to a gentle boil; reduce the heat to a simmer and cook uncovered for 1 hour. Skim frequently as the sediment comes to the top. For a concentrated stock, do not replenish the water as it evaporates.

Add the salt, onions, carrots, and celery and return to a simmer. Continue cooking for a total of 3 hours.

Bundle the cloves, garlic, bay leaves, peppercorns, thyme and parsley *in a small piece of cheesecloth*. Add the bundle to the pot ¹/₂ hour before the end of the cooking time.

When stock has finished cooking, remove from heat and set aside to cool. Chicken stock is very susceptible to spoiling, so the temperature should be reduced quickly. Set the pot in a sink with 3 to 4 inches of water for faster cooling. Strain the stock by pouring through a sieve. Straining through cheesecloth a second time will remove all the sediment. Stock can be refrigerated for 2 to 3 days, but must be brought to a boil if kept longer.

All soups begin with stock, which is the liquid from boiled meat, poultry, seafood, or vegetables, plus seasonings. Stocks are the foundation not only for soups and stews, but also for sauces and gravies. Stocks can be homemade or store-bought, with

the results differing based on recipes and combinations of flavors. On supermarket shelves, stocks are called consommés, bouillons, and broths, and they come bottled, canned, cubed, and granulated. They differ in strength and salt content, although many are robust and full-bodied.

Vegetable Stock

Yield: 4 to 5 quarts

> 2 tablespoons vegetable oil or butter
> 1 tablespoon salt
> 3 ounces white cider vinegar
> 2 cups chopped onions
> 1 cup coarsely chopped (but not peeled) carrots
> 1 cup chopped celery, including leaves
> 6 sprigs parsley
> 6 sprigs fresh dill, if available
> 2 bay leaves, crumbled
> 1 teaspoon black peppercorns
> 5 quarts water

Place the oil or butter in a large (8 to 10 quart) stockpot over medium heat. Add all the ingredients except the water; cover tightly and cook for 10 minutes over medium-low heat or until vegetables are limp.

Cover with 5 quarts of water, place over medium heat, and bring to a boil. Remove the sediment as it rises to the top. Heat may be reduced slightly, but stock should be kept boiling rather than simmering until

flavors are pronounced—about 45 minutes to 1 hour.

Strain the stock through a triple thickness of moistened cheesecloth held in a sieve. Chill, unless it is to be used immediately. Refrigerate or freeze until needed.

Cauliflower with Coriander Soup

Servings: 4 to 6

> 3 tablespoons vegetable oil
> 2 onions, chopped
> 1-inch piece fresh gingerroot, peeled, sliced thin, and cut into thin strips
> 4 cloves garlic, chopped
> 1 teaspoon ground cumin
> 2 teaspoons ground coriander
> $^{1}/_{4}$ teaspoon turmeric
> $^{1}/_{8}$ teaspoon cayenne pepper, or to taste
> 2 potatoes (about $^{1}/_{2}$ pound)
> 2 heaping cups cauliflower florets (about $^{1}/_{2}$ pound)
> 8 cups chicken broth
> 1 teaspoon salt
> 1 cup heavy cream

In a large heavy saucepan heat oil over moderately high heat until hot but not smoking. Add onions, gingerroot, and garlic, and stir-fry until onions are golden brown. Add cumin, coriander, turmeric, and cayenne pepper; cook, stirring, for 1 minute.

(continued)

Peel potatoes and dice into 1/2-inch pieces. Stir the potatoes, cauliflower, broth, and salt into the onion mixture and simmer until potatoes are tender, about 10 minutes.

In a blender, purée the soup in batches. Stir in the cream and reheat the soup over moderate heat until ready to serve.

Navy Bean Soup

Servings: 6 servings

*1 pound dried white beans or black-eyed
    peas, soaked overnight in water*
Ham bone with some meat on it
2 large yellow onions, chopped
1 clove garlic
*12-ounce can tomatoes, or home-canned
    tomatoes*
1 carrot, grated
1 tablespoon chopped parsley
1/2 cup chopped celery
1/3 teaspoon thyme
1 bay leaf
salt and pepper to taste

Simmer the beans and ham bone in 4 to 5 cups of water for 3 hours.

Add all the remaining ingredients. Add enough water to make the desired consistency. Simmer 1 hour with vegetables.

Before serving, remove meat from bone, return the meat to the soup, and discard the bay leaf.

Russian Borscht

Servings: 6 to 8

*1 pound beets, fresh or canned, cut into
    julienne strips, about 5 cups*
2 tablespoons butter
*3 stalks celery, trimmed and cut lengthwise
    into julienne strips 1 1/2 inches long*
1/2 cup shredded carrots
1 turnip, diced
1 large onion, peeled and finely chopped
1 clove garlic, minced
5 cups beef, chicken, or vegetable stock
1/3 cup tomato paste
1 tablespoon white vinegar
salt to taste
1/4 teaspoon freshly ground black pepper
1/2 cup sour cream
1/2 cup heavy cream

If using fresh beets, wash them well. Break off the leaves and separate them from the ribs. Cut the leaves into fine shreds and chop the stalks and ribs finely. Reserve the leaves, stalks, and ribs for later. Peel the beets and cut into julienne strips.

Heat the butter in a medium (4-quart) saucepan to bubbling. Add the celery, carrots, turnip, onion, fresh beets, and garlic. (If using canned beets, reserve them till later.) Cover and cook over medium heat for 15 minutes, stirring frequently.

Pour in the stock and add the tomato paste, vinegar, and reserved beet leaves and stalks, if used. Bring to a boil; reduce heat

and simmer until the vegetables, especially the beets, are fork tender—about 30 minutes over medium-low heat. If using canned beets, add them only during the last 10 minutes of cooking. Stir occasionally. Add salt, if needed, and black pepper.

In a small bowl, combine the sour and heavy creams. Spoon the hot soup into heated bowls. Swirl a teaspoon or more of the cream blend in each serving. Pass additional cream to guests. Serve with coarse whole grain bread and plenty of butter.

Classic borscht is always thick with vegetables, but can be less robust if strained when finished cooking and served as a clear liquid. There are many varieties of borscht. Some are made with meat (beef or pork) and some with no vegetables other than beets. The name—which comes from an old Russian word for a wild parsnip plant—can be spelled borscht, borsch, borshch, or bortsch.

French Onion Soup

Servings: 6

1 pound white onions, thinly sliced
2 cups dry white wine
2 tablespoons unsalted butter
48-ounce can chicken broth, or homemade chicken stock
6 thick slices crusty baguette, toasted
2 cups shredded Gruyère cheese

Heat oven to 425°F. Combine onions, wine, and butter in a 13 x 9-inch baking pan. Bake until onion is very soft and most of the liquid is absorbed, about 45 minutes.

Preheat the broiler. Heat broth to a simmer in a saucepan. Divide the warm onions among 6 ovenproof soup bowls or crocks. Ladle the broth over the onions. Top each with 1 slice of baguette. Top with cheese. Place under the broiler 6 inches away from the heat source. Broil until the cheese melts, 2 to 3 minutes.

Lentil Soup

Servings: 8 to 10

1 whole clove
1 clove garlic, minced
2 bay leaves, crumbled
¹/₂ teaspoon black peppercorns
¹/₂ teaspoon thyme
¹/₂ teaspoon marjoram
¹/₃ teaspoon savory
6 sprigs parsley, tied
¹/₂ pound lean bacon
1 cup each finely chopped rutabaga, carrots, celery, onions, and leeks
¹/₂ teaspoon freshly ground black pepper
2 cups lentils, washed and picked over
2 tablespoons cider vinegar
6 cups chicken stock
6 cups beef stock
salt to taste
¹/₄ cup finely chopped chives

(continued)

Wrap all the seasonings (the first 8 ingredients) in a piece of cheesecloth. Tie the bundle with a string, leaving extra string at the end. Set aside.

Dice the bacon and place into a large (5 to 6 quart) soup pot. Sauté the bacon over medium heat about 8 minutes. Beginning with the rutabaga, add each vegetable to the pot, cover, and cook over medium heat, with about 4 minutes between additions. (By the end, the rutabaga will have cooked 20 minutes.) Cook for an additional 5 minutes after the leeks have been added. Add the lentils and vinegar, and cook for 8 minutes. Pour in the stocks. Add the spice bag, and tie the string to the pot handle for easy retrieval later. Season with salt and pepper. Bring to a boil and simmer for 30 minutes over medium heat.

Remove the spice bag and serve the soup with a chive garnish. (If a thicker soup is desired, purée 3 to 4 cups of the soup and return to the pot before serving.)

Miso Soup

Servings: 4 to 5

¼ cup red miso
3½ cups chicken stock
8 ounces tofu (bean curd), cubed
4 sprigs parsley, finely chopped
2 large shiitake mushrooms, sliced

Whisk the miso into 2 tablespoons of slightly warmed stock and blend well. Gradually ladle the miso liquid into the remaining stock. Bring the soup to a simmer. Add tofu cubes, parsley, and mushrooms. Maintain at a simmer until the mushrooms and tofu are heated. Do not boil or soup will become bitter and cloudy. Ladle the soup into individual bowls and serve immediately.

Miso is a fermented soybean paste, which can be found in most well-stocked supermarkets. Red miso is pungent and quite salty, while white miso is mellow and slightly sweet. Miso paste can be left at room temperature for a year or more, since its flavor improves with age. It should not be frozen.

Tomato Bread Soup

Servings: 2

1 tablespoon olive oil
1 leek, chopped (white part only)
4 cloves garlic, minced
2 cups peeled and chopped tomatoes
⅓ cup chopped fresh basil
1½ cups vegetable stock or chicken stock, divided
½ teaspoon salt
½ teaspoon pepper
2 cups cubed day-old Italian bread
2 tablespoons grated Parmesan cheese

In a heavy saucepan, heat oil over medium heat. Cook leeks and garlic, stirring occasionally, for 3 minutes or until softened. Stir in tomatoes and basil. Bring to boil. Boil gently for 5 to 10 minutes or until slightly thickened.

Add 1 cup of the stock and the salt and pepper. Bring to a boil, stirring. Remove from the heat. Stir in the bread. If necessary, warm the remaining stock and add enough to reach the desired consistency. Serve with sprinkled Parmesan cheese.

To peel tomatoes, plunge into boiling water for 30 to 60 seconds or until skins loosen. Chill in cold water, then drain and peel.

Leek and Potato Soup

Servings: 8

4 large leeks
2 tablespoons butter
2 potatoes, peeled and cubed
1 onion, chopped
4 cups chicken stock
1 cup milk
salt and pepper
2 tablespoons light cream
1/4 cup chopped fresh chives

Trim the outer leaves and dark green tops from the leeks. Cut lengthwise in half almost all the way through, leaving the root end intact. Spread the leaves and rinse in cold water. Shake off the water and chop to make about 4 cups. In a large, heavy saucepan, melt the butter over low heat. Add the leeks, potatoes, and onion. Cover and cook, stirring occasionally, for 15 minutes or until softened.

Add the stock and simmer gently, covered, for about 20 minutes or until the vegetables are tender.

In a blender or food processor, purée the soup, in batches if necessary, until smooth. Return to the saucepan. Add the milk and heat through. Season with salt and pepper to taste. Serve hot or chilled, garnished with a swirl of cream and a sprinkle of chives.

In a pinch, vegetable stock can simply be the water saved from boiling vegetables such as carrots and potatoes. Frozen vegetable stock is available in some specialty stores, and vegetable bouillon stock cubes and powders are also available.

Broccoli Soup

Servings: 5

1 medium-sized broccoli bunch
1 onion, chopped
2 cups peeled and diced potatoes
1 clove garlic, minced
1 1/2 cups vegetable stock or water
1/2 teaspoon dried thyme

(continued)

¹/₄ teaspoon pepper
pinch of nutmeg
1¹/₂ cups milk
salt

Separate the broccoli into florets. Set 2 cups aside for garnish. Peel the stems and chop coarsely. In a saucepan, combine the stems and remaining florets, onion, potatoes, garlic, stock, thyme, pepper, and nutmeg. Bring to a boil. Reduce the heat, cover, and simmer for 10 minutes or until potatoes are tender. Steam the reserved florets for 5 minutes or until tender.

In a blender or food processor, purée the soup, in batches if necessary, until smooth. Return to the saucepan. Add the milk. Heat through without boiling. Season with salt to taste. Divide florets among soup bowls. Pour soup over the florets.

Curried Zucchini Soup

Servings: 8

1 tablespoon olive oil
5 cups chopped zucchini (about 6 small)
2 onions, chopped
1 stalk celery, diced
1 clove garlic, minced
2 teaspoons curry powder
³/₄ teaspoon salt
¹/₂ teaspoon cinnamon
¹/₄ teaspoon pepper
1 teaspoon packed brown sugar
6 cups vegetable stock

In a large saucepan, heat the oil over medium heat; cook the zucchini, onions, celery, garlic, curry powder, salt, cinnamon, and pepper in the oil, stirring occasionally, for 10 minutes or until softened. Sprinkle with brown sugar. Pour in the stock and bring to boil. Reduce the heat to medium. Simmer, covered, for 20 minutes or until vegetables are very tender.

In blender or food processor, purée the zucchini mixture, in batches, until smooth. Pour into a clean saucepan. Reheat, but do not boil. Season with more salt and pepper to taste.

Portuguese Kale Soup

Servings: 6 to 8

1 pound kale
1 pound small red potatoes, scrubbed and diced, not peeled
1 pound chorizo sausage
1 cup chopped onions
¹/₂ cup chopped carrots
2 teaspoon chopped garlic
2 tablespoons olive oil
2 tablespoons butter
2 quarts chicken broth
3 pounds tomatoes, peeled, seeded, and chopped
salt and pepper to taste

Strip the leaves from the washed kale, and cut diagonally into wide slices (6 to 8 cups lightly packed kale). Set aside. Wash and chop the potatoes, and keep in cold water. Prick the sausage and blanch in boiling water for 5 to 10 minutes to release the fat. Drain and cut into ¹/₂-inch slices. Set aside.

In a large saucepan, sauté the onions, carrots, and garlic in the oil and butter, cooking until softened, about 5 minutes. Add the potatoes and broth, and simmer, partially covered, for 15 to 20 minutes or until the potatoes are cooked.

Mash the potatoes against the side of the pot. (Or purée with some of the broth and return to the pot.) Stir in tomatoes and simmer for 10 to 15 minutes. Add the kale and sausage, cook 5 to 10 minutes longer, and season to taste with salt and pepper.

Corn Chowder

Servings: 4 to 6

4 ounces bacon, chopped
1 medium onion
2 cups new red potatoes, scrubbed and
    diced, unpeeled
2 cups chicken stock
1 cup water
1 teaspoon salt
pepper to taste
2 cups scraped corn*

1 cup corn kernels
¹/₂ cup heavy cream
pepper to taste

Sauté the chopped bacon in large, heavy saucepan over medium heat until moderately crisp. Remove the bacon from the pan and drain all but 3 tablespoons of fat. Chop the onion and cook in the fat until softened and golden. Add the potatoes, bacon, onion, stock, water, salt, and scraped corn. Bring to a boil; reduce the heat, and cook, partially covered, until potatoes are tender.

Stir in the corn kernels and cook 5 minutes longer. Add the heavy cream. Cook until heated through. Add pepper to taste. For a smoother texture, purée the corn.

*Scraped corn is obtained by running a knife down the center of a row of kernels, slicing right down to the end of the ear. Continue until all the rows have been prepared. Place the corn over a bowl. Then, using the back of the knife, push or scrape down on the kernels. The flesh and milk will spurt out.

Mushroom Parmesan Soup

Servings: 6

1¹/₂ pounds fresh mushrooms
3 tablespoons olive oil
2 cups thinly sliced scallions
2 cloves garlic, minced
4 cups chicken stock

(continued)

339

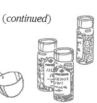

3 tablespoons butter
2 tablespoons flour
1 tablespoon Worcestershire sauce
1 teaspoon salt
freshly ground pepper to taste
$\frac{1}{4}$ cup Burgundy or Chianti
4 egg yolks
2 tablespoons chopped fresh parsley
$\frac{1}{2}$ cup grated Parmesan cheese

Clean the mushrooms with a brush or wipe with a damp cloth. (Do not wash in water.) Snap off the stems and chop the stems coarsely. Slice the caps thinly and set aside.

Heat the oil in a medium (3-quart) saucepan, and sauté the mushroom stems, scallions, and garlic. Cover and cook over medium heat for 15 minutes, stirring frequently. Set aside to cool slightly. Place in a food processor or blender, add 2 tablespoons of the stock, and purée into fine particles, but not into cream.

Return the purée to the heat and when simmering, add the butter. When melted, sprinkle in the flour. Blend into a smooth paste. Allow it to cook for 2 to 3 minutes. Add the stock and Worcestershire, whisk until smooth, and simmer for 5 minutes. Add the mushroom slices; return to a simmer and cook for 10 minutes. Add the salt and pepper to taste. Add the wine.

Blend together the egg yolks, parsley, and Parmesan cheese in a small bowl. Slowly stir the egg mixture into the simmering soup. Serve immediately and garnish with more Parmesan cheese.

Chicken Fennel Stew

Servings: 6

1 cup dry white beans
8 cups water
1 large yellow onion, chopped
2 large cloves garlic, pressed
2 celery ribs, chopped
1 small fresh fennel bulb, diced
$14\frac{1}{2}$-ounce can chicken broth
2 turkey sausages (medium-sized, about 2 ounces each)
1 large boneless, skinless chicken breast, cut into $\frac{1}{2}$-inch pieces
4–5 small new red potatoes, scrubbed and diced
1 teaspoon salt
$\frac{1}{2}$ teaspoon dried thyme
1 cup green beans, trimmed, cut into $\frac{1}{2}$-inch pieces

Rinse beans and soak overnight in cold water.

Drain, rinse, and drain again. Place in a large kettle and cover with 8 cups of water. Heat to boiling. Add onion, garlic, celery, fennel, and broth. Reduce heat to medium-low and simmer for $1\frac{1}{2}$ hours.

Make a slit in each sausage; remove the casings and discard them. Brown the sausage in a nonstick skillet, crumbling with a spoon, about 5 minutes. Add the chicken to the skillet and cook until brown around

the edges, about 5 minutes. Add sausage and chicken to the beans. Add potatoes, salt, thyme, and green beans. Return to a simmer and cook, covered, for 45 minutes.

 For best results, allow two days to make stews. Ingredients like dry beans and peas should soak overnight to increase their tenderness. The second day, add meats or poultry and remaining ingredients to make a hearty one-dish meal.

Veal Stew

Servings: 6

2 pounds boneless veal for stew
1 tablespoon olive oil
$^1/_2$ cup sliced yellow onion
1 clove garlic, minced
1 pound fresh mushrooms, stems and
 caps separated, stems chopped
$^3/_4$ cup dry sherry
1 teaspoon salt or seasoned salt
$^1/_4$ teaspoon lemon pepper
2 teaspoons parsley flakes
1 small bay leaf
2 cups water

Brown the veal in hot oil in a large nonstick frying pan. Add the onion, garlic, and chopped mushroom stems (reserve the caps). Sauté, stirring until the onion is limp. Add the sherry, salt, pepper, parsley, and

bay leaf and water and simmer, covered, about 30 minutes, or until veal is tender.

Add whole mushroom caps and continue simmering about 5 minutes or until mushrooms are the desired doneness. Remove bay leaf before serving.

Beef Burgundy Stew

Servings: 4 to 5

$2^1/_2$ pounds lean, boneless round steak
4 cloves garlic, minced
2 cups Burgundy or other dry red wine
$10^3/_4$-ounce can low-fat cream of mushroom
 soup, undiluted
$10^1/_2$-ounce can beef consommé, undiluted
1 envelope (1 ounce) onion soup mix
6 cups sliced fresh mushrooms
16-ounce package frozen pearl onions
3 tablespoons all-purpose flour
$^3/_4$ cup water
2 12-ounce packages medium egg noodles,
 uncooked
$^1/_4$ cup grated Parmesan cheese
$^3/_4$ cup nonfat sour cream

Trim fat from the steak and cut into $^1/_2$-inch cubes. Coat a large ovenproof Dutch oven with cooking spray. Place over medium heat until hot. Add steak and cook 9 minutes or until steak loses its pink color. Drain well and set aside. Wipe drippings from the pan.

(continued)

Preheat the oven to 350°F. Recoat the pan with cooking spray and place over medium heat. Add garlic and sauté 1 minute. Add wine, mushroom soup, beef consommé, and onion soup mix, stirring well and bringing to a boil. Return the steak to the pan. Stir in the mushrooms and onions. Remove from the heat and set aside.

Place the flour in a small bowl and gradually add water, blending with a wire whisk; add to the steak mixture. Cover and bake for 1½ hours. Cook the noodles according to package directions, omitting salt, and drain. Place in a large serving bowl; add cheese and sour cream. Toss gently to coat. Serve the steak stew over the noodles.

Beef Stew with Roasted Vegetables

Servings: 6

1¾–2-pound boneless beef chuck or
    shoulder
2½ tablespoons olive oil, divided
3 cloves garlic, crushed
¾ teaspoon pepper
13- to 14-ounce can ready to serve beef
    broth
2 teaspoons dried thyme leaves
12 medium mushrooms
6 plum tomatoes cut lengthwise into
    quarters and seeded

3 small white onions cut lengthwise into
    quarters
1½ cups baby carrots
1½ tablespoons, plus 2 teaspoons
    balsamic vinegar, divided
1 tablespoon cornstarch, dissolved in 2
    tablespoons water
fresh thyme, chopped, optional
3 cups cooked couscous

Trim the fat from the beef. Cut the beef into 1-inch pieces. In a Dutch oven, heat 1 tablespoon of the oil over medium heat until hot. Add half of the beef and garlic, and brown evenly, stirring occasionally. Brown the remaining beef and garlic. Pour off drippings. Return all the beef to the pan. Season with pepper. Stir in the broth and dried thyme. Bring to a boil, then reduce the heat to low. Cover tightly and simmer 1½ to 2 hours or until beef is tender.

Meanwhile, preheat oven to 425°F. Lightly spray a 15 x 10-inch jellyroll pan with cooking spray. Place the vegetables in the pan. Combine 1½ tablespoons oil with 1½ tablespoons of the vinegar and drizzle over the vegetables, tossing to coat. Roast 20 to 25 minutes or until tender.

Bring beef stew to a boil over medium-high heat. Add the cornstarch mixture and cook and stir 2 minutes or until sauce is slightly thickened and bubbly. Stir in the roasted vegetables and the remaining 2 teaspoons of vinegar. Sprinkle with fresh thyme if desired. Serve with couscous.

White Bean and Sage Cassoulet

Servings: 6

2 teaspoons olive oil
1 cup diced carrot
1 medium-sized fennel bulb, chopped
1 medium onion, diced
6 cloves garlic, minced
2 16-ounce cans cannellini beans, drained
4 ounces prosciutto or ham, sliced into thin strips
1/4 cup chicken broth or water
14 1/2-ounce can peeled tomato wedges
2 tablespoons finely chopped fresh sage
1/2–1 teaspoon fresh ground pepper
2 slices freshly cut French bread (1/2 inch)
fresh sage leaves (optional)

Preheat oven to 425°F. Heat the oil in a large nonstick skillet over medium-high heat. Add the carrot, fennel, onion, and garlic. Sauté 5 minutes. Spoon the carrot mixture into an 11 x 7-inch baking dish. Stir in the beans, prosciutto or ham, chicken broth, tomato wedges, sage, and pepper.

Trim the crusts from the bread and cut into 1-inch cubes. Lightly coat the cubes with cooking spray. Arrange the bread cubes in a single layer over the bean mixture, pressing the cubes gently into the mixture. Cover with foil, and bake. for 25 minutes. Uncover and bake an additional 5 minutes or until croutons are golden brown. Garnish cassoulet with fresh sage leaves, if desired.

Quick Turkey Cassoulet

Servings: 4

1 cup bread crumbs (3 slices of bread)
2 teaspoons olive oil
2 onions, chopped
1 carrot, chopped
2 cloves garlic, finely chopped
1/4 pound turkey kielbasa sausage, thinly sliced
1 1/2 cups diced cooked white turkey
16-ounce can great northern beans, drained and rinsed
28-ounce can whole tomatoes, drained and coarsely chopped
1 cup chicken stock
1/2 cup dry white or red wine
1 1/2 teaspoons chopped fresh thyme
1/2 teaspoon salt
1/2 teaspoon freshly ground black pepper

Preheat oven to 350°F. Spread bread crumbs on a baking sheet and bake for 6 to 8 minutes, stirring occasionally, until crisp and lightly colored. Set aside.

In a Dutch oven or flameproof casserole, heat oil over medium heat. Add onions, carrot, and garlic, and cook, stirring until just beginning to color, about 5 minutes. Add kielbasa and cook, stirring, until it is lightly browned, about 5 minutes longer. Add turkey, beans, tomatoes, chicken stock, wine, thyme, salt, and pepper. Bring the mixture to a simmer. Sprinkle the cassoulet with reserved bread crumbs and bake for 20 to 30 minutes, or until browned and bubbling.

Chicken Ragout

Servings: 4 to 6

2 tablespoons olive oil

*1½ pounds boneless, skinless chicken
thighs, cut in ½-inch pieces*

*6 ounces Italian sausages, casings
removed*

½ medium white onion, chopped

2 stalks celery, minced

2 carrots, peeled and minced

1 large clove garlic, minced

1 bay leaf

1 cup dry Marsala wine

½ pound fresh mushrooms, sliced

14-ounce can crushed tomatoes

1 cup chicken stock

1 tablespoon tomato paste

3 generous pinches ground cloves

Heat 2 tablespoons oil in a large skillet
over medium-high heat. Add chicken thighs
and Italian sausage. Stir and cook, breaking
sausage into small pieces, until chicken is
browned and sausage is no longer pink. Add
onion, celery, carrots, garlic, and bay leaf,
and continue to cook until the onion is softened. Stir in the Marsala. Bring to a boil,
scraping up any brown bits that are stuck to
the bottom of the skillet. Reduce heat and
simmer until half of the liquid has evaporated (about 15 minutes).

Transfer this mixture to a Dutch oven.
Mix in mushrooms, tomatoes, chicken
stock, tomato paste, and cloves. Bring to a
boil then reduce heat and simmer, stirring
occasionally for 45 minutes.

Serve as a stew with a salad and
French bread or serve as a sauce for your
favorite pizza.

Chicken Stew with Garlic

Servings: 4 to 5

1 head garlic

2 tablespoons + 1 teaspoon olive oil

3-pound chicken, cut into pieces

⅛ teaspoon garlic salt

⅛ teaspoon oregano

½ teaspoon freshly ground pepper, divided

1 red bell pepper cut into chunks

1 yellow bell pepper cut into chunks

1 orange bell pepper, cut into chunks

*2 fresh tomatoes, or 14-ounce can whole
tomatoes with juice, chopped*

14½-ounce can chicken broth

24 pearl onions

3 medium white potatoes

2 ears of corn

1 small yellow squash

1 tablespoon fresh sage

¼ teaspoon salt

Preheat oven to 400°F. Cut a 6-inch square piece of aluminum foil. Slice ½ inch off the top of the garlic head and discard. Place the remaining garlic on the foil. Drizzle garlic with 1 teaspoon olive oil; wrap in foil and bake for 40 minutes, until soft. Remove and set aside to cool.

Season chicken parts with garlic salt, oregano, and ¼ teaspoon pepper. In a large soup pot over medium-high heat, warm 2 tablespoons olive oil. Add the chicken and sauté until browned, about 5 minutes per side. Remove chicken and set aside. Pour off all but 1 tablespoon of liquid. Add bell peppers and sauté for 2 minutes.

When the garlic is done, open the foil and squeeze the garlic out of the skin, adding to the pot. Stir in the tomatoes with juice and broth. Replace the chicken. Bring to simmer over high heat. Reduce to low and let stew for 15 minutes.

While stew is simmering, peel pearl onions and potatoes. Cut potatoes into 1-inch chunks and cut corn into 2-inch chunks. Slice the squash. Stir the onions, potatoes, corn, squash, and sage into the stew. Cook for 15 more minutes.

Season with salt and the remaining ¼ teaspoon pepper. Serve immediately in shallow bowls.

Black Bean Chili

Servings: 4

2½ cups dried black beans
water
1 cup tomato sauce
6 tablespoons (¼ cup + 2 tablespoons) tomato paste
2 tablespoons lime juice
2 tablespoons red wine vinegar
1 cup chopped onions
1 cup chopped celery
1 cup chopped green bell pepper
1 cup chopped tomatoes
4 cloves garlic, finely chopped
1 tablespoon finely chopped fresh cilantro
1½ teaspoons ground cumin
1½ teaspoons chili powder
salt and pepper to taste
sour cream (optional)

Wash beans and place them in a large bowl. Cover with plenty of water to allow for expansion. (Beans will double in size while soaking.) Soak beans overnight.

Drain beans and place in a large soup pot. Add about 7½ cups of water. Bring beans to a boil and simmer for 2 hours or until beans are almost cooked.

Stir in tomato sauce, tomato paste, lime juice, vinegar, vegetables, and seasonings. Continue cooking until beans are soft, 45 minutes to an hour. Top each serving with a dollop of sour cream, if desired.

Beef and Kidney Bean Chili

Servings: 10

3 pounds lean ground beef
1 onion, chopped
28-ounce can tomato sauce
3 cups water
3 tablespoons chili powder
1 1/2 tablespoons cumin
3/4 teaspoon oregano
1 1/2 teaspoons paprika
1/4 teaspoon cayenne pepper
1 tablespoon salt
2 15-ounce cans kidney beans
1/4 cup masa flour (or 2 tablespoons flour
    and 2 tablespoons cornmeal)

Brown the meat and onion. Drain. Add the remaining ingredients except the masa. Simmer about 1 1/2 hours.

Mix the masa with enough water to make a thin paste. Add slowly to the simmering chili, stirring constantly. Cook 15 minutes more.

Meatless Chili

Servings: 4

1 tablespoon olive oil
2 Spanish onions, chopped
1 teaspoon cumin
1/2 teaspoon cinnamon
4 cloves garlic, minced
35-ounce can whole tomatoes with purée,
    drained, with liquid reserved

1/3 cup water
1 tablespoon Tabasco sauce
salt to taste
1 cup bulgur wheat
19-ounce can kidney beans, drained (or two
    8-ounce cans)

Heat the oil in a skillet over medium heat for 20 seconds. Add the onions and cook until translucent. Add the cumin, cinnamon, and garlic. Stir, then add the reserved tomato liquid along with the water, Tabasco, and salt. Cook for 5 minutes.

Add the bulgur; stir and cook for 5 more minutes. Chop the canned tomatoes and add to the skillet with the kidney beans. Reduce the heat; cover and cook for 10 more minutes.

Linguine with Beef and Black Bean Chili

Serves 4 to 6

2 tablespoons vegetable oil
1 pound ground beef
3/4 cup finely diced onion
1 jalapeño chili pepper, seeded and thinly
    sliced
2 tablespoons chili powder
1 tablespoon ground cumin
2 cloves garlic, finely chopped
One 16-ounce can black beans, well rinsed
    and drained
One 15-ounce can crushed tomatoes
2 tablespoons chopped fresh cilantro

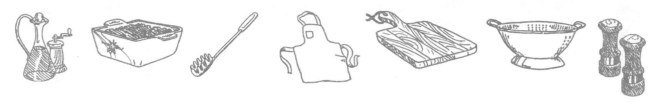

2 cups water
Salt and freshly ground pepper to taste
1 pound linguine

In a large, deep skillet, heat the oil over medium heat. Crumble the meat into the skillet and cook, stirring with a wooden spoon to break it up, until the meat begins to brown, about 5 minutes. Add the onion, jalapeño, chili powder, cumin, and garlic and cook until the onion changes color. Add the beans, tomatoes, cilantro, and water. Bring to a boil, reduce the heat to low, cover, and simmer for 15 minutes to blend the flavors. Season with salt and pepper.

In a large pot, bring at least 4 quarts water to a rolling boil. Add 1 tablespoon salt. Add the pasta, stir to separate, and cook until al dente. Drain and return to the pot. Add the bean mixture and stir over medium heat until the sauce simmers and the pasta is glazed with the sauce.

Roasted Corn-Chipotle Chowder

Servings: 12

5 ears fresh corn, husked
2 red bell peppers
7–8 small red new potatoes, scrubbed
6 slices bacon, diced
3 tablespoons butter
1 medium yellow onion, chopped

3 cloves garlic, minced
8 cups chicken broth
2 cans chipotle chilies, removed from sauce, seeded and diced
2 tomatoes, seeded and chopped
salt and freshly ground pepper to taste
1½ cups whipping cream

Roast corn on a grill in a heavy cast iron pan over low heat, or directly over a gas burner, turning until all kernels look slightly smoky, about 5 minutes. Cut kernels from 3 of the cobs, reserving 2 cobs. Roast the whole bell peppers on a grill or under an oven broiler, turning as the skin blackens on each side, about 8 minutes. Place the roasted peppers in a plastic bag and seal, allowing them to steam while other ingredients are prepared.

Dice 3 of the potatoes and set aside. Quarter the remaining potatoes and simmer the quartered potatoes just covered in water until tender, about 15 minutes. Mash coarsely with a fork and set aside. Fry the bacon until it's almost crunchy. Drain off bacon grease and remove. Melt butter in the bacon pan. Add onion and sauté until translucent, 7 to 10 minutes. Add garlic, and sauté 2 more minutes. Add sautéed bacon. Add broth, reserved corn cobs, diced potatoes, mashed potatoes, chipotle chilies, and tomatoes. Heat to a boil, and season with salt and pepper. Reduce heat to a simmer and cook until potato pieces are tender, about 25 minutes.

(continued)

While the soup is cooking, remove the loosened skin from the peppers. Discard the seeds and membrane. Cut the flesh into small pieces. Remove the cobs from the soup and discard. Add corn kernels, roasted red pepper, and cream. Simmer until heated through.

Most well-stocked supermarkets have canned chipotle chilies in the Mexican food section. Remove peppers from their sauce and slice them in half. Scrape off the seeds and mince the peppers to a pulp. Peppers remaining in the sauce can be kept for up to 2 weeks in the refrigerator.

Pinto Bean Soup

Servings: 6

1½ cups dried pinto beans
7 cups water
¼ cup olive oil
2 medium yellow onions, diced
1 teaspoon salt
½ teaspoon ground pepper
4 cloves garlic, crushed
¼ teaspoon dried thyme
6 cups vegetable stock or water
sour cream for garnish

Salsa:
3 ripe tomatoes, diced
½ small red onion, chopped
¼ cup coarsely chopped fresh cilantro
½ fresh green pepper, finely chopped
juice of 1 lime
salt and freshly ground pepper

Sort through the beans and rinse well. Place the beans in a saucepan with the water, and bring to a boil. Reduce the heat and simmer until the beans are cooked through and tender, about 1 ½ hours.

Remove beans from heat and set aside. In a large saucepan, warm the oil; add the onions, salt, and pepper, and sauté until the onions are lightly browned, about 10 minutes. Add the garlic and thyme and sauté for 1 to 2 minutes longer. Add the beans and their liquid and the stock or water. Bring to a boil; reduce heat and simmer uncovered, stirring occasionally, until the beans start to break apart, 20 to 30 minutes. Remove the beans from heat and cool slightly.

Meanwhile, make the salsa by stirring together all the salsa ingredients.

Working in batches, purée the beans until smooth. Transfer the purée to a clean saucepan and reheat over low heat, stirring occasionally, until hot. Ladle the soup into warmed shallow bowls and top each serving with a spoonful of salsa and a dollop of sour cream.

Chapter 14

Sandwiches and Pizzas

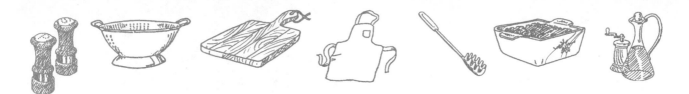

Sandwiches and pizzas are great for when you are in a hurry and need a quick, easy lunch or dinner. But they also make ideal finger food. Serve them bite-size at a luncheon, or as hors d'ouvres before a dinner. For the more exotic appetite, try a non-traditional recipe such as the leek and apple grilled pizza on your family for supper.

Vegetarian Pita Sandwiches

A great way to make a delicious vegetarian sandwich is to coat a whole-wheat pita with a Middle Eastern spread and top it with fresh vegetables to your liking—tomatoes, cucumbers, sprouts, carrots, and lettuce are great examples. Here are basic recipes for two such spreads: Baba Ghanouj and Hummus.

Baba Ghanouj Sandwich Spread

Yield: about 3 cups

2 large eggplants
2 tablespoons sesame or vegetable oil
3 cloves garlic
1 teaspoon salt
2 tablespoons extra-virgin olive oil
juice of 1 lemon
1 teaspoon cumin
¼ cup tahini
ground black pepper to taste

Preheat oven to 450°F.

Peel the eggplant and cut into 1-inch cubes. Toss with sesame oil, 1 chopped clove of garlic, and salt. Spread in a single layer on a baking sheet, and roast until soft and lightly browned, about 15 minutes. Allow to cool slightly.

In a blender or food processor, blend the eggplant, olive oil, lemon juice, remaining 2 cloves garlic (peeled and quartered), cumin, tahini, and pepper. (It may be necessary to do more than one batch; if so, divide ingredients evenly, then combine all batches well.) Refrigerate for at least an hour, or up to 4 days.

After refrigeration, the spread can be brought to room temperature for serving. Stir if any separation has occurred.

Pitas with Baba Ghanouj
Servings: 4

4 whole wheat pitas
¾ cup Baba Ghanouj (page 350)
1 cup fresh alfalfa sprouts

1 large vine-ripened tomato, thinly sliced
1 medium cucumber, peeled and
    thinly sliced

Preheat oven to 300°F.

Warm pitas in the oven for 3 to 4 minutes. Spread about 3 tablespoons Baba ghanouj in each warm pita and layer with sprouts, tomato, and cucumber.

Hummus

Yield: about 3 cups

2 cups dried garbanzo beans (chickpeas)*
6 cups water
4 cloves garlic, peeled and chopped
1 cup tahini
1 teaspoon dried cumin
1 teaspoon salt
3 tablespoons olive oil
1/2 cup lemon juice, divided

Soak garbanzo beans in cold water in a large kettle for 24 hours (or, alternatively, bring to a boil, boil for 1 minute, remove from heat, and allow to stand for 1 hour).

When beans have been soaked by one of these methods, bring them to a boil. Turn down the heat and simmer for 2 hours. Drain, picking out any shells. Rinse to clear off any thick juice.

In a food processor or blender, blend garbanzos until almost smooth. Add chopped garlic, tahini, cumin, salt, olive oil, and half

of the lemon juice. Blend until smooth. Taste, and add more lemon juice, salt, or cumin to taste. Hummus can be served at room temperature or cooler; refrigerate for up to 4 days.

*Canned garbanzo beans can also be used. Use 2 16-ounce cans, well drained.

Pitas with Hummus

Servings: 4

4 whole-wheat pitas
3/4 cup hummus (page 351)
1 large vine-ripened tomato, thinly sliced
1 cup freshly shredded carrots
1 avocado, peeled and thinly sliced

Preheat oven to 300°F.

Warm opened pitas in the oven for 3 to 4 minutes. Spread about 3 tablespoons hummus in each warm pita and layer with tomato, carrots, and avocado.

Chicken Parmesan Hoagies

Servings: 4

Sauce:
1 tablespoon olive oil
2 cloves garlic, finely chopped
1 small white onion (optional)
1 can diced tomatoes, lightly drained

(continued)

¹/₄ cup tomato paste
1 teaspoon garlic salt
1 teaspoon dried Italian seasoning

Chicken:

¹/₂ cup dry bread crumbs
¹/₂ cup grated Parmesan cheese
¹/₂ teaspoon freshly ground black pepper
1 egg, well beaten
4 boneless, skinless chicken breasts
vegetable oil

Other Ingredients:

4 hoagie rolls
6 ounces thinly sliced mozzarella

In a large saucepan, heat olive oil over medium-high heat. Add garlic and onion, and cook until onion is translucent, about 3 minutes. Add diced tomatoes, tomato paste, garlic salt, and Italian seasoning. Reduce heat to medium and stir occasionally until heated and thickened, about 10 to 12 minutes.

While sauce is cooking, combine bread crumbs, Parmesan cheese and black pepper in a wide-rimmed bowl. Dip both sides of the chicken breasts first in the egg and then in the bread crumb mixture. Cover a large skillet with about ¹/₄ inch vegetable oil, and heat to high. Fry chicken breasts for 12 to 14 minutes, or until no longer pink in the middle, turning once. Drain on paper towels.

Preheat oven to 400°F. Slice open the rolls. Layer each roll with sauce, fried chicken breasts, and mozzarella. Wrap indi-vidually in aluminum foil. Place wrapped sandwiches on the oven rack and heat for 7 to 8 minutes. Unwrap and serve hot.

Eggplant Parmesan Hoagies

Servings: 4

Sauce:

1 tablespoon olive oil
2 cloves garlic, finely chopped
1 small white onion (optional)
1 can diced tomatoes, lightly drained
¹/₄ cup tomato paste
1 teaspoon garlic salt
1 teaspoon dried Italian seasoning

Eggplant Coating:

2 large eggplants
¹/₂ cup grated Parmesan cheese
¹/₂ teaspoon freshly ground black pepper
2–3 tablespoons olive oil

Other Ingredients:

4 hoagie rolls
6 ounces thinly sliced mozzarella

Preheat oven to 450°F.

In a large saucepan, heat olive oil over medium-high heat. Add garlic and onion, and cook until onion is translucent, about 3 minutes. Add diced tomatoes, tomato paste, garlic salt, and Italian seasoning. Reduce heat to medium and stir occasionally until heated and thickened, about 10 to 12 minutes.

Spray a baking sheet with nonstick cooking spray. Peel the eggplants. Slice thinly, either vertically or horizontally. Combine the Parmesan cheese and black pepper in a wide-rimmed bowl. Brush the eggplant slices with olive oil on both sides. Dip into the Parmesan mixture and arrange in one layer on the baking sheet. Place in hot oven on top rack. Roast until eggplant is tender, about 12 to 14 minutes.

Reduce the oven temperature to 350°F. Slice open the rolls. Layer each roll with sauce, eggplant, and mozzarella. Wrap individually in aluminum foil. Place wrapped sandwiches on the oven rack and heat for 6 or 7 minutes. Unwrap and serve hot.

Original Egg Salad Sandwich

Servings: 3 generous

6 hard-boiled eggs, peeled
⅓ cup chopped celery
1 tablespoon pickle relish
1 teaspoon spicy mustard (such as Dijon)
⅔ cup mayonnaise
salt and pepper to taste
6 slices wheat or white bread
lettuce and sliced tomato (optional)

Run peeled eggs under water to make sure all shell is removed. Coarsely chop the eggs. In a mixing bowl, combine the eggs, celery, relish, mustard, mayonnaise, and salt and pepper. Chill thoroughly.

Spread on bread, and add lettuce and tomato, if desired.

Cholesterol-reducing hint: Use 8 hard-boiled egg whites and 4 egg yolks.

Add a kick suggestions:
• Add 1 teaspoon curry powder
• Replace mayo with cottage cheese
• Add 2 teaspoons garlic powder

Tuna Salad Sandwich

Servings: 2 generous sandwiches

1 can chunk light tuna in spring water
⅔ cup mayonnaise
1 teaspoon regular or spicy mustard
⅓ cup chopped celery
salt and pepper to taste
lettuce and sliced tomato
4 slices bread, any kind

Drain tuna thoroughly. In a mixing bowl, combine all ingredients except lettuce, tomato, and bread. Spread mixture evenly on bread, and add lettuce and tomato.

Variations:
• Add ⅓ cup shredded carrots to mixture
• Reduce mayo to ½ cup, and increase mustard to 1 tablespoon. Add 1 tablespoon balsamic vinegar.
• Soak ⅓ cup sun-dried tomatoes in warm water. Drain and chop. Add to mixture.

(continued)

Tuna Melt

Servings: 3

> 1 can chunk light tuna in spring water
> ²/₃ cup mayonnaise
> salt and pepper to taste
> 3 slices bread, any type
> 3 thin bread-sized slices of Swiss or
>   Cheddar cheese

Preheat oven to 400°F.

Drain the tuna well and mix with the mayonnaise, salt, and pepper. Lightly toast the bread in oven on the rack for 1 to 2 minutes, until lightly golden. Remove bread and place on a baking sheet. Scoop tuna mixture onto each slice of bread. Cover with

cheese. (*Option:* Stack tomatoes under the cheese.) Put the baking sheet in oven on top rack for 5 to 6 minutes, until cheese starts to bubble and is lightly browned. Serve immediately.

Vegetable Wrap with Dill Sauce

Servings: 4

Sauce:

> ¹/₂ cup plain (regular or low-fat) yogurt
> 1 medium cucumber, finely chopped
> 3 tablespoons chopped fresh dill or ¹/₂
>   tablespoon dried dill
> 1 teaspoon wine vinegar
> ¹/₂ teaspoon salt
> freshly ground black pepper to taste

Other Ingredients:

> 4 tortillas (spinach or whole-wheat
>   recommended)
> about 8 leaves romaine lettuce
> ¹/₂ pound sliced provolone or other
>   mild cheese
> 2 tomatoes, sliced
> 1 small red onion, sliced thin or chopped
> 1 medium avocado, peeled and sliced
> 1 cup alfalfa sprouts

In a small bowl or in a food processor, mix the yogurt, cucumber, dill, vinegar, salt, and pepper. If mixing by hand, be sure to chop the cucumber very finely.

Wraps

Wrap sandwiches are a cross between a burrito and a sandwich on bread. Instead of using bread, traditional sandwich ingredients are spread out and rolled in tortillas. Tortillas come in an assortment of flavors—try them and see what you like!

Spread a large spoonful of the sauce in the middle of a tortilla. Begin layering the rest of the ingredients. Roll the tortilla halfway from the bottom, fold one side in about an inch so that no ingredients can slip out that side, and continue to roll the rest of the way. Repeat with remaining tortillas. Serve immediately at room temperature, or chill before serving.

Salmon Cream Cheese Wrap

Servings: 4

   8 ounces. cream cheese, softened
   1 tablespoon capers, drained and slightly chopped
   1 teaspoon freshly ground black pepper
   3 tablespoons fresh or 2 teaspoons dried chives
   4 tortillas (plain or spinach)
   10 ounces smoked salmon, cut into strips
   1 small red onion, sliced or chopped
   2 medium tomatoes, sliced

In a small bowl, blend well the cream cheese, capers, pepper, and chives. Spread evenly on the tortillas. Layer with salmon, onion, and tomatoes. Roll the tortilla halfway from bottom to top, fold one side in about an inch so that no ingredient can slip out that side, and continue to roll the rest of the way way. Repeat for remaining tortillas. Chill before serving.

Steak and Cheese Wraps

An up-to-date variation on the cheese-steak sandwich

Servings: 4

   4 tortillas (herb or pepper flavor recommended)
   8 ounces Monterey Jack or Cheddar cheese
   2 large white onions
   2 large green peppers
   1 pound sirloin steak
   3 tablespoons olive oil
   2–3 teaspoons black pepper

Preheat oven to 350°F. On a baking sheet, layer tortillas with thinly sliced cheese; do not put cheese closer than 1 inch from the edges. Set aside.

Slice onions and green peppers thickly. Slice the steak into strips about $1/4$-inch thick and 2 inches long. Heat the olive oil in a grill pan or large skillet over medium-high heat. Add onions, green peppers, and black pepper. Stir and cook for about 3 to 4 minutes. Push vegetables to sides of pan and add the steak strips in the middle. Cook to the desired doneness, stirring occasionally. When about 4 minutes are left in cooking time, put the tortillas in the oven. Mix together the steak and onion/pepper mixture in the pan.

Remove the tortillas when the cheese is close to melted, and layer each tortilla with

(continued)

the steak mixture. Roll the tortilla halfway from bottom to top, fold one side in about an inch so that no ingredient can slip out that side, and continue to roll the rest of the way. Continue with remaining tortillas. Serve hot.

Sloppy Joes

Servings: 6

> 1 pound lean ground beef
> 1 medium onion, chopped
> 1/2 cup chopped celery
> 16-ounce can chili-flavored diced tomatoes*
> 2 teaspoons Worcestershire sauce
> dash hot pepper sauce
> salt and pepper to taste
> 6 hamburger buns
> shredded Cheddar cheese (optional)

In a large skillet, brown the ground beef together with the onion and celery, breaking up the beef, until beef is browned. Stir in the tomatoes, Worcestershire sauce, hot pepper sauce, salt, and pepper; and simmer at least 15 minutes, stirring occasionally. Skillet can be partially, but not tightly, covered to prevent splattering.

Serve on buns, and sprinkle with Cheddar cheese if desired.

*Or substitute 1 can of plain tomatoes, cut up, and 1 teaspoon chili powder, or more to taste.

Spicy Hot Beef Sandwiches

Servings: 10

> 1 tablespoon olive oil
> 2 white onions, chopped
> 1 can beef broth
> 1 cup tomato paste
> 3 1/2 to 4 pound chuck roast, braised, cooled, and shredded
> 3/4 cup chopped celery
> 3 tablespoons apple cider vinegar
> 3 tablespoons Worcestershire sauce
> 3 tablespoons packed brown sugar
> 1 teaspoon paprika
> 1 teaspoon dried red peppers
> 1 teaspoon black pepper
> 1 teaspoon chili powder
> 3 bay leaves
> 10 hamburger buns

In a large Dutch oven, heat oil over medium-high heat. Cook onions in the oil until translucent, about 3 to 4 minutes. Add broth and tomato paste, and cook for about 5 minutes, stirring until paste is well dissolved. Transfer broth mixture to a slow cooker or Crock-Pot. Add all remaining ingredients except the buns, and mix well. Cook on medium for 5 to 6 hours, turning bottom to top occasionally. Or cook on the stovetop by reducing heat to low, covering, and simmering for 2 hours, stirring often.

Serve hot on hamburger buns.

Classic Reuben Sandwich

Servings: 4

> 1 cup sauerkraut, very well drained
> 2 tablespoons unsalted butter, divided
> 8 slices rye bread
> ³/₄ cup Thousand Island or Russian
>   dressing
> ¹/₂ pound Swiss cheese, thinly sliced
> ¹/₂ pound corned beef, thinly sliced

Be sure the sauerkraut is well drained, using a paper towel if necessary. Heat 1 tablespoon of the butter in a large skillet over medium to medium-high heat. While butter is melting, spread one side of 4 pieces of bread with dressing. Lay the bread, dressing side up, in the skillet, moving the bread around to fully coat with butter. Layer the cheese, sauerkraut, and corned beef on the bread in the skillet.

With the remaining bread slices, butter one side and spread the other with dressing. Top the sandwiches in the skillet, placing the bread butter side up. Press down firmly. After the sandwiches have cooked for about 5 minutes on one side, carefully flip with a spatula. Press down firmly again. Cover the skillet for about 3 to 4 minutes, or until cheese has melted and the second side is golden. Serve hot with kosher dill pickles, if desired.

Grilled Swordfish Steak Sandwich with Roasted Peppers

Servings: 4

> 1 red bell pepper
> 1 yellow bell pepper
> 1 green bell pepper
> 1 small white onion (optional)
> 1 pound swordfish, halibut, or other white
>   fish fillet
> 1 tablespoon olive oil
> 1 teaspoon paprika
> salt to taste
> freshly ground black pepper to taste
> 3 tablespoons mayonnaise
> 1 teaspoon Dijon mustard
> Focaccia, home baked or purchased

Preheat the broiler. Cut the peppers in half; remove seeds and any white. Peel the onion and cut in thick slices. Place peppers and onions in the broiler cut side down. Broil until skin is charred, about 4 minutes. Cool until they can be handled. The charred pepper skin will peel off easily. Peel the pepper, and cut into narrow strips. Separate the onions into rings. Place in a bowl, mix, and cover to retain heat.

Preheat a grill pan or heavy skillet over medium-high heat. Brush the fish steak with the olive oil, and sprinkle with paprika and salt and pepper to taste. Place on the hot pan, and cook for a total of about 12

(continued)

minutes, depending on the thickness and desired doneness.

While the fish is grilling, mix together the mayonnaise and mustard. Slice the focaccia in half horizontally. Spread the mayo mixture on one side. Add a layer of the peppers and onion. Add the cooked fish steak, and top with more mayo mixture if desired.

Salmon Sandwich with Herb Mayonnaise

Servings: 4

¼ cup mayonnaise
1 teaspoon dried parsley

1 teaspoon dried tarragon
1 teaspoon marjoram
1 teaspoon red wine vinegar
2 teaspoons Dijon mustard
1 pound salmon fillets
1 tablespoon olive oil
4 large buns
4 large leaves of lettuce
4 slices red onion
8 slices tomato

Preheat oven to 350°F.

In a small bowl, mix the mayo, herbs, vinegar and mustard until well blended. Brush both sides of the salmon fillets with olive oil and spread the fillets in a baking dish. With half of the mayo mixture, coat the top side of the fillets. Bake for 17 to 20 minutes, or until the fish flakes easily with a fork.

Place the cooked fillets on buns and top with lettuce, onion, and tomato. Spread an extra layer of mayo on the top bun. Can be served warm, or chill and serve cold.

Muffulettas are serious sandwiches piled high with Italian meats and spread with an olive mixture to delight every sense. The sauce needs to marinate at least overnight, so plan ahead. This is a great choice to cut up into bite sized brunch or lunch party servings.

Fish Sandwiches

Usually, we think of fish as a dish on its own. But grilled, broiled, or fried fish sandwiches are a great way to add a little pep to any fish meal.

Muffuletta

Servings: 2 large sandwiches

Spread:
$\frac{1}{4}$ cup + 1 tablespoons olive oil
$\frac{1}{4}$ cup red wine vinegar
juice of $\frac{1}{2}$ lemon (about $1\frac{1}{2}$ tablespoons)
*2 tablespoons finely chopped black olives
   (such as the Kalamata type)*
*2 tablespoons finely chopped stuffed
   green olives*
1 tablespoon finely chopped red onion
1 tablespoon finely chopped celery
3 cloves garlic, finely chopped
$\frac{1}{4}$ teaspoon dried parsley
$\frac{1}{4}$ teaspoon crushed fennel seed
$\frac{1}{4}$ teaspoon oregano
$\frac{1}{4}$ teaspoon freshly ground black pepper

Other Ingredients:
2 large Italian hard rolls or loaves
$\frac{1}{2}$ pound hard salami
*$\frac{1}{2}$ pound spiced Italian sausage such as
   mortadella (or substitute ham)*
$\frac{1}{2}$ pound provolone cheese
6-8 leaves lettuce
$\frac{1}{2}$ red onion finely sliced

In a small bowl, mix all the spread ingredients. Cover and refrigerate at least overnight. (Mixture can be kept refrigerated for up to 3 days.)

When ready to assemble the sandwiches, slice the rolls in half lengthwise. Spread the olive mixture on the top and bottom of each roll. Layer the salami, sausage, cheese, lettuce, and onion slices.

Basic Pizza Dough

For the freshest taste, make your own pizza dough. However, if time is limited, good pizza crusts are now available at most groceries. Three recipes for great dough are printed here. Following that, we have listed some favorite pizza recipes. We make suggestions for the dough, but feel free to use any of these recipes for any of the pizzas.

No-Yeast Dough

Fast and easy, this dough also cooks quickly.

Yield: dough for 1 large or 2 small pizzas

2 cups all-purpose flour
1 teaspoon salt
$1\frac{1}{2}$ tablespoons baking powder
2 tablespoons olive oil
1 cup water, divided
2–3 tablespoons flour for kneading

In a large bowl, mix the flour, salt, and baking powder. Make a well in the center, and add the olive oil and $\frac{3}{4}$ cup water. Gradually work the flour and liquid mixture together, adding extra water as needed. Knead on a floured board about 5 minutes, or until dough feels smooth and sturdy. *This dough should be used immediately.*

Neapolitan Pizza Dough

Traditional Neapolitan pizza crust is very thin.

Yield: two 9-inch crusts

    1½ teaspoons active dry yeast
    ½ cup + ¼ cup lukewarm water
    1½ tablespoons olive oil
    1⅔ cups unbleached all-purpose flour
    ¾ teaspoon salt
    3–4 tablespoons flour for kneading

In a large mixing bowl, mix yeast into ½ cup lukewarm water. Allow it to stand until the mixture looks clouded and somewhat thickened. Stir in the olive oil. In a large bowl, combine flour and salt. Make a well and add the yeast mixture. Gradually work the flour and yeast mixture together, adding extra water as needed. Mix until the dough sticks together and can be easily formed.

Flour a large work surface and knead the dough until smooth and strong, about 8 to 10 minutes. Place it in an oiled bowl, cover with a clean cloth, and let the dough rest in a warm place (room temperature or above) for at least 15 minutes.

Divide the dough into 2 equal portions; knead each portion briefly and then roll each portion into a smooth round shape. To use immediately, place each ball on a floured work surface and cover with a clean cloth to rise for about an hour. When ready to bake, stretch each ball out into a 9-inch disk and add specific recipe toppings.

To store for up to 2 days, place the dough balls on a baking pan lined with a kitchen towel, cover them with another kitchen towel, and refrigerate. When ready to use, remove the balls from the refrigerator and allow to warm at room temperature for 10 to 15 minutes before making pizzas. For longer storage, place each dough ball into a small freezer bag and freeze for up to a month. When ready to use, place each ball into an oiled bowl, cover with plastic wrap and let thaw overnight in the refrigerator or at room temperature for about 2 hours. When ready to use, the dough should be soft to the touch and slightly rising.

Whole-Wheat Pizza Dough

Makes a soft, thick pizza crust

Yield: dough for 1 large or 2 small pizzas

    2½ teaspoons active dried yeast
    1½ teaspoons sugar
    1 teaspoon salt
    2 tablespoons olive oil
    ½ cup room temperature water
    2 cups whole-wheat flour
    2–3 tablespoons flour (whole wheat or
       all purpose) for kneading

Mix yeast, sugar, salt, olive oil, and water in a small bowl. Set aside for 10 minutes or until clouded and somewhat thickened. Put flour in

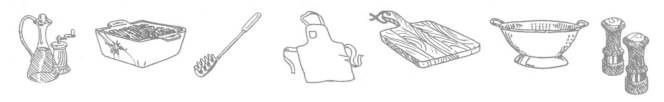

a large bowl and make a well in the center. Add the yeast mixture. Gradually work the flour and yeast mixture together, adding extra room-temperature water if needed.

Knead on a floured board about 5 minutes, or until dough feels smooth. Lightly oil a large bowl, place the dough in the bowl, and cover with a clean cloth. Place in a warm (at least room temperature) place for 30 minutes or until size doubles. Use immediately or store in a plastic bag for 2 days in the refrigerator or 3 weeks in the freezer.

Deep Dish Spinach-Cheese Pizza

Servings: 1 10-inch pizza

1 recipe Neapolitan Pizza Dough (page 360) or No-Yeast Dough, doubled (page 359)
½ pound mozzarella cheese, grated
½ pound provolone cheese, grated
½ package (about ⅔ cup) frozen spinach, thawed, drained, and squeezed
1½ cups Basic Tomato Sauce (page 117) or canned sauce
2–3 fresh tomatoes, sliced thinly
¼ pound Parmesan cheese, grated

Preheat oven to 500°F.
Make pizza dough as directed and flatten slightly. Spread the dough in a deep dish pizza pan, making sure the crust is brought

(continued)

Pizza

The pizza that we know today had its origins in Naples, Italy, as early as the 1st century A.D. Italian immigrants brought the "pizzaioli" to America, where it has become a national staple.

If you love garlic, add garlic. If you love mushrooms, add mushrooms. Very few ingredients will drastically alter the cooking time or other measurements of the pizza, but you may prefer to add more or less sauce depending on the ingredients you use. Basically, the key to a great pizza is to make it to order—**your** order!

up to the edge of the deep dish. Mix the mozzarella and provolone cheeses and spinach together well. Spread the spinach and cheese mixture evenly on the unbaked pizza crust. Top with the tomato sauce, slices of fresh tomato, and grated Parmesan cheese.

Bake on the middle rack of the oven 30 to 40 minutes, until cheese is bubbly and crust has browned.

Pizza Stones

For the best home-baked pizza, use a pizza stone. Heat it on the bottom rack of the oven while you prepare the pizza on a well-greased and floured baking sheet. While making the pizza, gently shake the baking sheet back and forth to make sure the pizza has not stuck to it. If it has, gently lift off the stuck section and sprinkle a little more flour underneath. When ready to bake the pizza, use the baking sheet like a large spatula to quickly slide the pizza onto the hot pizza stone.

Stuffed Spinach-Cheese Pizza

A variation on the deep dish, stuffed pizza houses the toppings between two layers of dough, rather than on top of one. This recipe is similar to the Deep Dish Spinach-Cheese Pizza, with a few minor adjustments to make the pizza more like a pizza pie.

Yield: 1 10-inch pizza

> Neapolitan Pizza Dough (page 360)
>   or Basic No-Yeast Dough,
>   doubled (page 359)
> 1/2 pound mozzarella cheese, grated
> 1/2 pound provolone cheese, grated
> 1/2 package (about 2/3 cup) frozen spinach,
>   thawed, drained, and squeezed
> 3 tablespoons olive oil
> 2–3 fresh tomatoes, sliced
> 1 1/2 cups Basic Tomato Sauce (page 117)
>   or canned sauce
> 1/4 pound Parmesan cheese, grated

Preheat oven to 500°F.

Prepare the pizza dough as directed, but divide into two balls, one about a third larger than the other. Spread the larger of the pizza dough balls into a deep dish pizza pan, making sure the crust is pushed up to the edges. Mix the mozzarella and provolone cheeses, spinach, and olive oil together well. Evenly spread the cheese and spinach mixture on top of the dough.

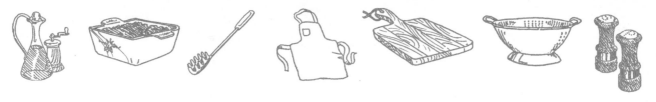

On a flat surface, form the remaining dough into a circle as large as the pizza pan, working from the middle outwards. Place the round dough on top of the spinach-cheese mixture and pinch the dough layers together around the circumference. On top of the top dough layer, spread the sliced tomatoes, and top with sauce. Sprinkle Parmesan cheese on top.

Bake on the middle rack of the oven 40 to 50 minutes or until cheese is bubbly and crust is golden brown.

Pizza with Sausage and Mushrooms

Yield: 9-inch pizza

*1/2 recipe Neapolitan Pizza Dough
    (page 360)*
2 tablespoons olive oil
1 small yellow onion, chopped
2 cloves garlic, finely sliced
1/4 pound lean sausage or ground beef
salt and freshly ground pepper to taste
*1 cup chopped fresh mushrooms
    (shiitake or Portobello works well)*
1 teaspoon oregano
*1/2 cup Basic Tomato Sauce (page 117) or
    canned sauce*
1/4 pound shredded mozzarella cheese
grated Parmesan cheese for sprinkling

Preheat oven to 500°F. Prepare dough as directed. Spread on an oiled and floured pizza pan or baking sheet.

Heat the olive oil in a large skillet over medium heat. Add the onion and garlic and cook for 3 to 4 minutes until onion are translucent. Add crumbled sausage or ground beef and salt and pepper to taste. Cook for about 5 minutes, stirring often to crumble beef. Lightly drain any excess grease; return to heat. Add the chopped mushrooms and oregano and cook 3 to 4 more minutes, stirring often, until mushrooms are reduced and beef is cooked through. Turn off the heat, add the sauce, and mix well.

Spread the beef mixture over the dough. Top evenly with mozzarella cheese. Bake until the edges are golden and the cheese is bubbly, 10 to 12 minutes. Remove the pizza with a large spatula. Sprinkle evenly with the Parmesan and serve immediately.

Whole-Wheat Pizza with Eggplant and Artichokes

Yield: 10-inch pizza

Whole-Wheat Pizza Dough (page 360)
6 tablespoons olive oil, divided
1 small eggplant, thinly sliced lengthwise
*1 6-ounce jar artichoke hearts, drained
    and sliced*
1 teaspoon dried rosemary

(continued)

1 teaspoon dried thyme
1 teaspoon dried thyme
1 teaspoon dried basil
2 cups crumbled feta cheese
1 cup cherry, grape, or plum tomatoes,
    thinly sliced

Preheat oven to 500°F.

Prepare dough as directed and form into a 10-inch circle on a floured pizza pan or baking sheet. In a medium skillet, heat 2 tablespoons of the olive oil over high heat. Sauté the eggplant on both sides in the oil for 2 to 3 minutes. Remove the eggplant and add 2 more tablespoons of olive oil to the pan.

Brush the dough with the remaining olive oil. Top evenly with eggplant and artichokes. Sprinkle with all the herbs. Spread the feta evenly over the pizza. Finish with evenly spaced tomato slices. Bake for 10 to 12 minutes, or until the crust is golden brown.

Zucchini and Squash Pizza with Pesto

Yield: 9-inch pizza

$^1/_2$ recipe Neapolitan Pizza Dough (page
    360) or No-Yeast Dough (page 359)
$^1/_4$ cup pesto (page 306) or use
    prepared pesto
1 medium zucchini, sliced
1 medium yellow squash, sliced
$^1/_2$ cup grated mozzarella cheese

Preheat oven to 500°F.

Prepare dough as directed and form a 9-inch circle on a floured pizza pan or baking sheet. Spread the pesto on the dough. Layer the zucchini and squash on the pesto. Spread the cheese on evenly. Bake for 15 minutes, or until the pizza is golden on the edges and the cheese is lightly browned.

Portobello and Swiss-Cheese Pizza

Yield: 10-inch pizza

$^1/_2$ recipe Neapolitan Pizza Dough (page
    360) or No-Yeast Dough (page 359)
1 tablespoon olive oil
2 cloves garlic, finely chopped
1 pound Portobello mushrooms, sliced thinly
1 large tomato, chopped
$^1/_2$ cup red wine
3 teaspoons rosemary
$^1/_2$ teaspoon salt
1 teaspoon freshly ground black pepper
$^1/_2$ pound Swiss cheese, grated or
    thinly sliced

Preheat oven to 500°F.

Prepare dough as directed and form a 10-inch circle on a floured pizza pan or baking sheet. In a large skillet, heat the olive oil over high heat. Add the garlic and cook for 2 minutes. Add the mushrooms.

Cook, stirring occasionally, until almost tender, about 4 minutes. Add tomato, wine, rosemary, salt, and pepper. Reduce the heat to medium and let cook for about 10 minutes or until liquid is largely evaporated.

Spread the mixture on the dough. Layer with Swiss cheese. Bake until the cheese is bubbly and the crust is golden, about 12 minutes.

Herb Pizza

Yield: 9-inch pizza

Herb-Flavored Focaccia (page 52) or store-bought focaccia
¹/₂ cup Basic Tomato Sauce (page 117) or canned sauce
¹/₄ cup grated Parmesan cheese
1 cup mixed chopped fresh herbs of your choice: rosemary, thyme, parsley, oregano, marjoram, chives, basil, etc.

Preheat oven to 500°F.

Prepare focaccia as directed. Spread the tomato sauce over the surface and sprinkle with Parmesan cheese. Evenly spread the fresh herbs over the top. Bake for 15 minutes, or until the crust is golden.

Leek and Apple Grilled Pizza

Yield: 10-inch pizza

¹/₂ recipe Neapolitan Pizza Dough (page 360)
2–3 Granny Smith or other tangy apples
1 large leek
2 tablespoons olive oil, divided
¹/₄ cup fresh basil
¹/₄ cup fresh thyme

Preheat oven to 500°F. Preheat an outdoor charcoal or gas grill.

Prepare the pizza dough as directed and bake for 5 minutes.

Slice the apples lengthwise (about ¹/₂ inch thick) to the core on both sides. Pull apart the leek, cutting off any hard bottom or browned top. Place the leeks and apples on the grill on a piece aluminum foil that has been lightly sprayed with cooking oil. Flip after 4 minutes, and continue to grill until slightly dried, about 4 minutes more.

Brush the pizza dough with 1 tablespoon olive oil and place on the grill. Flip after 2 or 3 minutes. Drizzle the remaining olive oil on top, and add the fresh herbs. Add the leeks and apples to the pizza. Continue grilling for 2 to 3 minutes more; remove and serve hot.

This pizza can also be prepared by using the broiler rather than an outdoor grill. Adjust the rack so it's 8 inches from the heating element, and prepare as above.

Herb-Flavored Focaccia

Focaccia bread has become a popular favorite for use in pizzas and as a delicious accompaniment to Italian or any meals. To make the bread more crispy, drizzle a little olive oil on the crust before baking; to make it softer, brush the crust with oil immediately after it comes out of the oven. Focaccia, a wonderful sandwich bread alternative, can transform a simple entree into a special treat. The recipe for Herb-Flavored Focaccia is in the Breads chapter on page 52.

Sun-Dried Tomato and Chicken Pizza

Yield: 9-inch pizza

8 ounces sun-dried tomatoes
½ recipe Neapolitan Pizza Dough (page 360) or No-Yeast Dough (page 359)
1 skinless, boneless chicken breast
2 tablespoons unsalted butter
⅓ cup Basic Tomato Sauce (page 117) or canned sauce
½ pound grated mozzarella cheese

Preheat oven to 500°F.

Soften the tomatoes in hot water, then drain well. Prepare the dough as directed and form a 9-inch circle on an oiled and floured pizza pan or baking sheet. Flatten the chicken breast and cut into 1-inch square pieces. Heat the butter over medium heat in a skillet. Add the chicken to the skillet and cook through, about 6 to 7 minutes. Spread the sauce on the dough, layer with chicken and drained tomatoes, and top with cheese. Cook for 12 to 14 minutes, or until the cheese is bubbly and the crust is golden.

Basic Cheese Calzone

Calzones are sandwich-pizza combinations

Servings: 4

> Neapolitan Pizza Dough (page 360)
> 1 cup ricotta cheese
> 1 cup shredded mozzarella cheese
> 2 tablespoons olive oil
> 2 eggs, divided
> 1 cup Basic Tomato Sauce (page 117) or
>   canned sauce
> 1/4 cup grated Parmesan cheese

Preheat oven to 400°F.

Divide the dough into four balls and flatten into 5-inch rounds. In a bowl, mix the ricotta, mozzarella, olive oil, and 1 slightly beaten egg. Spoon a fourth of the mixture onto the middle of each flattened dough ball. Beat the second egg well. Brush a 1/2-inch border on the edges of the dough with part of the egg. Gently fold the dough over the filling, covering the filling completely, and close by pressing the edges with a fork. Brush the tops with the remaining egg. Cut 2 small slits on the top for vents.

Bake for 20 to 25 minutes, or until a deep golden brown, on the middle rack of the oven.

Meanwhile, heat the tomato sauce if it's not already hot. Remove calzones from the oven, top generously with sauce and Parmesan cheese, and serve hot.

Variation: Stuff the basic cheese calzone with ingredients of your choice—mushrooms, tomatoes, sausage, spinach, garlic, zucchini, even fruit!

French Bread Pizzas

Serves: 4

> 1 loaf French bread
> 2 tablespoons olive oil
> 1 large onion, chopped
> 1 green bell pepper, chopped
> 2 garlic cloves, minced
> 2 teaspoons dried basil, crumbled
> 2 teaspoons dried oregano, crumbled
> 2 cups Basic Tomato Sauce (page 117)
> 2 large tomatoes, sliced
> 1 cup pitted black olives, sliced
> 2 cups finely grated carrots
> 1/3 cup grated Parmesan cheese

Preheat oven to 450°F.

Slice the bread in half lengthwise. Drizzle the cut sides of both halves with 1 tablespoon of the oil and place on a baking sheet. In a skillet, heat the remaining tablespoon of oil over medium heat. Add the onion, bell pepper, garlic, basil, and oregano and cook for 5 minutes, or until softened. Remove from heat. Spoon 1 cup of the spaghetti sauce on each piece of bread. Top evenly with the onion-pepper mixture, tomatoes, and black olives. Then sprinkle evenly with the carrots and Parmesan cheese.

Bake for 12 to 15 minutes, or until bubbly and the bread is lightly browned. Cut crosswise to serve. Serve hot.

Chapter 15

Desserts and Sweets

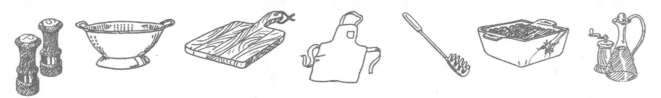

It is no coincidence that words commonly associated with dessert – honey, sweetie, sugar, cookie – are regularly used as terms of endearment. People everywhere love their sweets. Here you have a multitude of desserts to satisfy every craving that your sweet tooth may demand. Try personalizing a recipe with a sprinkle of walnuts here or a splash of coffee liqueur there, and you'll have them eating out of your hands.

Homemade Pie Crust

Yield: 4 pie crusts

4 cups flour, unsifted
2 cups lard (or white Crisco)
1 teaspoon baking powder
1 tablespoon sugar
1 teaspoon salt
1 egg
1 tablespoon cider vinegar
$\frac{1}{2}$ teaspoon water

Blend the first 5 ingredients with a pastry cutter or your hands. In a separate bowl, beat the egg slightly and add the vinegar and water. Add this to the flour mixture and form it into 4 balls, enough for two 2-crust pies. If you are only making one pie you can freeze the dough balls in plastic wrap until you need them.

To bake an unfilled pie crust: Preheat oven to 400°F. Bake 8 to 10 minutes, or until light golden brown.

Pastry Blender

Pastry Cutter

Glass Pie Dish

Glass Deep Pie Dish

370

Homemade Pie Crust

1 Use a pastry blender to blend the ingredients.

2 Flour the work surface. Using the rolling pin, roll the ball of dough out from the center out in all directions.

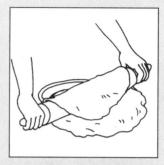

3 Roll the dough loosely around the rolling pin and transfer to the pie dish.

4 Carefully arrange the dough over the bottom and corners of the pie dish.

5 Pinch the dough on the rim of the pie dish. Trim away the excess dough with a knife.

6 To fix a tear in the dough, moisten a piece of dough and put it over the tear.

Rhubarb Custard Pie

Servings: 6

> 3 cups chopped fresh rhubarb
> 1½ cups sugar
> ¼ cup flour
> 3 whole eggs
> ¼ cup heavy cream
> sugar for sprinkling

Preheat the oven to 325°F. Place the rhubarb in a mixing bowl. Add the sugar, flour, eggs, and cream. Stir together, and pour into an unbaked pie crust. Cover with another pie crust or make a latticework upper crust. Sprinkle sugar on top before baking. Bake about 45 minutes to an hour. Don't overbake, but be sure the pie juices are bubbly before removing from the oven.

To make a latticework crust: Roll out the dough for a regular crust; use a sharp knife to make cuts about an inch apart, creating strips of dough. Starting with the middle and longest strip, place it across the middle of the pie filling. Place a second strip parallel to the first; then place a third strip perpendicular to the first two, laying it under one of them. Continue weaving the strips until the pie is covered. Seal the edges and press into decorative waves.

Banana Cream Pie

Servings:

Pudding:
> 2 tablespoons butter
> ¾ cup sugar
> ⅛ teaspoon salt
> ⅓ cup flour
> 2 eggs, well beaten
> 2 cups 2% milk, scalded*
> ½ teaspoon vanilla flavoring
> fresh sliced bananas
>
> baked pie shell

Meringue:
> 3 egg whites
> ⅓ cup sugar
> ¼ teaspoon cream of tartar

Combine butter, sugar, salt, flour, and eggs. Add hot milk slowly, stirring constantly. Cook over hot water in a double boiler until thick and smooth; stir constantly, as it will burn or get lumpy very easily. Remove from the heat and add the vanilla.

Slice the bananas into the baked pie shell. Pour the pudding mixture over the bananas.

Preheat the oven to 350°F. Beat the egg whites until almost stiff. Add the sugar and

(continued)

Pie Dough Tips

- Have the butter, shortening, and water as cold as possible.
- Using a pastry blender, cut the butter into the flour until it becomes crumbly, then add the shortening. Mix only enough for moist crumbs to form.
- Add the water a few drops at a time and mix until the dough just sticks together when you press it between your hands.
- Don't overwork the dough! The more you work it, the tougher it will be.
- To make rolling easier, form the dough into a ball or disk, cover, and refrigerate 15 minutes or more.
- Lightly dust the surface of the dough, the board, and the rolling pin with flour. Roll the dough from the center out. Lift and turn it occasionally to help you roll it evenly.
- Pie crust should be rolled about ⅛-inch thick.
- Do not stretch or pull the dough when fitting to the pan. Prick the dough with fork tines, *unless* it is to be rebaked after filling, as with pumpkin pies.
- Cover the edges with strips of aluminum foil to prevent excess browning, pressing the foil gently onto the crust. Remove the foil during the last 15 minutes of baking.
- Do not use shiny pans to bake pies; use dull metal or glass pans. Dull metal and glass absorb heat, and will help the bottom crust to bake completely.
- To prevent the crust for a one-crust pie from shrinking when baked, do not use a nonstick pan.
- It is not necessary to grease pie pans, because pastry dough contains a large amount of fat and will not usually stick.

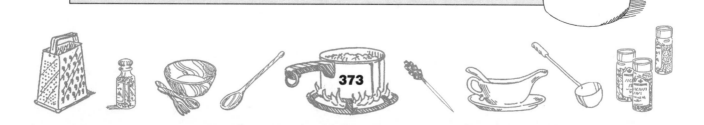

cream of tartar. Continue beating until it looks shiny and has some texture. Spoon it on top of the pie, spreading the meringue out and making little peaks with it. Bake for about 10 minutes until set.

Variation: To make coconut cream pie, add coconut instead of bananas and prepare as above.

*Heat the milk to very warm, but not boiling.

Pan Placement

Place a cake pan or cookie sheet in the middle of an oven rack that has been centered in the oven. It's best to bake only one large pan or cookie sheet at a time, but if you must bake more than one:

- Arrange the pans so there is at least 1 inch of space between the pans and between the pans and the oven walls if they are on the same rack.
- If the pans are on different racks, do not place them directly under each other; stagger them.

Pecan Pie

Servings: 4 to 5

3 eggs
²/₃ cup sugar
1 cup dark corn syrup
½ teaspoon salt
⅓ cup butter, melted
1 teaspoon vanilla
1 cup pecan halves

9-inch pie crust

Preheat oven to 375°F.

Beat the eggs until they're light yellow and fluffy. Add the sugar, corn, syrup, salt, melted butter, vanilla, and pecan halves. Place the mixture in the unbaked pie crust and bake for 40 to 50 minutes, or until edges are bubbly.

Old-Fashioned Pound Cake

Yield: large tube cake

1 cup butter
5 eggs
2 cups sugar
2 cups flour
*1 teaspoon vanilla, almond, or
    citrus extract*

Preheat oven to 300°F. Butter a large tube pan well.

Cream the butter well. Add the eggs, one at a time, beating 1 minute after each. While beating continuously, gradually add the sugar, then the flour, then the flavoring. Pour into the tube pan, and bake for $1\frac{1}{2}$ to $1\frac{3}{4}$ hours, or until a toothpick or knife inserted in the middle comes out clean. Serve with strawberries or other berries if desired.

Estelle's Cream Cheese Pound Cake

Yield: large bundt cake

$1\frac{1}{2}$ cups butter
3 cups sugar
8 ounce package cream cheese
6 eggs
1 teaspoon vanilla
3 cups cake flour
powdered sugar

Preheat oven to 300°F. Grease a bundt pan well.

Cream together the butter, sugar, and cream cheese until light and fluffy. Add the eggs one at a time, beating well after each, then add the vanilla. Add the flour slowly. Bake in the bundt pan for $1\frac{1}{2}$ hours.

Dust with sifted powdered sugar before serving. Cake may be served when cool, but is even better the second day.

Strawberry-Banana Shortcake

Yield: 8-inch-square cake

1 quart strawberries
$\frac{3}{4}$ cup sugar, divided
1 cup flour
$1\frac{1}{2}$ teaspoons baking powder
$\frac{1}{4}$ teaspoon salt
1 large ripe banana
1 tablespoon lime juice
$\frac{1}{4}$ cup butter
1 egg
$\frac{1}{2}$ teaspoon vanilla
$\frac{1}{2}$ cup chopped walnuts

Preheat oven to 350°F.

Hull and slice the strawberries. Sprinkle with $\frac{1}{4}$ cup of the sugar and allow to stand for at least 1 hour at room temperature before serving. Set aside and stir occasionally.

Sift together the flour, baking powder, and salt and set aside. In a small bowl, mash the banana and mix in the lime juice. Cream the butter and remaining $\frac{1}{2}$ cup sugar until light and fluffy, then add the egg and vanilla and mix well. Without stopping the mixer, add the banana mixture. Stir in the dry ingredients, then the nuts. Spread the batter in a lightly greased 8- or 9-inch square baking pan and bake about 30 minutes, or until center tests done. Cool completely.

To serve, cut cake into squares and top with strawberries.

Wella's White Cake

Yield: 9 x 13 cake

2¼ cups cake flour
1½ cups sugar
1 tablespoon baking powder
1 teaspoon salt
½ cup solid shortening, room temperature
1 cup milk, divided
1 teaspoon vanilla
2 eggs
coconut (optional)

Preheat oven to 350°F.

Sift the dry ingredients together. Add the shortening, ⅔ of the cup milk, and vanilla, and beat for 2 minutes with an electric mixer on medium-low speed. Add the remaining ⅓ cup milk and the eggs, and beat 2 minutes at medium speed. Bake in a greased, floured 9 x 13 pan for 30 to 35 minutes.

Frost with Seven-Minute Frosting (page 380) and sprinkle with coconut if desired.

Texas Sheet Cake

Yield: 15 x 10 cake

Cake:
1 cup butter
1 cup water
¼ cup cocoa powder
2 cups flour
2 cups sugar
½ teaspoon salt
2 eggs
½ cup sour cream
1 teaspoon baking soda

Frosting:
½ cup butter
¼ cup cocoa
6 tablespoons (¼ cup +
*   2 tablespoons) milk*
16-ounce package powdered sugar
1 teaspoon vanilla
½ cup chopped walnuts (optional)

Is It Done?

To test a cake, insert a toothpick or cake tester (an inexpensive kitchen gadget) in the center of the cake. If it comes out clean, the cake is done. If crumbs or batter stick to it, it needs to bake longer.

Some cooks prefer the "touch" method. Touch the cake lightly in its center. If it springs back, the cake is done. If the indentation from your finger remains, it needs to bake longer.

When done, the cake will also begin to shrink slightly away from the sides of the pan.

(continued)

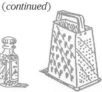

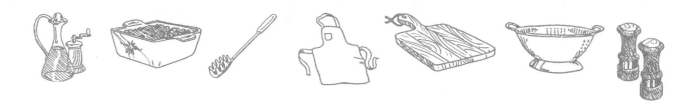

Cake Pan Tips

- The best pans for cake baking are shiny metal. If using dark coated (nonstick) or glass pans, follow the manufacturer's directions; if the directions are not available, reduce the oven temperature by 25 degrees. Glass and dark pans absorb the heat instead of reflecting it.

- To prevent sticking, grease both the bottom and sides of the pan generously. Dust the bottom with flour; shake the pan to coat the bottom, then turn over and discard the excess flour.

- For chocolate cakes, dust the baking pan with cocoa powder instead of flour.

- Even if using a cooking spray, dust the pan with flour if the recipe instructs you to do so. Sprays containing flour are also available specifically for baking.

- The bottom of the pan can also be lined with waxed paper to help cakes release without sticking.

- Solid shortening is the best choice for greasing pans. Butter browns or burns at a lower temperature, and will sometimes result in a browner "crust" on the bottom and sides of the cake.

several cake pans

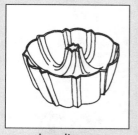

bundt pan

greasing the pan

flouring the pan

Preheat the oven to 375°F.

Make the cake: In a large saucepan, bring to a boil the butter, water, and cocoa. Remove from the heat and mix in the flour, sugar, and salt; beat about 1 minute at medium speed with an electric mixer. In a separate bowl, beat together the eggs, sour cream, and baking soda, then add to the flour mixture in the saucepan, beating until well combined. Pour into a greased jellyroll pan (15 x 10 x 1) and bake 20 to 22 minutes. Allow to cool partially.

Make the frosting: In a medium saucepan, bring to a boil the butter, cocoa, and milk. Remove from the heat and add the powdered sugar and vanilla, beating until smooth. Allow to cool partially, then spread over the cake while still warm. Sprinkle with nuts.

Fudge Cake

Yield: 9 x 13 cake

$^1/_2$ cup boiling water
$^1/_2$ cup cocoa powder
2 cups cake flour
1 teaspoon soda
1 teaspoon baking powder
$^1/_2$ teaspoon salt
$^1/_2$ cup solid shortening
$1^1/_2$ cups sugar
2 egg yolks
1 teaspoon vanilla
$^3/_4$ cup buttermilk or sour milk
2 egg whites

Preheat oven to 350°F.

Add the boiling water to the cocoa and make a smooth paste; set aside and allow to cool. Sift together the flour, soda, baking powder, and salt, and set aside. Cream together the shortening and sugar, beating until light and fluffy. Add the unbeaten egg yolks and vanilla and beat well, then stir in the vanilla. Add the flour mixture alternately with the milk, beating well after each addition. Stir in the cocoa mixture, combining well. Beat the egg whites until stiff peaks form, then fold them into the batter. Turn into a greased and floured 9 x 13-inch pan and bake about 45 minutes.

Aunt Louise's Boiled Spice Cake

Yield: 9 x 13 cake

2 cups sugar
2 eggs
$^3/_4$ cup vegetable oil
2 cups raisins
2 teaspoons cinnamon
2 teaspoons cloves
2 cups water
1 teaspoon salt
2 teaspoons baking soda
3 cups flour

In a heavy saucepan, heat the sugar, eggs, oil, raisins, cinnamon, cloves, water, and salt to a boil. Remove from the heat and let cool.

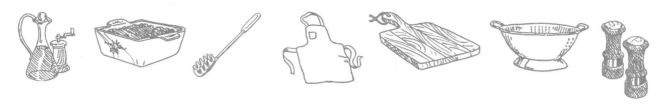

When cool preheat the oven to 325°F. Add the baking soda and flour. Pour into a greased 9 x 13-inch baking pan and bake at 325°F. for 30 to 40 minutes.

Carrot Cake

Yield: large bundt cake

3 cups flour
2 cups sugar
2 teaspoons baking soda
1 teaspoon cinnamon
$\frac{1}{2}$ teaspoon salt
3 eggs
2 teaspoons vanilla
$1\frac{1}{2}$ cups vegetable oil
8-ounce can crushed pineapple (undrained)
2 cups grated carrots
$1\frac{1}{2}$ cups walnuts
$\frac{1}{2}$ cup coconut

Preheat oven to 350°F.

In a large bowl, stir together the dry ingredients. Beat the eggs lightly and add with the oil to the dry ingredients, beating well. Stir in the undrained pineapple and the carrots, then the nuts and coconut. Turn into a greased and floured bundt pan and bake for 1 hour, or until cake tests done.

Cool, then frost with cream cheese frosting (page 380). If desired, sprinkle frosting with chopped walnuts or coconut, or both.

Substituting Tips

- Do not substitute vegetable oil spread for butter or margarine if the label indicates the spread has less than a 65 percent fat content. Your results will be affected.

- Do not use tub or whipped butters or margarines in recipes. They contain more air and water than stick butters, and will affect the results.

- Do not substitute oil for solid shortening or butter, even if the recipe calls for the shortening or butter to be melted before adding.

- If a recipe calls for cake flour, you can substitute 1 cup minus 2 tablespoons of all-purpose flour, sifted.

Cream Cheese Frosting

Yield: frosts 1 bundt or 9 x 12 cake

¹/₂ cup butter
8-ounce package cream cheese
2 teaspoons vanilla
16-ounce package powdered sugar
milk

Cream the butter and cream cheese together, then add the vanilla. Mix in the powdered sugar. If the frosting is too thick, add milk, a teaspoon at a time, until the desired consistency is reached. Cakes frosted with this icing should be refrigerated.

Seven-Minute Frosting

Yield: frosts a 9 x 13 cake

2 egg whites
1¹/₂ cups sugar
¹/₃ cup cold water
¹/₄ teaspoon cream of tartar
dash salt
1 teaspoon vanilla

In the top of a double boiler (at the counter), combine all ingredients except vanilla; then beat for about 1 minute with an electric mixer at low speed. Place on the stove over boiling water (in the bottom of the double boiler) and continue beating at high speed for 7 minutes, or until the frosting forms stiff peaks. Remove from the heat and stir in the vanilla, then beat for 2 or 3 more minutes, or until thick enough to spread.

Butter Frosting

Yield: frosts a 9 x 12 cake

¹/₃ cup butter
*2 cups powdered sugar, sifted after
    measuring*
1 teaspoon vanilla
2 tablespoons heavy or light cream

Cream together the butter and sugar, adding the sugar gradually. Continue beating and stir in the vanilla and cream until the frosting reaches a spreading consistency.

Chocolate butter frosting: Melt 2 ounces unsweetened chocolate and allow to cool. While creaming the butter and sugar, add in the chocolate after about half the sugar has been added.

Sugar Cookies

Yield: 5 dozen large cookies

5¹/₂ cups flour
1¹/₂ teaspoons baking soda
1 teaspoon cream of tartar
1¹/₂ cups sugar
1¹/₂ cups powdered sugar
1¹/₂ cups butter

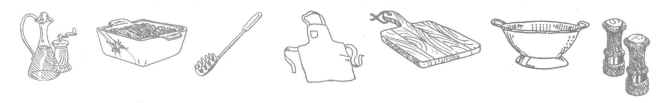

3 eggs
2 teaspoons vanilla
¾ cup vegetable oil
sugar for rolling cookies

Preheat oven to 350°F.

Sift the flour, soda, and cream of tartar together and set aside. Cream together the sugars and butter until light and fluffy. Add the eggs one at a time, beating well after each, then add the vanilla. Add the oil and beat until smooth. Slowly add the dry ingredients, blending well.

Roll dough into balls about 1½ inches in diameter, roll in sugar, then place on a cookie sheet 3 inches apart. (If the dough is too soft, refrigerate until it can be easily worked.) Flatten cookies slightly with a glass bottom dipped in sugar, and bake 10 to 12 minutes, or until the edges are golden brown.

Buttermilk Cutter Cookies

Yield: 3 dozen cookies

2½ cups flour
1 teaspoon baking powder
¼ teaspoon salt
½ teaspoon soda
½ cup shortening (do not substitute)
1 cup sugar
1 egg
½ cup buttermilk
½ teaspoon vanilla extract

(continued)

Cookie Tips

- If a cookie recipe calls for solid shortening, it is possible to substitute butter. Butter will have a good flavor, but it can sometimes affect the structure and texture of the cookies. Experiment to find the result you prefer in a particular recipe.

- Chill the dough for 15 to 30 minutes before shaping cookies. Work with a small amount of dough at a time, and allow the rest to remain in the refrigerator until you are ready to use it.

- If you take the time to make the cookies uniform in size, they will bake evenly.

- When rolling cookie dough, use as little flour as possible for dusting the board and the rolling pin. Too much flour can give cookies a tough texture.

Preheat oven to 350°F.

Sift together the dry ingredients and set aside. Cream the shortening and sugar together well, then add the egg and beat well. Add the dry ingredients alternately with the buttermilk and vanilla. Roll on a lightly floured board to no more than ¼-inch thickness. Cut with cookie cutters and bake on a greased cookie sheet about 15 minutes. If desired, cookies can be sprinkled with plain or colored sugars before baking, or can be iced after they're cool.

Det's Butter Cookies

Yield: 2½ dozen cookies

3 cups flour
1 tablespoon baking soda
½ cup butter
½ cup solid shortening
1 cup sugar
½ cup brown sugar
2 eggs
1 teaspoon vanilla

Preheat oven to 375°F.

Sift the flour and soda together and set aside. Cream together the butter, shortening, and sugars well. Add the eggs, one at a time, then the vanilla, beating well. Mix in the dry ingredients. Chill the dough for 2 hours.

Roll the dough into small balls and bake on an ungreased cookie sheet for 12 to 15 minutes.

Applesauce Cookies

Yield: 5 dozen cookies

2 cups flour
1 teaspoon baking powder
1 teaspoon baking soda
½ teaspoon salt
1 teaspoon cinnamon
1 teaspoon ground cloves
¼ cup butter
¼ cup solid shortening
1 cup sugar
1 egg
1 cup thick applesauce
1 cup raisins
1 cup chopped nuts

Preheat oven to 375°F.

Sift the dry ingredients together and set aside. Cream the butter, shortening, and sugar well. Mix in the egg and applesauce. Add the dry ingredients, blending well, then stir in the raisins and nuts. Drop by spoonfuls onto well-greased cookie sheets and bake 7 to 10 minutes.

Date Cookies

Yield: 2½ dozen

1 cup sugar
½ cup butter, softened
1 egg
1 teaspoon vanilla
2 teaspoons cream of tartar

1 teaspoon baking soda
2 teaspoons heavy cream
3 cups flour

Filling:
12-ounce package pitted dates
1 cup sugar
¹/₂ cup water
1 teaspoon flour

Preheat oven to 325°F. With an electric mixer or food processor, blend the sugar, butter, egg, and vanilla until blended. In a separate bowl, blend the cream of tartar and baking soda into the cream. Add to the sugar mixture. Add the flour slowly, mixing between additions.

For the filling, blend the four filling ingredients in a food processor or mixer until just blended. Roll out the cookie dough (to ¹/₄-inch thickness) with a rolling pin on a pastry cloth or pastry surface. Cut into 4-inch-diameter circles. Place a little filling on half of each circle, fold over the other half, and seal by pinching the edges. Bake the filled cookies on a nonstick cookie sheet for 7 to 8 minutes, or until the cookies are slightly browned.

Butterscotch Cookies

Yield: 8 dozen cookies

3¹/₂ cups all-purpose flour, sifted
¹/₂ tablespoon baking soda
¹/₂ tablespoon cream of tartar

2 eggs, slightly beaten
¹/₂ teaspoon vanilla
¹/₂ cup butter, softened
2 cups brown sugar
¹/₂ cup finely chopped walnuts

Preheat oven to 425°F. Sift together the flour, baking soda, and cream of tartar, and vanilla. Add the eggs and beat well. Add vanilla and flour mixture to eggs, butter and sugar mixture. Mix well. Shape in a square loaf, wrap in wax paper, and refrigerate overnight.

Slice the loaf thinly and place cookies on a nonstick cookie sheet. Sprinkle with the chopped walnuts. Bake the cookies for 8 minutes.

Peanut Blossom Cookies

Yield: 4 dozen cookies

2 8-ounce packages Hershey's
  chocolate kisses*
¹/₂ cup peanut butter
¹/₂ cup sugar
¹/₂ cup butter
¹/₂ cup brown sugar
1 egg
1 teaspoon vanilla
1³/₄ cups all-purpose flour
¹/₂ teaspoon baking soda
¹/₂ teaspoon salt
sugar for rolling

(continued)

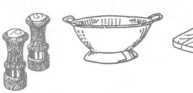

Preheat oven to 375°F. Unwrap chocolate kisses and set aside.

Blend peanut butter, sugar, butter, and brown sugar in a food processor or electric mixer. Add the egg and vanilla and blend for 1 more minute. Combine flour, baking soda, and salt together. Add to peanut butter mixture and blend well. Shape cookies into small balls, roll in white sugar and place on nonstick cookie sheets.

Bake 8 minutes, then remove from the oven. Place a chocolate kiss in the center of each cookie, pressing down slightly. Return the cookies to the oven and bake for an additional 2 to 5 minutes.

*Note: Mini Reese's peanut butter cups can be substituted for the Hershey's Chocolate Kisses.

Katherine's Marriage Proposal Lemon Bars

Yield: 3 dozen bars

1¼ cups all-purpose flour, divided
1 cup sugar, divided
⅓ cup butter, softened
¾ cup white chocolate chips
2 eggs
¼ cup fresh lemon juice
2 tablespoons lemon zest
powdered sugar

Preheat oven to 350°F. In a medium-sized bowl, stir together 1 cup of the flour and ¼ cup of the sugar. With a pastry blender cut in the butter until the mixture resembles coarse crumbs. Press the mixture into the bottom of a 9-inch-square pan. Bake 15 minutes or until lightly browned. Sprinkle vanilla chips over the crust.

In a medium-sized bowl, stir together the eggs, lemon juice, lemon zest, remaining ¼ cup flour and ¾ cup sugar. Carefully pour over chips and crust. Bake 15 minutes or until set. Cool in the pan on a wire rack. Sprinkle with powdered sugar. Cool completely. Cut into bars and serve.

Mel's Easy Cheesy Blintz Bars

Yield: 9 x 13 pan of bars

2 packages refrigerated crescent-style rolls
12 ounces cream cheese
½ cup sugar
1 egg
1 teaspoon vanilla

Topping:

½ cup sugar
¼ cup butter
1 teaspoon cinnamon

Preheat oven to 350°F.
Spray a 9 x 13-inch pan with cooking spray. Unroll 1 package of roll dough and

spread evenly over the bottom of the pan. Stretch to fit and press seams together. In a small bowl, beat together the cream cheese, sugar, egg, and vanilla, then spread evenly over the dough in the baking pan.

Unroll the second package of roll dough, spread it out, stretch it, and place over the top of the cream cheese mixture. In a separate bowl, use a fork to mix the topping ingredients together, then sprinkle over the dough. Bake for 20 to 25 minutes.

Meltaway Toffee Bars

Yield: 9 x 13 pan of bars

Crust:
½ cup butter
½ cup sugar
½ teaspoon salt
1 cup all-purpose flour

Second Layer:
14-ounce can sweetened condensed milk
2 tablespoons butter
¼ teaspoon salt
2 teaspoons vanilla

Frosting:
2 tablespoons butter
1-ounce square unsweetened chocolate
1½ cups sifted powdered sugar
1 teaspoon vanilla
hot water

Preheat oven to 350°F.

To make the crust: Cream together the butter, sugar, and salt. Mix in the flour. Pat into an ungreased 9 x 13-inch baking pan, and bake until lightly browned, about 12 to 15 minutes.

To make the second layer: In a heavy saucepan, combine the condensed milk, butter, salt, and vanilla. Cook over low heat, stirring constantly, for about 5 minutes or until the mixture thickens and becomes smooth and pourable. Spread over the baked layer. Bake until golden brown, 12 to 15 minutes.

To make the frosting: In a medium saucepan, melt the butter and unsweetened chocolate over low heat; stir constantly. Remove from heat; stir in the powdered sugar and vanilla. Blend in about 2 tablespoons hot water, or more if needed, till almost a pourable consistency. Spread warm cookies with fudge frosting. While warm, cut into bars and remove from the pan. Leftover bars should be refrigerated.

Chocolate Chip Brownies

Yield: 9 x 13 pan of brownies

2 cups semisweet chocolate chips, divided
⅔ cup butter
1 cup sugar
2 eggs
1 teaspoon vanilla

(continued)

1¹/₄ cups flour
1 teaspoon baking powder
1 cup rolled oats

Preheat oven to 350°F.

Melt 1 cup of the chocolate chips and allow to cool slightly. Cream together the butter and sugar. Add the eggs and vanilla, and beat until smooth. Add the melted chips and mix well. Stir in the flour, baking powder, rolled oats, and remaining 1 cup of unmelted chocolate chips. Spread the batter in a lightly greased 9 x 13 baking pan, and bake 25 to 30 minutes or until brownies begin to leave the side of the pan. Cool before cutting into bars.

Peanut Butter Brownies

Yield: 9 x 13 pan of brownies

Filling:

2 3-ounce packages cream cheese
¹/₂ cup creamy peanut butter
¹/₄ cup sugar
1 egg
2 tablespoons milk
³/₄ cup peanut butter chips

Batter:

1 cup butter
2 cups sugar
2 teaspoons vanilla
3 eggs
³/₄ cup cocoa powder
1¹/₄ cups flour
¹/₂ teaspoon baking powder
¹/₄ teaspoon salt
1 cup milk chocolate chips

Preheat oven to 350°F.

To make the filling: Soften the cream cheese and beat together with the peanut butter and sugar. Add the egg and milk and beat until smooth. Stir in the peanut butter chips. Set aside.

To make the batter: Melt the butter and stir in the sugar and vanilla. Beat by hand rather than electric mixer: add the eggs one at a time, and beat well after each; add the cocoa and beat well. Add the flour, baking powder, and salt and beat well. Stir in the chips. Reserve 1 cup of batter, and turn the remainder into a lightly greased 9 x 13-inch baking pan.

Spoon the filling over the batter, then spoon the reserved batter over the filling. Using a table knife, gently swirl through the batter to create a marbling of the filling. Bake about 40 minutes, or until the center tests done. Cool completely before cutting into bars.

Really Good Plain Cheesecake

Yield: 9-inch cheesecake

Crust:
1³/₄ cups fine graham cracker crumbs
¹/₄ cup finely chopped walnuts
1 teaspoon cinnamon
¹/₂ cup melted butter

Cheesecake:
3 eggs, well beaten
16 ounces cream cheese, at room temperature
1 cup sugar
¹/₄ teaspoon salt
2 teaspoons vanilla
¹/₂ teaspoon almond extract
3 cups sour cream (24 ounces)

Preheat oven to 375°F. Cover the *outside* of a 9-inch springform pan with aluminum foil, shiny side out (for even baking). Mix together the graham cracker crumbs, chopped walnuts, cinnamon, and melted butter. Press into the bottom and sides of the pan.

Combine the eggs, cream cheese, sugar, salt, vanilla, and almond extract. Beat until well combined and lumps are gone from the cream cheese. Blend in the sour cream. Pour into the crumb crust. Bake for at least one hour or until set. During baking, the center may crack and the edges may brown a little. The center should still look soft.

Turn off the heat and let the cake remain in the oven for another 30 minutes. Chill about 4 to 5 hours or overnight. Top with fresh strawberries if desired.

To make low-fat cheesecakes, use an egg substitute, low-fat cream cheese, and low-fat sour cream.

Chocolate Espresso Cheesecake

Yield: 9-inch cheesecake

Crust:
1³/₄ cups crushed Oreo cookies, filling removed
¹/₂ cup sugar
¹/₂ cup butter, melted

Cheesecake:
24 ounces cream cheese
12 ounces semisweet chocolate chips
2 tablespoons instant espresso coffee or ¹/₄ cup instant regular coffee
1 tablespoon hot water
1 cup sugar
3 tablespoons all-purpose flour
3 eggs
2 egg yolks
1 cup heavy cream, not whipped

Let the cream cheese warm to room temperature in a large mixing bowl. Set aside. Blend the crushed chocolate wafers,

(continued)

sugar, and melted butter in a medium-sized bowl. Press firmly over the bottom and sides of a lightly buttered 9-inch springform pan. Chill briefly before filling.

Preheat oven to 375°F. Melt the chocolate in the top of a double boiler over hot, not boiling water and let cool slightly. Dissolve the espresso coffee in the hot water. Beat the cream cheese until smooth. Add the sugar gradually, beating until light and fluffy. Sprinkle the flour over the mixture and blend thoroughly. Add the eggs and egg yolks one at a time, beating well after each addition. Beat in the chocolate, coffee, and heavy cream at low speed. Pour into the prepared pan.

Bake for 1 hour. Turn off the heat and let cake remain in the oven with the door closed for 40 more minutes. Remove the cake from the oven and cool completely on a rack. Refrigerate several hours or overnight before serving.

Chocolate Amaretto Cheesecake

Yield: 10-inch cheesecake

Crust:
¹/₄ cup butter
1 cup graham cracker crumbs
¹/₄ cup cocoa powder
2 tablespoons sugar

Filling:
8 ounces semisweet chocolate
16 ounces cream cheese
¹/₂ cup sugar
3 large eggs
8 ounces sour cream
1 teaspoon vanilla
1 teaspoon almond extract
¹/₃ cup amaretto liqueur

Topping (optional):
2 ounces semisweet chocolate
2 tablespoons butter

Preheat the oven to 300°F.

To make the crust: Melt the butter and combine with the other crust ingredients. Press the mixture into the bottom and 1 inch up the sides of a 10-inch springform pan.

To make the filling: Melt the chocolate and allow it to cool. Soften the cream cheese and beat it with the sugar until the mixture is smooth. Add the eggs, one at a time, beating well after each addition. Stir in the sour cream, chocolate, vanilla, almond extract, and amaretto.

Turn the mixture into the crust and bake for 1 hour. Turn the oven off and let the cheesecake cool in the oven for 1 hour. Remove to a rack and allow to cool completely, then cover loosely and chill for at least 12 hours.

To make the topping: Melt the chocolate and stir in the butter. Spread the mixture over the chilled cheesecake and chill an additional hour before serving.

Cheesecake Tips

- Before mixing, bring all ingredients to room temperature.

- If too much air is added to the batter, the cheesecake is likely to crack when done. Beat at a low speed, and for as little time as necessary. If you have a paddle attachment with your electric mixer, use it for cheesecakes.

- Allow cheesecake to cool very slowly, away from drafts. Quick temperature changes cause cracks in the surface. If the recipe allows, cool in the oven with the heat off and the door ajar.

- For best results, allow cheesecake to "set" 12 hours or overnight, in the refrigerator, before serving. If you cannot, allow at least 3 hours for complete cooling; otherwise the cheesecake will be extremely difficult to cut.

- Do not cover cheesecakes that are cooling; moisture will form on the top. Fully cooled and leftover cheesecakes should be covered, however, to prevent drying.

- Cut with a sharp, wet knife.

- Refrigerate leftover cheesecake.

Chocolate Pudding Cake

Yield: 9-inch cake

> 1 cup flour
> 1¼ cups sugar, divided
> 2 teaspoons baking powder
> ⅛ teaspoon salt
> ½ cup cocoa powder, divided
> ¼ cup butter
> ½ cup milk
> 1 teaspoon vanilla
> ½ cup brown sugar
> 1½ cups cold water

Preheat oven to 350°F.

Stir together the flour, ¾ cup of the sugar, baking powder, salt, and ¼ cup of the cocoa. Melt the butter and combine with the milk and vanilla, then add to the dry ingredients, mixing just until blended. Turn into a greased 9-inch baking pan.

Over the top of the batter, sprinkle the brown sugar, then the remaining ½ cup granulated sugar, then the remaining ¼ cup cocoa. Pour the water over all. Bake 40 minutes. Allow to cool at room temperature before serving.

Variation: For mocha pudding cake, substitute strong cold coffee for the cold water.

Baked Rice Pudding

Servings: 4 to 5

> 4 cups 2% milk
> 4 large eggs
> 2 cups cooked rice
> ½ cup sugar
> ¼ teaspoon salt
> ½ cup raisins
> 1 teaspoon vanilla
> dash of nutmeg

Preheat oven to 350°F.

Heat the milk until it's very warm, but not boiling; place in 3-quart baking dish. With an electric mixer, beat the eggs until light yellow and fluffy. Add the rice, sugar, salt, raisins, and vanilla. Stir slightly. Sprinkle with nutmeg. Place the dish in another shallow baking dish with 1½ inches of water. Bake for 45 to 60 minutes, or until pudding is set.

Grace's Date Pudding

Yield: 8-inch-square dessert

Cake:

> 1½ cups flour
> ½ teaspoon salt
> 1 teaspoon baking powder
> 1 teaspoon baking soda
> 1 cup chopped dates
> 1 cup sugar

³/₄ cup chopped nuts
1 tablespoon butter
1 cup boiling water
1 egg

Topping:

1 cup brown sugar
³/₄ cup chopped dates
1 cup boiling water

Preheat oven to 350°F.

Sift together the flour, salt, baking powder, and baking soda; set aside. Combine the dates, sugar, nuts, and butter; add the boiling water, and mix. Beat the egg lightly and stir into the date mixture. Add the dry ingredients and combine well. Spread the batter in a greased and floured 8 x 8- inch baking pan and bake 25 minutes. Cool.

To make the topping: In a large saucepan, mix the brown sugar, dates, and boiling water, and cook until thickened. Cool. When cooled, spread on the cake.

Fruit Crisp

Yield: 9-inch-square dessert

Topping:

³/₄ cup brown sugar
¹/₂ cup flour
¹/₄ cup rolled oats
¹/₃ cup butter
¹/₂ teaspoon cinnamon

Fruit Filling:

4 cups sliced cooking apples or peaches,
    or fresh blueberries
1 tablespoon lemon juice
1 tablespoon water

Preheat oven to 375°F.

Combine topping ingredients, mixing well. Place the fruit in a 9-inch-square pan and sprinkle with the lemon juice and water. Sprinkle the topping evenly over the fruit. Bake about 45 minutes. Can be served warm or cold, with whipped cream or ice cream if desired.

Variation: Substitute a 21-ounce can of cherry pie filling or other fruit pie filling of your choice for the fresh fruit, and reduce the brown sugar to ²/₃ cup.

Date Loaf Candy

Servings: 8 to 10

2¹/₂ cups sugar
1 cup milk
12-ounce package pitted dates, chopped
1 cup chopped pecans

In a heavy saucepan, combine the sugar and milk and heat to boiling. Boil gently until a small amount forms a soft ball in a glass of water, about 20 minutes. Add the chopped dates and continue boiling, stirring constantly, until dates are dissolved. Remove

(continued)

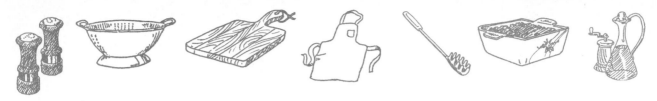

from the heat and add the pecans; beat by hand until cool.

Pour candy onto a wet cloth and shape into a roll. When cold, cut into slices and serve.

Erica's Taffy

Yield: 2 dozen candies

2 cups sugar
$^1/_2$ cup light corn syrup
$^1/_2$ cup water
$^1/_4$ teaspoon cream of tartar
1 teaspoon vanilla

Mix all ingredients in a large saucepan and cook over medium heat until the sugar dissolves. Simmer gently without stirring until the mixture reaches the firm ball stage. Pour the mixture onto a well-greased platter and allow to cool. Shape into oblong balls.

Variation: For pink mint taffy, substitute $^3/_4$ teaspoon peppermint extract and $^1/_4$ teaspoon vanilla for the 1 teaspoon vanilla; add a few drops of red food coloring.

The Cold Water Test for Candy Doneness

If you do not use a candy thermometer to make candy, you can use the "ball drop" method. Using a glass of very cold water drop a small amount of the hot candy mixture into the water, then test with your fingers. If the candy does not pass the test, continue cooking.

- Soft ball—the candy forms a soft ball that flattens, when removed from the cold water.
- Firm ball—the candy forms a ball that holds its shape, but can be pressed with the fingers.

Index

A

We Have EVERYTHING!

Everything® **After College Book**
$12.95, 1-55850-847-3

Everything® **American History Book**
$12.95, 1-58062-531-2

Everything® **Angels Book**
$12.95, 1-58062-398-0

Everything® **Anti-Aging Book**
$12.95, 1-58062-565-7

Everything® **Astrology Book**
$12.95, 1-58062-062-0

Everything® **Baby Names Book**
$12.95, 1-55850-655-1

Everything® **Baby Shower Book**
$12.95, 1-58062-305-0

Everything® **Baby's First Food Book**
$12.95, 1-58062-512-6

Everything® **Baby's First Year Book**
$12.95, 1-58062-581-9

Everything® **Barbeque Cookbook**
$12.95, 1-58062-316-6

Everything® **Bartender's Book**
$9.95, 1-55850-536-9

Everything® **Bedtime Story Book**
$12.95, 1-58062-147-3

Everything® **Bicycle Book**
$12.00, 1-55850-706-X

Everything® **Breastfeeding Book**
$12.95, 1-58062-582-7

Everything® **Build Your Own Home Page**
$12.95, 1-58062-339-5

Everything® **Business Planning Book**
$12.95, 1-58062-491-X

Everything® **Candlemaking Book**
$12.95, 1-58062-623-8

Everything® **Casino Gambling Book**
$12.95, 1-55850-762-0

Everything® **Cat Book**
$12.95, 1-55850-710-8

Everything® **Chocolate Cookbook**
$12.95, 1-58062-405-7

Everything® **Christmas Book**
$15.00, 1-55850-697-7

Everything® **Civil War Book**
$12.95, 1-58062-366-2

Everything® **Classical Mythology Book**
$12.95, 1-58062-653-X

Everything® **Collectibles Book**
$12.95, 1-58062-645-9

Everything® **College Survival Book**
$12.95, 1-55850-720-5

Everything® **Computer Book**
$12.95, 1-58062-401-4

Everything® **Cookbook**
$14.95, 1-58062-400-6

Everything® **Cover Letter Book**
$12.95, 1-58062-312-3

Everything® **Creative Writing Book**
$12.95, 1-58062-647-5

Everything® **Crossword and Puzzle Book**
$12.95, 1-55850-764-7

Everything® **Dating Book**
$12.95, 1-58062-185-6

Everything® **Dessert Book**
$12.95, 1-55850-717-5

Everything® **Digital Photography Book**
$12.95, 1-58062-574-6

Everything® **Dog Book**
$12.95, 1-58062-144-9

Everything® **Dreams Book**
$12.95, 1-55850-806-6

Everything® **Etiquette Book**
$12.95, 1-55850-807-4

Everything® **Fairy Tales Book**
$12.95, 1-58062-546-0

Everything® **Family Tree Book**
$12.95, 1-55850-763-9

Everything® **Feng Shui Book**
$12.95, 1-58062-587-8

Everything® **Fly-Fishing Book**
$12.95, 1-58062-148-1

Everything® **Games Book**
$12.95, 1-55850-643-8

Everything® **Get-A-Job Book**
$12.95, 1-58062-223-2

Everything® **Get Out of Debt Book**
$12.95, 1-58062-588-6

Everything® **Get Published Book**
$12.95, 1-58062-315-8

Everything® **Get Ready for Baby Book**
$12.95, 1-55850-844-9

Everything® **Get Rich Book**
$12.95, 1-58062-670-X

Everything® **Ghost Book**
$12.95, 1-58062-533-9

Everything® **Golf Book**
$12.95, 1-55850-814-7

Everything® **Grammar and Style Book**
$12.95, 1-58062-573-8

Everything® **Guide to Las Vegas**
$12.95, 1-58062-438-3

Everything® **Guide to New England**
$12.95, 1-58062-589-4

Everything® **Guide to New York City**
$12.95, 1-58062-314-X

Everything® **Guide to Walt Disney World®, Universal Studios®, and Greater Orlando, 2nd Edition**
$12.95, 1-58062-404-9

Everything® **Guide to Washington D.C.**
$12.95, 1-58062-313-1

Everything® **Guitar Book**
$12.95, 1-58062-555-X

Everything® **Herbal Remedies Book**
$12.95, 1-58062-331-X

Everything® **Home-Based Business Book**
$12.95, 1-58062-364-6

Everything® **Homebuying Book**
$12.95, 1-58062-074-4

Everything® **Homeselling Book**
$12.95, 1-58062-304-2

Everything® **Horse Book**
$12.95, 1-58062-564-9

Everything® **Hot Careers Book**
$12.95, 1-58062-486-3

Everything® **Internet Book**
$12.95, 1-58062-073-6

Everything® **Investing Book**
$12.95, 1-58062-149-X

Everything® **Jewish Wedding Book**
$12.95, 1-55850-801-5

Everything® **Job Interview Book**
$12.95, 1-58062-493-6

Everything® **Lawn Care Book**
$12.95, 1-58062-487-1

Everything® **Leadership Book**
$12.95, 1-58062-513-4

Everything® **Learning French Book**
$12.95, 1-58062-649-1

Everything® **Learning Spanish Book**
$12.95, 1-58062-575-4

Everything® **Low-Fat High-Flavor Cookbook**
$12.95, 1-55850-802-3

Everything® **Magic Book**
$12.95, 1-58062-418-9

Everything® **Managing People Book**
$12.95, 1-58062-577-0

Everything® **Microsoft® Word 2000 Book**
$12.95, 1-58062-306-9

Everything® **Money Book**
$12.95, 1-58062-145-7

Everything® **Mother Goose Book**
$12.95, 1-58062-490-1

Everything® **Motorcycle Book**
$12.95, 1-58062-554-1

Everything® **Mutual Funds Book**
$12.95, 1-58062-419-7

Everything® **One-Pot Cookbook**
$12.95, 1-58062-186-4

Everything® **Online Business Book**
$12.95, 1-58062-320-4

Everything® **Online Genealogy Book**
$12.95, 1-58062-402-2

Everything® **Online Investing Book**
$12.95, 1-58062-338-7

Everything® **Online Job Search Book**
$12.95, 1-58062-365-4

Everything® **Organize Your Home Book**
$12.95, 1-58062-617-3

Everything® **Pasta Book**
$12.95, 1-55850-719-1

Everything® **Philosophy Book**
$12.95, 1-58062-644-0

Everything® **Playing Piano and Keyboards Book**
$12.95, 1-58062-651-3

Everything® **Pregnancy Book**
$12.95, 1-58062-146-5

Everything® **Pregnancy Organizer**
$15.00, 1-58062-336-0

Everything® **Project Management Book**
$12.95, 1-58062-583-5

Everything® **Puppy Book**
$12.95, 1-58062-576-2

Everything® **Quick Meals Cookbook**
$12.95, 1-58062-488-X

Everything® **Resume Book**
$12.95, 1-58062-311-5

Everything® **Romance Book**
$12.95, 1-58062-566-5

Everything® **Running Book**
$12.95, 1-58062-618-1

Everything® **Sailing Book, 2nd Edition**
$12.95, 1-58062-671-8

Everything® **Saints Book**
$12.95, 1-58062-534-7

Everything® **Selling Book**
$12.95, 1-58062-319-0

Everything® **Shakespeare Book**
$12.95, 1-58062-591-6

Everything® **Spells and Charms Book**
$12.95, 1-58062-532-0

Everything® **Start Your Own Business Book**
$12.95, 1-58062-650-5

Everything® **Stress Management Book**
$12.95, 1-58062-578-9

Everything® **Study Book**
$12.95, 1-55850-615-2

Everything® **Tai Chi and QiGong Book**
$12.95, 1-58062-646-7

Everything® **Tall Tales, Legends, and Outrageous Lies Book**
$12.95, 1-58062-514-2

Everything® **Tarot Book**
$12.95, 1-58062-191-0

Everything® **Time Management Book**
$12.95, 1-58062-492-8

Everything® **Toasts Book**
$12.95, 1-58062-189-9

Everything® **Toddler Book**
$12.95, 1-58062-592-4

Everything® **Total Fitness Book**
$12.95, 1-58062-318-2

Everything® **Trivia Book**
$12.95, 1-58062-143-0

Everything® **Tropical Fish Book**
$12.95, 1-58062-343-3

Everything® **Vegetarian Cookbook**
$12.95, 1-58062-640-8

Everything® **Vitamins, Minerals, and Nutritional Supplements Book**
$12.95, 1-58062-496-0

Everything® **Wedding Book, 2nd Edition**
$12.95, 1-58062-190-2

Everything® **Wedding Checklist**
$7.95, 1-58062-456-1

Everything® **Wedding Etiquette Book**
$7.95, 1-58062-454-5

Everything® **Wedding Organizer**
$15.00, 1-55850-828-7

Everything® **Wedding Shower Book**
$7.95, 1-58062-188-0

Everything® **Wedding Vows Book**
$7.95, 1-58062-455-3

Everything® **Weight Training Book**
$12.95, 1-58062-593-2

Everything® **Wine Book**
$12.95, 1-55850-808-2

Everything® **World War II Book**
$12.95, 1-58062-572-X

Everything® **World's Religions Book**
$12.95, 1-58062-648-3

Everything® **Yoga Book**
$12.95, 1-58062-594-0

Visit us at everything.com

EVERYTHING.

Trade Paperback, $12.95
1-58062-488-X, 352 pages

The Everything® Quick Meals Cookbook
By Barbara Doyen

The Everything® *Quick Meals Cookbook* features 300 easy-to-follow recipes for cooks with gourmet tastes and limited time. You'll learn to prepare delicious and nutritious meals faster and easier than ever before. From a one-course dinner for the family to an elaborate feast for special guests, this book provides mouth-watering recipes that will satisfy any appetite. It also features dozens of valuable time-saving tips, and complete instructions so that your favorite meals turn out perfect every time.

Trade Paperback, $12.95
1-58062-186-4, 288 pages

The Everything® One-Pot Cookbook
By Lisa Rojak

What could be easier than cooking an entire meal using just one pot? One-pot cuisine is characterized by hearty, satisfying dishes that can be prepared using only one of a variety of conventional cooking techniques: a single baking pan, skillet, crock pot, or conventional stovetop pot. *The Everything*® *One-Pot Cookbook* features hundreds of exciting recipes that are guaranteed crowd pleasers, with minimal mess. From appetizers to entrees and even desserts, these one-pot meals are quick, simple, and delicious.

Available wherever books are sold!
To order, call 800-872-5627, or visit everything.com
Adams Media Corporation, 57 Littlefield Street, Avon, MA 02322. U.S.A.